P9-ELR-025

Warriner's High School Handbook

Holt, Rinehart and Winston, Inc.

Harcourt Brace Jovanovich, Inc.

Austin · Orlando · San Diego · Chicago · Dallas · Toronto

Printed in 2009

Printed in the United States of America

ISBN 0-03-054009-7

19 20 1083 09

Acknowledgments

For permission to reprint copyrighted material, grateful acknowledgment is made to the following sources:

Childrens Press: "How Can You Show That Sound Waves Travel Through Air?" from *Discovering Science on Your Own* by Illa Podendorf. Copyright © 1962 by Childrens Press,® Inc.

Commentary and David Herbert Donald: From "Family Chronicle" by David Herbert Donald in *Commentary,* December 1976. All rights reserved.

Delacorte Press/Seymour Lawrence: From *Wamperters Foma & Granfalloons* by Kurt Vonnegut Jr. Copyright © 1974 by Kurt Vonnegut Jr.

Doubleday, a division of Bantam, Doubleday, Dell Publishing Group, Inc.: From "Architecture and Building" by John Burchard from *An Outline of Man's Knowledge of the Modern World,* edited by Lyman Bryson. From *Speech Can Change Your Life* by Dorothy Sarnoff. Copyright © 1970 by Dorothy Sarnoff.

Dutton, an imprint of New American Library, a division of Penguin Books USA Inc.: From "On Golden Swamp" by Pauline Kael from *The New Yorker,* October 3, 1983. Copyright © 1983 by Pauline Kael. Originally published in *The New Yorker.*

Farrar, Straus & Giroux, Inc.: From "Some Dreamers of the Golden Dream" by Joan Didion from *Slouching Towards Bethlehem.* Copyright © 1966 by Joan Didion. From *Life Among the Savages* by Shirley Jackson. Copyright © 1953 by Shirley Jackson; copyright renewed © 1981 by Laurence Hyman, Barry Hyman, Mrs. Sarah Webster, and Mrs. Joanne Schnurer.

Harcourt Brace Jovanovich, Inc.: From *The Enjoyment of Literature* by Ralph P. Boas and Edwin Smith. Copyright 1934 by Harcourt Brace Jovanovich, Inc., copyright renewed © 1962 by Edwin Smith and L.S. Boaz. From *Language in Thought and Action*, Fourth Edition, by S. I. Hayakawa. Copyright © 1978 by Harcourt Brace Jovanovich, Inc.

HarperCollins, Publishers Inc.: From pp. 49–50 from *A Childhood: Biography of a Place* by Harry Crews. Copyright © 1978 by Harry Crews. From p. 35 from *House Made of Dawn* by N. Scott Momaday. Copyright © 1966, 1967, 1968 by N. Scott Momaday. From *The Story of the English Language* by Mario Pei. Copyright 1952, © 1967 by Mario Pei.

Harvard University Press: From *One Writer's Beginnings* by Eudora Welty. Copyright © 1983, 1984 by Eudora Welty. Published by Harvard University Press.

Historical Society of Saratoga Springs, NY: Adapted from "The Cliché Expert Reveals Himself In His True Colors" by Frank Sullivan.

Houghton Mifflin Company: From "A Little Incident in the Rue de l'Odeon" in *The Collected Essays and Occasional Writings of Katherine Anne Porter.* Copyright © 1970 by Katherine Anne Porter.

Alfred A. Knopf, Inc.: From *A Distant Mirror: The Calamitous 14th Century* by Barbara Tuchman. Copyright © 1978 by Barbara W. Tuchman. From *The March of Folly: From Troy to Vietnam* by Barbara Tuchman. Copyright © 1984 by Barbara W. Tuchman.

Little, Brown and Company, Inc., in association with the Atlantic Monthly Press: From *Never Cry Wolf* by Farley Mowat. Copyright © 1963 by Farley Mowat Ltd. "The Purist" from *Verses from 1929 On* by Ogden Nash. Copyright 1935 by Ogden Nash. First appeared in *The Saturday Evening Post.*

The Miami Herald Publishing Company: From "Results of National Sports Survey" from *The Miami Herald,* November 25, 1984, p. 24A.

William Morrow & Company, Inc.: From p. 231 from *The Ways of My Grandmothers* by Beverly Hungry Wolf. Copyright © 1980 by Beverly Hungry Wolf.

National Audubon Society: From "For Migrants, No Winter Home?" by Frank Graham, Jr. from *Audubon* Magazine, November 1980.

The New Republic, Inc.: From "Gettysburg Address in Eisenhowerese" by Oliver Jensen from *New Republic,* June 17, 1957. Copyright © 1957 by The New Republic, Inc.

The New York Times Company: From "Dizzy Dean" in *The New York Times,* July 26, 1946. Copyright © 1946 by The New York Times Company. From "Ways to Offset Lack of Light in the Shorter Days of Winter" by Jane E. Brody from *The New York Times,* November 14, 1984. Copyright © 1984 by The

New York Times Company. From "The Post-Holiday Strip" by William Safire from *The New York Times*, January 6, 1985. Copyright © 1985 by The New York Times Company.

W. W. Norton & Company, Inc.: From *The Ever-Present* by Edith Hamilton. Copyright © 1964 by W. W. Norton & Company, Inc.

Harold Ober Associates, Inc.: From "The Alerting of Mr. Pomerantz" from *Eleven Blue Men and Other Narratives of Medical Detection* by Berton Roueché. Copyright 1947 by The New Yorker Magazine, Inc.; copyright renewed © 1975 by Berton Roueché.

Peachtree Publishers Ltd.: From "Me and My Guccis" from *Won't You Come Home, Billy Bob Bailey?* by Lewis Grizzard. Copyright © 1980 by Lewis Grizzard.

Random House, Inc.: From *Persons of Consequence: Queen Victoria and Her Circle* by Louis Auchincloss. Copyright © 1979 by Louis Auchincloss. Entry "masterpiece" from *The Random House College Dictionary*, Revised Edition. Copyright © 1975 by Random House, Inc.

Reader's Digest: From "Soft Contact Lenses—How Good Are They?" by James H. Winchester from *Reader's Digest*, November 1975.

Charles Scribner's Sons: From *The Great Gatsby* by F. Scott Fitzgerald. Copyright 1925 by Charles Scribner's Sons; copyright renewed © 1953 by Frances Scott Fitzgerald Lanahan.

Smithsonian Institution Press: From "Recollections of a Childhood Friend Named Crowcrow" by Rudolph Chelminski from *Smithsonian*, September 1982.

Rosemary A. Thurber: From "University Days" from *My Life and Hard Times* by James Thurber. Copyright © 1933, 1961 by James Thurber. Published by Harper & Row, Publishers, Inc.

United Press International, Inc.: From "Hayes: 'There Is So Much to Do'" by Helen Hayes.

Viking Penguin, a division of Penguin Books USA Inc.: From "Ego" from *Letters from a Distant Land* by Philip Booth. Copyright © 1956 and renewed © 1984 by Philip Booth. Originally published in *The New Yorker*. From "Flight" from *The Long Valley* by John Steinbeck. Copyright 1938 and renewed ©1966 by John Steinbeck.

Wallace Literary Agency, Inc.: From *Strangers and Pilgrims* by Ann Cornelisen. Copyright © 1980 by Ann Cornelisen.

Webster's New World Dictionaries/A Division of Simon & Schuster, Inc.: Entry for "brave" from *Webster's New World Dictionary of the American Language*, Third College Edition. Copyright © 1988 by Webster's New World Dictionaries/A Division of Simon & Schuster, Inc.

The H. W. Wilson Company: Entries "BALL, George Wildman" through "National Ballet of Canada" from p. 47 from *Reader's Guide to Periodical Literature*, May 10, 1980, v. 80, no. 5. Copyright © 1980 by The H. W. Wilson Company.

To the Student

This textbook is designed to help you master the skills required for the effective use of standard English. Beginning with the basics in grammar, usage, and mechanics (capitalization, punctuation, and spelling), each chapter provides you with instruction and practice in specific skills.

The numerous exercises throughout the book enable you to check your understanding of important concepts, rules, and guidelines. In addition, various writing exercises and activities offer you opportunities to apply what you have learned.

The three chapters on composition lead you step by step through the writing process, showing you how to create successful paragraphs, compositions, and research reports.

The final section of the book acquaints you with a range of valuable information on the library, reference books, the dictionary, and vocabulary study. You may be particularly interested in the last chapter because it gives a number of useful tips on studying and on taking a variety of tests.

The organization of your textbook also makes it a useful reference source. By familiarizing yourself with the book's contents and by using the index, you can easily find what you need to know to avoid mistakes in your writing. Keep this book nearby whenever you write, not only in your English class but also in any other class or in any other situation inside or outside school.

CONTENTS

Part Two: USAGE

Part Four: SENTENCE STRUCTURE

Part Five: COMPOSITION

25. Writing a Research Paper 431

RESEARCH, WRITING, DOCUMENTATION

Part Six: RESOURCES FOR WRITING AND STUDYING

PART 1

GRAMMAR

CHAPTER 1

The Parts of Speech

THEIR IDENTIFICATION AND FUNCTION

In your study of English, certain aspects will already be familiar from your English courses of previous years. Among these is grammar.

Grammar is important. It gives you the wherewithal to talk about language by providing a terminology and a system of classification. Also, by making you aware of the basic patterns of English sentences, it can help you develop a varied and interesting style in your speaking and writing. This is one of the main goals of the study of English.

The next few chapters will give you the opportunity to review and refine what you have learned in previous years. Chapter 1 deals with the parts of speech—the building blocks of language.

DIAGNOSTIC TEST

Identifying the Parts of Speech of Words. Number your paper 1–20. Write the numbered words from the following passage and the part of speech, using these abbreviations: *n.* (noun), *pron.* (pronoun), *adj.* (adjective), *v.* (verb), *adv.* (adverb), *conj.* (conjunction), *prep.* (preposition), *interj.* (interjection). Base your answers on the way each word is used in the sentence.

EXAMPLE Writing can be (1) *inventive* and original.
1. *inventive, adj.*

GRAMMAR

For less than five dollars (1) *you* can get to know yourself better! How can such a wonder be accomplished? Purchase a (2) *blank* notebook (3) *and* begin to keep a personal journal. Within a short time you will be amazed to see what you (4) *learn* (5) *about* yourself.

Keeping a journal is (6) *simple.* There is only one rule: date all entries. (7) *Usually* your mood will determine length. One type of entry is the (8) *daily* log, in which you record (9) *what* you did and how you felt on a particular day. Another is a (10) *record* of favorite songs and poetry. (11) *Most* important are those entries that have nothing to do with your "outer life," (12) *but* that (13) *record* your "inner life": your dreams, your thoughts, your questions, your goals, and especially your feelings. (14) *Because* the journal is a personal book, which no one else reads, it becomes a "free place" to say (15) *anything* you want. Most people find that writing four or five entries a week is a realistic goal. Rereading your entries (16) *later* will show you how you once were.

Does the journal really work? (17) *Wow!* You bet it does! One girl in (18) *Connecticut* wrote to her teacher that keeping a journal was "the closest I've come to knowing myself." The journal is an adventure (19) *in* self-awareness. (20) *Try* keeping one yourself.

THE NOUN

1a. A *noun* is a word used to name a person, place, thing, or idea.

Nouns may be classified in two ways: *proper* or *common* and *abstract* or *concrete.* A further classification for some nouns is *collective.*

A *proper noun* names a particular person, place, or thing and is capitalized: *Ann, New Mexico, Sears Tower.*

A *common noun* does not name a particular person, place, or thing. Common nouns are not capitalized: *woman, district, chair.*

An *abstract noun* names a quality, a characteristic, or an idea: *peace, civilization, honor, justice.*

A *concrete noun* names an object that can be perceived by the senses: *star, whisper, gravel, cinnamon.*

A *collective noun* names a group: *jury, band, family.*

> ☞ **NOTE** A *compound noun* is a noun composed of more than one word: *County Savings and Loan Association, roller coaster, weekend, forget-me-not.*

EXERCISE 1. Identifying and Classifying Nouns. After the proper number, write the nouns in the following sentences in order. After each noun, indicate its classification: proper or common.

1. Last summer our family drove to Chicago in our new van.
2. Because of their intelligence and athletic ability, Karen Cornell and Leonard Johnson were named "Scholar Athletes."
3. In one afternoon the crew repaired eleven helicopters.
4. We purchased tomatoes, lettuce, and corn grown by local farmers.
5. Congress debated the merits of a tax bill late into the night.
6. My goal is to visit every state in the United States.
7. When they saw the beauty of the snow-capped Rockies, the hikers paused and silently enjoyed the scene.
8. Her valuable experience as last year's class treasurer convinced a majority of the students to vote for her for class president.
9. Blunt honesty, quick wit, and fierce loyalty are the qualities I most admired in Huck Finn.
10. The crowd roared enthusiastically as Chip sank the winning basket just one second before time ran out.

WRITING APPLICATION A:
Defining Abstract Nouns

An abstract noun refers to something that cannot be pictured or heard or felt.

EXAMPLES hope, freedom, awe, regret, success

Writing Assignment

Great writers usually focus on abstract ideas. For example, William Shakespeare explores *ambition* in *Macbeth* and *indecision* in *Hamlet.* Define an abstract noun in a clear, specific way and use an anecdote or a concrete illustration to make it meaningful for your readers.

THE PRONOUN

1b. A *pronoun* is a word used in place of a noun or of more than one noun.

EXAMPLE The commuters complained to the mayor about the fare increase. **They** said that **he** had not warned **them** about **it.**

In the preceding example, the pronouns *they* and *them* take the place of the noun *commuters;* the pronoun *he* takes the place of the noun *mayor;* and the pronoun *it* takes the place of the noun *increase.*

Sometimes a pronoun takes the place of another pronoun.

EXAMPLE **One** of the film projectors is broken. **It** has been sent out for repair. [The pronoun *it* takes the place of the pronoun *one.*]

The word to which a pronoun refers (whose place it takes) is the *antecedent* of the pronoun. In the preceding example *one* is the antecedent of *it.*

Pronouns are classified as *personal, reflexive, intensive, relative, interrogative, demonstrative,* or *indefinite.*

Personal Pronouns

I, me	he, him	it	they, them
you	she, her	we, us	

Possessive Forms of Personal Pronouns

my, mine	his	its	their, theirs
your, yours	her, hers	our, ours	

Some of the possessive forms—*my, your, his, her, its, our, their*—are used before a noun in the same way that adjectives are used to limit the meaning of a noun: *my* parents, *your* home, *her* coat, etc. They are possessive pronouns functioning as adjectives. In this book these words are called pronouns. However, your teacher may prefer to have you call them possessive adjectives.

Reflexive and Intensive Pronouns

myself	ourselves
yourself	yourselves
himself, herself, itself	themselves

Personal pronouns combined with *-self, -selves* may be used in two ways:

1. They may be used *reflexively.*

   Miranda explained **herself.**

2. They may be used *intensively* for emphasis.

   Miranda **herself** made the explanation.

Relative Pronouns

who	which	whose
whom	that	

Relative pronouns are used to introduce subordinate clauses (see Chapter 4, pages 58–60).

EXAMPLES The college **that** I chose is in Texas.
Do you know the woman **whose** writing was mentioned?

Interrogative Pronouns

who	which	what
whom	whose	

Interrogative pronouns are used in questions.

EXAMPLES **Who** borrowed my pen?
Which do you prefer?

Demonstrative Pronouns

this	these	that	those

Demonstrative pronouns are used to point out persons or things.

EXAMPLES **That** is an excellent question.
This is the correct answer.

Most Commonly Used Indefinite Pronouns

all	everybody	no one
another	everyone	one
any	few	other
anybody	many	several
anyone	most	some
both	neither	somebody
each	nobody	someone
either	none	such

Pronouns that do not usually refer to a specific antecedent are called *indefinite pronouns*. Most indefinite pronouns express the idea of quantity: *all, few, none.*

EXAMPLES **Most** of the members have voted.
Everyone favors a weekly meeting.

EXERCISE 2. Identifying Pronouns. Number your paper 1–10. After the proper number, write the pronouns in the order in which they occur in the sentence.

1. Last year our school gave two photography courses, neither of which had been offered before.
2. The course that I took dealt with the ways in which people perceive their environment.
3. Most of us block out our everyday surroundings.
4. You can prove to yourselves how blind all of us become to our surroundings.
5. Which of you, upon returning home from a trip, suddenly notices how different all of the rooms look to you?
6. Some of your possessions may look unfamiliar to you, and a few of them may seem totally alien.
7. Eventually your house takes on its familiar appearance again.
8. Each of us can regain the ability to see freshly if we make full use of our sense of sight.
9. We must see the objects themselves as shapes instead of thinking about their function.
10. Claude Monet, a French impressionist painter, stated that we must forget the names of the things that we are looking at.

THE ADJECTIVE

1c. An *adjective* is a word used to modify a noun or a pronoun.

To modify means "to limit," or "to make the meaning of a word more definite." Adjectives may modify nouns or pronouns in any one of three different ways:

1. By telling *what kind:* **green** apples, **small** car, **capable** student
2. By pointing out *which one:* **this** woman, **that** play
3. By telling *how many:* **some** birds, **two** squirrels

As the preceding examples show, the normal position of an adjective is directly before the word it modifies. Occasionally, for stylistic reasons, a writer may use adjectives after the word they modify.

EXAMPLE The hikers, **tired** and **hungry**, straggled into camp.

A *predicate adjective* (see Chapter 2, page 32) is separated from the word it modifies by a verb.

EXAMPLES Deborah is **practical.**
His stew tasted **delicious.**

Articles

The most frequently used adjectives are *a, an,* and *the*. These words are usually called *articles.*

A and *an* are indefinite articles; they refer to one of a general group.

EXAMPLES **A** book fell down.
We worked **an** hour.

A is used before words beginning with a consonant sound; *an* is used before words beginning with a vowel sound. Notice in the second example above that *an* is used before *hour,* which begins with a consonant; that is because the *h* in *hour* is not pronounced. Remember that the *sound* of the noun, not the spelling, determines which indefinite article should be used.

The is the definite article. It indicates that a noun refers to someone or something in particular.

EXAMPLES **The** book fell down.
Margaret ate **the** orange.
The hour passed quickly.

The Same Word as Adjective and Pronoun

A word may be used as more than one part of speech. This rule is especially true of the words in the list below, which may be used both as pronouns and as adjectives.

all	many	that
another	more	these
any	neither	this
both	one	those
each	other	what
either	several	which
few	some	

ADJECTIVE **These** books are overdue. [*These* modifies the noun *books.*]
PRONOUN **These** are overdue. [*These* takes the place of a noun previously mentioned.]

ADJECTIVE We chose **neither** candidate. [*Neither* modifies the noun *candidate.*]
PRONOUN We chose **neither.** [*Neither* takes the place of a noun previously mentioned.]

Nouns Used as Adjectives

Nouns are sometimes used as adjectives.

sofa cushion   **hotel** lobby   **bread** pudding

When you are identifying parts of speech and you encounter a noun used as an adjective, label it as an adjective.

EXERCISE 3. Identifying Adjectives and the Words They Modify. Write the adjectives in the following sentences in order after the numbers of the sentences in which they appear. After each adjective, write the word(s) modified. Do not list articles (*a, an,* and *the*).

1. The first person to walk on the moon was Neil Armstrong, the American astronaut.
2. Young people admire the sleek look of a new car.
3. Nine players are needed to form a baseball team.
4. "That engine will work for many years," said Mr. Sanchez.
5. On a sultry July afternoon we enjoyed sitting under the branches of a beautiful willow tree.
6. The rich soil of Kansas accounts for the high agricultural yield of that state.
7. Eager fans waited for several hours to buy tickets for the rock concert.
8. Some regard Jim Thorpe, an Oklahoma Indian, as the greatest all-around athlete America has yet produced.
9. On an ordinary day the major television networks offer serious and comic programs.
10. Sharon made a narrow vase, a deep bowl, and a coffee mug in her pottery class; she was proud of these accomplishments.

EXERCISE 4. Identifying Nouns, Pronouns, and Adjectives. For each sentence below, write the italicized words in order in a column, numbering them as in the example. After each word, tell what part of speech it is. If a word is an adjective, write in parentheses the word that the adjective modifies. Do not list articles (*a, an,* and *the*).

EXAMPLE 1. *Everyone* in class is writing a poem about a *famous American.*
1. *Everyone, pron.*
famous, adj., (*American*)
American, n.

1. *Some* students are writing *theirs* about well-known Presidents; *others* have chosen *military* heroes as *their* subjects.
2. *Most* of *us* are writing about *someone whom* we admire.
3. The *aviator* Amelia Earhart is a *popular* subject; *another* choice is Harriet Tubman, the *courageous* woman who led *many* people to *freedom* on the Underground Railroad.
4. *Both* of *these* women made lasting *impressions* in their time.
5. On Earhart's attempted around-the-world *flight, radio* contact aboard her plane was broken and never resumed.
6. *Speculation* about the *nature* of Earhart's flight continues; *many* believe that she was on an *intelligence* mission.
7. Tubman was *one* of *many* former slaves *who* devoted their lives to the *cause* of freedom and to the *advancement* of their people.
8. The *abolitionist* John Brown referred to her as "*General Tubman.*"
9. Although she *herself* was *free,* she could not be happy while even *one* member of her family remained a *slave;* once she brought as many as *twenty-five* slaves to freedom in a *single* band.
10. *Nobody* in our class seems *unhappy* with his or her choice of *subject.*

WRITING APPLICATION B:
Replacing Drab Adjectives with Fresh, Lively Ones

You use adjectives to make nouns and pronouns more definite. Adjectives tell what kind, which one, or how many. Try to replace the old worn-out adjectives with fresh, even startling ones. For example, look at the fresh, vivid adjectives Gerard Manley Hopkins uses to describe a falcon in his poem "The Windhover": ". . . *dapple-dawn-drawn* Falcon . . . how he rung upon the rein of the *wimpling* wing. . . ."

Writing Assignment

Select a childhood experience that had particular meaning for you. As you describe this experience, try to use fresh, lively adjectives.

THE VERB

1d. A *verb* is a word that expresses action or otherwise helps to make a statement.

All verbs help to make a statement. Some help to make a statement by expressing action. The action expressed may be physical, as in *hit, play,* and *run,* or it may be mental, as in *think, imagine, believe.*

Transitive and Intransitive Verbs

Action verbs may or may not take an *object*—a noun or pronoun that completes the action by showing *who* or *what* is affected by the action. Verbs that have an object are called *transitive.* The verbs in the following examples are transitive:

EXAMPLES The rain **lashed** the windows. [*Windows* is the object of *lashed.*]
My cousin **bought** a new car. [*Car* is the object of *bought.*]

Verbs that express action without objects are called *intransitive.*

EXAMPLES The rain **fell.**
My cousin **drove.**

Some action verbs are transitive only (*ignore, complete*) and some intransitive only (*arrive, exist*). Most verbs in English can be either.

EXAMPLES The chorus **sang** patriotic *songs.* [transitive]
The chorus **sang.** [intransitive]

> **NOTE** Most dictionaries group the meanings of verbs according to whether they are transitive (*v.t.* in most dictionaries) or intransitive (*v.i.*).

Linking Verbs

Some verbs express a state or condition. These verbs link to the subject a noun, a pronoun, or an adjective that describes or identifies the subject. They are called *linking verbs.* These verbs are *intransitives.* The word that is linked to the subject is called a *subject complement.*

EXAMPLES This **is** *she.* [*She* refers to the subject *this.*]
She **looks** *serious.* [*Serious* refers to the subject *she.*]

The subject complement always refers to the subject of the linking verb. It may identify the subject, as in the first example, or describe the subject, as in the second one.

The most common linking verb is the verb *be,*[1] which has the

[1] The verb *be* can also be followed by certain adverbs and adverb phrases: We were *there;* the men were *at work.* In this situation, *be* is not considered a linking verb.

following forms: *am, is, are, was, were, be, being, been* (and all verb phrases ending in *be, being,* or *been,* such as *can be, is being,* and *could have been*). Other common linking verbs are listed below.

Common Linking Verbs

appear	grow	seem	stay
become	look	smell	taste
feel	remain	sound	

Many of the verbs in the preceding list can also be used as action verbs—that is, without a subject complement.

LINKING The singer **appeared** nervous.
ACTION The singer **appeared** on television.

In general, a verb is a linking verb if you can substitute some form of the verb *seem* for it.

EXAMPLES The audience **looked** [seemed] sympathetic.
The singer gradually **grew** [seemed] more relaxed.

The Helping Verb and the Verb Phrase

A *verb phrase* is made up of a main verb and one or more *helping verbs* (sometimes called *auxiliary verbs*). Helping verbs *help* the main verb to express action or make a statement. The helping verbs in the following phrases are printed in boldfaced type:

has played	**will be** coming
should have paid	**must have been** injured

In other words, a verb phrase is a verb of more than one word.

Common Helping Verbs

am	has	can (may) have
are	had	could (would, should) be
is	can	could (would, should) have
was	may	will (shall) have been
were	will (shall) be	might have
do	will (shall) have	might have been
did	has (had) been	must
have	can (may) be	must have
		must have been

The parts of a verb phrase may be separated from one another by words; i.e., the helping verb may be separated from the main verb.

GRAMMAR

EXAMPLES **Did** you **see** Lorraine Hansberry's play?
We **have** not **seen** it yet.

EXERCISE 5. Identifying and Classifying Verbs and Verb Phrases. Write in order the verbs and verb phrases in the following sentences. After each verb, tell whether it is transitive (*v.t.*), intransitive (*v.i.*), or linking (*l.v.*). List all the words in a verb phrase.

GRAMMAR

1. The Statue of Liberty, which has become a major American landmark, may well be the best-known structure in the world.
2. It possesses a twofold magic: it symbolizes human liberty, and it unfailingly awes the visitor by its sheer size.
3. Moreover, it has never fallen down and has survived everything that wind and weather can throw at it.
4. Although Frederic-Auguste Bartholdi designed the statue, the supporting framework came from the drawing board of Alexandre-Gustave Eiffel.
5. The copper statue has an intricate inner network that supports Liberty's somewhat awkward pose.
6. The statue itself was a gift from the people of France, but American contributions paid for the construction of the pedestal.
7. In newspaper editorials, Joseph Pulitzer persuaded the American people that they needed this statue.
8. They agreed, and in 1886 celebrated the dedication of the Statue of Liberty on what was then Bedloe's Island in New York Bay.
9. Bartholdi had borrowed his mother's features for Liberty's face.
10. Those features have remained symbols of quiet determination.

WRITING APPLICATION C: Selecting Precise Verbs

The particular verb you choose can transform a vague idea into a highly specific one. Notice the shades of meaning suggested by the following verb changes: He *talked* (*negotiated, chattered*) for an hour.

Writing Assignment

An incident that on the surface seems unimportant may actually be quite significant. Write a journal entry describing such an event. Use fresh, specific verbs.

THE ADVERB

1e. An *adverb* is a word used to modify a verb, an adjective, or another adverb.

The adverb is used most commonly as the modifier of a verb. It may tell *how, when, where,* or *to what extent* (*how often* or *how much*) the action of the verb is done.

EXAMPLES She reads **quickly.** [*Quickly* tells *how* she reads.]
She reads **early** and **late.** [*Early* and *late* tell *when* she reads.]
She reads **everywhere.** [*Everywhere* tells *where* she reads.]
She reads **thoroughly.** [*Thoroughly* tells *to what extent* she reads.]
She reads **frequently.** [*Frequently* tells *how often* she reads.]

Some adverbs, such as *really, actually, truly, indeed,* are used chiefly for emphasis. Classify these adverbs as adverbs of extent.

EXAMPLES Rosa can **really** skate. [*Really* emphasizes the fine quality of Rosa's skating.]
She is **truly** a fine skater. [*Truly* emphasizes the fact that she is a fine skater.]
She can **actually** fly over the ice. [*Actually* emphasizes the fact that she can fly over the ice, which is apparently a surprise to the speaker.]

An adverb may modify an adjective.

EXAMPLE She is a **really** intense competitor. [*Really* modifies the adjective *intense,* telling to what extent she is competitive.]

An adverb may modify another adverb.

EXAMPLE She skated **very** well. [The adverb *very* modifies the adverb *well,* telling how well she skated.]

> ☞ **NOTE** The word *not* is classified as an adverb; it tells *to what extent.*

Nouns Used as Adverbs

Some nouns may be used adverbially.

EXAMPLES My parents left **yesterday.**
They will return **Saturday.**

In identifying parts of speech, label nouns used in this way as adverbs.

EXERCISE 6. Identifying Adverbs and the Words They Modify. Write the adverbs in the following sentences in order after the proper number. After each adverb, write the word or words it modifies and state whether the adverb tells *how, when, where,* or *to what extent.*

1. Dr. Rosalyn Yalow is an American physicist who helped develop an extremely sensitive biological technique.
2. Radioimmunoassay is now used in laboratories here and abroad and can readily detect infinitesimal biological substances.
3. Dr. Yalow writes, "If you ever have a new idea, and it's really new, you have to expect that it will not be widely accepted immediately."
4. In other words, unlike Archimedes, scientists do not leap excitedly from the bath crying, "Eureka!"
5. Dr. Yalow and her colleague accidentally discovered radioimmunoassay while they were observing two patients.
6. They then carefully interpreted their observations and arrived at their exciting discovery.
7. Although her collaborator was deceased, the Nobel Prize Committee promptly excepted its rule and awarded Dr. Yalow the undeniably prestigious Nobel Prize for Medicine.

8. Radioimmunoassay was an unquestionably important discovery; it soon became a scientifically basic tool for investigation in widely different areas of medicine.
9. According to Dr. Yalow, the technique was not quickly accepted because people ordinarily resist change.
10. She is convinced that progress can not be obstructed forever and that eventually a highly original idea is accepted.

EXERCISE 7. Identifying the Parts of Speech of Words. Write the numbered, italicized words. After each word, tell what part of speech it is; then, after each adjective or adverb, tell what word or words it modifies.

Lizards may be sleek, slender, and (1) *graceful;* or they may be (2) *fantastically* ugly, with grotesque (3) *horns,* spines, and frilly collars. (4) *They* have startling habits. They may snap off (5) *their* tails when they are seized. (6) *Some* may rear up and run (7) *away* on their hind legs. (8) *Certainly*, there (9) *is* nothing (10) *commonplace* about lizards.

(11) *Warmer* portions of the earth (12) *have* the (13) *greatest* number and variety of lizards, but (14) *they* are (15) *also* found in temperate latitudes. There are about 125 (16) *different* kinds in the United States.

(17) *One* of the most familiar is the little chameleon, also called the anolis. (18) *It* (19) *belongs* to the iguana family and is (20) *quite* different from the (21) *true* chameleon family of Africa.

THE PREPOSITION

1f. A *preposition* is a word used to show the relation of a noun or pronoun to some other word in the sentence.

In the following sentences the prepositions are shown in boldfaced type. The words between which the prepositions show relationships are italicized.

> The first *speaker* **on** the *program* is my mother.
> Her cousin *will teach* **in** *San Diego* next year.
> The *two* **of** *us* edited the *article* **for** the *magazine*.

Object of a Preposition

A preposition appears at the beginning of a phrase (see Chapter 3, page 37). The noun or pronoun at the end of a prepositional phrase is the *object* of the preposition that begins the phrase.

EXAMPLES before **lunch** at the **game**

Commonly Used Prepositions

about	between	over
above	beyond	past
across	but (meaning "except")	since
after	by	through
against	concerning	throughout
along	down	to
amid	during	toward
among	except	under
around	for	underneath
at	from	until
before	in	unto
behind	into	up
below	like	upon
beneath	of	with
beside	off	within
besides	on	without

A group of words may act as a preposition: *on account of, in spite of.*

GRAMMAR

EXERCISE 8. Writing Sentences With Prepositions. Write five sentences, each containing a different one of the following prepositions. Underline each prepositional phrase and circle the object of each preposition.

1. against 2. below 3. during 4. into 5. until

THE CONJUNCTION

1g. A *conjunction* is a word that joins words or groups of words.

The conjunctions below are printed in boldfaced type; the words or groups of words that the conjunctions join are italicized.

The bear *turned* **and** *lumbered* off into the woods.
We can use a *pickup truck* **or** a *jeep*.
She helped **both** *Carrie* **and** *me* with our applications.
The doctor will call back **after** *he has studied the X-rays.*

There are three kinds of conjunctions: *coordinating* conjunctions, *correlative* conjunctions, and *subordinating* conjunctions.

Coordinating Conjunctions

and but or nor for so yet

Correlative Conjunctions

either . . . or	not only . . . but (also)
neither . . . nor	whether . . . or
both . . . and	

Correlative conjunctions are always used in pairs.

These shirts are available **not only** in small sizes **but also** in outsizes.
The speech was **neither** eloquent **nor** convincing.

Commonly Used Subordinating Conjunctions[1]

after	before	provided	unless
although	how	since	until
as	if	than	when
as much as	inasmuch as	that	where
because	in order that	though	while

[1] Some of these words may be used as prepositions: *after, before, since, until;* others may be used as adverbs: *how, when, where. That* is often used as a relative pronoun.

Subordinating conjunctions are used to begin subordinate clauses (see Chapter 4, pages 64–66), usually adverb clauses.

In the following sentences, the subordinate clauses are italicized, and the subordinating conjunctions are in boldfaced type.

This computer is even better **than** *we had anticipated.*
The sun had already set **when** *we reached Grand Canyon National Park.*

A subordinating conjunction does not always come between the sentence parts that it joins. It may come at the beginning of the sentence.

If the price is right, I will buy your bicycle.
Since you can't help me, I will do it myself.

EXERCISE 9. Identifying and Classifying Conjunctions. Number your paper 1–10. After each number, write the conjunction(s) in the sentence. Then classify the conjunction(s) as coordinating, correlative, or subordinating.

1. Our old car needs either a valve job or a new engine.
2. Before you write your paper, you must submit an outline.
3. I don't know whether I'll take physics or economics next year.
4. Taritha excels not only as a swimmer but also as a musician.
5. After I had read the novel *The Return of the Native,* I became a Thomas Hardy fan.
6. Workers here pay city, state, and federal income taxes.
7. Because the Tsang family had installed a smoke detector in their home, their lives were saved.
8. Both Mike and Sue work at the same supermarket.
9. Are you going to the movies or not?
10. When I looked in my wallet, I was amazed to find five dollars.

THE INTERJECTION

1h. An *interjection* is a word that expresses emotion and has no grammatical relation to other words in the sentence.

EXAMPLES Oh! My goodness! Ah! Ouch!

THE SAME WORD AS DIFFERENT PARTS OF SPEECH

Many words in English may be used as more than one part of speech. For example, *these* may be an adjective (*these books*) or a pronoun (*I want these*); *Tuesday* may be a noun (*Tuesday is my birthday*) or an adverb (*Come Tuesday*). Thousands of words like these can be classified by part of speech only when you see them in sentences.

EXAMPLES The **plant** was growing in a terrarium. [*Plant* names a living thing; it is a noun.]
We usually **plant** tomatoes in the spring. [*Plant* expresses action; it is a verb.]
Bacteria cause many **plant** diseases. [*Plant* modifies *diseases;* it is an adjective.]

REVIEW EXERCISE. Identifying the Parts of Speech of Words. In a column on your paper, write the italicized words in the following paragraphs. Determine the use of each word, and write its part of speech.

One summer (1) *night* (2) *several* years ago I was (3) *suddenly* awakened (4) *by* the noisy clatter of garbage cans. I quickly ran (5) *outside* (6) *where* I heard scratching noises from inside the large can (7) *that* held (8) *most* of our garbage. I cautiously (9) *removed* the lid and (10) *out* popped a family of raccoons.

Since then I have learned that a (11) *myth* about raccoons is (12) *untrue:* raccoons (13) *are* not (14) *fastidious.* True, they (15) *wash* their food before they eat (16) *it.* The purpose, however, is not improved hygiene (17) *but* improved taste. Moreover, raccoons will greedily eat (18) *everything* in sight. (19) *Among* their favorite dishes are berries, small birds, and, of course—(20) *ugh!*—garbage.

CHAPTER 1 REVIEW: POSTTEST 1

Identifying the Parts of Speech of Words. Number your paper 1–20. Each of the following sentences contains at least one word of the kind specified. Find those words and write them after the proper number. Base your answers on the way each word is used in the sentence.

EXAMPLES 1. I have an interesting job. (*noun*)
1. *job*

2. Did they hunt and fish yesterday? (*verb*)
2. *hunt, fish*

1. Dr. Samuel Johnson compiled the first dictionary in the English language. (*adjective*)
2. Did Elizabeth's parents want her to try out for the squad? (*pronoun*)
3. My keys were sitting on the table, but I was convinced that I had lost them in the yard. (*pronoun*)
4. Although she was blind and deaf, Helen Keller learned to communicate effectively with other people. (*noun*)
5. At the end of the game, neither the coach nor the team members could account for the lopsided score. (*conjunction*)
6. Drivers in the Indianapolis 500 must stay continuously alert and be extremely skillful. (*adverb*)
7. How can you best prepare yourself for an effective interview? (*noun*)
8. The ads for the movie *Summer Mystery* ironically promised that the film would be "a chilling thriller." (*adverb*)
9. We wanted to eat at the Russian Tea Room, but we couldn't afford the prices. (*conjunction*)
10. John Updike's novels have met with praise from critics and public alike. (*preposition*)
11. Mr. and Mrs. Lopez spent three snowy winters in Vermont. (*adjective*)
12. After her successful concert, Heidi said that the praise of her teacher, Ms. Hawkins, was her greatest reward. (*verb*)
13. The evening air felt rather cool as we opened the door of the densely packed gymnasium and stepped outside. (*adverb*)
14. A man with a full beard slipped a note to a sinister-looking character during the first intermission of the show. (*preposition*)
15. Oh, what a magnificent performance of *Faust*! (*interjection*)
16. The blurb on the jacket of the novel promised "the intense emotional experience of both sorrow and joy." (*noun*)
17. The detectives thought that there might have been a burglary when they noticed that the lock had scratch marks around it. (*verb*)
18. This antique clock chimes a soulful note every hour. (*adjective*)
19. When I had finished the test, I handed Ms. Martello my paper, returned to my seat, and became calmer. (*verb*)
20. At the start of the movie, I wondered about the sound effects that came toward me from all sides. (*preposition*)

CHAPTER 1 REVIEW: POSTTEST 2

Writing Sentences with Words Used as Specific Parts of Speech. Write twenty sentences according to the following guidelines. Use the dictionary for help.

1. Use *yesterday* as an adverb.
2. Use *when* as a subordinating conjunction.
3. Use *sound* as a noun.
4. Use *all* as a pronoun.
5. Use *fire* as a verb.
6. Use *leather* as an adjective.
7. Use *terrific* as an interjection.
8. Use *up* as a preposition.
9. Use *hard* as an adverb.
10. Use *both* as an adjective.

SUMMARY OF PARTS OF SPEECH

Rule	*Part of Speech*	*Use*	*Examples*
1a	noun	names	man, Iowa, corn, justice, cattle
1b	pronoun	takes the place of a noun	he, us, herself, mine, this, who
1c	adjective	modifies a noun or pronoun	red, large, two
1d	verb	shows action or helps to make a statement	is, does, have, wanted, seems
1e	adverb	modifies a verb, an adjective, or another adverb	rapidly, well, somewhat, too
1f	preposition	relates a noun or a pronoun to another word	into, below, from, of
1g	conjunction	joins words or groups of words	and, but, or, for, after, as, until
1h	interjection	shows strong feeling	Ow!

GRAMMAR

CHAPTER 2

The Parts of a Sentence

SUBJECTS, PREDICATES, COMPLEMENTS

With only two terms—*subject* and *predicate*—you could describe most English sentences. However, to achieve a fuller understanding of the structure of English sentences, you also need to know the name and function of some other important sentence elements: *object, predicate nominative,* and *predicate adjective,* to name only the most important. You have met all of these terms in previous English classes. Use the following diagnostic test to see which terms, if any, you need to review.

DIAGNOSTIC TEST

Identifying Subjects, Predicates, and Complements. Number your paper 1–20. For each sentence, identify the italicized word or words using these abbreviations: *s.*(subject), *v.*(verb), *d.o.* (direct object), *i.o.* (indirect object), *p.n.* (predicate nominative), and *p.a.* (predicate adjective).

EXAMPLE 1. Jim's *sarcasm* made him unpopular.
1. *s.*

1. *Some* of your classmates will attend.
2. This experience taught me a valuable *lesson.*

3. Out of the darkness came a huge, lumbering *creature.*
4. To everyone's surprise, Jane and I *were* not late.
5. The water in the bay seemed very *cold.*
6. The only people in the water were the *children.*
7. This morning the mail carrier *left* this letter for you.
8. He gave *me* this one, too.
9. Lee Trevino is an excellent *golfer.*
10. Mechanics had just assembled and checked all *parts* of the motor.
11. Cheryl gave *me* her paper to proofread.
12. Yolanda is the *valedictorian* of her class.
13. Please put the *dishes* away.
14. Yesterday seemed rather *dreary.*
15. I *wrote* that essay in less than an hour.
16. Examples of religious music are *Gregorian chants, church hymns,* and *gospel singing.*
17. There are only fifteen *problems* for tonight's assignment.
18. Please do not omit any necessary *punctuation.*
19. Brian told *Arnie* some very funny stories.
20. In the middle of the road was a large *patch* of ice.

2a. A *sentence* is a group of words expressing a complete thought.

SENTENCE	The significance of the computer as a message carrier is often ignored.
NOT A SENTENCE	The significance of the computer as a message carrier
SENTENCE	A computer can instantly scan its entire library for documents of interest to the user.
NOT A SENTENCE	A computer instantly scanning its entire library for documents of interest to the user

SUBJECT AND PREDICATE

2b. A sentence consists of two parts: the *subject* and the *predicate.* The *subject* of the sentence is the part about which something is being said. The *predicate* is the part that says something about the subject.

SUBJECT	PREDICATE
Computers and electronic calculators	can solve problems quickly.

PREDICATE	SUBJECT
Ahead of us may lie	a universal computer language.

A subject or a predicate may consist of a single word or of many words. The whole subject is called the *complete subject;* the whole predicate, the *complete predicate.* However long a subject or predicate may be, it always has a core, or an essential part.

The Simple Subject

2c. The *simple subject* is the principal word or group of words in the subject.

EXAMPLES The most distinguished participant at the ceremonies was the President. [subject: *The most distinguished participant at the ceremonies;* simple subject: *participant*]

The Memorial Coliseum in Los Angeles was filled to capacity. [subject: *The Memorial Coliseum in Los Angeles;* simple subject: *Memorial Coliseum*]

> **NOTE** Throughout this book the term *subject,* when used in connection with the sentence, refers to the simple subject; the term *verb* refers to the simple predicate.

The Simple Predicate, or Verb

2d. The principal word or group of words in the predicate is called the *simple predicate,* or the *verb.*

EXAMPLE The athletes were greeted with cheers. [predicate: *were greeted with cheers;* simple predicate: *were greeted*]

Compound Subjects and Verbs

2e. A *compound subject* consists of two or more subjects that are joined by a conjunction and have the same verb. The usual connecting words are *and* and *or.*

EXAMPLE Jomo and Ahmed wore long, flowing robes. [compound subject: *Jomo . . . Ahmed*]

2f. A *compound verb* consists of two or more verbs that are joined by a conjunction and have the same subject.

GRAMMAR

EXAMPLE Mary McLeod Bethune founded Bethune-Cookman College and served twice as its president. [compound verb: *founded . . . served*]

How to Find the Subject of a Sentence

To find the subject of a sentence, first find the verb (the simple predicate); then ask yourself the question "Who or what . . . ?" For instance, in the sentence "Outside the wall walked an armed guard," the verb is *walked.* Ask the question, "Who or what walked?" The answer is *guard walked. Guard* is the subject of the sentence.

In addition to this simple formula for locating the subject, here are some other facts you should keep in mind:

1. In sentences expressing a command or a request, the subject is always *you,* even though the word *you* may not appear in the sentence.

(You) Proofread your report after typing it.
(You) Please submit a cover sheet with your report.

2. The subject of a sentence is never in a prepositional phrase.

Neither of these books has an index. [verb: *has* What has? *Neither. Neither* is the subject. *Books* is not the subject. It is in the prepositional phrase *of these books.*]

The rules of punctuation are sometimes frustrating. [verb: *are* What are? *Rules. Rules* is the subject. *Punctuation* is the object of the preposition *of.*]

3. To find the subject in a question, turn the question into statement form.

QUESTION What subject did you choose for your speech?
STATEMENT You did choose what subject for your speech? [subject: *you;* verb: *did choose*]

4. *There* and *here* are not usually the subjects of a verb. Except in a statement like the previous sentence, *there* and *here* are either adverbs or expletives.

Here is your pencil. [verb: *is;* subject: *pencil* In this sentence the word *here* is an adverb telling where.]
There are several good points in your argument. [verb: *are;* subject: *points*]

In this last use, *there* is an *expletive,* a word used to get the sentence started. The word *it* may also be used as an expletive. *It is senseless to leave.*

EXERCISE 1. Identifying Subjects and Verbs. Number your paper 1–10. Write the subject and the verb of each sentence after the proper number. Underline subjects once and verbs twice. Include all parts of compound subjects and verbs, as well as all words in a verb phrase.

1. Researchers at Harvard and Stanford universities studied the exercise patterns of 17,000 subjects and reported the results.
2. Participants climbed stairs, walked, and engaged in sports.
3. High blood pressure and cardiovascular disease have been blamed on the lack of physical fitness.
4. However, until recently no scientific proof had been offered of the link between exercise and fitness.
5. Now scientists from Harvard and Stanford urge regular exercise.
6. Even brisk walks four times a week may prevent serious diseases.
7. The real discovery of this research is the presence of cardiovascular disease in sedentary people.
8. For years physicians have been aware of this connection but have not always succeeded in convincing their patients of it.
9. Carefully consider your own physical activities.
10. There could be changes in your approach to physical fitness.

COMPLEMENTS

Some sentences express a complete thought by means of a subject and verb only.

S V — She won. S V — The spectators cheered.

Most sentences, however, have one word or more in the predicate that completes the meaning of the subject and verb. These completing words are called *complements.*

She won	the **race.**
Someone sent	**me** a **rose.**
She is	the **mayor** of our town.
The ripest ones are	**those.**
They seem	**industrious.**

He called **me overconfident.**
Who made **you boss?**

> **NOTE** An adverb modifying the verb is not a complement. Only nouns, pronouns, and adjectives function as complements.

Dr. Ames is **here.** [The adverb *here* modifies the verb *is.* It is not a complement.]
Dr. Ames is **brilliant.** [The adjective *brilliant* is a complement.]

Direct and Indirect Objects

Complements that receive, or are affected by, the action of the verb are called *objects.* There are two kinds: the *direct object* and the *indirect object.*

2g. The *direct object* of the verb receives the action of the verb or shows the result of the action. It answers the question *What?* or *Whom?* after an action verb.

We drove **Jim** to the train station. [We drove *whom*?]
He was carrying a large **suitcase.** [He was carrying *what*?]

Except when it ends in *-self* (*myself, himself*), the object of a verb never refers to the same person or thing as the subject.

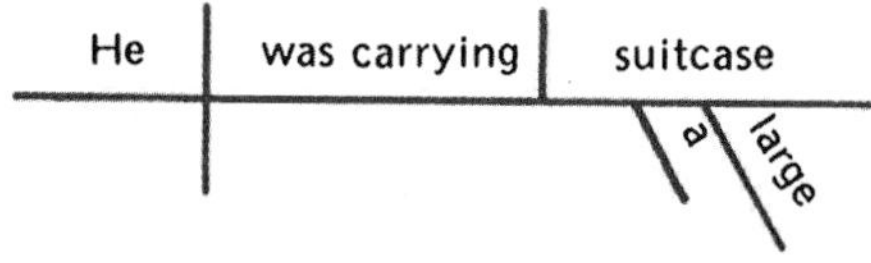

> **NOTE** Sentence diagrams are "pictures" of the structure of a sentence. They are used in this book as aids so that the functions of words and word groups in a sentence can be more easily seen.

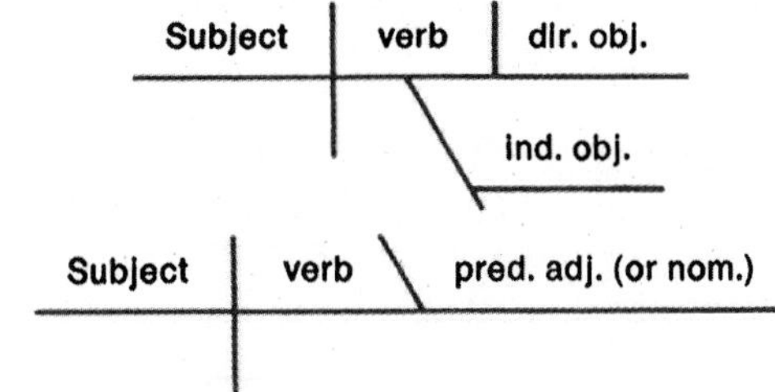

2h. The *indirect object* of the verb precedes the direct object and usually tells to whom or for whom the action of the verb is done.

If the word *to* or *for* is used, the noun or pronoun following it is part of a prepositional phrase; it is not an indirect object.

Mr. Bates promised me a job. [*Me* is an indirect object.]
Mr. Bates promised a job to me. [*Me* is part of the phrase *to me.*]

EXAMPLES He gave **us** his permission. [gave *to* us]

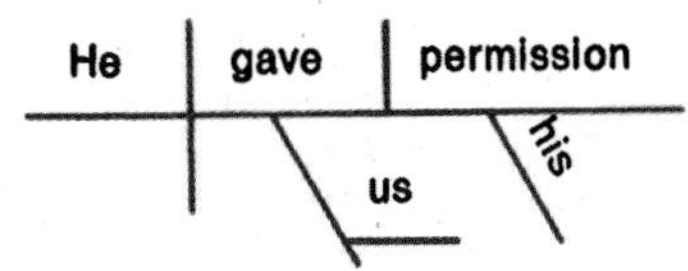

Bob made his **mother** a writing desk. [made *for* his mother]

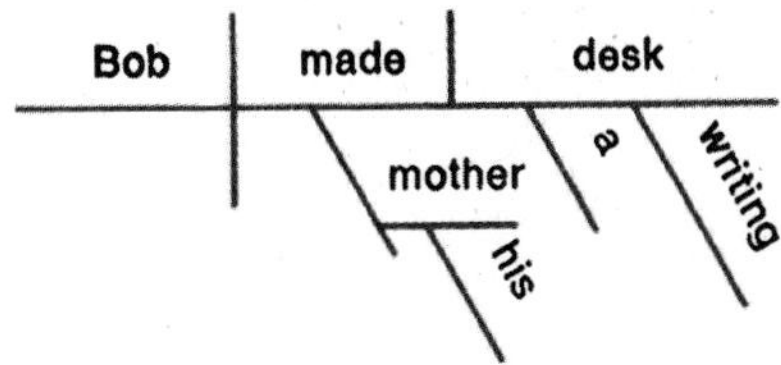

Objects of the verb may be compound.

Mrs. Spiers praised the stage **crew** and the **cast.**

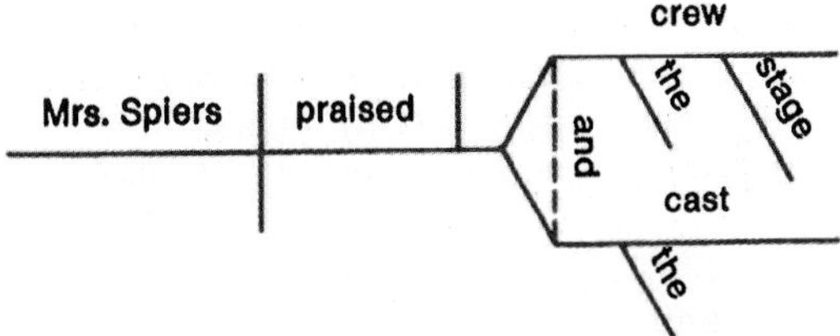

She gave **George** and **me** several suggestions.

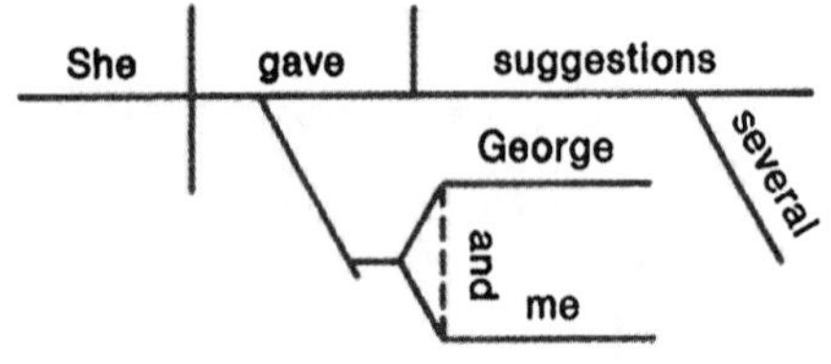

The Objective Complement

To complete their meaning, some action verbs require an additional complement following their objects. This additional complement is called an *objective complement* because it refers to the object; it may be a noun or an adjective.

They elected Mary **chairwoman**. [The noun *chairwoman* refers to the direct object *Mary* and helps to complete the meaning of the verb *elected*. It is an objective complement.]

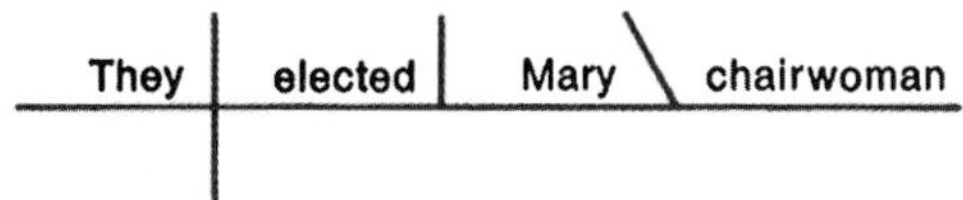

You made her **angry.** [The adjective *angry* modifies the direct object *her* and helps to complete the meaning of the verb *made*. It is an objective complement.]

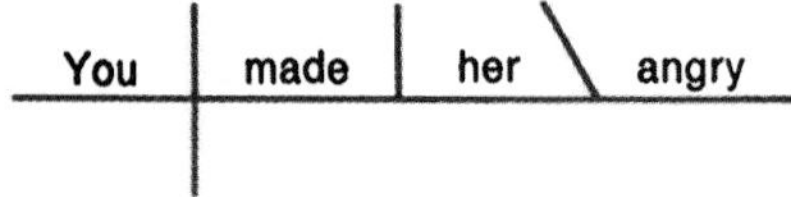

Only a few verbs take an objective complement. They usually mean "make" or "consider": *elect, appoint, name, choose, render, make, consider,* etc.

The cat licked its paws **clean.** [*made* its paws clean]
We painted my room **green.** [*made* my room green]
I thought the joke **tasteless.** [*considered* the joke tasteless]

EXERCISE 2. Identifying Direct Objects, Indirect Objects, and Objective Complements. Number your paper 1–10. After the proper number, write the objects in the sentence. After each object, write *i.o.* for indirect object, *d.o.* for direct object, or *o.c.* for objective complement.

1. Computers may have created the automobile revolution of the 1980's.
2. A spokesperson for the industry showed reporters several examples of computerized cars.
3. One car has a computer display for its speedometer and its turn signals.
4. Another makes trips a pleasure with computerized information.
5. Some cars have seven computers on board.
6. A voice synthesizer in one car warns the driver of drowsiness.
7. According to engineers, computers can give us an amazing amount of detailed and accurate information about a car.
8. Car computers can make predictions about engine failure.
9. One computer even makes a car burglarproof.
10. On the negative side, some safety experts consider colorful computer panels a driving hazard.

Subject Complements

Complements that refer to (describe, explain, or identify) the subject are *subject complements.* There are two kinds: the *predicate nominative* and the *predicate adjective.*

Subject complements follow linking verbs only. The common linking verbs are the forms of the verb *be* (see page 13) and the following verbs: *become, seem, grow, appear, look, feel, smell, taste, remain, sound,* and *stay.*

2i. A *predicate nominative* is a noun or pronoun complement that refers to the same person or thing as the subject of the verb. It follows a linking verb.

New York is our largest **city.** [*City* refers to the subject *New York.*]

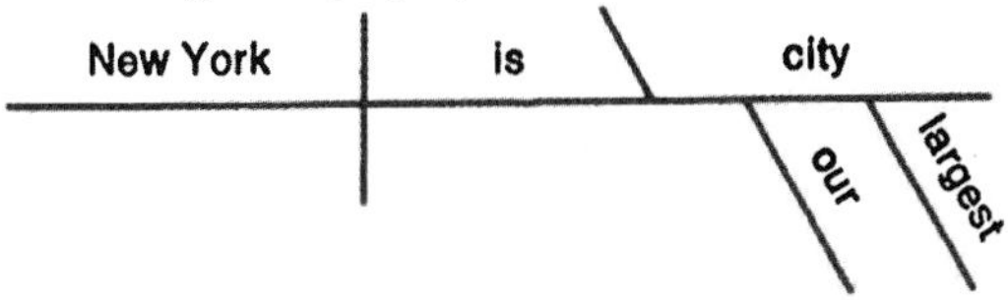

New York | is \ city
our
largest

GRAMMAR

My favorite authors are **Austen** and **she.** [Compound predicate nominative: *Austen* and *she* refer to the same people as the subject *authors.*]

2j. A *predicate adjective* is an adjective complement that modifies the subject of the verb. It follows a linking verb.

This book is **dull.** [The predicate adjective *dull* modifies the subject *book.*]

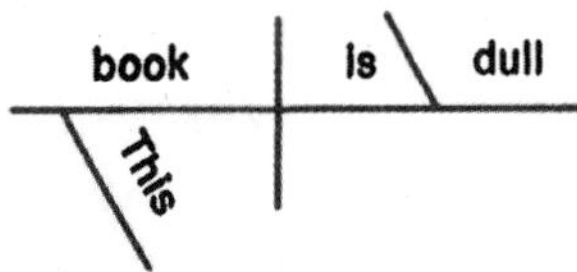

His speech seemed **repetitious** and **tiresome.** [Compound predicate adjective modifying the subject *speech.*]

In the normal order of an English sentence, complements follow the verb. However, a complement may precede the verb.

This **song** he wrote in 1980. [*Song* is the direct object of the verb *wrote.*]

Fortunate are those who can learn from their mistakes. [*Fortunate* is a predicate adjective modifying the subject *those.*]

EXERCISE 3. Identifying Predicate Nominatives and Predicate Adjectives. Number your paper 1–10. After the proper number, write any predicate nominatives or predicate adjectives in the sentence; identify each complement with the abbreviation *p.n.* or *p.a.* Some sentences contain more than one complement.

1. Her nominating speech was both effective and convincing.
2. In 1817, Monroe became the fourth President from Virginia.
3. Iago grew increasingly more ruthless and cunning.
4. The witness' account of the accident seems plausible.
5. The cats appeared nervous during the storm.
6. Pablo Casals was not only a famous cellist but also a respected conductor.
7. The spray tasted salty and the wind felt cold.
8. The rooms in the restored guardhouse smelled musty.
9. Those strawberries look ripe and delicious.
10. That reflector was once the most powerful telescope in the entire world.

REVIEW EXERCISE. Identifying Subjects, Verbs, and Complements. Number your paper 1–10. After the proper number, write the subject, the verb, and any complements in the sentence. After each complement, identify as follows: *d.o.* (direct object); *i.o.* (indirect object); *p.n.* (predicate nominative); *p.a.* (predicate adjective); or *o.c.* (objective complement).

1. "Mark Twain" is the pseudonym of the American writer Samuel Langhorne Clemens.
2. He became famous for his stories about the Mississippi.
3. Through his writings he has given us homespun pictures of America and tales of life in the mining camps of the West.
4. At his death in 1910, many critics considered him the most prominent American writer of his generation.
5. Twain had some curious notions about his life story.
6. Over the years those ideas became even more curious.
7. He told William Dean Howells the scheme of his autobiography.
8. That scheme was apparently a haphazard one.
9. The first published autobiographies were fragmentary and imperfect.
10. Charles Neider's edited version is, however, a magnificent document of value both as literature and as entertainment.

WRITING APPLICATION:
Using Complete Sentences in Your Writing

Add variety to your writing by experimenting with the placement of subjects and verbs.

EXAMPLE From out of the misty darkness, swaying and undulating around a steaming pot, appeared three filthy witches. [The verb *appeared* and the subject *witches* are at the end of the sentence.]

Writing Assignment

In literature, *an epiphany* is a sudden realization. Experiencing an epiphany is like turning a light on in a darkened room. Suddenly, you see what you didn't see before, perhaps about your own strengths and weaknesses. Write about an epiphany—your own, a friend's, or a fictional character's. At some point, vary subject and verb placement.

CHAPTER 2 REVIEW: POSTTEST 1

Identifying Subjects, Verbs, and Complements. Number your paper 1–20. For each sentence, identify the italicized word as follows: *s.* (subject), *v.* (verb), *d.o.* (direct object), *i.o.* (indirect object), *p.n.* (predicate nominative), *p.a.* (predicate adjective), or *o.c.* (objective complement).

EXAMPLE 1. Studying the map carefully, we *decided* on the shortest route.
1. *v.*

1. The gymnastics team elected Terry *captain.*
2. *Robert Frost* became famous as a poet.
3. The desk *was moved* to a corner of the room.
4. My little sister has an interesting coin *collection.*
5. The directions on the package were *clear.*
6. Rob gave *her* a smile.
7. The home economics class hosted a *luncheon* for their parents.
8. I *read* the newspaper for news of sales and bargains.
9. Margaret received a ten-speed *bicycle* for her birthday.
10. The factory owner gave his *employees* a raise in pay.
11. Each spring, millions of people *watch* the Academy Awards on television.
12. One of the most valuable experiences of my life was *scouting.*
13. Did you give *Ming Chin* directions to the beach?
14. My grandfather got a *part* in an amateur play.
15. After work, will *you* call me so that we can make plans?
16. I felt *energetic* after my exercise workout.
17. Alice Walker has become a well-known *writer.*
18. *Place* the disk in the disk drive first.
19. My mother is *taller* than any of her four sisters.
20. Without warning, out jumped a *mouse*!

CHAPTER 2 REVIEW: POSTTEST 2

Writing Sentences. Write your own sentences, one of each of the following kinds, and underline the subjects and verbs.

1. A sentence with a compound subject and a compound verb
2. A sentence with a direct object and an indirect object
3. A sentence with a direct object and an objective complement
4. A sentence with a predicate nominative
5. A sentence with a predicate adjective

SUMMARY OF SENTENCE PATTERNS

You have learned that every sentence has two basic parts—subject and predicate. Within the subject there is a simple subject, commonly called the subject; within the predicate there is a simple predicate, commonly called the verb. The pattern of some sentences consists of subject and verb only.

S	V
Artists	paint.

Modifiers may be added to the subject and verb without changing the basic pattern of such a sentence.

Several artists (S) from the Senior Citizen Center paint (V) in the mountains.

You have learned also that certain additions to the predicate, called complements, create other sentence patterns. These complete the meaning begun by the subject and verb. The different kinds of complements produce the different sentence patterns. These are the seven common sentence patterns:

S	V
Artists	paint.

S	V	D.O.
Artists	paint	landscapes.

S	V	I.O.	D.O.
She	gave	them	supplies.

S	V	D.O.	OBJ.COMP.(ADJ.)
These	made	the artists	happy.

S	V	D.O.	OBJ.COMP.(NOUN)
They	named	her	resident artist.

S	V	P.N.
She	is	their resident artist.

S	V	P.A.
She	seems	talented.

GRAMMAR

CHAPTER 3

The Phrase

KINDS OF PHRASES AND THEIR FUNCTIONS

Words in a sentence act not only individually but also in groups. The grouped words act together as a unit that may function as a modifier, a subject, a verb, an object, or a predicate nominative. The most common group of related words is the phrase. In Chapter 1 you learned about the verb phrase, which is a verb of more than one word (*is coming, might have been*). This chapter provides a review of other kinds of phrases.

DIAGNOSTIC TEST

Identifying Phrases. Number your paper 1–20. Next to each number, identify the kind of phrase italicized in each sentence. Write *adj.* for a prepositional phrase used as an adjective, *adv.* for a prepositional phrase used as an adverb, *part.* for a participial phrase, *ger.* for a gerund phrase, *inf.* for an infinitive phrase, or *appos.* for an appositive phrase. Do not identify separately any phrases within a larger italicized phrase.

EXAMPLE 1. We had a tossed salad *with fresh tomatoes* at lunch.
1. *adj.*

1. Marnie made an appointment *to audition for a part in the play.*
2. For a split second, the football sat balanced *on the goal-post bar.*

3. Dr. Martin, *the pediatrician,* has advertised for a receptionist.
4. *Sitting in the sun for three hours* gave Rebecca a headache.
5. *Smiling broadly,* the television commentator praised the work of the 4-H Club.
6. I saw the beautiful bouquet *of roses* on the table.
7. William Golding, *the British novelist,* was awarded the Nobel Prize for literature in 1983.
8. The biology class had mixed emotions about *dissecting the frog.*
9. Kai's ambition is *to drive a tractor-trailer truck.*
10. Shakespeare's plays are performed *in numerous languages* throughout the world.
11. *Moving their cars to the right,* the drivers let the ambulance pass.
12. Marianne and Fred intend *to run for class offices.*
13. *Filled with joy and happiness,* the bride and groom greeted their family and friends after the wedding ceremony.
14. Two clowns *from the circus* gave a benefit performance.
15. My friends *Alecca and Leon* sent me a postcard from Rome.
16. You can get help in an emergency by *dialing the operator.*
17. Donya wants to ride her bicycle from Washington, D.C., *to Seattle, Washington.*
18. The public library is a valuable resource for anyone who wants *to do research.*
19. My teacher recommended a book *about the Industrial Revolution.*
20. We watched three experts *discussing the economy* on television.

3a. A *phrase* is a group of words not containing a verb and its subject. A phrase is used as a single part of speech.

Five kinds of phrases are explained in the following pages: *prepositional phrases, participial phrases, gerund phrases, infinitive phrases,* and *appositive phrases.*

THE PREPOSITIONAL PHRASE

3b. A *prepositional phrase* is a group of words beginning with a preposition and ending with a noun or pronoun.

for Lisa and you **in** the park **after** the game

The noun or pronoun that concludes the prepositional phrase is the object of the preposition that begins the phrase.

on the **way** from **Angela** and **me** with a **shout**

Prepositional phrases are usually used as modifiers—as adjectives or adverbs. Occasionally, a prepositional phrase is used as a noun:

Before lunch will be convenient. [The prepositional phrase is the subject of the sentence; it is used as a noun.]

GRAMMAR

The Adjective Phrase

3c. An *adjective phrase* is a prepositional phrase that modifies a noun or a pronoun.

Tucson has been the locale **of many Westerns.**

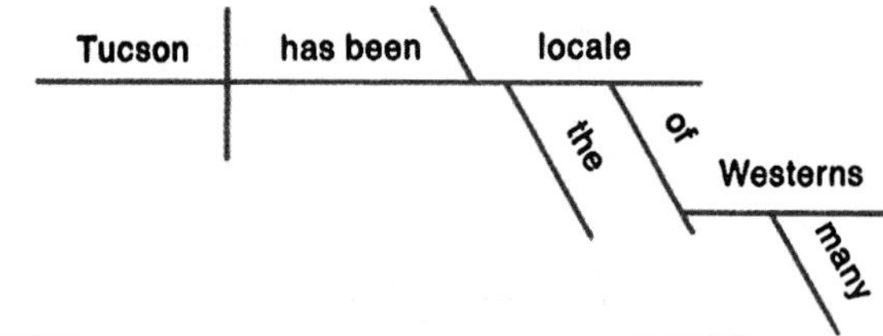

Tourists **from the East** visit the old frontier towns **in the West.**

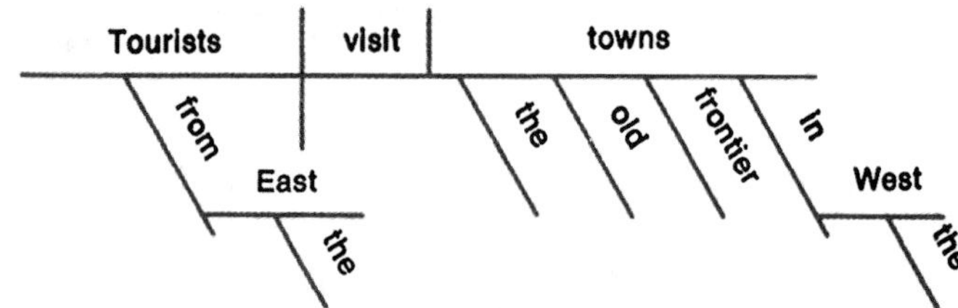

EXERCISE 1. Identifying Adjective Phrases and the Words They Modify. After each sentence number, list the adjective phrases in the sentence. Next to each phrase, write the noun modified.

1. The rivers of New Guinea are now popular areas for rafting enthusiasts.
2. A series of nearly continuous rapids crosses jungles of primeval beauty.

3. Twenty-eight major rapids on the Tua River make it a course for rafters with experience and courage.
4. There are butterflies with brilliant colors, and the metallic whine of cicadas almost drowns out the roar of the river.
5. The banks are a chaos of tumbled boulders and uprooted trees.

The Adverb Phrase

3d. An *adverb phrase* is a prepositional phrase that modifies a verb, an adjective, or another adverb.

The following sentences show the ways in which an adverb phrase can modify a verb.

> Tina exercises **with care.** [*how* Tina exercises]
> She exercises **before a meet.** [*when* she exercises]
> She exercises **in the gym.** [*where* she exercises]
> She exercises **to her capacity.** [*to what extent* she exercises]
> She exercises **for her health.** [*why* she exercises]

Note the following diagram.

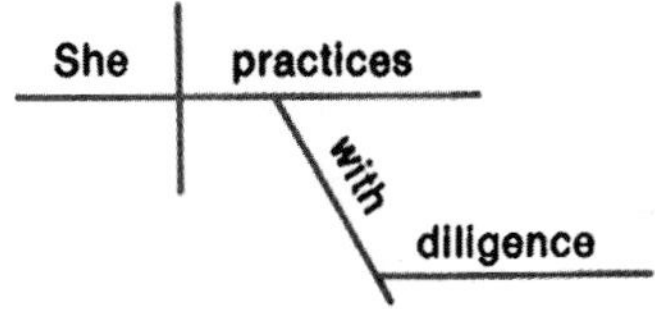

In the following sentence, the adverb phrase modifies a predicate adjective.

> He was true **to his word.**

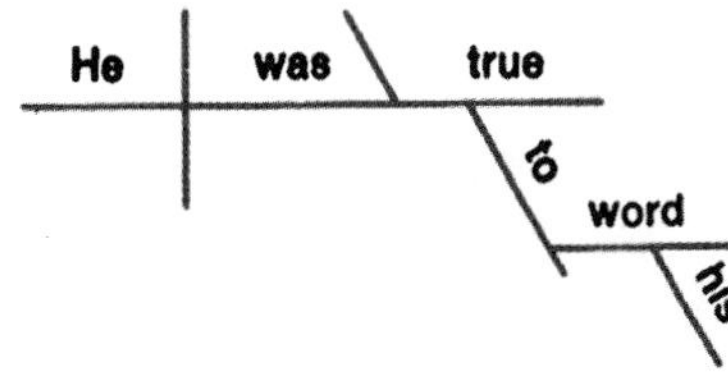

The following sentence illustrates the placement of an adverb phrase that modifies an adverb.

He threw the ball far **to the left.**

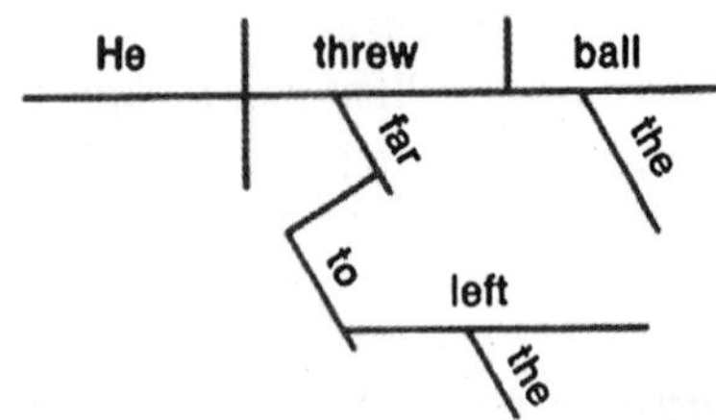

EXERCISE 2. Identifying Adverb Phrases and the Words They Modify. Number your paper 1–10. After the proper number, list the adverb phrases in the sentence and the word(s) modified.

1. Nothing in Dutch memory compares with the flood of February 1953.
2. Some 50,000 houses were swept out to sea; 70,000 people were evacuated from their homes.
3. As a result of that deluge, engineers are erecting a massive coastal barrier.
4. Work on the barrier was not begun until 1978 but should be complete by 1990.
5. By that time this masterpiece of engineering will have cost Dutch taxpayers nearly three billion dollars.
6. From a distance the odd-looking structures resemble skyscrapers.
7. They are located near the Dutch town of Zierikzee and symbolize Holland's centuries-old struggle against the sea.
8. The barriers will be positioned between two islands and will reach from shore to shore.
9. These massive pillars were constructed in dry dock and will be moved into place by a special ship.
10. Holland may remain safe from the sea forever.

PHRASES CONTAINING VERBALS

Less common than the prepositional phrase but still very useful to a writer are verbal phrases: the *participial phrase,* the *gerund phrase,* and the *infinitive phrase.* These phrases are called verbal phrases because the most important word in them is a verbal. Verbals are formed from verbs; they may express action, have modifiers, and be followed by complements. However, verbals do not function as verbs in a sentence. They function as nouns, as adjectives, or as adverbs.

On the following pages you will find an explanation of each kind of verbal, followed by a discussion of the verbal as it is most commonly used—in a phrase.

The Participle and the Participial Phrase

3e. A *participle* is a verb form that can be used as an adjective.

The rapidly **developing** storm kept small boats in port.
Developing rapidly, the storm kept small boats in port.
The storm, **developing** rapidly, kept small boats in port.

In these sentences, *developing,* which is formed from the verb *develop,* is used as an adjective modifying the noun *storm.*

In the following sentence the participle *crying* is used as an adjective modifying the pronoun *him.*

I found him **crying.**

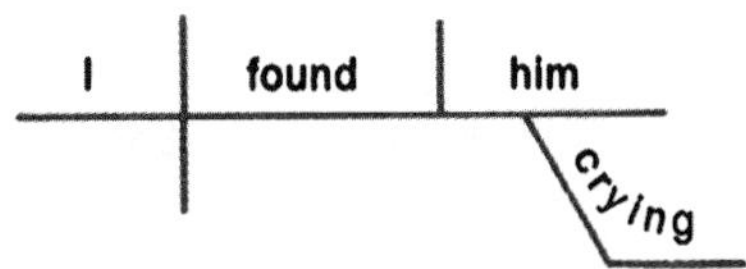

There are two basic kinds of participles: *present participles* and *past participles.* A present participle, like those in the preceding examples, ends in *-ing.* A past participle may end in *-ed, -d, -t, -en,* or *-n:* ask*ed,* save*d,* deal*t,* eat*en,* see*n.*

PRESENT PARTICIPLE We watched the puppies **playing.**
PAST PARTICIPLE The puppies, **exhausted,** collapsed in the grass.

Although participles are formed from verbs, they cannot be used by themselves as verbs. A participle may, however, be used with a helping verb to form a verb phrase.

PARTICIPLE The **barking** dogs followed the colts into the barn. [*Barking* modifies *dogs.*]

VERB PHRASE The dogs **were barking** excitedly. [The verb phrase *were barking* consists of the helping verb *were* plus the present participle *barking.*]

When participles are used in verb phrases, they are considered part of the verb and are not considered adjectives.

3f. A *participial phrase* is a phrase containing a participle and any complements or modifiers it may have.[1]

Removing his coat, Jack rushed to the river. [The participial phrase is made up of the participle *removing* and the complement *coat,* which is the direct object of *removing.* Like verbs, participles may take an object.]

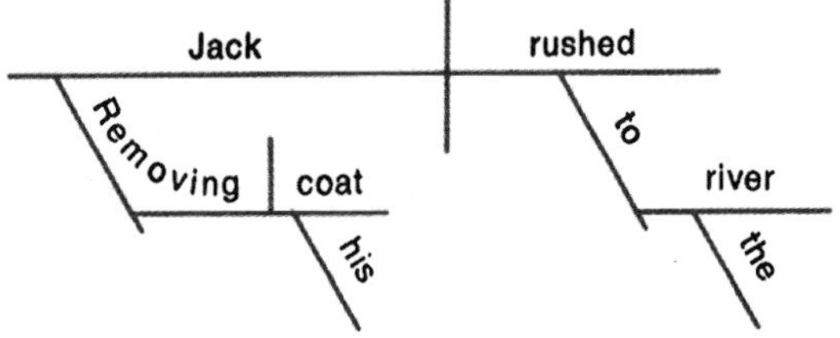

Hesitating there for a moment, he quickly grasped the situation. [The participial phrase is made up of the participle *hesitating* plus its modifiers —the adverb *there* and the adverb phrase *for a moment.*]

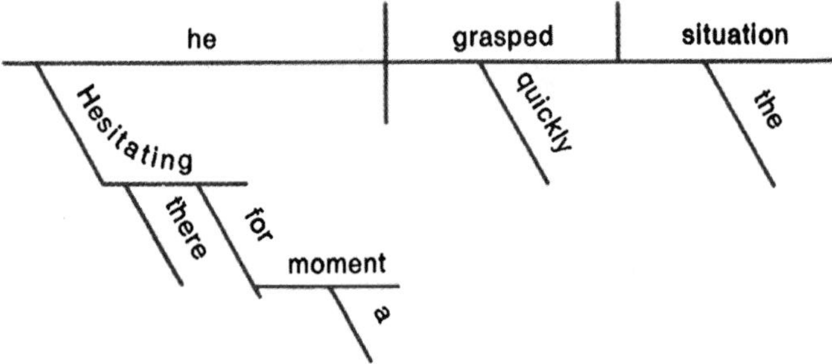

The participle usually introduces the phrase, and the entire phrase acts as an adjective to modify a noun or pronoun.

We saw Carl Lewis **receiving his first gold medal** in the 1984 Olympics.

Swaying rhythmically, the snake raised its head.

Spread with white linen, the table glowed in the candlelight.

EXERCISE 3. Identifying Participial Phrases and the Words They Modify. Write on your paper the participial phrases in the following

[1] For work on the participial phrase as a sentence fragment, see pages 278–80. For exercises on the dangling participle, see pages 302–303.

sentences. Be sure to include all complements and modifiers. Before each phrase, write the number of the sentence in which it appears. After each phrase, write the word the phrase modifies.

1. High-school graduates replying to a questionnaire about their college courses often mention freshman English as the course giving them the most trouble.
2. Facing college standards, the graduates realize that they did not work hard enough on the themes assigned in high school.
3. Statistics reported by the National Education Association revealed that the vast majority of American colleges offer remedial English classes emphasizing composition.
4. Handicapped by their writing deficiencies, graduates seeking employment or advancement are often denied opportunities.
5. Recognizing the importance of practice, teachers of composition, imitating the athletic coach, conduct regular practice sessions.

WRITING APPLICATION A:
Using Participial Phrases in Your Writing

Participial phrases contribute to sentence variety while supplying pertinent information for the reader.

EXAMPLE *Reflecting a deep love of Ireland,* the poems of William Butler Yeats were awarded the Nobel Prize.

Writing Assignment

What does the word *heroic* mean to you? Are there still heroes? Does it have to be someone prominent, or can it be an ordinary person? Define what you think a hero is; then illustrate this definition with an example. Use at least three participial phrases. Underline these phrases.

REVIEW EXERCISE A. Identifying Participial Phrases, Adjective Phrases, and Adverb Phrases. For each of the following sentences, write the italicized phrases in order on your paper. Place each phrase on a separate line. After each phrase, write the word it modifies and tell whether it is a *participial* phrase, an *adjective* prepositional phrase, or an *adverb* prepositional phrase. Include prepositional phrases within a larger italicized phrase with the larger phrase.

EXAMPLE 1. *Living far from the city,* I developed an interest *in nature at an early age.*

1. *Living far from the city, I, participial*
in nature, interest, adjective
at an early age, developed, adverb

GRAMMAR

1. *Having studied hard,* Karen walked rapidly *to school,* confident that she would do well on her test *in chemistry.*
2. *By next week* all of the students *trying out for the soccer team* will have heard *from the coach or his assistant.*
3. Today's newspaper, *printed last night,* made no mention *of this morning's traffic tie-up.*
4. Many *of the articles written for a newspaper* are based *on news-wire reports.*
5. *Annoyed by the mosquitoes,* Mr. Sims went *into his house for a while.*
6. *Rinsed with hot water,* the dishes were stacked up, *waiting to be washed.*
7. The gift *given to our principal, Mrs. Scott,* was a necklace *made of silver and turquoise.*
8. *Addressing her audience,* the principal spoke encouraging words.

The Gerund and Gerund Phrase

3g. A *gerund* is a verb form ending in *-ing* that is used as a noun.

Walking is healthful exercise. [*Walking* is formed from the verb *walk* and, as the subject of the sentence, is used as a noun.]

A gerund is a verbal noun. It may be used just as a noun may be used.

Good **writing** comes from much practice. [gerund used as subject]

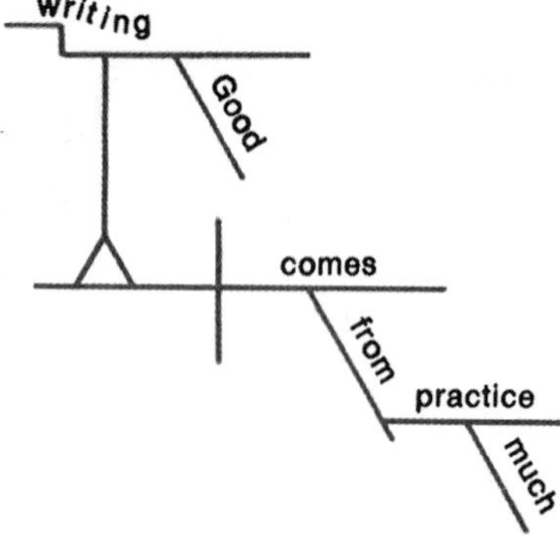

They do not appreciate my **singing.** [gerund used as object of verb]

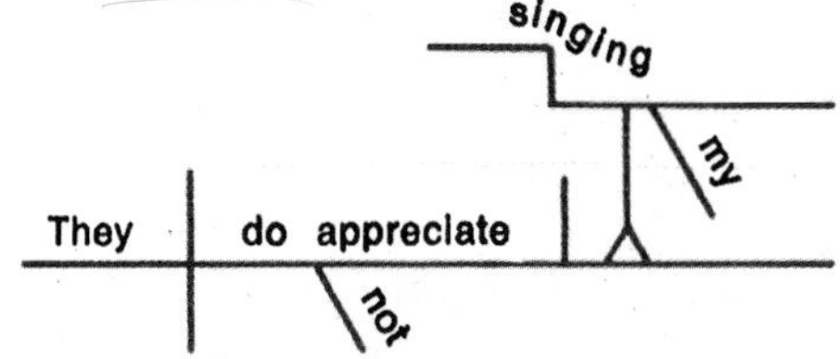

By **studying** you can pass the course. [gerund used as object of a preposition]

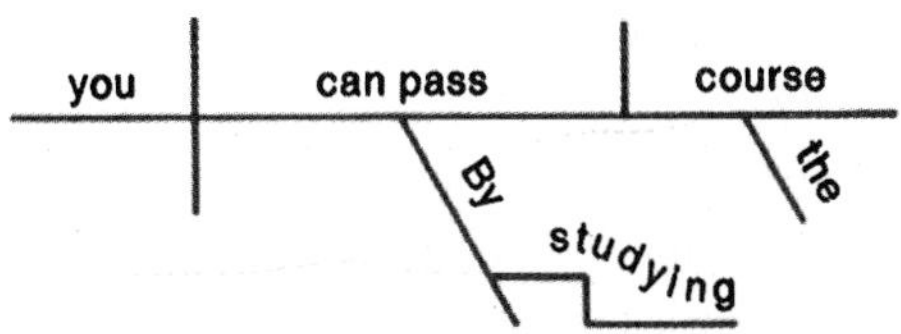

3h. A *gerund phrase* is a phrase consisting of a gerund and any complements or modifiers it may have.

Carrying coals to Newcastle is a traditional example of the unnecessary. [The gerund *Carrying* has *coals* as its direct object and is modified by the adverb phrase *to Newcastle.*]

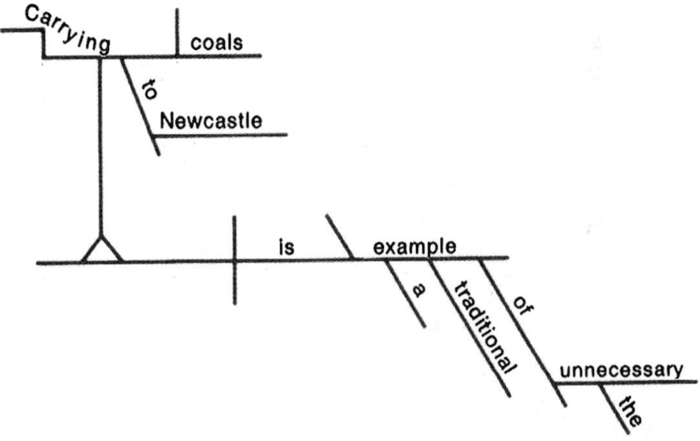

Like the gerund alone, the gerund phrase may be used in any way that a noun may be used.

Writing that letter was a good idea. [gerund phrase as subject]
My cousin enjoys **working as a lifeguard.** [gerund phrase as direct object]
We were fined for **parking there.** [gerund phrase as object of preposition.]
Her most publicized achievement was **winning three gold medals.** [gerund phrase as predicate nominative]

GRAMMAR

EXERCISE 4. Identifying Gerund Phrases and Their Functions. Number your paper 1–10. Identify the gerund phrase in each sentence. Then identify as subject (*s.*), predicate nominative (*p.n.*), direct object (*d.o.*), indirect object (*i.o.*), or object of a preposition (*obj. prep.*).

EXAMPLE 1. Learning to type is one of my most practical accomplishments.
1. *Learning to type, s.*

1. Solving crossword puzzles is one of Geraldo's favorite pastimes.
2. Sylvia's method of making decisions reveals a great deal about her.
3. My grandparents enjoy walking briskly.
4. In making any changes, please notify our secretary, Ms. Erikson.
5. Producing a movie for Mr. Hisoka's cinematography course requires the ability to organize and communicate.
6. Ms. Sanapaw finished writing her paper.
7. Gaining the vote for women was Susan B. Anthony's mission.
8. One of the most interesting characteristics of bees is their dancing to communicate the location of distant food sources.
9. Hector earns money on the weekends by giving guitar lessons.
10. My brother's singing in the shower adds mirth and music to our morning routine.

WRITING APPLICATION B:
Using Gerund Phrases in Describing a Process

Gerund phrases are particularly useful in describing a process because a process involves action.

EXAMPLE You can improve your vocabulary by *keeping a notebook, listing new words, and making an effort to use these words.*

Writing Assignment

Jot down the steps a person should follow to complete a process (use one you are familiar with). Write down the process, using gerund phrases. Underline them.

GRAMMAR

The Infinitive and the Infinitive Phrase

3i. An *infinitive* is a verb form, usually preceded by *to,* that can be used as a noun or a modifier.

to study   to write   to hope   to be

An infinitive is generally used as a noun, but it may also be used as an adjective or an adverb.

The infinitive used as a noun:

To leave would be rude. [infinitive as subject]
No one wants **to stay.** [infinitive as direct object]
Her goal is **to win.** [infinitive as predicate nominative]

The infinitive used as an adjective:

She is the candidate **to watch.** [The infinitive modifies *candidate.*]

The infinitive used as an adverb:

We came **to cheer.** [The infinitive modifies the verb *came.*]

> NOTE Do not confuse the infinitive, a verbal of which *to* is a part, with a prepositional phrase beginning with *to,* which consists of *to* plus a noun or pronoun.

INFINITIVES	PREPOSITIONAL PHRASES
to go	to them
to sleep	to bed

The word *to,* called the sign of the infinitive, is sometimes omitted.

The clowns made her [to] **laugh.**
Help me [to] **clean** the car.

3j. An *infinitive phrase* consists of an infinitive and any complements or modifiers it may have.[1]

They promised **to return soon.** [*Soon* is an adverb modifying the infinitive *to return.*]
We have time **to walk to the concert.** [The prepositional phrase *to the concert* modifies the infinitive *to walk.*]
I saved enough money **to buy a car.** [*Car* is the object of *to buy.*]

[1] For exercises on the use of the infinitive phrase to reduce wordiness, see pages 319–21.

Like infinitives alone, infinitive phrases can be used as nouns or as modifiers.

We tried **to reason with her.** [The infinitive phrase *to reason with her* is the object of the verb *tried.*]
There must be a way **to solve this problem.** [The infinitive phrase modifies the noun *way.*]
His plan is **to go to college for two years.** [The infinitive phrase is a predicate nominative, referring back to *plan.*]

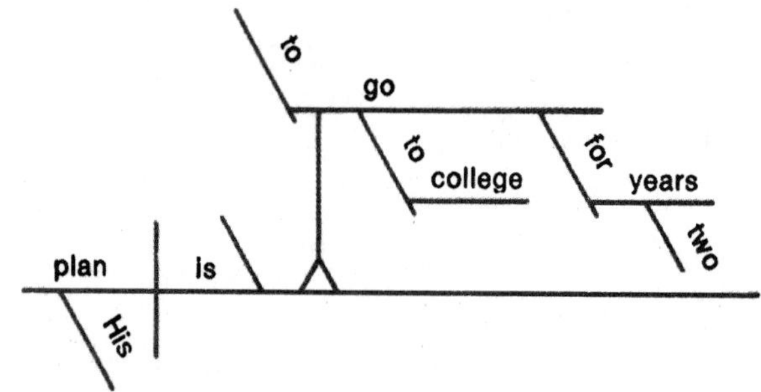

The Infinitive Clause

Unlike other verbals, an infinitive may have a subject as well as complements and modifiers.

Everyone expected **Gina to win the nomination.** [*Gina* is the subject of the infinitive *to win.*]
We asked **her to lead the discussion.** [*Her* is the subject of the infinitive *to lead.*]
We believe **Andrew to be the winner.** [*Andrew* is the subject of the infinitive *to be; winner* is a predicate nominative referring to *Andrew.*]
I found **it to be difficult.** [*It* is the subject of the infinitive *to be; difficult* is a predicate adjective referring back to *it.*]

When an infinitive has a subject, as in the preceding examples, the construction is called an *infinitive clause.* Notice that the subject of an infinitive is in the objective case.[1]

EXERCISE 5. Identifying Infinitive Phrases and Their Functions. Number your paper 1–10. Identify the infinitive phrase in each sentence and indicate whether the phrase is used as a noun, an adjective, or an adverb. If it is used as a noun, identify it as the subject

[1] For rules concerning the use of the objective case, see pages 104–107.

(*s.*), direct object (*d.o.*), predicate nominative (*p.n.*), or object of a preposition (*obj. prep.*).

EXAMPLE 1. I like to compose music for the guitar.
1. *to compose music for the guitar, noun, d. o.*

GRAMMAR

1. To win an Olympic gold medal is the dream of every member of the women's ski team.
2. The candidate had the courage to speak on a controversial issue.
3. We went to Italy to see Michelangelo's statue, the *David.*
4. The Latin and French Clubs try to work together on projects.
5. Martin Luther King's dream was that all people should be free to exercise their rights as American citizens.
6. Louis Pasteur experimented for years to discover a method for preventing rabies.
7. The ability to speak distinctly is an advantage in job interviews.
8. To open the box required a hammer and a crowbar.
9. Alana's hobby is to spend hours each day developing original computer programs.
10. Marvella has always wanted to learn about horseback riding.

REVIEW EXERCISE B. Identifying Prepositional, Participial, Gerund, and Infinitive Phrases. Number your paper 1–20. In the following passage, most prepositional, participial, gerund, and infinitive phrases are numbered and italicized. Study the phrase, and after the corresponding number on your paper, write what kind of phrase it is. If it is a prepositional phrase, tell whether it is an adjective phrase or an adverb phrase. Include the prepositional phrase within a larger italicized phrase with the larger phrase.

(1) *Having read several poems by Robert Frost,* I suddenly saw the difference between (2) *enjoying prose and enjoying poetry.* (3) *Reading poetry* does not require the same kind (4) *of skill* as reading prose. Inexperienced readers (5) *of poetry* try (6) *to find* "messages." Many readers race (7) *through a poem* (8) *to seek that elusive nugget* (9) *of wisdom.* It is misleading (10) *to equate the enjoyment of a poem* with (11) *finding its central thought.* (12) *Enjoying a poem to its fullest* is somewhat like (13) *watching a baseball game.* (14) *During a game,* most fans are eager (15) *to participate vicariously in the pleasure* of

(16) *hitting a home run* or of (17) *making a double play.* (18) *Awaiting the outcome of a game,* the average fan also responds to the total experience of the game itself. (19) *To read a poem for meaning alone* can be compared to (20) *attending a baseball game and watching the scoreboard.*

GRAMMAR

THE APPOSITIVE[1]

3k. An *appositive* is a noun or pronoun—often with modifiers—set beside another noun or pronoun to explain or identify it.

My cousin **Maria** is an accomplished violinist.
Riboflavin, a **vitamin,** is found in leafy vegetables.

An *appositive phrase* is a phrase consisting of an appositive and its modifiers.

My brother's car, **a sporty red hatchback with bucket seats,** is the envy of my friends.

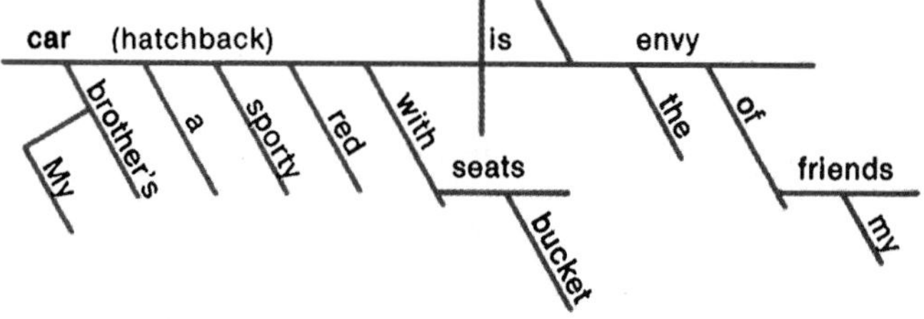

An appositive phrase usually follows the word it explains or identifies, but may precede it.

Once a pagan **feast,** Valentine's Day is now celebrated as a day of love.

REVIEW EXERCISE C. Identifying Phrases. Number your paper 1–20. In the following passage, most of the phrases have been numbered and italicized. After the proper number, identify each phrase as prepositional, participial, gerund, infinitive, or appositive. In the case of a prepositional phrase, write whether it is an adjective phrase or an adverb phrase. Include prepositional phrases within a larger italicized phrase as part of the larger phrase.

[1] For rules on the punctuation of appositives, see page 228. For the use of the appositive in subordination of ideas, see page 291.

Altamont Pass, (1) *an area of grassy hills* (2) *surrounding San Francisco Bay,* is producing a new cash crop. Energy entrepreneurs are hurrying (3) *to lease wind rights on acreage* (4) *throughout the Altamont.* One rancher owns several hundred acres (5) *dotted with tall white wind machines.* (6) *Standing in rows on the windswept hills,* this crop is expected (7) *to produce electricity.* (8) *With any luck,* the wind-power industry may soon spread (9) *to other parts* of the country. The temperature differences (10) *between the cool coast and the hot valley* can create air surges (11) *funneling inland through natural gaps* (12) *like the Altamont.* According to some energy experts, there will be several hundred wind machines (13) *producing thirty million kilowatts per year,* the power (14) *used by 4,800 homes.* (15) *An economist and a trained engineer,* John Eckland has advocated (16) *generating electricity* by (17) *using these updated windmills.* Not until the oil shortages of the 1970's did a serious effort begin (18) *in the United States* (19) *to develop a wind industry.* Modern wind turbines may someday become as numerous (20) *in the United States* as windmills were in Holland.

CHAPTER 3 REVIEW: POSTTEST 1

Identifying Phrases. Number your paper 1–25. For each sentence, write the italicized phrase. Then identify it as a prepositional, participial, gerund, infinitive, or appositive phrase. If it is a prepositional phrase, indicate whether it is used as an adjective or an adverb. Include phrases or verbals occurring within a longer italicized phrase as part of that phrase.

EXAMPLE: 1. The sunlight shimmering *on the lake* was beautiful.
1. *on the lake, prepositional, adverb*

1. Juanita likes *to take candid pictures of her friends.*
2. *Arriving late at school,* Bill stopped in the office to get a pass.
3. The sound *of the band* made everyone want to dance.
4. *Made in Ireland,* Waterford crystal is admired throughout the world.
5. By *inventing the telephone,* Alexander Graham Bell assured himself a place in history.
6. Try *to finish your work before dinner.*
7. Luciano Pavarotti, *the great Italian tenor,* received a standing

ovation at the end of his concert.

8. Ruth's secret ambition is *to do research in space.*
9. We stood on the deserted street *looking in vain for a taxi.*
10. Raul has the talent *to sculpt and design beautiful objects.*
11. Francine's hobby is *collecting earrings;* she has thirty pairs!
12. For great performers, *interpreting music* is an art as well as a skill.
13. *Having suffered through three days of a heat wave,* we decided to purchase an air conditioner.
14. In Cleveland, we visited our friend Barbara, *a prosecuting attorney.*
15. At the rodeo, I always enjoy *watching the courageous riders.*
16. "It is a pleasure to be with you today," remarked the mayor *at the beginning of her talk.*
17. Swaggering cowboys and daring sheriffs are stereotypes that appear *in many old western movies.*
18. Dr. Acevedo, *a noted cardiologist,* assured the patient's family that the operation had been successful.
19. Many pioneer women kept diaries and journals *of their experiences* settling the American wilderness.
20. *To speak freely on any issue* is a right guaranteed to all Americans.
21. *Speaking before a large audience*, the President delivered an important foreign policy speech.
22. We stood on the deserted street *looking in vain for a taxi.*
23. As Captain Williams stood *on the deck of the boat*, he scanned the horizon.
24. While the witness gave her testimony, the members *of the jury* listened carefully.
25. Karan went to the Upper Peninsula in Michigan *to swim in Lake Superior.*

CHAPTER 3 REVIEW: POSTTEST 2

Writing Sentences with Phrases. Write your own sentences according to the following guidelines:

1. Use *with patience* as an adverb phrase.
2. Use *for my friend Margaret* as an adverb phrase.
3. Use *from Chicago* as an adjective phrase.
4. Use *with vegetables* as an adjective phrase.

5. Use *looking from a distance* as a participial phrase.
6. Use *studying hard* as a gerund phrase that is the object of a preposition.
7. Use *writing letters* as a gerund phrase that is the subject.
8. Use *to dream* as an infinitive phrase that is the object of a verb.
9. Use *to study the piano* as an infinitive phrase that is the subject.
10. Use *our local newspaper* as an appositive phrase.

GRAMMAR

CHAPTER 4

The Clause

THE FUNCTION OF CLAUSES

By now you know that most sentences are made up not only of single words functioning as parts of speech but also of word groups functioning as single parts of speech. The phrase is one such word group; the clause is another. This chapter reviews the subordinate clause; your use of this word group will help you vary your sentences and so improve your writing.

DIAGNOSTIC TEST

A. Identifying Clauses. Identify each italicized group of words as an independent or a subordinate clause. If it is a subordinate clause, identify it as an adjective clause, an adverb clause, or a noun clause.

EXAMPLE 1. *As he cruised along the tranquil beach on his bicycle,* Warren could hear the waves beating on the rocky shore.
1. *subordinate clause—adverb clause*

1. Most Americans are not sufficiently familiar with American Indian culture; *yet it is rich and interesting.*
2. Why is it that I can never find a pencil *when I need one*?
3. As we walked along the road, *we saw the wheat waving in the wind.*
4. I don't care *what you think*!

5. Do you know *that Dr. Robert Goddard was the pioneer of the liquid-fuel rocket*?
6. I'm so happy *that I could dance and sing*!
7. *Because his art work received wide recognition*, Pablo Picasso became famous and wealthy.
8. I have concluded *that personal freedom involves both self-realization and service to others.*
9. *The pitcher read the catcher's signals* and then struck out the hitter with a fastball.
10. Please do not talk *while the test is in progress.*

B. Classifying Sentences. Classify each sentence as simple, compound, complex, or compound-complex and then as declarative, interrogative, imperative, or exclamatory.

EXAMPLE 1. I can swim, but my sister can't, because she hasn't learned yet.
1. *compound-complex—declarative*

11. On your way here, look for a group of strange people wearing space-age outfits.
12. Did the coach realize that she was looking at her strongest softball team in years?
13. As the lights dimmed in the theater, a hush fell over the audience, and the overture began.
14. "Mitosis" and "meiosis" are technical terms for most people, but they are merely everyday words for cellular biologists.
15. Set in the rural South, Flannery O'Connor's short stories present an assortment of odd characters.
16. Given to the United States by France in 1886, the Statue of Liberty stands in New York Harbor and is regarded as a symbol of American freedom.
17. Jerome has had a job as a chef for six months; he hopes to own his own restaurant in the future.
18. The realtor said the price of the house has been lowered by $100,000!
19. Is it true that Jack, who lives in Sacramento, California, works in San Francisco?
20. After the hurricane had destroyed many homes, the townspeople bravely began a difficult clean-up operation.

4a. A *clause* is a group of words containing a subject and a predicate and is used as part of a sentence.

Clauses are classified according to grammatical completeness. Those that can stand alone if removed from their sentences are called *independent clauses.* Those that do not express a complete thought and cannot stand alone are called *subordinate clauses.*

GRAMMAR

INDEPENDENT CLAUSES

When removed from its sentence, an independent clause[1] makes complete sense. Written with a capital at the beginning and a period at the end, it becomes a simple sentence. It is referred to as an independent *clause* only when combined with one or more additional clauses, independent or subordinate, into a larger sentence.

When two or more independent clauses are joined into a single sentence, the usual connecting words are *and, but, or, nor,* or *for.*

EXAMPLES It was a hot, sunny weekend, **and** all the beaches were packed. [The conjunction *and* joins two independent clauses.]

The soup was delicious, **but** the main course tasted bland. [The independent clauses are joined by *but.*]

SUBORDINATE CLAUSES

Subordinate clauses,[2] which cannot stand alone as sentences, are used as nouns or modifiers in the same way as single words and phrases are. A subordinate clause is always combined in some way with an independent clause. The following examples are subordinate clauses.

whoever knows the song
which is my favorite song
as she has always insisted

Combined with an independent clause, each of these subordinate clauses plays its part in a sentence:

Whoever knows the song may join in.
We sang "Green Grow the Lilacs," **which is my favorite song.**
As she has always insisted, Mother will not sing at parties.

[1] Independent clauses are sometimes called *main* clauses.
[2] Subordinate clauses are sometimes called *dependent* clauses.

EXERCISE 1. Identifying Independent and Subordinate Clauses. In each of the following sentences, a clause is printed in italics. If the italicized clause is an independent clause, place *I* after the proper number. If it is a subordinate clause, place *S*.

1. Egyptology is the branch of learning *that is concerned with the language and culture of ancient Egypt.*
2. *Until the Rosetta Stone was discovered in 1799,* the ancient Egyptian language was an enigma to scholars.
3. Boussard, *who was a captain under Napoleon,* found the stone in the trenches near Rosetta, a city near the mouth of the Nile.
4. Before the French had a chance to analyze its inscriptions, *the stone was captured by the British.*
5. Because the stone contained the same message in two kinds of Egyptian writing and in Greek script, *it provided the needed key for deciphering the Egyptian language.*
6. *When the Rosetta Stone was found,* part of the hieroglyphic portion was missing.
7. Scholars could easily read the Greek inscription, *which was nearly complete.*
8. *In 1818 Thomas Young succeeded in isolating a number of hieroglyphics* that he took to represent names.
9. *The message* that was written on the stone *was not very exciting.*
10. Since the priests of Egypt were grateful for benefits from the king, *they were formally thanking the king for his generosity.*

The Adjective Clause

Like a phrase, a subordinate clause acts as a single part of speech—as an adjective, an adverb, or a noun.

4b. An *adjective clause* is a subordinate clause that, like an adjective, modifies a noun or a pronoun.

EXAMPLES She is someone **who has shown remarkable courage.**

This book, **which I read for my history report,** is about Africa.

Since a subordinate clause, like a sentence, has a verb and a subject and may contain complements and modifiers, it is diagramed very much like a sentence. Adjective and adverb clauses are placed on a horizontal line below the main line. An adjective clause is joined to the word it modifies by a broken line drawn from the modified word to the relative pronoun at the beginning of the clause.

EXAMPLE Students **whose work represents their second-best** are not real students. [The subordinate clause *whose work represents their second-best* modifies the noun *students.*]

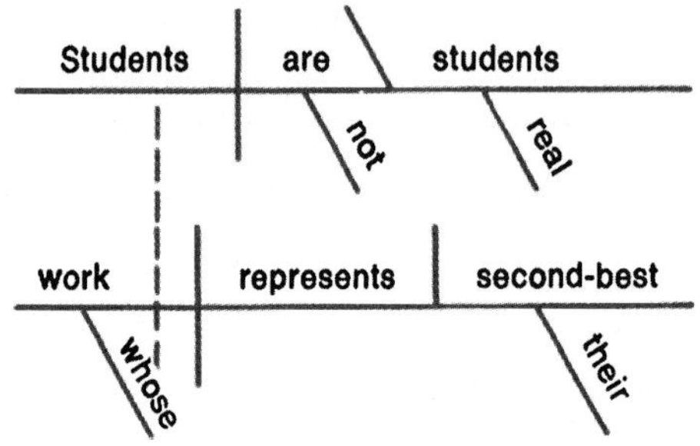

Relative Pronouns

Adjective clauses often begin with the pronouns *who, whom, whose, which,* or *that.* These pronouns refer to, or are *related* to, a noun or pronoun that has come before.

4c. A *relative pronoun* is a pronoun that begins a subordinate adjective clause and is related to a noun or a pronoun already mentioned or understood. The word to which the relative pronoun is related is its *antecedent.*

A relative pronoun does three things:

1. It refers to a preceding noun or pronoun:

The amplifier was one **that we had seen before.**
Let's listen to a weather forecaster **whom we can trust.**

2. It connects its clause with the rest of the sentence:

Ms. Lopez is a counselor **who never betrays a confidence.** [The relative pronoun *who* joins the subordinate clause to the independent clause.]
You should find a source **that is more up-to-date.** [The subordinate clause is joined to the independent clause by the relative pronoun *that.*]

3. It performs a function within its own clause by serving as the subject, object, etc., of the subordinate clause:

The principal appointed George, **who is a reliable student.** [*Who* is the subject of the verb *is* in the adjective clause *who is a reliable student.*]

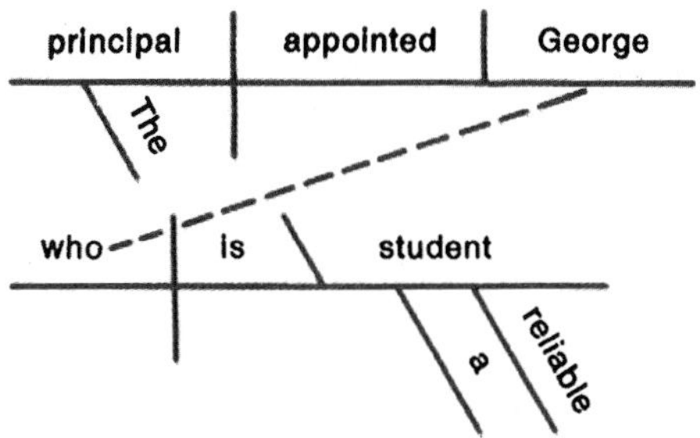

Show me the book **that you read.** [That is the object of the verb *read* (read what?).]

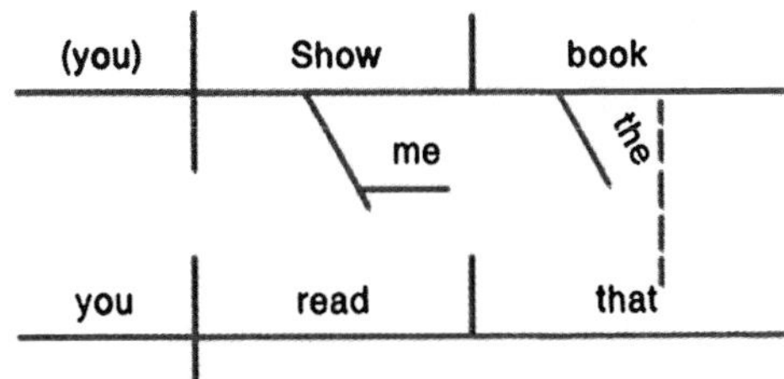

These are the assignments **for which you are responsible.** [*Which* is the object of the preposition *for.*][1]

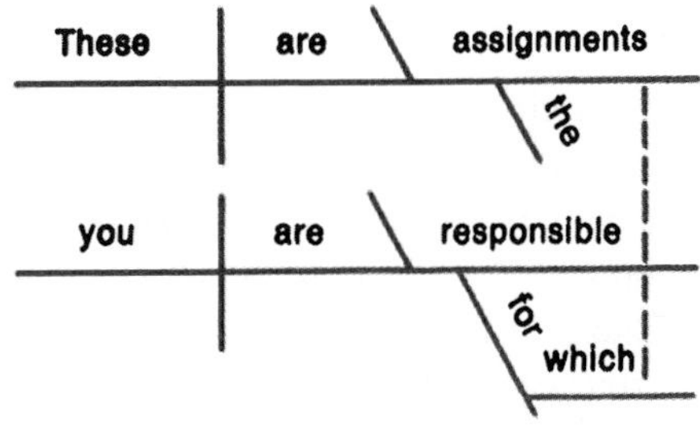

An adjective clause may also begin with the relative adjective *whose* or with the relative adverb *where* or *when.*

[1] In this sentence two words—*for* and *which*—begin the clause. Other two-word combinations of a preposition and a relative pronoun to begin a clause are *in which, by whom, for whom, from whom,* etc.

He is a coach **whose record has been amazing.** [*Whose,* the possessive form of the relative pronoun *who,* functions as an adjective modifying *record.*]

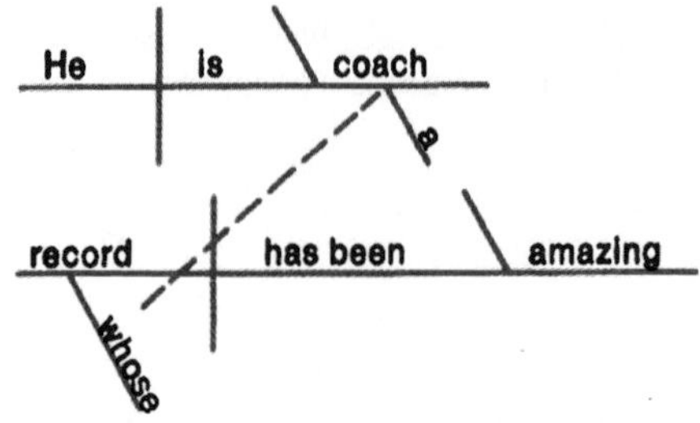

Do you remember the restaurant **where we ate lunch?** [*Where* acts as an adverb modifying *ate,* the verb in the clause. The antecedent is *restaurant.*]

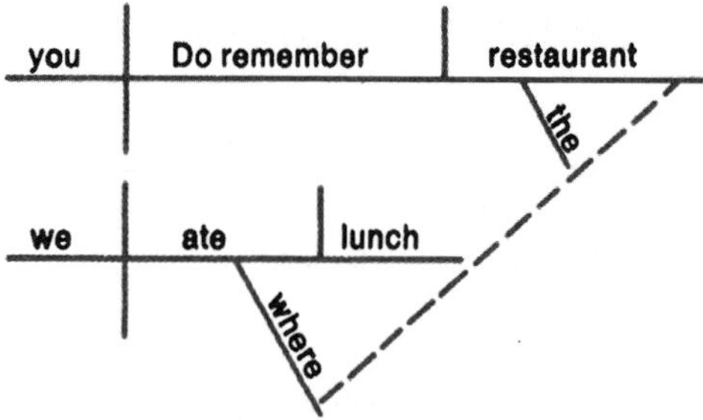

EXERCISE 2. Identifying Adjective Clauses and the Words They Modify. After the proper number, write in order the adjective clauses in the following sentences. After each clause, write the noun or pronoun that the clause modifies. Be prepared to state whether the relative pronoun or adverb is used as a subject, an object of a verb, an object of a preposition, or a modifier.

1. The Mars of the nonscientist is a planet of the imagination, where an ancient civilization has left its mark and where maps blossom with romantic place names like Utopia and Elysium.
2. "Earthlings," who were awed by the planet's red glow in the evening sky, looked on Mars as a home for creatures who might someday cross cosmic barriers and visit planet Earth.
3. Such thinking was encouraged by an Italian astronomer who observed the planet through a telescope and saw a series of fine lines that crisscrossed its surface.
4. He called the lines *canali,* which is Italian for "channels"; the word was erroneously translated into English as "canals."

5. A planet where there are canals must, of course, be inhabited by people who are capable of building not only canals but also the cities that presumably sprang up at their intersections.
6. Percival Lowell, the astronomer who founded the reputable Lowell Observatory in Flagstaff, Arizona, vitalized the Martian myths with nonscientific observations that most astronomers disputed.
7. Lowell reported a total of 437 canals, of which a large number were discovered by his own team of astronomers.
8. A writer whose interest was drawn to Mars was Edgar Rice Burroughs, whom we remember as the creator of Tarzan.
9. In his Martian books, Burroughs recounts the adventures of John Carter, who could get to Mars by standing in a field and wishing.
10. Burroughs' best-known literary successor is Ray Bradbury, who wrote *The Martian Chronicles,* published in 1950.

The Noun Clause

4d. A *noun clause* is a subordinate clause used as a noun.

In diagraming, a noun clause is pictured as a unit by placement at the top of a vertical line rising from the part of the diagram (subject, object, predicate nominative) to which the clause belongs.

EXAMPLE **Whoever wins the election** will have many problems.

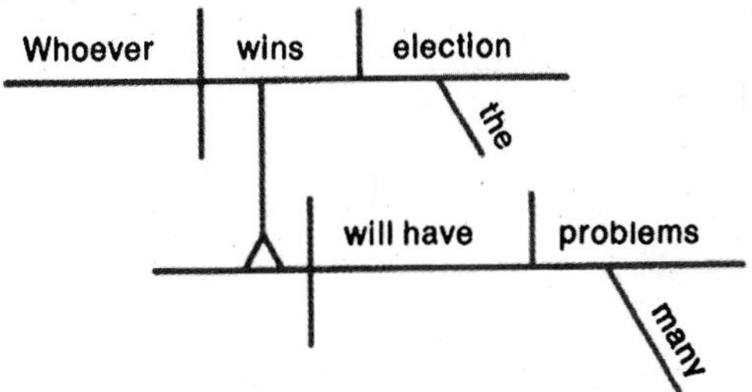

The entire noun clause *whoever wins the election* is the subject of the verb *will have.* Study the following pairs of sentences to see how a noun clause functioning in the same way that a noun functions may be a predicate nominative, an object of a verb, or an object of a preposition.

This is the **solution.** [*Solution* is a noun used as a predicate nominative after the linking verb *is.*]

This is **what we have been looking for.** [*What we have been looking for* is a noun clause used as a predicate nominative.]

We learned an interesting **fact.** [*Fact* is a noun used as the object of the verb *learned.*]
We learned **that she is a physicist.** [*That she is a physicist* is a noun clause used as the object of a verb.]

Here is a draft of my **proposal.** [*Proposal* is a noun used as the object of the preposition *of.*]
Here is a draft of **what I am proposing.** [*What I am proposing* is a noun clause used as the object of a preposition.]

GRAMMAR

A noun clause may begin with an indefinite relative pronoun—*that, what, whatever, who, which, whoever, whichever.* Unlike most relative pronouns, an indefinite relative pronoun does not have an antecedent in its sentence.

EXAMPLE He gave me **whatever I wanted.**

A noun clause may also begin with an indefinite relative adjective—*whose, which, whatever*—or an indefinite relative adverb—*where, when, how, etc.*

I know **whose car this is.**

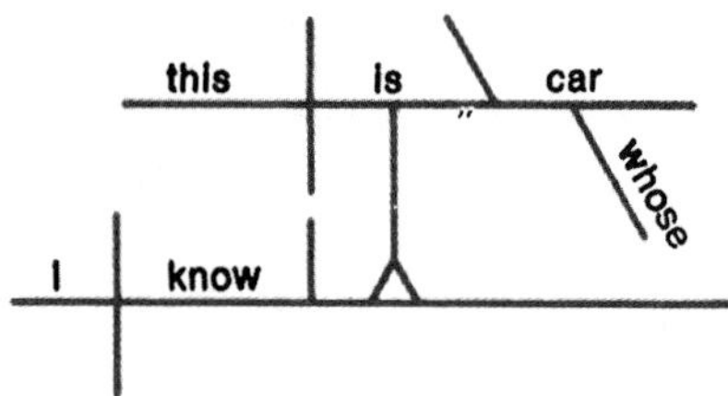

I know **where she went.**

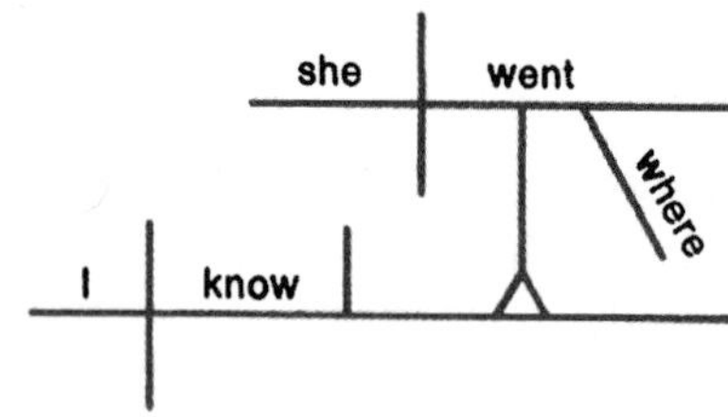

☞ **NOTE** Adjective and noun clauses are sometimes used without an introductory word. Note that the introductory word is omitted in the second sentence in each of the following pairs:

I. M. Pei is an architect **whom most critics praise.**
I. M. Pei is an architect **most critics praise.**

She says **that James Earl Jones was once a pre-med student.**
She says **James Earl Jones was once a pre-med student.**

EXERCISE 3. Identifying Noun Clauses and Their Functions. On your paper, write the noun clauses in the following sentences. Before each clause, write the number of the sentence in which it appears. After each clause, write its function in the sentence: *subject, direct object, predicate nominative, object of a preposition.*

EXAMPLE 1. I don't know what to think.
1. *what to think—direct object*

1. The problem is that my finances don't quite allow me to live in style; in fact, I'm broke!
2. Do you know what the referee says to the opponents at the start of a boxing match?
3. What I like most about Harriet is that she never complains.
4. Scientists disagree about why dinosaurs died out.
5. Sometimes I am amused and sometimes I am amazed by what I read in the newspaper's advice column.
6. Through scientific research, psychologists have learned that everyone dreams during sleep.
7. What the dancers Agnes de Mille and Martha Graham did was to create a new form of American dance.
8. Can you tell me where the Museum of African Art is located?
9. Do you know whether Sakima has tried out for the track team?
10. I know how you are feeling, and I am happy for you.

EXERCISE 4. Identifying Adjective and Noun Clauses. Each sentence below contains at least one subordinate clause. List the clauses in order after the proper number. After each clause, tell what kind it is: adjective or noun. Be prepared to tell what word each adjective clause modifies and how each noun clause is used in the sentence.

1. A person has found that toys are not meant only for children.
2. Athelstan Spilhaus, an oceanographer, admits he has sometimes been unable to distinguish between his work and his play.
3. Some of the toys he collects are simply to be admired; his favorites are those that can be put into action.
4. Some of his collectibles are put into intensive care, where he skillfully replaces parts that have been damaged or lost.
5. Dr. Spilhaus says that a toy is anything that enables us to tarry during the fast whip of ordinary life.
6. What is appealing about some toys is that they can make us laugh.
7. Someone once suggested that many physical principles began as playthings.
8. For example, the toy monkey that is activated by squeezing a rubber bulb uses the same principle as the jackhammer that digs up our streets.
9. Only those who have lost touch with childhood question what a toy is worth in dollars and cents.
10. Ask someone who knows toys what their enchantment is worth.

The Adverb Clause

4e. An *adverb clause* is a subordinate clause that, like an adverb, modifies a verb, an adjective, or an adverb.

In the following examples each adverb clause illustrates one of the typical adverbial functions of telling *how, how much, when, where, why, to what extent,* or *under what conditions.*

She practices **as though her life depended on it.** [*how* she practices]
She practices **whenever she has time.** [*when* she practices]
She practices **wherever the team travels.** [*where* she practices]
She practices **because she wants to win.** [*why* she practices]
She practices more **than anyone else does.** [*how much* more]
She practices on weekends **if her schedule permits.** [*under what conditions* she practices]

In diagraming, an adverb clause is written on a horizontal line below the main line of the diagram. The subordinating conjunction beginning the clause is written on a slanting broken line which links the verb of the clause to the word the clause modifies.

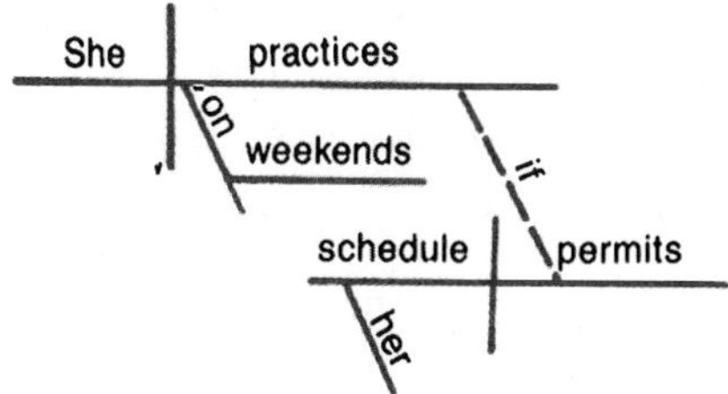

Adverb clauses may also modify adjectives and other adverbs.

She is certain **that she will make the team.** [The adverb clause *that she will make the team* modifies the adjective *certain.*]
He runs faster **than I do.** [The adverb clause *than I do* modifies the adverb *faster.*]

The Subordinating Conjunction

Adverb clauses often begin with a word like *after* or *because* that expresses the relationship between the clause and the rest of the sentence.

4f. A conjunction that begins an adverb clause is called a *subordinating conjunction.* It joins the clause to the rest of the sentence.

The following words are subordinating conjunctions. (Some may also be used as other parts of speech.)

Common Subordinating Conjunctions

after	because	so that	whenever
although	before	than	where
as	if	though	wherever
as if	in order that	unless	whether
as long as	provided that	until	while
as though	since	when	

The Elliptical (Incomplete) Clause

Sometimes we do not complete an adverb clause.

EXAMPLES I am much taller **than you [are].**
While [I was] running for the bus, I dropped my books.

In these adverb clauses the part of the clause given in brackets has been omitted. The missing part, however, could be readily provided by a reader or listener. Such incomplete clauses are said to be "elliptical."[1]

EXERCISE 5. Identifying Adverb Clauses. Write on your paper the adverb clauses in the following sentences. Before each clause, write the number of the sentence in which it appears. Draw a line under the subordinating conjunction that introduces the clause. After each clause, write what the clause tells: *how, how much, when, where, why, to what extent,* or *under what conditions.*

1. Because company was coming for dinner, Lola Gomez and her father prepared a special treat of Cuban-style black beans, one of their specialties.
2. After Lola had soaked a pound of black beans overnight, she drained them and covered them with fresh water; that makes the beans more easily digestible.
3. Before she lit the stove, she added chopped onion and green pepper, a bay leaf, coriander leaves, oregano, and salt pork to the beans.
4. While the mixture was simmering, Mr. Gomez prepared the sofrito, a necessary ingredient in many Latin American dishes.
5. Whenever a recipe calls for sofrito, you finely chop some onion, green pepper, and garlic.
6. Then you fry these vegetables in a little oil until they are tender, and add herbs such as basil, coriander, cumin, and black and white pepper.
7. As soon as the sofrito was ready, Mr. Gomez added it to the bean mixture.
8. He then crushed some of the beans against the side of the pot so that the bean mixture would become thicker.
9. When the mixture was thick, Lola put in some vinegar and sugar, which gives it that extra "tang."
10. Although this dish is usually served with rice, Lola and her father prepared a green salad instead.

[1] The definition of *ellipsis,* as applied to grammar, is an omission of one or more words obviously understood but necessary to make the expression grammatically complete. For the correct usage of pronouns in elliptical clauses, see page 112.

WRITING APPLICATION A: Using the Adverb Clause to Express Cause-and-Effect Relationships

One of the most important skills of reasoning is the ability to determine *why* something happens or *why* people act the way they do. Once the question has been answered, the answer usually includes an adverb clause. In addition to telling *why*, adverb clauses also tell *how, when, where, how much,* and *under what conditions.*

EXAMPLE Frank Lloyd Wright's building was the only large building standing in Tokyo after the earthquake of 1923 *because he used steel and concrete and floated it on a sea of mud.* (In this cause-and-effect sentence, the cause is placed in a subordinate adverb clause.)

Writing Assignment

Think of a *why* question that you would like to answer. Either do the research or conduct interviews to find the answer. In your topic sentence, use an adverb clause to express this cause-and-effect relationship. Some ideas are the following:

1. Why are some scientists concerned about a "greenhouse effect"?
2. Why are high levels of cholesterol dangerous?
3. Why do students take Latin, which is called a "dead" language?
4. Why can't anything travel faster than the speed of light?

REVIEW EXERCISE A. Identifying Adjective, Noun, and Adverb Clauses. Each of the following sentences contains at least one subordinate clause. Write the clauses in order on your paper. Before each, write the number of the sentence in which it appears. After each, write what kind it is—adjective, noun, or adverb.

1. When a group of scholars first applied computer science to the study of literature, their colleagues expressed what can only be described as polite skepticism.
2. What, they asked, would the computer do?
3. Enraged scholars argued that measuring the length of Hemingway's sentences was dreary enough when it was done without computers.

4. Would precise mathematical profiles of style determine whether Thomas More wrote one of Shakespeare's plays?
5. Because initial studies were indeed made along these lines, they provided controversy when published.
6. Although such controversy raged for years, computers have won increasing support that has become more and more impressive.
7. Researchers use the computer whenever a project involves such mechanical tasks as compiling an index or a bibliography.
8. Since all of ancient Greek is now available on computer tape, scholars can make analyses that shed light on etymology.
9. There are certain elements in literary research that computers can pick up faster than readers can.
10. Many eminent scholars believe that the use of the computer as a literary tool has already produced results that are both significant and intelligible.

SENTENCES CLASSIFIED BY STRUCTURE

4g. Classified according to their structure, there are four kinds of sentences: *simple, compound, complex,* and *compound-complex.*

(1) A *simple sentence* is a sentence with one independent clause and no subordinate clauses.

Great literature stirs the imagination.

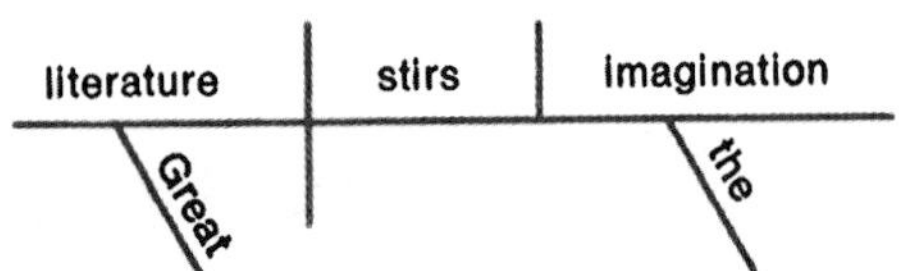

(2) A *compound sentence* is a sentence composed of two or more independent clauses but no subordinate clauses.[1]

Great literature stirs the imagination, and it challenges the intellect.
Great literature stirs the imagination; moreover, it challenges the intellect.

> **NOTE** Do not confuse the compound predicate of simple sentences with the two subjects and verbs of compound sentences.

[1] For rules concerning the punctuation of compound sentences, see pages 221–22 and 238–40.

Study the following diagrams.

Great literature **stirs** the imagination and **challenges** the intellect. [simple sentence with compound predicate]

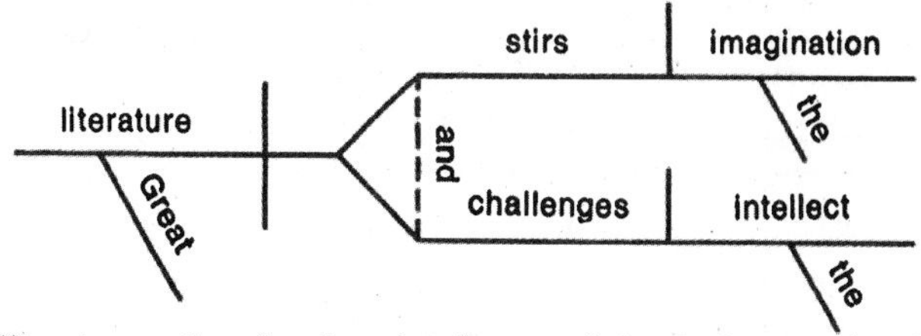

Great **literature stirs** the imagination, and **it challenges** the intellect. [compound sentence with two subjects and two verbs]

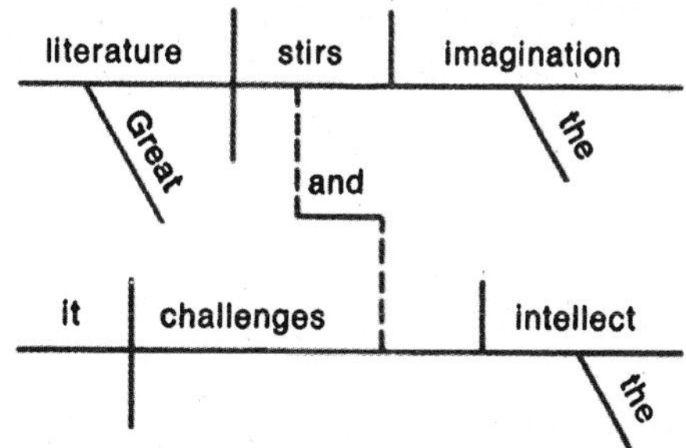

Independent clauses are joined by semicolons, coordinating conjunctions, or conjunctive adverbs.

Conjunctive Adverbs

also	furthermore	nevertheless	therefore
besides	however	otherwise	thus
consequently	moreover	then	still

(3) A *complex sentence* is a sentence that contains one independent clause and at least one subordinate clause.

Great literature, which stirs the imagination, also challenges the intellect.

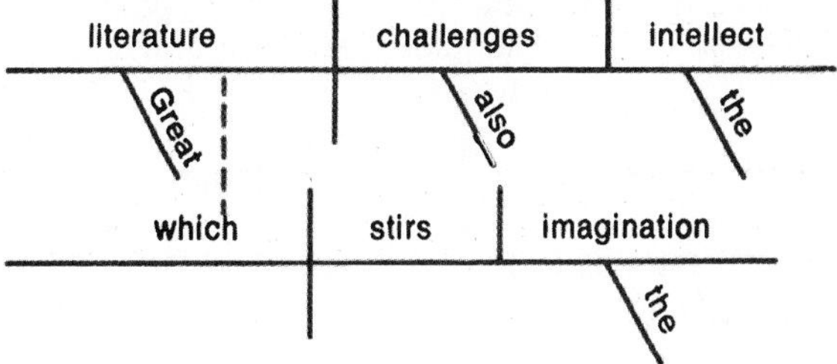

GRAMMAR

(4) A *compound-complex sentence* is a sentence that contains two or more independent clauses and at least one subordinate clause.

Great literature, which challenges the intellect, is sometimes difficult, but it is also rewarding. [The independent clauses are *Great literature is sometimes difficult* and *it is also rewarding*. The subordinate clause is *which challenges the intellect*.]

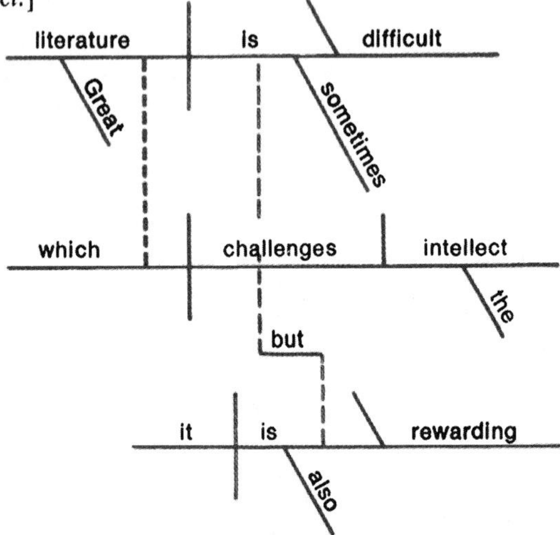

WRITING APPLICATION B:
Using a Variety of Sentence Structures in Your Writing

Notice in the following paragraph that the writer has used a variety of sentence structures to add vitality to his writing.

> When he was far up toward the top, he lay down and slept for a little while. [CX] The withered moon, shining on his face, awakened him. [S] He stood up and moved up the hill. [S] Fifty yards away he stopped and turned back, for he had forgotten his rifle. [CD] He walked heavily down and poked about in the brush, but he could not find his gun. [CD] At last he lay down to rest. [S] The pocket of pain in his armpit had grown more sharp. [S] His arm seemed to swell out and fall with every heartbeat. [S] There was no position lying down where the heavy arm did not press against his armpit. [CX]
>
> JOHN STEINBECK

Writing Assignment

Write a narrative paragraph of a memorable experience in your life. Use a variety of sentence structures to enliven your writing.

SENTENCES CLASSIFIED BY PURPOSE

4h. Classified according to their purpose, there are four kinds of sentences: *declarative, imperative, interrogative,* and *exclamatory.*

(1) A *declarative sentence* is a sentence that makes a statement.

Homes should be made safer for the elderly.

(2) An *imperative sentence* is a sentence that gives a command or makes a request.

Close that book and pay attention.
Please lower the volume.

(3) An *interrogative sentence* is a sentence that asks a question.

What was the name of that song?

(4) An *exclamatory sentence* is a sentence that expresses strong feeling.

How happy I am!

EXERCISE 6. Classifying Sentences According to Structure and Purpose. Number your paper 1–10. Classify each sentence in two ways: (1) according to its structure and (2) according to its purpose.

EXAMPLE 1. Look at this article I'm reading.
1. *complex—imperative*

1. Are you aware that there is a worldwide demand for butterflies?
2. Millions are caught and sold each year to museums, entomologists, private collectors, and factories.
3. The plastic-encased butterflies that are used to decorate ornamental objects such as trays, tabletops, and screens are usually common varieties, most of which come from Taiwan, Korea, and Malaysia.
4. There is a difference, however, between what goes on there and what goes on in Papua.
5. Papua, which was administered by Australia until it gained its independence in 1975, is taking advantage of a growing interest in tropical butterflies.
6. Here butterfly ranchers gather, raise, and sell high-quality specimens that are accompanied by scientific data.

7. Because biologists have not yet detailed the life cycles of the Papuan butterflies, the villagers have become the experts; and as a result, butterfly ranching has improved the economy in many otherwise impoverished villages.
8. Some Papuan butterflies are quite small, but others are larger than an adult human hand.
9. As you examine these photographs, observe that a carefully stocked pasture of butterflies looks like a flower garden.
10. What rich, vibrant colors Papuan butterflies have!

GRAMMAR

REVIEW EXERCISE B. Classify each sentence as simple, compound, complex, or compound-complex and then as declarative, interrogative, imperative, or exclamatory.

EXAMPLE 1. Whenever I need a piece of golfing equipment, I know that the To a Tee Shop is certain to have it in stock.
1. *complex—declarative*

1. Do you know that imaginative teachers who are enthusiastic about their work can make school pleasurable for their students?
2. Last year, when I took a social studies elective, Law and Order, I found myself looking forward to fourth period each day.
3. What our teacher, Ms. Schiavone, did to enrich our course was to bring the outside world into the classroom.
4. In addition to assigning reading, homework, and tests, she invited guest speakers to share their experiences with us throughout the school year.
5. By the end of three months, the class had met with a defense attorney, a prosecutor, and several local police officers; and we had interviewed the first FBI agent we had ever met.
6. In addition, Ms. Schiavone also arranged to have four prisoners, accompanied by police, tell us about how they were coping with prison life.
7. After we had listened to these men and women telling of their experiences, we all agreed that a career in crime is definitely not attractive!
8. In addition to bringing these people and experiences into the classroom, Ms. Schiavone set up a schedule of field trips, and she then took the classroom "into the world."

9. For example, on one day we visited the local jail; and on another, when we attended a session of a jury trial, we spoke personally with the judge.
10. I am glad that I was in Ms. Schiavone's class, and I was pleased when she was voted "Outstanding Educator of the Year."

CHAPTER 4 REVIEW: POSTTEST 1

A. Identifying Clauses. Identify each italicized group of words as an independent or a subordinate clause. If it is a subordinate clause, identify it as an adjective clause, an adverb clause, or a noun clause.

EXAMPLE 1. *While we were talking on the telephone,* our conversation was drowned out by noise on the line.
1. *subordinate—adverb*

1. *Tamara applied for the job last Monday,* and each day since then she has been waiting for a call from the company.
2. Do you think *that your parents will approve of your spending so much money for a stereo*?
3. *Please give me a break.*
4. Amelia Earhart, *who was the first woman to fly solo over the Atlantic and Pacific Oceans,* had great courage.
5. *Though he was a paraplegic because of injuries sustained in an auto accident,* Mr. Benoit was the best coach at Central High School.
6. As you wait for the signal, concentrate only on *what you have to do to win.*
7. Since last year Maureen and Jim have been rotating household tasks, and as a result, *each has become more understanding and more helpful.*
8. *If you study patterns of stock market transactions,* you will notice that prices often fall as interest rates rise.
9. How was I ever going to get the parts of the engine reassembled *before my father got home*?
10. *I won a soccer ball* when I was ten because I had raked more leaves than my brother and sister had in a "contest" devised by our clever parents.

11. Tired from a long day in the hot sun, the lifeguard reported *that there had been no accidents.*
12. In high school, Counsuelo Garcia set an all-city scoring record in basketball, *and she later went to college on a scholarship.*
13. Can you tell me *why there is still famine in parts of the world*?
14. After World War II, *President Harry Truman authorized the Marshall Plan,* which was a massive program designed to speed economic recovery in Europe.
15. The Vietnam memorial, a black granite wall engraved with the names of those *who died in the Vietnam War,* was designed by Maya Lin when she was a student at Yale University.

B. Classifying Sentences. Classify each sentence according to its structure (simple, compound, complex, or compound-complex) and according to its purpose (declarative, interrogative, imperative, or exclamatory).

EXAMPLE 1. How long have you been collecting old records?
1. *simple—interrogative*

16. Even though it has been years since his death, Elvis Presley's records still show good sales.
17. Where are you going in such a hurry that you have forgotten to put on your shoes?
18. Please proceed to the auditorium with your homeroom class and take the seats assigned to you.
19. President Lyndon Johnson, the thirty-sixth president, is credited with the passage of the Civil Rights Act of 1964, which is a landmark piece of legislation.
20. This morning the bank approved our loan, and this afternoon we began work on the new solar addition to our house.
21. As the molten lava moved down the mountain, residents who lived within a ten-mile radius were asked to evacuate their homes.
22. I am so relieved because the ordeal is over at last!
23. My friend Kaya likes to solve puzzles that are challenging; cryptograms are what he enjoys most.
24. When Bart says he will arrive at noon, I know I can expect him at any time between one o'clock and four.
25. Sometimes, on rainy Sunday afternoons, Carmen enjoys watching an old movie on television.

CHAPTER 4 REVIEW: POSTTEST 2

Writing Sentences. Write your own sentences, one of each of the following kinds:

1. A complex sentence with an adjective clause beginning with the relative adverb *where*
2. A complex sentence with a noun clause used as the subject of the sentence
3. A complex sentence with a noun clause used as the object of the main verb of the sentence
4. A complex sentence with an adjective clause beginning with the relative pronoun *who*
5. A complex sentence with an adverb clause beginning with the subordinating conjunction *because*
6. A complex sentence with an adverb clause beginning with the subordinating conjunction *while*
7. A compound-complex sentence
8. A complex sentence with an elliptical clause
9. An interrogative compound sentence
10. An imperative sentence

PART 2

USAGE

CHAPTER 5

Agreement

SUBJECT AND VERB, PRONOUN AND ANTECEDENT

USAGE

Some words in English have matching forms to show grammatical relationships. Forms that match in this way are said to *agree.* For example, a subject and verb agree if both are singular or both are plural. Pronouns also agree with their antecedents, which are the words the pronouns stand for.

DIAGNOSTIC TEST

Selecting Verbs That Agree with Their Subjects and Pronouns That Agree with Their Antecedents. Number your paper 1–20. After the proper number, write the word in parentheses that correctly completes the sentence. Follow the practices of formal usage.

EXAMPLE 1. Neither of the pitchers (was, were) able to stop the Seagulls from winning the baseball game.
1. *was*

1. Each of the air traffic controllers (was, were) communicating with departing and arriving pilots.
2. Both of your answers (is, are) correct.
3. A team with too many superstars (has, have) trouble working as a unit.
4. "(Is, Are) mumps contagious?" I asked when my sister got the disease two days before I was to star in our school play.

5. Laura is one of those students who always (takes, take) good notes.
6. Luis' greatest problem before a race (is, are) nerves.
7. Ms. Caplice, in addition to Mr. Ruiz and Ms. Rogers, (was, were) asked to attend the conference.
8. Many a financial investor (has, have) a headache on a day when the stock market drops.
9. An adventure novel, *The Three Musketeers* (has, have) been made into a movie many times.
10. Kathy (doesn't, don't) look like her sister Missy at all.
11. Each of the students had brought (his, their) notes to the meeting.
12. When we got to the picnic grounds, we discovered that neither Fred nor Bill had brought (his, their) radio.
13. The number of people seeking jobs in the computer industry (is, are) rising rapidly.
14. Jane or the twins (is, are) sure to be home when you call.
15. At the dance, some of the food served during the breaks (was, were) home cooked.
16. Our city is proud of (its, their) cultural activities.
17. My mother thought that twenty-five dollars (was, were) too much to pay for the designer T-shirt.
18. As I shaded my eyes from the bright orange, yellow, and green plaid material, Doug said, "(Here's, Here are) my new trousers. What do you think?"
19. One of the women hurt (her, their) foot in the race.
20. The twin towers of the World Trade Center in New York City (is, are) an awesome sight.

USAGE

AGREEMENT OF SUBJECT AND VERB

5a. A word that refers to one person or thing is *singular* in number. A word that refers to more than one is *plural* in number.

SINGULAR	PLURAL
car	cars
ox	oxen
this	these
either	both
he, she, it	they

5b. A verb agrees with its subject in number.

(1) Singular subjects take singular verbs.

A young **woman lives** next door.
This bake **sale was sponsored** by the Pep Club.

(2) Plural subjects take plural verbs.

Young **women live** next door.
These bake **sales were sponsored** by the Pep Club.

Most verbs ending in a single *s* are present-tense singular forms: he *is*, she *has*, he *thinks*, she *works*, etc. Most present-tense verbs not ending in a single *s* are plural: They *are*, *have*, *think*, *work*, etc. The exceptions, which should cause little difficulty, are verbs used with *I* and singular *you:* I *think*, you *work*, etc.

Notice that all the verbs given as examples in the preceding paragraph are in the present tense. Past tense verbs have the same form in the singular and plural. The exception is the verb *be*, which has a special form *was* that is used with *I*, *he*, *she*, and *it*, and all singular nouns.

SINGULAR	PLURAL
I threw	they threw
he applied	we applied
I was	we were

If English is your native language, you probably have little trouble in making verbs agree with their subjects when they directly follow the subjects. You will encounter sentences, however, in which it is not so easy to identify the subject correctly or determine whether it is singular or plural. These constructions, which create most agreement problems, are taken up separately on the following pages.

Intervening Phrase

5c. The number of the subject is not changed by a phrase following the subject.

A phrase that comes between a singular subject and its verb can easily mislead you if it contains a plural word. Remember that the verb agrees with its subject, not with any modifiers the subject may have.

EXAMPLES The **counselor was** very helpful.
The **counselor** for the senior students **was** very helpful. [*Counselor*, not *students*, is the subject of the sentence.]
A **solution has been found.**
A **solution** to these problems **has been found.** [*solution has,* not *problems have*]

In formal writing, singular subjects followed by phrases beginning with *together with, as well as, in addition to,* and *accompanied by* take singular verbs.

EXAMPLE The **singer**, as well as the musicians, **was** pleased with the recording.

EXERCISE 1. Selecting Verbs That Agree with Their Subjects. Number your paper 1–10. Write after the proper number the subject of the sentence. After the subject, write the verb in parentheses that agrees in number with the subject.

1. The theory of plate tectonics (has, have) explained causes of earthquake activity throughout the world.
2. Enormous plates of rock (is, are) moving constantly beneath the earth's surface.
3. The movements, in addition to the pressure of molten rock, (causes, cause) the plates to collide.
4. The pressure of colliding plates (forces, force) the rock to bend until it breaks.
5. A ridge of these breaks (is, are) called a fault.
6. The cause of most earthquakes (is, are) the release of stress along a fault.
7. The Richter scale, as well as other measurements, (has, have) been used to record the magnitude of earthquakes.
8. The tremors of the great San Francisco earthquake (was, were) estimated to have measured 8.3 on the Richter scale.
9. California, with the San Andreas and Garlock faults, (has, have) about ten times the world average of earthquake activity.
10. The scientific community, especially seismologists and geologists, (is, are) studying the effects of earthquakes.

Indefinite Pronouns as Subjects

Pronouns like *everybody, someone, everything, all,* and *none,* which are more or less indefinite in meaning, present special usage problems.

USAGE

Some of them are always singular, some are always plural, and others may be singular or plural, depending on the meaning of the sentence. In addition, such pronouns are often followed by a phrase. Therefore, you must first determine the number of the pronoun and then remember the rule about phrases that come between subjects and verbs.

5d. The following common words are singular: ***each, either, neither, one, no one, every one, anyone, someone, everyone, anybody, somebody, everybody.***

EXAMPLES **Each does** his own cooking.
Each of the boys **does** [not *do*] his own cooking.
Everyone enjoys the summertime.
Every one of the campers **enjoys** [not *enjoy*] the summertime.

5e. The following common words are plural: ***several, few, both, many.***

EXAMPLES **Several** of the students **were** transferred.
Few on the committee **attend** meetings.
Both of the teams **play** very well.
Many were impressed by the guest speaker.

5f. The words ***some, any, none, all,*** **and** ***most*** **may be singular or plural, depending on the meaning of the sentence.**

Usually, when the words *some, any, none, all,* and *most* refer to a singular word, they are singular; when they refer to a plural word, they are plural.[1] Compare these examples:

Some of the show **was** hilarious. [*Some* is singular because it refers to *show,* which is singular.]

Some of the actors **were** hilarious. [*Some* is plural because it refers to *actors,* which is plural.]

All of the workout **seems** simple.
All of the exercises **seem** simple.

Most of the program **was** new to me. [the major part of one program]
Most of the programs **were** new to me. [a number of separate programs]

Is any of the salad left?
Are any of the shirts clean?

None of the story **makes** sense.
None of the movies **were** exciting. [see note on page 84]

[1] Since the word referred to appears in a phrase following the subject, this rule is an exception to rule 5c.

> ☞ USAGE NOTE *Was* could have been used in the last example, but modern usage prefers a plural verb in this situation. If you want the subject to be singular in such a sentence, use *no one* or *not one* instead of *none*.

WRITING APPLICATION A: Observing Agreement Rules in Recording Observations

Indefinite pronouns can be tricky. They can be singular, plural, or either, depending upon the meaning of the sentence. Words like *each* are singular; words like *several* are plural; and words like *some* may be singular or plural, depending on the sentence.

Writing Assignment

Think of yourself as eyewitness to an important event. It could be a disaster, an impressive ceremony, or any other striking situation. Record your observations, following agreement rules carefully. In your written account, include at least four indefinite pronouns (such as *each, all, several, both, many,* etc.) used as subjects.

USAGE

EXERCISE 2. Selecting Verbs That Agree with Their Subjects. Number your paper 1–10. Write the subject of each sentence. After it, write the verb in parentheses which agrees in number with the subject.

1. Each of the pictures (was, were) in a silver frame.
2. One of my friends (play, plays) the tuba.
3. All of our belongings (is, are) still unpacked.
4. Some of these rare books (has, have) leather covers.
5. None of the people in the theater (was, were) pleased with the film.
6. Every one of these jeans (is, are) too small.
7. A few in my class (was, were) asked to help out.
8. The lack of funds (present, presents) a problem.
9. Everybody living in Lewis Heights (go, goes) to George Washington Carver High School.
10. A band with two trumpet players and thirty-five clarinetists (sound, sounds) terrible.

EXERCISE 3. Writing Verbs That Agree with Their Subjects. Revise these ten sentences, following the instructions that appear in brackets after each of them. Sometimes the addition will affect agreement. Be sure to make the subject and verb of the new sentence agree. Underline each subject once and each verb twice.

EXAMPLE 1. Each of the contestants was confused by the question. [Change *Each* to *Several.*]
1. *Several of the contestants were confused by the question.*

1. All of the fruit has spoiled. [Change *fruit* to *oranges.*]
2. Each of my friends was angry about the election. [Change *Each* to *Many.*]
3. Has anybody joined the choir? [Change *anybody* to *any of the new students.*]
4. The class leaves tomorrow on the field trip. [Add *accompanied by two chaperons* after *class.* Put a comma before and after the added phrase.]
5. Our team is going to Austin for the debate tournament. [Add *Three members of* before *Our team.*]
6. Most of the classrooms were equipped with new microcomputers. [Change *Most* to *None.*]
7. The pitcher was disappointed in the coach's decision. [Add *as well as the other players* after *pitcher.* Set off the addition with commas.]
8. Every one of the smoke detectors was broken. [Change *Every one* to *All but two.*]
9. Both of them usually expect the worst to happen. [Change *Both of them* to *Everyone.*]
10. Some of her plan has been approved. [Change *plan* to *suggestions.*]

USAGE

EXERCISE 4. Determining Subject-Verb Agreement. Number your paper 1–10. Read each of the following sentences. If the verb in a sentence agrees with its subject, write a + after the proper number on your paper; if the verb does not agree, write the correct form of the verb.

1. The mayor, as well as her aides, were in the parade.
2. Neither of the groups follow parliamentary procedure.
3. Some of the essay wasn't coherent.
4. The cause of the recent fires are being investigated.

5. Each of the computers run a different program.
6. None of the students has disagreed with my suggestion.
7. Only a few on any committee do all the work.
8. Luckily every one of the students have passed the test.
9. Most of his lectures holds my interest.
10. Either of your ideas seems reasonable.

Compound Subjects

As you will recall from Chapter 2, two words or groups of words may be connected to form the subject of a verb. These words, usually joined by *and* or *or,* are called a *compound subject.* Compound subjects may take singular or plural verbs, depending on whether the words joined are singular or plural and what the connecting word is.

USAGE

5g. Subjects joined by *and* take a plural verb.

EXAMPLES A **horse and** an **elephant are** mammals.
Hannah and Dot have been friends for years.

EXCEPTION When the parts of a compound subject are considered as a unit or when they refer to the same thing, a singular verb is used.

EXAMPLES **Bread and butter comes** with every meal.
Joe's **brother and** best **friend is going** to college in New Mexico.

5h. Singular subjects joined by *or* or *nor* take a singular verb.

EXAMPLES A **jacket or** a **sweater is** warm enough at night.
Neither the **coach nor** the **trainer was** sure of the starting time.

5i. When a singular and a plural subject are joined by *or* or *nor,* the verb agrees with the nearer subject.

ACCEPTABLE Either the singer or the musicians are off-key.

It is usually possible to avoid this awkward construction altogether:

BETTER Either the singer is off-key, or the musicians are.

Another reason for avoiding this construction is that the subjects may be different in person. If this is so, the verb must agree with the nearer subject in person as well as number. In the following example, the verb must not only be singular to agree with *I*, but it must also have the form (am) that matches *I* as a subject.

ACCEPTABLE Neither my girl friends nor I am working part-time.
BETTER My girl friends are not working part-time and neither am I.

USAGE NOTE The rules in this chapter are consistently followed in standard formal English but are often disregarded in informal speaking and writing. Formal usage requires a singular verb after a singular subject. Informal usage, however, often permits the use of a plural verb if the meaning is clearly plural.

FORMAL Neither Ellen nor Lola has a video camera.
INFORMAL Neither Ellen nor Lola have a video camera. [Although joined by *nor*, which strictly calls for a singular verb, the meaning of the sentence is essentially plural: both Ellen and Lola lack cameras.]

FORMAL The conductor, as well as a soprano and many stagehands, was trapped in the theater fire.
INFORMAL The conductor, as well as a soprano and many stagehands, were trapped in the theater fire. [Although the construction calls for a singular verb, the meaning is clearly plural—all of them were trapped, not just the conductor. It is usually wise to avoid constructions that set up a conflict. The example would be better if it were written as "The conductor, a soprano, and many stagehands were. . . ."]

In some of the exercise sentences in this chapter, you will encounter such differences between formal and informal usage. For the purposes of these exercises, follow the rules of formal usage.

EXERCISE 5. Determining Subject-Verb Agreement. Number your paper 1–20. Read each of the following sentences. If the verb in a sentence agrees with its subject, write a + after the proper number. If the verb does not agree, write the correct form of the verb. Follow the practices of formal usage.

1. One of the most precious resources in the nation is water.
2. The abundance and use of water vary greatly among the regions of the United States.
3. The water supply for all the states come from either surface water or underground water.
4. Unfortunately, neither overuse nor contamination of water supplies has stopped completely.

5. Not one of the water sources are free from pollution.
6. After years of study, pollution of lakes, rivers, and streams continue to be a serious problem.
7. Lake Erie, as well as the Potomac and Cuyahoga Rivers, have been saved by clean-up efforts.
8. The government, in addition to environmentalists, are also worried about the quality and abundance of ground water.
9. Aquifers, a source of ground water, is layers of rock, sand, and soil that hold water.
10. About 88 billion gallons of water is pumped out of the ground each day.
11. In some regions, the drinking water for hundreds of people come from aquifers.
12. Every one of the recent studies of aquifers has revealed contamination to some degree.
13. The causes of contamination are varied.
14. Salt for melting ice on city streets cause pollution.
15. The chemicals that sometimes leak out of a sewer system or waste dump contaminates aquifers.
16. Fertilizers used on a farm also add pollutants to the water.
17. The extent of the damages from contamination are not known.
18. Another problem, according to scientists, is uncontrolled use of water sources.
19. Ground water in some areas are being used faster than the supply can be renewed.
20. Each one of the fifty states have a stake in preserving sources of water.

USAGE

Other Problems in Subject-Verb Agreement

5j. When the subject follows the verb, as in questions and in sentences beginning with *here* and *there*, be careful to determine the subject and make sure that the verb agrees with it.

NONSTANDARD How's Al and Roberta feeling?
STANDARD How **are Al and Roberta** feeling?

NONSTANDARD There's seven vegetables in the salad.
STANDARD There **are** seven **vegetables** in the salad.

5k. Collective nouns may be either singular or plural.

A collective noun names a group: *crowd, committee, jury, class.* A collective noun takes a plural verb when the speaker is thinking of the individual members of the group; it takes a singular verb when the speaker is thinking of the group as a unit.

The **audience were entering** the theater. [The speaker is thinking of the individuals in the audience.]
The **audience was** one of the best. [The speaker is thinking of the audience as a whole, a single unit.]
The **team have voted** eighteen to three to buy new uniforms.
The **team has won** the semifinals.

SOME COMMON COLLECTIVE WORDS

army	crowd	orchestra
audience	flock	public
class	group	swarm
club	herd	team
committee	jury	troop

5l. Expressions stating amount (time, money, measurement, weight, volume, fractions) are usually singular when the amount is considered as a unit.

EXAMPLES **Five years has been** a long time to wait.
Twenty pounds seems a lot to gain in a month.
Two thirds of the day is spent in school.

However, when the amount is considered as a number of separate units, a plural verb is used.

EXAMPLES The **last six miles were** the most scenic.
There **are thirteen days** left in the month.
Two thirds of the holidays fall on a Friday or a Monday.

5m. The title of a book or the name of an organization or country, even when plural in form, usually takes a singular verb.

EXAMPLES ***Lilies of the Field* is** on the late show tonight.
Friends of the Earth has held a membership drive.
The United States was represented at the summit conference.

EXCEPTION Some names of organizations (Veterans of Foreign Wars, New York Yankees, Chicago Bears, etc.) customarily take a plural verb when you are thinking of the members and a singular verb when you mean the organization.

The **Veterans of Foreign Wars attend** this meeting.
The **Veterans of Foreign Wars is** a large organization.

5n. A few nouns, such as *mumps, measles, civics, economics, mathematics, physics,* although plural in form, take a singular verb.

EXAMPLES The **mumps** usually **lasts** three days.
Nuclear **physics is** a controversial branch of science.

The following similar words are more often plural than singular: *athletics, acoustics, gymnastics, tactics*. The word *politics* may be either singular or plural, and *scissors* and *trousers* are always plural.

For more information on the use of words ending in *-ics,* look up *-ics* in your dictionary.

USAGE

5o. When the subject and the predicate nominative are different in number, the verb agrees with the subject, not with the predicate nominative.

ACCEPTABLE The last **act** featured **was** the singers and dancers.
ACCEPTABLE The **singers and dancers were** the last act featured.
BETTER The **singers and dancers were** featured last.

Although the first two examples are acceptable, it is usually better to avoid writing sentences in which the subject and predicate nominative are different in number.

5p. *Every* or *many a* before a word or series of words is followed by a singular verb.

EXAMPLES **Every waitress, busboy,** and **cashier was** pleased with the new schedule.
Many a young **runner finishes** the grueling race in less than five hours.

5q. *Don't* and *doesn't* must agree with their subjects.

With the subjects *I* and *you,* use *don't* (*do not*). With other subjects, use *doesn't* (*does not*) when the subject is singular and *don't* (*do not*) when the subject is plural.

EXAMPLES **I don't** like her painting.
You don't talk too much.
It [He, She, This] doesn't work anymore.
They don't agree.

By using *doesn't* after *it, he,* and *she*, you can eliminate most of the common errors in the use of *don't.*

5r. In formal English, verbs in clauses that follow *one of those* are almost always plural.

Even though informal usage often permits a singular verb in the clause following *one of those*, the plural verb is almost always correct. Use a singular verb only when *one of those* is preceded by *the only.*

EXAMPLES This is **one of those** assignments that **require** research in the library.
Naomi is **one of those** players who **are** good losers.
Ron is the **only one of those students** who **has** permission to leave.

5s. The word *number* when followed by the word *of* is singular when preceded by *the*; it is plural when preceded by *a*.

EXAMPLES **The number** of volunteers **is** surprising.
A number of volunteers **are** signing up right now.

EXERCISE 6. Selecting Verbs That Agree with Their Subjects. Number your paper 1–20. After the proper number, write the correct verb in parentheses.

1. Neither the knife nor the scissors (was, were) sharp enough.
2. Forty dollars (is, are) too much to pay for jeans.
3. (Where's, Where are) her coat and boots?
4. Many a gymnast (dreams, dream) of participating in the Olympic Games.
5. There (seems, seem) to be something for everyone.
6. Every one of her quilts (has, have) been sold.
7. The captain of the football team and the president of the senior class (represents, represent) the students.
8. Macaroni and cheese (is, are) on the menu again.
9. *A Tale of Two Cities* (was, were) made into a movie for television.
10. The Chicago Cubs is one of those teams that (rallies, rally) in the late innings.
11. Neither civics nor mathematics (is, are) his best subject.
12. Each of the packages (contains, contain) a surprise gift.
13. Every volunteer in the city's hospitals (is, are) being honored at the banquet.

14. One half of the receipts (was, were) found in a shoe box.
15. The Society of Procrastinators (has, have) postponed the annual meeting.
16. That was one of those jokes that (offends, offend) everyone.
17. None of the peaches (was, were) bruised in shipping.
18. The acoustics in the auditorium (has, have) been improved.
19. Not one of the accusations (was, were) ever proved in court.
20. Some short stories by O. Henry (is, are) Ken's favorite book.

REVIEW EXERCISE A. Determining Subject-Verb Agreement. Number your paper 1–10. If the verb in a sentence agrees with its subject, write + after the proper number. If the verb does not agree, write the correct form of the verb.

EXAMPLES 1. Here's two letters for you.
1. *Here are*
2. The display in the auto dealer's showrooms represents more than $150,000 worth of cars.
2. +

1. Each year, a faculty member and a student talks to the student body during an assembly on the opening day of school.
2. In the United States, there are a wide variety of ethnic groups in the population.
3. Can you believe that Leo don't go anywhere without his pocket calculator?
4. My sister Latrice is one of those people who make guests feel at ease.
5. As employers demand more skills from employees, the importance of studies after high school are evident to most seniors.
6. Some of the criticism aimed at children's cartoons are perceptive and accurate.
7. From my experience with team sports, I know that when neither the coach nor the team members has the will to win, there is little chance of victory.
8. The number of serious accidents that happen at home is surprisingly large.
9. The musical *Cats* was based on a group of poems by T. S. Eliot.
10. Every morning during swim season, each of the girls on the team were at the pool by 6 A.M.

WRITING APPLICATION B:
Writing Sentences with Subject-Verb Agreement

Writers make "agreement errors" when they do not see the *true* subjects of their sentences. You should always analyze your sentences for the *true* subjects so that you can make the verbs agree with their subjects.

INCORRECT The players, as well as the coach, was disappointed.
CORRECT The players, as well as the coach, **were** disappointed. [*Players*, not *coach*, is the subject of the sentence.]

Writing Assignment

Write ten sentences, each beginning with a different one of the following groups of words. Make sure that the verbs agree with their subjects.

1. *Great Expectations*
2. Five dollars
3. Neither of the sofas
4. The critics' reviews
5. Many a doctor
6. The man talking to the children
7. My aunt and uncle
8. Some of the salespeople
9. Peanut butter and jelly
10. Everyone in the contests

AGREEMENT OF PRONOUN AND ANTECEDENT

5t. A pronoun agrees with its antecedent in number and gender.[1]

The antecedent of a pronoun is the word to which the pronoun refers. In the following examples, the antecedents and the pronouns referring to them are in boldfaced type. As a rule the pronoun is singular when the antecedent is singular and plural when the antecedent is plural. The pronoun is masculine (*he, him, his*) when the antecedent is masculine; feminine (*she, her, hers*) when the antecedent is feminine; neuter (*it, its*) when the antecedent is neither masculine nor feminine. This kind of agreement is agreement in *gender*.

She should have done it **herself.**
Keith hit **his** first home run today.
The **Fishers** returned from **their** fishing trip.
The **company** advertises **its** products on television.

[1] Pronouns also agree with their antecedents in *person* (see page 102). Agreement in person rarely presents usage problems.

(1) The words *each, either, neither, one, everyone, everybody, no one, nobody, anyone, anybody, someone, somebody* are referred to by a singular pronoun—*he, him, his, she, her, hers, it, its.*

The use of a phrase after the antecedent does not change the number of the antecedent.

EXAMPLES **Each** of the women designed **her** own pattern.
Neither of the men left **his** coat on the seat.
One of the girls took **her** umbrella with **her**.

> **USAGE NOTE** Sometimes the antecedent may be either masculine or feminine; sometimes it may be both. Some writers use the masculine form of the personal pronoun to refer to such antecedents. Other writers prefer to use both the masculine and feminine forms in such cases.

EXAMPLES Everyone has handed in **his** paper.
Everyone has handed in **his or her** paper.

You can often avoid the awkward *his or her* construction by rephrasing the sentence in the plural.

The **students** have handed in **their** papers.

In conversation, you may find it more convenient to use a plural personal pronoun when referring to singular antecedents that can be either masculine or feminine. This form is becoming increasingly popular in writing as well and may someday become acceptable as standard written English.

EXAMPLES If **anyone** calls, tell **them** I'll call back.
Someone left **their** umbrella.

Strict adherence to the rule of pronoun-antecedent agreement may lead to a construction so absurd that no one would use it:

ABSURD Did *everybody* leave early because *he* wasn't enjoying *himself*?

In instances of this kind, use the plural pronoun or recast the sentence to avoid the problem:

BETTER Did **everybody** leave early because **they** weren't enjoying **themselves**?
or
Did the **guests** leave early because **they** weren't enjoying **themselves**?

(2) Two or more singular antecedents joined by *or* or *nor* should be referred to by a singular pronoun.

Neither **Sue nor Maria** left **her** books on **her** desk.

(3) Two or more antecedents joined by *and* should be referred to by a plural pronoun.

Sue and Maria presented **their** reports.

> ☞ NOTE Like some of the rules for agreement of subject and verb, the rules for agreement of pronoun and antecedent show variations between formal and informal usage. Standard informal usage follows meaning rather than strict grammatical agreement. The sentences below marked "informal" are acceptable in informal writing and speaking. In exercises, however, follow the practices of formal English.

FORMAL **Neither** of the women carried **her** purse with **her**.
INFORMAL Neither of the women carried their purses with them.
FORMAL **Every one** of the contestants was instructed to place **his** scorecard on the table in front of **him**.
INFORMAL Every one of the contestants was instructed to place their scorecards on the table in front of them.

WRITING APPLICATION C:
Making Pronouns Agree with Their Antecedents

Writers often use pronouns to avoid repeating nouns. Always check to make sure that the pronouns agree with their antecedents. Use the rules on pages 93–94 and this page to help you.

Writing Assignment

Write a narration about a humorous or light-hearted incident in which you and a friend or relative were involved. Wherever appropriate, use pronouns to avoid repeating nouns. When you proofread, check to see that the pronouns agree with their antecedents.

USAGE

EXERCISE 7. Determining Pronoun-Antecedent Agreement. Number your paper 1–10. If a pronoun in a sentence does not agree with its antecedent, write the pronoun on your paper and next to it write the correct form. If a sentence is correct, write a + after the proper number. Follow the practices of formal usage.

EXAMPLES
1. Neither Elena nor Barbara made any errors on their test.
1. *their—her*
2. Neither Stan nor Len wanted to endanger themselves.
2. *themselves—himself*

1. Each of the skiers waxed their skis before leaving the lodge.
2. All of the senior citizens enjoyed their trip to Boston, where they walked the Freedom Trail.
3. Every one of the reporters at the press conference asked their questions too quickly.
4. I believe that anybody should be free to express their opinion.
5. No one brought their camera to the party.
6. Neither of the male soloists pronounced their words very clearly.
7. Neither of the newborn kittens seemed very steady or secure on its feet.
8. If anyone loses their way while exploring Salt Lake City, they should use the special street maps available from the tour guide.
9. As far as I could see, neither of the women made a mistake while presenting their argument during the debate.
10. One of the interesting quirks of American history is that neither President Gerald Ford nor Vice-President Nelson Rockefeller was elected to his high office.

REVIEW EXERCISE B. Determining Subject-Verb Agreement and Pronoun-Antecedent Agreement. Number your paper 1–20. If a sentence is correct, write a + after the proper number; if it is incorrect, write the correct form of the verb or pronoun.

1. The number of accidents have been startling.
2. Each one of the terrorists were captured in a daring rescue attempt.
3. How's the heat and the humidity in Florida?
4. Has either of the brothers traveled before?
5. This is one of those cars that has a fuel injection system.
6. Anyone who speaks a foreign language increases their chance for a high-paying job.

USAGE

7. Neither of the restaurants serves customers who aren't wearing shoes.
8. The experience of sailing the Great Lakes builds character in the young women.
9. Every part-time employee at the store was thanked for their help with taking the inventory.
10. She is one of the engineers that is working on the new design for the space shuttle.
11. When the bank's computer breaks down, every one of the tellers holds their breath.
12. The increase in taxes have met resistance.
13. A person who admits his mistakes is respected by all.
14. Three fourths of the audience always stay until the last note is played.
15. Each student needs a chance to think for himself.
16. Is there film and batteries in the camera?
17. All but three games in the final round was held at the community center.
18. A large number of scientists is studying the 843 pounds of rock and soil from the moon.
19. When one of the teachers retire, the students give him an engraved plaque.
20. The factory of the future will have robots working on its assembly line.

REVIEW EXERCISE C. Writing Verbs That Agree with Their Subjects. Revise the following sentences according to the directions given for each. Be sure to make changes or additions in verb forms, pronouns, etc. if necessary.

1. Some famous sports stars have made television commercials. [Change *Some famous sports stars* to *Many a famous sports star.*]
2. Where's my book? [Add *and my pen* after *book.*]
3. Both of the candidates have promised to reduce taxes. [Change *Both* to *Neither.*]
4. She writes neatly. [Add *is one of those students who* after *She.*]
5. Our basketball team has won the championship. [Add *Neither our football team nor* at the beginning of the sentence.]
6. People need friends to confide in. [Change *People* to *A person.*]

7. An application blank is required by the state university. [After *blank* add *together with a recent photograph and an autobiographical essay*. Put a comma before *together* and after *essay*.]
8. The tigers are growling ferociously. [At the beginning of the sentence, add *Either the lion or*.]
9. The movie screen is hard to see. [At the beginning of the sentence, add *The captions on*.]
10. A day in the library is all the time I need to finish my research. [Change *A day* to *Two days*.]

CHAPTER 5 REVIEW: POSTTEST

USAGE

Determining Subject-Verb Agreement and Pronoun-Antecedent Agreement. Number your paper 1–25. If a sentence is correct, write a + after the proper number; if it is incorrect, write the correct form of the verb or pronoun.

EXAMPLE: 1. In September, the new teacher was delighted because the class were enthusiastic and cooperative.
1. *was*

1. One of the South's great ecological treasures are the estuary and flatlands of Galveston Bay.
2. Twenty miles are too far for someone to walk unless he can stop and rest frequently.
3. Neither Melinda nor Greta answered their phone yesterday.
4. During the five hours of deliberation, the jury was often in disagreement.
5. Public relations and advertising is exciting but often stressful work.
6. Anyone earning such a low salary will have trouble paying their bills.
7. Everyone who was at the tennis championship saw Chris Evert Lloyd and Martina Navratilova play their best match ever.
8. Is there any milk and apple pie in the refrigerator?
9. A completed application, in addition to a full financial statement, are required of students seeking college scholarships.
10. Every file cabinet, bookcase, and desk drawer were crammed with books and papers.

11. Where there's people and excitement, you're sure to find the twins Kazuo and Yori.
12. Not one of those nature programs that were shown on television this year have dealt with walruses.
13. Some of the information found in reference books need to be updated every year.
14. You might be surprised to know that many a city dweller grows vegetables in their own small yard.
15. Is Dolores one of the cheerleaders who are receiving a school letter at the sports banquet?
16. Each of the boys got a bonus for their hard work.
17. The Murphy family has made plans to visit relatives in Iowa.
18. Did you know that the city of Savannah, Georgia, has their own spectacular parade on St. Patrick's Day?
19. "Neither of the movies seem to have much hope of making the millions the producers want," commented the film critic.
20. All of the battalion was transfered to Fort Bliss in Texas.
21. Are the Lesser Antilles near Puerto Rico?
22. None of the competitors knew what his own chances of winning were.
23. A gentle snowfall is one of those winter events that is guaranteed to put me into a peaceful mood.
24. The number of people investing in companies that manufacture robots is increasing.
25. One junior, as well as four seniors, have been invited to attend the Milford Youth Council each month.

CHAPTER 6

Correct Use of Pronouns

NOMINATIVE AND OBJECTIVE CASE; SPECIAL PROBLEMS

DIAGNOSTIC TEST

Selecting Pronouns to Complete Sentences. Number your paper 1–20. From the parentheses, select the pronoun that correctly completes the sentence and write it after the proper number on your paper. Base your answer on formal standard usage.

EXAMPLE 1. Jose and (her, she) completed the math test first.
1. *she*

1. Greg and (I, myself) got our driver's licenses on the same day.
2. My Uncle Bill, (who, whom) I greatly admire, worked in the Peace Corps for two years after he had finished college.
3. As we waited at the starting line, I knew in my heart that the race was really going to be between Ted and (I, me).
4. At the town meeting, Ellen McCarthy asked, "If (we, us) voters don't vote, how can we expect the situation to change?"
5. I thought Manuel was in Kansas City; so when he walked into the restaurant, I could hardly believe it was (he, him).
6. Even though we are twins, Julie has always been taller than (I, me).
7. Does anyone know (who, whom) was using the computer?
8. My parents have a low tolerance for (me, my) playing rock music.

9. "May I help you?" asked the receptionist. "(Who, Whom) do you wish to see?"
10. The bus driver always greeted (us, we) students with a smile.
11. Owen said that for the first time the soccer team had elected co-captains, Mario and (he, him).
12. When you get to the airport, give your ticket to the person (who, whom) is at the check-in counter.
13. I remember (us, our) exploring the rocky coast of Maine when I was fifteen, and I have wanted to return there ever since.
14. Many people, adults as well as teen-agers, waste time worrying about (who, whom) is more popular in their social group.
15. "Does anyone dance better than (she, her)?" I wondered, as I watched Twyla Tharpe on the stage.
16. "When you and Regina were young children," said my grandfather, "I used to enjoy watching you and (she, her) playing Monopoly."
17. Knowing Noel and Bruce, I thought it had to be (they, them) who had played the practical joke on me.
18. Do you know that Stacy and (me, I) applied for the same job?
19. The President-elect knew exactly (who, whom) he wanted to appoint as Secretary of State.
20. I was so happy to see the new car that I could only gasp to my friend Danielle, "These wheels were made for you and (I, me)!"

The function of a pronoun in a sentence is shown by the case form of the pronoun. Different functions demand different forms. For instance, a pronoun that acts as a subject is in the *nominative case;* a pronoun that acts as an object is in the *objective case;* and a pronoun that shows possession is in the *possessive case.*

PRONOUN AS SUBJECT	**We** called the doctor.
PRONOUN AS OBJECT	The doctor called **us**.
POSSESSIVE PRONOUN	**Our** call was an emergency.

Observe that the pronoun has a different form (*we, us, our*) in each case.

☞ **NOTE** Since they are used in the same ways that pronouns are used, nouns may also be said to have case. The following sentence illustrates the three cases of nouns.

The *sculptor's statue* won an *award.*
sculptor's noun in the possessive case
statue noun in the nominative case—subject
award noun in the objective case—direct object

However, nouns have identical forms for the nominative and objective cases, and they form the possessive in a regular way. Thus, case presents no problems as far as nouns are concerned.

6a. Learn the case forms of pronouns and the uses of each form.

Personal pronouns are those pronouns that change form in the different persons. There are three persons—first, second, and third—which are distinguished as follows:

First person is the person speaking: *I* (*We*) work.
Second person is the person spoken to: *You* are working.
Third person is a person or thing other than the speaker or the one spoken to: *He* (*She, It, They*) will work.

Personal Pronouns

Singular	NOMINATIVE CASE	OBJECTIVE CASE	POSSESSIVE CASE
FIRST PERSON	I	me	my, mine
SECOND PERSON	you	you	your, yours
THIRD PERSON	he, she, it	him, her, it	his, her, hers, its

Plural	NOMINATIVE CASE	OBJECTIVE CASE	POSSESSIVE CASE
FIRST PERSON	we	us	our, ours
SECOND PERSON	you	you	your, yours
THIRD PERSON	they	them	their, theirs

Since *you* and *it* do not change their forms, ignore them. Memorize the following lists of nominative and objective forms.

NOMINATIVE CASE	OBJECTIVE CASE
I	me
he	him
she	her
we	us
they	them

USES OF NOMINATIVE FORMS

6b. The subject of a verb is in the nominative case.

This rule means that whenever you use a pronoun as a subject, you should use one of the pronouns from the left-hand column on page 102. Ordinarily, you do this without thinking about it. When the subject is compound, however, many persons do make mistakes in their selection of pronouns. Whereas they would never say "Me am seventeen years old," they will say "Myra and me are seventeen years old." Since the pronoun is used as a subject in both sentences, it should be in the nominative case in both: "*Myra and I* are seventeen years old."

(1) To determine the correct pronoun in a compound subject, try each subject separately with the verb, adapting the form as necessary. Your ear will tell you which form is correct.

NONSTANDARD Her and me are teammates. [*Her* is a teammate? *Me* am a teammate?]
STANDARD **She** and **I** are teammates. [*She* is a teammate. *I* am a teammate.]

NONSTANDARD Either Joe or him was in the gym. [*Him* was in the gym?]
STANDARD Either **Joe** or **he** was in the gym. [*He* was in the gym.]

(2) When the pronoun is used with a noun (*we girls, we seniors,* etc.), determine the correct form by reading the sentence without the noun.

EXAMPLE **We girls** painted the house. [*We* (not *Us*) painted the house.]

6c. A predicate nominative is in the nominative case.

A predicate nominative is a noun or pronoun in the predicate that refers to the same thing as the subject of the sentence. For the present purpose, think of a predicate nominative as any pronoun that follows a form of the verb *be*.

COMMON FORMS OF *BE*		PREDICATE NOMINATIVE
am is, are was, were may be, can be, will be, etc. may have been, etc. must be, might be	are followed by	I he she we you they

EXAMPLES I am **she.**
Can it be **he?**
It might have been **they** in the store.

> ☞ **USAGE NOTE** It is now perfectly acceptable to use *me* as a predicate nominative in informal usage: *It's me.* The plural form (*It's us*) is also generally accepted. However, using the objective case for the third person form of the pronoun (*It's him, It's them*) is still often frowned on in standard English. When you encounter any of these expressions in the exercises in this book or in the various tests you take, you will be wise to take a conservative attitude and use the nominative forms in all instances.

EXERCISE 1. Using Pronouns in the Nominative Case. Number your paper 1–10. After the proper number, write the personal pronoun that can be substituted for each italicized expression. In those sentences calling for [1st person pron.], use the appropriate one of the following pronouns: *I, we.*

EXAMPLES 1. Carl and *Sue Ann* are always happy.
1. *she*
2. Terri and [1st person pron.] were at the picnic.
2. *I*

1. Jorge and *Mike* are tied for third place.
2. *Donna* and her parents have moved to San Antonio.
3. [1st person pron.] seniors will take the exam.
4. Can it be *some choir members* in that picture?
5. Either Ellen or *Sally* will be in charge.
6. The team and *Mr. Knight* have chartered a bus.
7. [1st person pron.] varsity men earned our trophies.
8. Neither *Carolyn* nor Michele has change for the bus.
9. Did you know that Greg and [1st person pron.] are leaving?
10. I am sure it was *Ed* and you on the dance floor.

USES OF OBJECTIVE FORMS

6d. The object of a verb is in the objective case.

The object of a verb answers the question "What?" or "Whom?" after an action verb.

EXAMPLE We thanked **her.** [Thanked whom? Answer: *her,* which is the object.]

As their name suggests, the objective forms (*me, him, her, us, them*) are used as objects.

EXAMPLES I helped **him** with the report.
She surprised **us** last night.
Him I have always admired.

Since both direct and indirect objects are in the objective case, there is no point in distinguishing between them in applying this rule.

EXAMPLES They hired **her.** [direct object]
They gave **her** a present. [indirect object]

Like the nominative forms of pronouns, the objective forms are troublesome principally when they are used in compounds. Although you would hardly make the mistake of saying, "I helped *he* with the report," you might say, "I helped *Rod and he* with the report." Trying each object separately with the verb will help you to choose the correct pronoun for compound objects: "I helped *him* with the report."

When a pronoun is used with a noun (*we girls, us girls*), determine the correct form by omitting the noun.

It annoys **us** runners. [It annoys *us,* not *we.*]

EXERCISE 2 Using Pronouns in the Objective Case. Referring to the list of objective forms, supply the correct pronouns for the italicized words in the following sentences. In sentences calling for [1st person pron.], use the appropriate one of the following: *me, us.*

1. Did you tell the superintendent or *Ms. Marshal?*
2. Carla and *Dave* I would never doubt.
3. Leave [1st person pron.] girls alone for a while.
4. Michelle will be inviting both you and [1st person pron.] to her birthday party.
5. Did you see Lois or *Andy* today?
6. I sent the admissions director and *her assistant* a letter.
7. The coach chose Joan and *Carmen and me.*
8. The principal should have notified *Sven* and Gail about the schedule change.
9. Ron just passed Tina and [1st person pron.] in the hall.
10. Please don't ask [1st person pron.] athletes about last Saturday's game.

EXERCISE 3. Selecting Pronouns in the Nominative or Objective Case to Complete Sentences. This exercise covers the use of personal pronouns as subjects of verbs, predicate nominatives, and objects of verbs. Number your paper 1–20. Write the correct pronoun in parentheses in each sentence.

1. The guests thanked Rita and (she, her).
2. Gloria and (I, me) have matching outfits.
3. That's (he, him) standing on the corner.
4. (We, Us) girls are studying self-defense.
5. What were you telling Chuck and (we, us) earlier?
6. Of course, I remember Monica and (she, her).
7. We knew it was (he, him).
8. Did Jean and (he, him) sing in the musical?
9. Give (we, us) girls the message as soon as possible.
10. My grandparents took Donna and (I, me) to the symphony.
11. Who will tell Georgia and (I, me) the truth?
12. I didn't hear the teacher and (they, them) arrive.
13. Jana and (she, her) are active members.
14. It's either you or (he, him).
15. I will call Jody and (they, them) tomorrow.
16. The teacher gave her friend and (she, her) more homework.
17. We are glad it wasn't Edna and (she, her) in the accident.
18. The volunteers and (I, me) distributed the posters.
19. You and (he, him) have been practicing every day.
20. I thought it was (she, her) on the stage.

6e. The object of a preposition is in the objective case.

Prepositions, as well as verbs, take objects. The noun or pronoun at the end of a prepositional phrase is the object of the preposition that begins the phrase. In the following prepositional phrases the objects are printed in boldfaced type:

from **Los Angeles**   at the **bottom**   to **them**

Errors in the use of the pronoun as the object of a preposition usually occur when the object is compound. Since you would not say "I gave the ticket to *she*," you should not say "I gave the tickets to *Jenny* and *she*." By omitting the first of the two objects in a compound object, you can usually tell what the correct pronoun should be.

NONSTANDARD We got the keys from Len and he.
STANDARD We got the keys **from** Len and **him.** [from *him*]

NONSTANDARD Dwayne sat behind Norman and I.
STANDARD Dwayne sat **behind** Norman and **me.** [behind *me*]

EXERCISE 4. Selecting Pronouns in the Objective Case to Complete Sentences. Number your paper 1–10. Find the preposition in each sentence, and write it after the proper number on your paper. After the preposition, write the correct pronoun in parentheses. Remember to choose the objective form.

1. The chess team sent a challenge to Don and (he, him).
2. The slide show was presented by my sister and (I, me).
3. We are planning to leave with (they, them) and Alice.
4. I dedicated my poem to both Marcia and (she, her).
5. Frank arrived right after Juanita and (I, me).
6. The responsibility has fallen upon (we, us) students.
7. Were you sitting near Tony and (she, her)?
8. The matter is strictly between Ms. James and (they, them).
9. Consuelo has been asking about you and (she, her).
10. Would you draw a cartoon for the girls and (we, us)?

REVIEW EXERCISE A. Selecting Pronouns in the Nominative or Objective Case to Complete Sentences. Number your paper 1–20. Select the correct pronoun in parentheses and write it on your paper. After each pronoun, write its use in the sentence, using these abbreviations: s. (subject of a verb), p.n. (predicate nominative), d.o. (direct object), i.o. (indirect object), and o.p. (object of a preposition).

EXAMPLE 1. Leave the pamphlets with Kim and (he, him).
1. *him, o.p.*

1. The coach chose Darrell and (he, him).
2. Luckily, the Smiths and (we, us) missed the heavy traffic.
3. I haven't heard from Mark and (she, her) in ages.
4. Is it really (she, her) walking down the road?
5. Mr. Weaver chaperoned the boys and (we, us).
6. It could be (they, them) across the street.
7. Ms. Grant, the Dodges, and (she, her) went to the reunion.
8. During the busy season, the boss relies on (we, us) workers.
9. The mayor granted (she, her) an interview.

10. (We, Us) science students did our experiment at the fair.
11. (She, Her) and Heather always sit in the last row.
12. Mrs. Lemon said that (we, us) girls inspired her.
13. Would you please stop bothering Marla and (I, me)?
14. Adele painted a picture for (they, them) and (we, us).
15. Who is running toward (he, him)?
16. Neither the Spartans nor (we, us) Cougars play today.
17. Flora visited (she, her) and (I, me) in the hospital.
18. I thought it was Rob and (they, them) in the center aisle.
19. The team and (they, them) work well together.
20. The referee gave Manny and (he, him) a warning.

USES OF *WHO* AND *WHOM*

Like the personal pronouns, the pronouns *who* and *whoever* have three different case forms:

NOMINATIVE	OBJECTIVE	POSSESSIVE
who	whom	whose
whoever	whomever	whosever

Who and *Whom* as Interrogative Pronouns

Who and *whom* are interrogative pronouns when they are used to ask a question. The four rules on pages 103–106 governing the case forms of the personal pronouns apply also to *who* and *whom.*

EXAMPLES **Who** broke his leg? [The nominative form is required because *who* is the subject of *broke.*]
Whom did Nora choose? [The objective form is required because *whom* is the object of *did choose.*]

You may find it helpful, at first, to substitute *he, she—him, her* for *who—whom,* respectively. If *he* or *she* (nominative) fits the sentence, then *who* (also nominative) will be correct. If *him* or *her* fits, then *whom* will be correct.

EXAMPLES *(Who, Whom)* broke his leg? [**He** broke his leg. Hence, **Who** broke his leg?]
(Who, Whom) did Nora choose? [Nora did choose **him**. Hence, Nora did choose *whom.* **Whom** did Nora choose?]

Interrogative pronouns appear in both direct and indirect questions. A direct question uses the exact words of the speaker and is followed by a question mark. An indirect question does not use the exact words of the speaker and is not followed by a question mark.

DIRECT QUESTION	**Who** washed the dishes?
INDIRECT QUESTION	Joni asked **who** washed the dishes.
DIRECT QUESTION	**Whom** did she see?
INDIRECT QUESTION	I asked **whom** she had seen.

When the interrogative pronoun is used immediately after a preposition, *whom* is always the correct form.

EXAMPLES **On whom** does it depend?
For whom did you bake the bread?

> ☞ **USAGE NOTE** In informal usage, *whom* is not usually used as an interrogative pronoun. *Who* is used regardless of the case. In formal usage, however, the distinction between *who* and *whom* is still recognized.

INFORMAL	FORMAL
Who were you calling?	**Whom** were you calling?
Who did the club elect?	**Whom** did the club elect?

Who and *Whom* as Relative Pronouns

When *who* and *whom* (*whoever* and *whomever*) are used to begin a subordinate clause, they are relative pronouns. Their case is governed by the same rules that govern the case of a personal pronoun. Although *whom* is becoming increasingly uncommon in spoken English, the distinction between *who* and *whom* in subordinate clauses is usually observed in writing.

6f. The case of the pronoun beginning a subordinate clause is determined by its use in the clause. The case is not affected by any word outside the clause.

In order to analyze a *who—whom* problem, follow these steps:

1. Pick out the subordinate clause.
2. Determine how the pronoun is used in the clause—subject, predicate nominative, object of a verb, object of a preposition—and decide its case according to the rules.
3. Select the correct form of the pronoun.

PROBLEM Harry Houdini, (who, whom) audiences adored, performed daring escape tricks.
Step 1 The subordinate clause is *(who, whom) audiences adored.*
Step 2 In the clause the subject is *audiences;* the verb is *adored;* and the pronoun is the object of the verb *adored.* As an object it is in the objective case.
Step 3 The objective form is *whom.*
SOLUTION Harry Houdini, **whom** audiences adored, performed daring escape tricks.

PROBLEM Do you remember (who, whom) the escape artist was?
Step 1 The subordinate clause is *(who, whom) the escape artist was.*
Step 2 In the clause, *artist* is the subject and *was* is the verb; the pronoun is a predicate nominative. As a predicate nominative it is in the nominative case.
Step 3 The nominative form is *who.*
SOLUTION Do you remember **who** the escape artist was?

In writing the sentence above, one might tend to use *whom,* thinking it the object of the verb *remember,* but *remember* is outside the clause and cannot affect the case of a word in the clause. The object of the verb *remember* is the entire clause *who the escape artist was.*

USAGE

> ☞ **USAGE NOTE** In determining whether to use *who* or *whom,* do not be misled by a parenthetical expression like *I think, he said,* etc.

EXAMPLES We are the only ones **who,** I think, are taking jazz dance. [*who* are taking jazz dance]
She is the student **who** Mr. Hines thinks should be a chemist. [*who* should be a chemist]

EXERCISE 5. Selecting the Correct Case Form of *Who* and *Whoever* to Complete Sentences. Number your paper 1–20. Using the three steps described on pages 109–110, determine the pronoun's correct form for each of the following sentences.

1. The two people (who, whom) I liked most were Will and Angela.
2. Someone called last night, but I don't know (who, whom) she was.
3. The announcer said that (whoever, whomever) finishes in the top ten can compete in the final round.
4. We did not hear (who, whom) the principal had named.
5. Neither of the two pianists was the musician (who, whom) the audience cheered.

6. Anybody (who, whom) orders now will receive a free gift.
7. She is the teacher (who, whom) Al thinks will be our substitute.
8. The science club wants to find an astronomer (who, whom) will be an exciting guest speaker.
9. They are curious about (who, whom) you talked to so angrily.
10. Harriet Tubman was a woman (who, whom) we should revere.
11. The pedestrian (who, whom) the car hit suffered only minor cuts.
12. The police have not caught (whoever, whomever) stole my bike.
13. Several of the women (who, whom) had served on committees were considered for the position.
14. Anyone (who, whom) she can corner will be treated to a lecture on buying a home computer.
15. Allen is the only person in school (who, whom), I believe, has lived in a foreign country.
16. I never found out (who, whom) the driver was.
17. It does not matter (who, whom) wins, as long as you do your best.
18. I cannot find the person to (who, whom) this package belongs.
19. The player's reaction was to shout at the referee (who, whom) charged him with the penalty.
20. Ralph Bunche was a man (who, whom) many people respected.

WRITING APPLICATION A:
Using *Who* and *Whom* Correctly in Subordinate Clauses

When you are writing about characters in fiction, you are usually using formal English. In formal English, the distinction is still made between *who* and *whom*. These pronouns often introduce subordinate clauses in complex sentences that discuss literary characters.

EXAMPLE The character *whom* the people hate in *An Enemy of the People* is Dr. Thomas Stockmann.
The son *who* closely resembles Willy Loman in *Death of a Salesman* is Happy.

Writing Assignment

Select a short story, poem, play, or novel you have read and discuss one or more of its important characters. At some point, use *who* and *whom* correctly in subordinate clauses. Underline these pronouns.

PRONOUNS IN INCOMPLETE CONSTRUCTIONS

An "incomplete construction" occurs when something is omitted after the word *than* or *as* in a comparison. To avoid repetition, we say "The tenor sang louder than he" (than he *sang*). "The crash hurt Tim as much as her" (as *it hurt* her).

The meaning of the sentence may actually depend on the form of the pronoun.

EXAMPLE We trust Jane more than **she.** [than she trusts Jane]
We trust Jane more than **her.** [than we trust her]

6g. After *than* and *as* introducing an incomplete construction, use the form of the pronoun you would use if the construction were completed.

USAGE

EXERCISE 6. Selecting Pronouns in Incomplete Constructions. Number your paper 1–10. Write the part of each sentence beginning with *than* or *as,* using the correct pronoun and completing the sentence to show that the pronoun is correct. In several sentences either pronoun may be correct, depending on how the sentence is completed; in those cases, write the sentences both ways.

EXAMPLE 1. Nolan has worked longer than (he, him).
1. *than he has worked*

1. Have you lived in this city as long as (they, them)?
2. I don't know Brenda as well as (she, her).
3. Eva is shorter than (I, me).
4. The senior class scored higher than (they, them).
5. The trip will benefit Roger more than (I, me).
6. Is she six months older than (I, me)?
7. The results show that I do better on essay tests than (he, him).
8. Can they hit safely as often as (we, us)?
9. I understand him better than (she, her).
10. Can Ms. Edwards tutor Paula as well as (I, me)?

REVIEW EXERCISE B. Identifying and Correcting Errors in Pronoun Usage. Number your paper 1–10. Each sentence contains one error in pronoun usage. Write the incorrectly used pronoun and next to it, write the correct form.

EXAMPLE 1. Do you know who they gave the money to?
1. *who—whom*

1. The two students whom the committee nominated were Genevieve and me.
2. Geraldine announced to Joe and me that Cleon and her would do the inventory.
3. If you can't trust Ed and her, who can you trust?
4. "We kids are better than the kids on Central's team," Phil said. "So why aren't we doing better than them?"
5. Brenda sat between Sheryl and I.
6. The two people in this class whom you can always rely on are Dave and her.
7. Oscar, whom I believe is the smartest member of our family, shares the evening newspaper with Tammy and me.
8. When Ann and I were young, us kids used to love to ride the tractor with my father.
9. When Laura told Greg and I that Ms. Cohen was going to retire, all three of us seniors felt sad.
10. When Andy and I study together, nobody in our class does better than us.

MINOR PROBLEMS IN THE USE OF PRONOUNS

6h. In standard formal English the pronouns ending in *-self, -selves* are usually used only to refer to another word in the sentence or to emphasize another word.

EXAMPLES **I** hurt **myself**. [*Myself* refers to *I*.]
She planned the party **herself.** [*Herself* emphasizes *she*.]
The **boys themselves** invented the game. [*Themselves* emphasizes *boys*.]

Avoid the use of pronouns ending in *-self, -selves* in place of other personal pronouns if the pronouns do not refer to or emphasize another word in the sentence.

EXAMPLES Joanne and **I** [not *myself*] are club members.
Ms. Markham gave skating lessons to Al and **me** [not *myself*].
The tickets belong to them and **us** [not *ourselves*].

6i. An appositive is in the same case as the word with which it is in apposition.

NONSTANDARD Two seniors, Abe and her, made the best speeches.
STANDARD Two seniors, **Abe and she,** made the best speeches.

Abe and *she* are in apposition with *seniors,* the subject of the sentence. Since the subject of a verb is nominative, the appositive is also nominative; hence, *she* is correct.

STANDARD For the lead roles, the director chose two people, **Abe and her**.

In apposition with *people*, which is the object of *chose, Abe* and *her* are also in the objective case; hence, *her* is correct.

6j. Use the possessive case of a noun or a pronoun before a gerund.

USAGE

This use of the possessive case will appear reasonable if you understand that a gerund is a noun form.

EXAMPLES We were flattered by the **critic's praise.**
We were flattered by the **critic's giving** such praise.
Did you object to **my comments?**
Did you object to **my making** the comments?

Sometimes a participle ending in *-ing* may be confused with a gerund. Use the objective case before a participle.

EXAMPLES I followed **him hiking** through the woods.
I hear **them talking** outside.

The use of the possessive *his* in the first sentence would change the meaning to a far less likely idea: *I followed his hiking through the woods.* The second sentence identifies *them,* not *talking; I hear their talking outside* is an unlikely emphasis.

Whether or not you should use the possessive form before a word ending in *-ing* often depends on which word you wish to emphasize. If you wish to emphasize the action in the *-ing* word, you use the possessive. If you wish to emphasize the preceding word (the noun or pronoun), you do not use the possessive.

What did they say about Mary's jogging? [In this sentence the emphasis is on the kind of jogging Mary does.]
Can they imagine Mary jogging? [In this sentence the emphasis is on Mary, who apparently is not a jogger.]

WRITING APPLICATION B:
Using the Possessive Form Before a Gerund

In both your speech and writing you often use gerunds, which are simply verb forms used as nouns. Gerunds end in *-ing*. Participles ending in *-ing* can therefore be confused with gerunds. You must decide whether the *-ing* word is a participle or a gerund in determining whether to use the possessive form in front of it. If you wish to emphasize the **action** in the **-ing** word, use the possessive form of the noun or pronoun that precedes it.

EXAMPLES I saw *him* taking the ACT this morning. (The word emphasized is *him,* not *taking;* therefore, the possessive form is not used before the *-ing* word.)

There is some question about *his* taking the ACT again to improve his score. (The word emphasized is *taking;* therefore, the possessive form is used before the *-ing* word.

Writing Assignment

An important characteristic of mature people is the ability to listen carefully to advice, to weigh its merits, and then to decide whether or not to follow it. Think of some advice you have been given. How did you feel about it? Did you follow it or not? What has been the result? Write a summary of this important incident. Illustrate the use of the possessive form before a gerund. Underline the possessive.

EXAMPLE I resented *their* urging me to watch the football game every Sunday.

EXERCISE 7. Identifying and Correcting Errors in Pronoun Usage. Some of the following sentences contain errors in pronoun usage. Number your paper 1–10. Write + after the proper number for each correct sentence; write 0 for each incorrect sentence. After each 0, write the correct form of the pronoun.

1. The store's being closed annoyed us.
2. Both Ruth and myself take piano lessons.
3. We all looked forward to their singing.
4. The coach tried to understand him striking out.
5. My close friends, Alicia and her, joined the choir.

6. After him promising to drive us, his car broke down.
7. Someone, either Irene or he, talked to the doctor.
8. They had not been told about us staying overnight.
9. The reporters interviewed his uncle and himself.
10. Their dancing thrilled the audience.

CHAPTER 6 REVIEW: POSTTEST

Selecting Pronouns to Complete Sentences Correctly. Number your paper 1–25. From the words in parentheses, select the pronoun that correctly completes the sentence and write it after the proper number on your paper. Base your answer on formal standard usage.

EXAMPLE 1. After a pause, I heard Tara say into the phone, "Yes, this is (she, me)."
1. *she*

1. Last summer, my friend Megan and (I, me) worked in a factory that produces microchips for computers.
2. Before we began, we made a pact that (we, us) teen-agers would show the adults that we were responsible workers.
3. For the first two weeks, everything ran smoothly because our supervisor, Mr. Karas, was a person (who, whom) we thought was firm and just.
4. In fact, we were surprised by (him, his) showing interest in our progress and going out of his way to train us.
5. When Mr. Karas went on vacation, we doubted that his assistant, Ms. Sullivan, would be as firm as (he, him).
6. Our first mistake was in thinking that Mr. Karas and (she, her) would have different sets of standards.
7. Also, we thought wrongly that (she, her) sitting in for him would decrease our work load.
8. Well, I'm sure you can guess (who, whom) the situation taught a lesson to.
9. We started giving (us, ourselves) ten extra minutes during our morning break just a week after Ms. Sullivan took over.
10. One morning Ms. Sullivan walked up to us at our job stations and said, "Megan and Rick, until now I had thought you were workers (who, whom) took pride in your work."

11. "In fact, I received a post card from Mr. Karas this morning, and he asked if (his, him) being away has affected your work in any way."
12. "Between you and (I, me)," she said, "he'll never know you failed a test this morning by taking extra time during your morning break."
13. "If you're late again," Ms. Sullivan said calmly, "we, Mr. Karas and (I, me), will be looking for two other trainees for this station after he gets back."
14. It's funny how even an assistant supervisor can make her meaning clear to people like (us, ourselves) in just a few sentences.
15. For the rest of that morning, you couldn't find two other workers concentrating as well as Megan and (I, me).
16. (Who, Whom) do you think we talked about during our lunch break? Right!
17. We, Megan and (I, me), agreed that we had made not just one but several mistakes.
18. First, (us, our) deliberately taking extra time was wrong.
19. Second, we had let Mr. Karas down because it was (he, him) who had hired us, trained us, and trusted us.
20. Third, we had stereotyped Ms. Sullivan, thinking that because she was a woman she wouldn't do her job as well as (he, him).
21. Fourth, we had let (us, ourselves) down by failing to do our best.
22. (Who, Whom) had we been kidding when we had said that we wanted to prove to the adults that teen-agers were mature and responsible?
23. In the two weeks that followed, Megan and (I, me) did our work conscientiously and punctually, keeping our goal in mind.
24. We also watched how Ms. Sullivan did her job, and we soon saw that Mr. Karas and (she, her) shared many of the same strengths we had admired in Mr. Karas.
25. Shaking hands with Mr. Karas and Ms. Sullivan at the end of the summer, (we, us) two agreed that we had earned good money, but that we had also learned important lessons for life.

USAGE

CHAPTER 7

Correct Form and Use of Verbs

PRINCIPAL PARTS; TENSE, VOICE, MOOD

DIAGNOSTIC TEST

A. Using Verbs Correctly. The sentences in this exercise contain problems with verbs which will be discussed in this chapter. Number your paper 1–15. After the proper number, write the correct form of the verb in parentheses.

EXAMPLE 1. In a hurry to go to work, I couldn't remember where I had (laid, lain) my keys.
1. *laid*

1. During the political rally, several balloons filled with helium (burst, bursted) as they rose from the ground.
2. Whenever Joan sits down to watch television, her Samoyed puppy (lies, lays) down at her feet.
3. If I (was, were) President, I would make world peace my first priority.
4. Mary Ann (swam, swum) the hundred-meter race in record time.
5. If I (had, would have) told the truth in the first place, the situation would have been much easier to handle.
6. (Cooking, Having cooked) a delicious Thanksgiving meal together, the newlyweds received many compliments from their guests.

7. When the math team came in second, the team members were upset because they (hoped, had hoped) to take first place.
8. Because we did not add the proper amount of yeast, the loaves of bread failed to (raise, rise).
9. The tree died because it (was hit, had been hit) by lightning.
10. The five riders are pleased (to qualify, to have qualified) for the equestrian team.
11. After I had (wrote, written) my autobiographical essay for my college application, I heaved a sigh of relief.
12. I wished that there (was, were) a good movie playing in town.
13. Because he had starred in four high-school productions, David hoped (to pursue, to have pursued) an acting career.
14. (Lie, Lay) your work aside and relax for a few minutes.
15. In 1984, Joaquim Cruz, whose right leg is slightly shorter than his left leg, was happy when he (won, had won) Brazil's first gold medal in the 800-meter run.

B. Recognizing Incorrect Verbs in Sentences. Each sentence below has an incorrect or awkward verb form. Rewrite each sentence correctly.

16. After running six miles, Nick said he could have drank a gallon of water.
17. The calculator was put together by Kristi with almost no assistance.
18. I was born in this town, and I lived here all my life.
19. If Mrs. Wyn has twins, she will have four children in three years.
20. The trip was taken by Mr. Jenson because of his poor health.

A verb is a word that expresses action or otherwise helps to make a statement.

KINDS OF VERBS

All verbs help to make statements about their subjects. Those that do so by expressing action, either physical or mental, are called *action verbs.*

ACTION VERBS Arthur **dashed** across the busy street.
She **wondered** about their strange behavior.

USAGE

Some verbs help to make statements by linking the subject with a word in the predicate. Such verbs are called *linking verbs.*

LINKING VERBS Their future **looked** bright. [*Bright,* an adjective, modifies the subject *future.*]
Elsa **is** my friend. [*Friend,* a noun, identifies Elsa.]

Some verbs can be either action verbs or linking verbs:

ACTION VERB They **felt** the snake's smooth, dry skin. [*Felt* expresses action.]
LINKING VERB I **felt** tired today. [This time, *felt* links the subject, *I,* with a word that describes it, *tired.*]

There are many fewer linking verbs than action verbs. (You will find a list of the most common linking verbs on page 13.) The verb used most often as a linking verb is *be*, whose forms are *am, is, are, was, were,* and all verb phrases ending in *be, being,* or *been: may be, was being, has been,* etc.

In addition to functioning as a linking verb, *be* can also be followed by an adverb or adverb phrase:

Rachel was **here.**
The cottage is **in the north woods.**

Although it resembles an action verb in this use, *be* is not generally classified as one. Just remember that *be* is always a linking verb except when followed by an adverb.

USAGE

THE PRINCIPAL PARTS OF A VERB

Every verb has four basic forms called principal parts: the *infinitive, present participle, past,* and *past participle.* All other forms are derived from these principal parts.

INFINITIVE	PRESENT PARTICIPLE	PAST	PAST PARTICIPLE
talk	(is) talking	talked	(have) talked

The words *is* and *have* are given with the present participle and past participle forms to remind you that these forms are used with a helping verb: *am, is, are, was, were, has been, will be, have, has, had,* etc.

Regular Verbs

A regular verb is one that forms its past and past participle by adding *-d* or *-ed* to the infinitive form.

INFINITIVE	PAST	PAST PARTICIPLE
care	care**d**	(have) care**d**
jump	jump**ed**	(have) jump**ed**

Irregular Verbs

An irregular verb is one that forms its past and past participle in some other way than by adding *-d* or *-ed*.

This "other way" may involve changing the spelling of the verb or making no change at all.

INFINITIVE	PAST	PAST PARTICIPLE
drive	drove	(have) driven
ring	rang	(have) rung
set	set	(have) set

The major problem in the correct use of verbs is the choice of the correct past and past participle forms of irregular verbs. Since irregular past tenses and past participles are formed in a variety of ways, you must know the principal parts of each irregular verb.

Three principal parts of common irregular verbs are given in the following alphabetical list (infinitive, past, and past participle). Use this list for reference. For the principal parts of other irregular verbs, consult a dictionary. Drill exercises on irregular verbs frequently misused are given following the list.

Principal Parts of Irregular Verbs

INFINITIVE	PAST	PAST PARTICIPLE
bear	bore	(have) borne
beat	beat	(have) beaten *or* beat
begin	began	(have) begun
bite	bit	(have) bitten
blow	blew	(have) blown
break	broke	(have) broken
bring	brought	(have) brought
burst	burst	(have) burst
catch	caught	(have) caught
choose	chose	(have) chosen
come	came	(have) come
creep	crept	(have) crept
dive	dived[1]	(have) dived

[1] Also, *dove*.

USAGE

INFINITIVE	PAST	PAST PARTICIPLE
do	did	(have) done
draw	drew	(have) drawn
drink	drank	(have) drunk
drive	drove	(have) driven
eat	ate	(have) eaten
fall	fell	(have) fallen
fling	flung	(have) flung
fly	flew	(have) flown
freeze	froze	(have) frozen
get	got	(have) got *or* gotten
give	gave	(have) given
go	went	(have) gone
grow	grew	(have) grown
know	knew	(have) known
lay	laid	(have) laid
lead	led	(have) led
lend	lent	(have) lent
lie	lay	(have) lain
lose	lost	(have) lost
ride	rode	(have) ridden
ring	rang	(have) rung
rise	rose	(have) risen
run	ran	(have) run
say	said	(have) said
see	saw	(have) seen
set	set	(have) set
shake	shook	(have) shaken
shine	shone *or* shined	(have) shone *or* shined
sing	sang *or* sung	(have) sung
sink	sank *or* sunk	(have) sunk
sit	sat	(have) sat
speak	spoke	(have) spoken
steal	stole	(have) stolen
sting	stung	(have) stung
swear	swore	(have) sworn
swim	swam	(have) swum
swing	swung	(have) swung
take	took	(have) taken
tear	tore	(have) torn
throw	threw	(have) thrown
wear	wore	(have) worn
write	wrote	(have) written

7a. Learn the principal parts of common irregular verbs.

USAGE

To help you learn the correct use of irregular verbs, those which are commonly misused are presented on the following pages in four groups. Memorize the principal parts of the verbs in each group. In doing the exercises, remember that the past participle is used with helping, or auxiliary, verbs: *is, are, was, were, have, has, had, have been,* etc. As you say the principal parts, place *have* before the past participle: *begin, began, have begun.*

Group I

INFINITIVE	PAST	PAST PARTICIPLE
beat	beat	(have) beaten *or* beat
begin	began	(have) begun
blow	blew	(have) blown
break	broke	(have) broken
burst	burst	(have) burst
choose	chose	(have) chosen
come	came	(have) come
do	did	(have) done

EXERCISE 1. Using the Past and the Past Participle Forms Correctly. Number your paper 1–10. After the proper number, write either the past or the past participle of the verb given, whichever will correctly complete the sentence.

EXAMPLE 1. *do* I —— nothing yesterday.
1. *did*

1. *begin* They had —— to argue.
2. *choose* Have the players —— a captain for the basketball team yet?
3. *beat* You —— me at tennis last Friday.
4. *do* Has Erica —— her chores yet?
5. *break* Milt has —— the school track record.
6. *burst* During the freeze last March, the water pipes at school —— .
7. *blow* John's shed had been —— over in the storm.
8. *do* The dancers —— their warm-up exercises.
9. *begin* I was so scared that I —— to tremble.
10. *come* Jennifer has —— to spend the weekend.

Group II

INFINITIVE	PAST	PAST PARTICIPLE
draw	drew	(have) drawn
drink	drank	(have) drunk
drive	drove	(have) driven
fall	fell	(have) fallen
fly	flew	(have) flown
freeze	froze	(have) frozen
give	gave	(have) given
go	went	(have) gone

EXERCISE 2. Using the Past and Past Participle Forms Correctly. Number your paper 1–10. Complete each sentence by writing either the past or the past participle of the given verb.

1. *drink* We have —— spring water for years.
2. *fall* My ring has —— into the dishwater.
3. *freeze* They have —— a peck of beans for next winter.
4. *fly* Have you —— in a helicopter?
5. *drive* Ellie has never —— a jeep.
6. *draw* Toni —— pictures on the wall when she was two.
7. *go* Becky has —— to the rodeo with friends.
8. *drink* I worked hard, but he —— more water than I did.
9. *go* He —— out the door before I could stop him.
10. *give* We should have —— Donna a surprise party.

EXERCISE 3. Using the Past and Past Participle Forms Correctly. *This exercise covers the verbs in Groups I and II.* Write a + for each sentence in which the italicized verb is correct; if the verb is incorrect, write the correct form of the verb.

EXAMPLE 1. They *have* often *drove* to the mountains.
1. *have driven*

1. I *gave* her my last dime.
2. They *should have went* to Hawaii for vacation.
3. The guests *have drank* all the punch.
4. It was so cold in the basement, the water *had froze.*
5. Henry *done* his best yesterday.
6. Some of the sketches *were drew* with pen and ink.

7. She wondered if she *had chose* the right one.
8. Why *have* you *came* home so early?
9. During the cold weather the water pipe *had bursted.*
10. Mr. Donahue *flew* to Africa last summer.
11. One of the children *could have fell* down the rickety stairs.
12. The thunder crashed and the lights *begun* to flicker.
13. Our team *has* not *beat* them in three years.
14. I'll never know why he *done* it.
15. The crystal vase *has broke* in a million pieces.
16. They never *would have begun* if you hadn't helped them.
17. The wind *blowed* gently through the pines.
18. At last we *have chosen* a mascot for our club.
19. We *gone* beyond the exit ramp on the highway.
20. The farmer *has drived* that old tractor nearly every day for twenty years.

Group III

INFINITIVE	PAST	PAST PARTICIPLE
grow	grew	(have) grown
know	knew	(have) known
ride	rode	(have) ridden
ring	rang	(have) rung
run	ran	(have) run
see	saw	(have) seen
sing	sang *or* sung	(have) sung
speak	spoke	(have) spoken

EXERCISE 4. Using the Past and Past Participle Forms Correctly. Number your paper 1–10. Complete each sentence by writing either the past or the past participle of the verb given.

1. *run* The shortstop —— toward third base.
2. *sing* Have you ever —— a round before?
3. *speak* We had —— to the plumber about the leak.
4. *know* No one could have —— the outcome.
5. *grow* Our baby hamster has —— rapidly.
6. *see* We —— the parade on television.
7. *ride* A few of us had —— on the roller coaster.
8. *ring* Has the bell —— yet?

9. *see* I —— a flash of lightning just now.
10. *ring* If my alarm clock hadn't —— , I would still be sleeping.

Group IV

INFINITIVE	PAST	PAST PARTICIPLE
spring	sprang *or* sprung	(have) sprung
steal	stole	(have) stolen
swim	swam	(have) swum
swing	swung	(have) swung
take	took	(have) taken
tear	tore	(have) torn
throw	threw	(have) thrown
write	wrote	(have) written

USAGE

EXERCISE 5. Using the Past and Past Participle Forms Correctly. Number your paper 1–10. Complete each sentence by writing either the past or the past participle of the verb given.

1. *spring* The rabbit had —— out of the bushes.
2. *tear* Why have they —— up the newspapers?
3. *write* Has Penny —— the editorial for the next issue?
4. *throw* Connie finally —— away her old tennis shoes.
5. *swim* She should not have —— so soon after lunch.
6. *take* I wish I had —— your advice.
7. *swing* The trapeze artists —— high above the crowd.
8. *steal* Why would anyone have —— your notebook?
9. *swim* The children were like fish; they —— for hours.
10. *throw* Make a wish after you have —— a coin into the well.

EXERCISE 6. Using the Past and Past Participle Forms Correctly. *This exercise covers the verbs in Groups III and IV* Write a + for each sentence in which the italicized verb is correct; if the verb is incorrect, write the correct form of the verb.

EXAMPLE 1. The bells *rung* loudly two hours ago.
1. *rang*

1. I *have ran* too far to turn back now.
2. *Had* the children *rang* the bell as a prank?
3. Little Tommy *has growed* two inches taller than I.

4. Ms. Owens *seen* the hit-and-run accident.
5. He *has tore* his shirt on that rusty nail.
6. *Had* she *knew* they were here, she would have stayed home.
7. You *should* not *have took* the biggest slice for yourself.
8. Jory Ann *swung* the lariat and roped the calf.
9. Are you sure he *swum* fifty lengths of the pool?
10. They're sorry they *had* not *spoke* up sooner.
11. He *has* always *rode* the bus to school.
12. I'm afraid the pool *has sprang* a leak.
13. How many times *has* Bobby *stole* second base?
14. The startled burglar *sprang* out of the window.
15. *Has* Gladys ever *sang* a cappella?
16. I *seen* that movie twelve times.
17. Sam *would have wrote,* but he misplaced his address book.
18. The children's choir *sung* as well as could be expected.
19. Who *throwed* out my old comic books?
20. We *were torn* between the two candidates.

EXERCISE 7. Using the Past and Past Participle Forms Correctly. *This exercise covers the verbs in Groups I – IV.* Number your paper 1–50. Complete each sentence by writing either the past or the past participle of the verb at the beginning of the sentence.

1. *burst* The firefighters —— open the door.
2. *freeze* Waiting for the bus, we almost —— .
3. *break* Have the movers —— anything?
4. *fly* They could have —— to Dallas in two hours.
5. *blow* A sudden gust of wind —— out all the candles.
6. *fall* She could not have —— more than two meters.
7. *begin* The networks —— the new season last Monday.
8. *know* We have —— them since grade school.
9. *beat* They —— us fair and square.
10. *ring* I opened the door, but no one had —— the bell.
11. *drive* We were —— by our sense of justice.
12. *ride* Carlton has finally —— in a trolley car.
13. *drink* During the recent flood, we —— bottled water.
14. *run* They —— five miles yesterday evening.
15. *do* Edith and I —— much better than we had hoped.

16. *swim* Holly has —— the 100-meter butterfly race.
17. *come* Shortly after you called, Rudy —— home.
18. *steal* She discovered that the microfilm had been —— .
19. *choose* We should have —— seats closer to the stage.
20. *sing* I have —— professionally since I was ten.
21. *grow* The number of entrants in the annual speech tournament has —— tremendously.
22. *speak* We have —— to the judges on your behalf.
23. *go* I arrived early, but Gloria had already —— .
24. *see* Do you think he —— us buying his gift?
25. *give* What in the world —— them such a crazy idea?
26. *take* Brenda could have —— a longer vacation.
27. *tear* I have —— the coupons out of the magazine.
28. *throw* Greg was furious when Billy —— the golf clubs into the swimming pool.
29. *tear* The photograph had been —— in half.
30. *write* Thomas Hardy —— many novels and poems.
31. *throw* The pitcher has —— six curve balls to me.
32. *go* I —— to my friend's recital last Sunday.
33. *see* Haven't you —— the abstract art exhibit?
34. *freeze* Water had —— on the inside of the window.
35. *run* Time has —— out on the deadline.
36. *come* When I was sick, Maria —— to the hospital to visit me every day.
37. *write* How many postcards have you —— ?
38. *drink* Someone —— the last glass of orange juice.
39. *know* Iris was never —— for her singing.
40. *break* The children —— their promise to behave.
41. *begin* As soon as the play started, Lynne —— to cough.
42. *swim* It was so hot, the adults —— in the "kiddy" pool.
43. *fall* We were told that Don had —— off the ladder.
44. *beat* The blacksmith —— the hot metal into shape.
45. *see* We —— him perform in the band concert.
46. *throw* The club has —— its support behind the mayor.
47. *run* Sue Ann has —— into this problem often.
48. *speak* They —— to Carolyn about the scholarship.
49. *come* We have —— to apologize for our rudeness.
50. *write* You or Beth should have —— the new bylaws.

THREE TROUBLESOME PAIRS OF VERBS

Three pairs of verbs require special study because they are difficult to use correctly. These special verbs are *lie* and *lay, sit* and *set, rise* and *raise.*

Lie and Lay

The verb *lie* means "to assume a lying position" or "to be in a lying position." Its principal parts are *lie, (is) lying, lay, (have) lain.*

The verb *lay* means "to put" or "to place something." Its principal parts are *lay, (is) laying, laid, (have) laid.*

The verb *lie* is intransitive (see page 12); that is, it never has an object. You never "lie" anything down.

The verb *lay* is transitive; that is, it may have an object or be in the passive voice. (See page 12.)

INTRANSITIVE	The pattern **lies** on top of the fabric. [no object]
TRANSITIVE	You **lay** the fabric on a flat surface. [object: *fabric*]
TRANSITIVE	The fabric **is laid** on a hard, flat table. [passive voice]

Memorize the principal parts of these verbs:

INFINITIVE	PRESENT PARTICIPLE	PAST	PAST PARTICIPLE
lie (to recline)	(is) lying	lay	(have) lain
lay (to put)	(is) laying	laid	(have) laid

Take time to think through each form carefully to establish the habit of using the verbs correctly. When faced with a *lie-lay* problem, ask yourself two questions:

1. What is the meaning I intend? Is it "to be in a lying position," or is it "to put something down"?

2. What is the time expressed by the verb and which principal part is required to express this time?

PROBLEM	Ginny (lay, laid) her new dress on the bed.
Question 1	Meaning? The meaning here is "to put." The verb which means "to put" is *lay*.
Question 2	Principal part? The time is past and therefore requires the past form, which is *laid*. [lay, *laid*, laid]
SOLUTION	Ginny **laid** her new dress on the bed.

PROBLEM The cat is (lying, laying) on my good coat.

Question 1 Meaning? The meaning here is "to be in a lying position." The verb which means "to be in a lying position" is *lie*.

Question 2 Principal part? The time here requires the present participle, which is *lying*.

SOLUTION The cat is **lying** on my good coat.

It will pay you to use this two-question formula each time you are in doubt about a problem in the use of *lie* and *lay*. Of course, you must memorize the principal parts of the verbs before you can use the formula.

Two facts about the use of *lie* and *lay* may be of additional help.

1. Most errors in the use of these verbs are made when the speaker means "to assume or to be in a lying position." When this is the meaning you intend, be especially cautious.

2. When you wish to express the idea of "putting or placing something" in the past tense, always use *laid*.

EXERCISE 8. Using *Lie* and *Lay* Correctly. Number your paper 1–10. After the proper number, write the correct one of the two words in parentheses. Use the two-question formula.

1. If you are sick, you should be (lying, laying) down.
2. They (lay, laid) the heavy crate on the handcart.
3. She had (lain, laid) a great deal of emphasis on usage.
4. Amy (lay, laid) down for a while.
5. I left my gloves (lying, laying) on the counter.
6. She had just (lain, laid) down when the doorbell rang.
7. They (lay, laid) their plans before the committee.
8. The calf (lay, laid) on a pile of straw.
9. She (lay, laid) her pen down and closed her notebook.
10. Don't leave your shoes (lying, laying) under the table.

EXERCISE 9. Using *Lie* and *Lay* Correctly. Choose the correct form of *lie* or *lay* to fill the blank in each sentence. Use the two-question formula.

EXAMPLE 1. I have —— the ribbons on the counter.
1. *laid*

1. The letters are —— on the table for you to read.
2. Why don't you —— down for a few minutes?
3. Be careful when you are —— the new carpeting.

4. The mysterious package —— on the park bench.
5. Tomorrow we will —— new tiles in the hallway.
6. After an exhausting day, Carla —— on the sofa.
7. Danny —— the vase down and repaired the crack.
8. She —— on the track while the trainer taped her ankle.
9. The driftwood had —— on the beach for years.
10. Nina had not —— the keys by the telephone.

Sit and *Set*

Sit usually means "to assume or to be in an upright, sitting position."[1] The principal parts of *sit* are *sit,* (*is*) *sitting, sat,* (*have*) *sat. Sit* is almost always an intransitive verb; it rarely takes an object.

Set usually means "to put, to place something." The principal parts of *set* are *set,* (*is*) *setting, set,* (*have*) *set.* Like *lay*, *set* is a transitive verb; it may take an object.

Since all forms of *set* are made without changing the vowel, the problem of using these two verbs is rather simple. When you mean "to put something down," use *set* or *setting*. For all other meanings, use *sit* or *sat* or *sitting.*[2]

INFINITIVE	PRESENT PARTICIPLE	PAST	PAST PARTICIPLE
sit (to rest)	(is) sitting	sat	(have) sat
set (to put)	(is) setting	set	(have) set

EXERCISE 10. Using *Sit* and *Set* Correctly. Number your paper 1–10. Write the correct verb in parentheses in each sentence.

EXAMPLE 1. Don't (sit, set) on the wet paint!
1. *sit*

1. After he had struck out, Pete (sat, set) on the bench.
2. My little sister (sits, sets) quietly when we have company.
3. Where were the packages (sitting, setting) this morning?
4. We had (sat, set) the packages on the plush chairs.
5. I never (sit, set) in the balcony at the Bijou.
6. They were (sitting, setting) placemats on the table.
7. It makes no difference to me where you (sit, set).
8. We (sat, set) up folding chairs for the guests.
9. Mr. Han told me to (sit, set) the equipment on his desk.

[1] Such expressions as "Sit the baby in the high chair" or "Sit him up" really mean "to put" or "to place," and these expressions, which are acceptable, are exceptions to the rule.
[2] The expressions "The sun sets," "the setting hen," and "Wait for the cement to set" are exceptions to the rule.

10. I may never know who had (sat, set) on my glasses.

Rise and *Raise*

The verb *rise* means "to go up." Its principal parts are *rise, (is) rising, rose, (have) risen.* In other words, when the subject of the verb is itself moving upward, use *rise*. *Rise* is intransitive; it never takes an object.

The verb *raise* means "to force something to move upward." Its principal parts are *raise, (is) raising, raised, (have) raised.* When the subject of the verb is acting on something, forcing it upward, use *raise*. *Raise* is transitive; it usually takes an object.

INFINITIVE	PRESENT PARTICIPLE	PAST	PAST PARTICIPLE
rise (to go up)	(is) rising	rose	(have) risen
raise (to force up)	(is) raising	raised	(have) raised

EXERCISE 11. Using *Rise* and *Raise* Correctly. Number your paper 1–10. Write the correct verb in parentheses in each sentence.

1. Air bubbles have been (rising, raising) to the surface.
2. Increasing the import duty will (rise, raise) retail prices.
3. The speaker (rose, raised) from her chair and took the mike.
4. This month, the star has been (rising, raising) in the east.
5. The rooster (rises, raises) early.
6. During the Revolutionary War, many American colonists decided to (rise, raise) up against King George III.
7. Balloons can (rise, raise) because they contain heated air, which is less dense than the surrounding air.
8. The Wilsons (rose, raised) six adopted children.
9. Mist was (rising, raising) from the ground.
10. The dough has been (rising, raising) for the past hour.

EXERCISE 12. Using *Lie-Lay, Sit-Set,* and *Rise-Raise* Correctly. For each of the following verbs, write a brief sentence in which the verb is correctly used.

1. lie	3. laying	5. lay (past)	7. rose	9. risen
2. raising	4. raised	6. has laid	8. setting	10. sat

EXERCISE 13. Using *Lie-Lay, Sit-Set,* and *Rise-Raise* Correctly. Number your paper 1–20. Write the correct word in parentheses in each sentence.

EXAMPLE 1. Please (sit, set) wherever you like.
1. *sit*

1. All week that box has (lain, laid) unopened on the desk.
2. We (rose, raised) our hats to salute the astronauts.
3. The injured deer (lay, laid) motionless in the road.
4. Our applications were (lying, laying) in front of the file.
5. Would you please (sit, set) with us?
6. I always (lie, lay) the phone book on this table.
7. We arrived late and had to (sit, set) at the top of the bleachers.
8. Kathy hummed as she (lay, laid) the baby in the crib.
9. Clean up the mess that's (lying, laying) on your floor.
10. Last night's victory really (rose, raised) the team's spirit and confidence.
11. If you (sit, set) the pie on the ledge, it may vanish.
12. Fred should (lie, lay) on his side to stop snoring.
13. After the fire, the museum (lay, laid) in a heap.
14. Tempers (rose, raised) as the debate progressed.
15. The police are (lying, laying) in wait for the crooks.
16. Never (sit, set) anything on the seat next to you.
17. Our St. Bernard often (lies, lays) in my lap.
18. Billows of dust (rose, raised) up from the field.
19. Haven't they (sat, set) down the piano yet?
20. You must (lie, lay) on a padded surface to do exercises.

USAGE

REVIEW EXERCISE A. Using Verb Forms Correctly. Number your paper 1–10. In each sentence, identify any verb used incorrectly. Write it on your paper, and next to it write the form of the verb needed to correct the sentence.

EXAMPLE 1. The helicopter raised from the airstrip and headed north.
1. *raised—rose*

1. As I watched the horror movie, I could feel fear rising in my throat; I knew I had chose the wrong way to relax.
2. Aretha had taken her younger sister to the circus; things went well until the little girl's balloon bursted.
3. When we woke, we saw that the pond was froze.
4. When their parents had went shopping, the twins decided to play some computer games.

5. The defendant, who had been found guilty, was brung before the judge for sentencing.
6. After we had donated blood, we laid down for a few minutes and were then given coffee and doughnuts.
7. Before we knew what was happening, Marvin had dove through the ice to rescue the child who had fallen into the lake.
8. If you hadn't been so careless, you wouldn't have broke that vase.
9. While Jessica was in surgery, her concerned parents set in the waiting room and kept their hopes high.
10. Jorge walked up to the door and rung the bell, waiting nervously for the girl he had driven two hours to see.

TENSE

Verbs change in form to show the time of their action or of the idea they express. The time expressed by a verb (present, past, future) is its tense. There are six tenses. As the following conjugations of the verbs *go* and *be* will show you, the six tenses are formed from the principal parts of the verb. Study these conjugations and use them for reference in your work on tense.

7b. Learn the names of the six tenses and how the tenses are formed.

Conjugation of the Verb Go

Present infinitive: *to go* Perfect infinitive: *to have gone*

Principal Parts

INFINITIVE	PRESENT PARTICIPLE	PAST	PAST PARTICIPLE
go	going	went	gone

Present Tense

Singular	*Plural*
I go	we go
you go	you go
he, she, it goes	they go

Present progressive: *I am going,* etc.

Past Tense

Singular	*Plural*
I went	we went
you went	you went
he, she, it went	they went

Past progressive: *I was going,* etc.

Future Tense

(*will* or *shall* + the infinitive[1])

Singular	*Plural*
I will (shall) go	we will (shall) go
you will go	you will go
he, she, it will go	they will go

Future progressive: *I will* (*shall*) *be going,* etc.

Present Perfect Tense

(*have* or *has* + the past participle)

Singular	*Plural*
I have gone	we have gone
you have gone	you have gone
he, she, it has gone	they have gone

Present perfect progressive: *I have been going,* etc.

Past Perfect Tense

(*had* + the past participle)

Singular	*Plural*
I had gone	we had gone
you had gone	you had gone
he, she, it had gone	they had gone

Past perfect progressive: *I had been going,* etc.

Future Perfect Tense

(*will have* or *shall have* + the past participle)

Singular	*Plural*
I will (shall) have gone	we will (shall) have gone
you will have gone	you will have gone
he, she, it will have gone	they will have gone

Future perfect progressive: *I will have* (*shall have*) *been going,* etc.

[1] For a discussion of the use of *shall* and *will,* see page 189.

Conjugation of the Verb Be

Present infinitive: *to be*   Perfect infinitive: *to have been*

Principal Parts

INFINITIVE	PRESENT PARTICIPLE	PAST	PAST PARTICIPLE
be	being	was, were	been

Present Tense

Singular	*Plural*
I am	we are
you are	you are
he, she, it is	they are

Present progressive: *I am being,* etc.

Past Tense

Singular	*Plural*
I was	we were
you were	you were
he, she, it was	they were

Past progressive: *I was being,* etc.

Future Tense

(*will* or *shall* + the infinitive)

Singular	*Plural*
I will (shall) be	we will (shall) be
you will be	you will be
he, she, it will be	they will be

Present Perfect Tense

(*have* or *has* + the past participle)

Singular	*Plural*
I have been	we have been
you have been	you have been
he, she, it has been	they have been

Past Perfect Tense

(*had* + the past participle)

Singular	*Plural*
I had been	we had been
you had been	you had been
he, she, it had been	they had been

Future Perfect Tense

(*will have* or *shall have* + the past participle)

Singular	*Plural*
I will (shall) have been	we will (shall) have been
you will have been	you will have been
he, she, it will have been	they will have been

7c. Learn the uses of each of the six tenses.

Each of the six tenses has its own particular uses, some of which require explanation. Study the following explanations, and use them for reference when you are confronted by a problem in your own writing.

(1) The *present tense* is used to express action (or to help make a statement about something) occurring now, at the present time.

EXAMPLES We **wait** patiently.
We **are waiting** patiently. [progressive form]
We **do wait** patiently. [The verb with *do* or *did* is called the emphatic form.]

> ☞ NOTE In all tenses, as in the second example, continuing action may be shown by the use of the progressive form, which ends in *-ing*. The third example illustrates the emphatic form, consisting of a form of *do* plus the first principal part of a verb. The normal way of making a sentence emphatic is to pronounce the helping verb with stress. When there is no helping verb, *do* or *did* is added to carry this stress. These emphatic forms can be used in the present and past tenses only.

The present tense is also used to indicate habitual action.

EXAMPLE We **wait** for the bus every morning.

The present tense is often used to express a general truth, something which is true at all times.

EXAMPLES Amy agreed with her mother that honesty **is** [instead of *was*] the best policy.
I have read that Alaska **is** [instead of *was*] the only state without an official nickname.

The present tense is used occasionally to achieve vividness in writing about past events. This use of the present tense is known as the *historical present.*

EXAMPLE Queen Elizabeth I **strengthens** England's power and **leads** the country through its greatest era.

(2) The *past tense* is used to express action (or to help make a statement about something) that occurred in the past but did not continue into the present. The past tense is formed regularly by adding *-d* or *-ed* to the verb.

EXAMPLES We **waited** for you yesterday.
We **were waiting** for you yesterday.
We **did wait** for you yesterday.

The past tense may also be shown by *used to:*

EXAMPLE We **used to wait** for the bus.

(3) The *future tense* is used to express action (or to help make a statement about something) occurring at some time in the future. The future tense is formed with *will* or *shall.*

EXAMPLES We **will wait** for you tonight.
We **will be waiting** for you tonight.

The future may also be indicated in other ways:

EXAMPLES We **are going to wait** outside.
We **are about to wait** outside.
We **wait** outside **later.** [present with another word indicating future time]

(4) The *present perfect tense* is used to express action (or to help make a statement about something) occurring at no definite time in the past. It is formed with *have* or *has.*

EXAMPLE Ted **has waited** for us often.
We **have waited** for them before.

The present perfect tense is also used to express action (or to help make a statement about something) occurring in the past and continuing into the present.

EXAMPLES We **have waited** for an hour. [We are still waiting.]
We **have been waiting** for an hour. [We are still waiting.]

(5) The *past perfect tense* is used to express action (or to help make a statement about something) completed in the past before some other past action or event. It is formed with *had*.

EXAMPLES After we **had waited** for an hour, we **left.** [The waiting preceded the leaving.]
After we **had been waiting** for an hour, we **left.**

(6) The *future perfect tense* is used to express action (or to help make a statement about something) which will be completed in the future before some other future action or event. It is formed with *will have* or *shall have*.

EXAMPLES By the time the bus **arrives,** we **will have waited** for an hour. [The waiting precedes the arriving of the bus.]
By the time the bus **arrives,** we **will have been waiting** for an hour.

EXERCISE 14. Understanding the Uses of the Six Tenses. Explain the difference in meaning between the sentences in the following pairs. The sentences are correct. Then name the tense used in each sentence.

EXAMPLE 1. I met you at 3:00.
I will have met you at 3:00.
1. *In the first sentence, the action occurred once and ended. In the second sentence, the action will be completed in the future before another action will be completed.*
past, future perfect

1. Marga lived in Brazil for eight years.
   Marga has lived in Brazil for eight years.
2. Why had she gone to the theater?
   Why has she been going to the theater?
3. Have the directions been explained clearly?
   Had the directions been explained clearly?
4. Was she driving?
   Had she been driving?
5. As of June 30, they will have raised taxes twice this year.
   As of June 30, they will be raising taxes twice this year.

EXERCISE 15. Understanding the Uses of the Six Tenses. In each of the following items you are given the meaning of a sentence. Two sentences then follow. Only one of these sentences matches the given meaning. Number your paper 1–10. Next to the appropriate number, write the *letter* of the sentence that matches the *meaning*. Be prepared to name the tenses used in each sentence.

EXAMPLE 1. *Meaning:* It is not snowing now.
a. It had been snowing all afternoon.
b. It has been snowing all afternoon.
1. a

1. *Meaning:* John still works for Mr. Porzio.
   a. John has worked for Mr. Porzio for a year.
   b. John had worked for Mr. Porzio for a year.
2. *Meaning:* Ann Rosine could be on her way to Worcester right now or could be going later.
   a. Ann Rosine is moving to Worcester, Massachusetts.
   b. Ann Rosine will be moving to Worcester, Massachusetts.
3. *Meaning:* Jaime is still in school.
   a. Jaime has been studying pharmacy since last summer.
   b. Jaime studied pharmacy last summer.
4. *Meaning:* Elena was born on Mary and David's wedding day.
   a. Barbara and Steven had had their first child, Elena, when Mary and David got married.
   b. Barbara and Steven had their first child, Elena, when Mary and David got married.
5. *Meaning:* Sabina will have finished working two jobs by the time she graduates.
   a. When she graduates from college, Sabina will have worked on a farm and in a department store.
   b. When she graduates from college, Sabina will have been working on a farm and in a department store.
6. *Meaning:* Lionel is not in law school yet.
   a. Lionel is going to attend Columbia University Law School in September.
   b. Lionel is attending Columbia University Law School.
7. *Meaning:* Alison takes a bus to work on a regular basis.
   a. Alison takes the bus to work.
   b. Alison is taking the bus to work.

USAGE

8. *Meaning:* I don't know whether my work has paid off.
   a. After I had passed the test, I knew my work had paid off.
   b. After I pass the test, I know my work will have paid off.
9. *Meaning:* Rayae was a bank officer at the age of twenty-four.
   a. When Rayae turned twenty-five, she had been promoted to the position of bank officer.
   b. When Rayae turned twenty-five, she was promoted to the position of bank officer.
10. *Meaning:* The children will not miss the anniversary celebration.
   a. I'm sure Eva and Claude will celebrate their anniversary when their children come home from college.
   b. I'm sure that Eva and Claude will have celebrated their anniversary when their children come home from college.

WRITING APPLICATION A:
Making Writing Clear Through the Use of Correct Tenses

Time is extremely important in your daily life. When you write, the time your verbs express is equally important. The tense of a verb signals the time for your reader. The incorrect tense can cause considerable confusion.

Writing Assignment

As you near the end of high school, you are probably considering several different options for the future. You may be thinking about a vocational school, college, a job, or the military service. Jot down the steps you plan to take after graduation to reach a long-range goal. Use these notes to write a summary of your plans. Check your paper for correct use of tense.

SPECIAL PROBLEMS OF TENSE USAGE

The Past Perfect Tense

The past perfect tense requires special consideration because inexperienced writers frequently fail to use it in expressing two actions that happened at different times in the past. The function of the past perfect tense is to make clear which of the actions came first.

7d. Use the past perfect tense for the earlier of two past actions.

NONSTANDARD Sue mentioned (past) that she invited (past) the neighbors to her party. [The two actions did not happen at the same time. Since the inviting preceded the mentioning, the past perfect form of *invite* should be used.]

STANDARD Sue **mentioned** (past) that she **had invited** (past perfect) the neighbors to her party.

NONSTANDARD There was (past) a parking lot where the brick house was (past). [Since the two verbs in this sentence are in the same tense, the sentence suggests that the lot and the house were there together.]

STANDARD There **was** (past) a parking lot where the brick house **had been** (past perfect). [The past perfect *had been* makes it clear that the house was there before the lot.]

STANDARD There **had been** (past perfect) a parking lot where the brick house **was** (past). [Making the other verb past perfect reverses the time order; the lot preceded the house.]

USAGE

7e. Avoid the use of *would have* in "if clauses" expressing the earlier of two past actions. Use the past perfect.

NONSTANDARD If he would have taken more time, he would have won.

STANDARD If he **had taken** more time, he would have won.

NONSTANDARD If we would have stopped by, we would have met your cousin.

STANDARD If we **had stopped** by, we would have met your cousin.

EXERCISE 16. Using Tenses Correctly. Correct the following sentences, which all contain errors in the use of tenses. Refer, if necessary, to the tense rules on pages 137–142.

EXAMPLE 1. If I knew the last answer, I would have had a perfect test.
1. *had known*

1. Pam finally appreciated the old saying that every cloud had a silver lining.
2. By the time we graduate in June, Ms. O'Connell will be teaching Latin for twenty-four years.
3. Although Denny's skill was demonstrated during the season, he was not selected to play in the City All-Star game.
4. If they would have called sooner, I would have given them a ride.

5. When I finally got to the dentist, my tooth already stopped hurting.
6. The company hired Ms. Littmann because she lived for many years in Japan.
7. When I presented my speech before the committee, the members previously studied several reports on nuclear waste disposal.
8. Mr. Frey already complained to the neighbors many times before he called the police.
9. By then I will receive my first paycheck.
10. If she forgot the directions, we could have been lost.
11. The judges declared that we made the most interesting exhibit at the science fair.
12. If they had enough money, they could have taken a taxi.
13. As I thought about our argument, I was sure you lost your temper first.
14. By tomorrow we will be living in Los Angeles five years.
15. When we reviewed the videotapes of the game, we saw that the other team committed the foul.
16. The clerk remembered that the manager has ordered the new shipment last Tuesday.
17. How could I have forgotten that Great Britain included England, Wales, and Scotland?
18. We estimate that when we're in our forties, we will be working more than twenty years.
19. If Gary would have read the advertisement, he could have saved a hundred dollars on that camera.
20. Walt would have done much better on the exam if he was present at our study sessions.

Having with the Past Participle

7f. In participial phrases, use *having* with the past participle to express action completed before another action.

NONSTANDARD Being absent for the midterm exam, I was given a makeup test. [The present participle *being* is incorrectly used to express an action which has obviously been completed *before* the second action in the sentence.]

STANDARD **Having been** absent for the midterm exam, I **was given** a makeup test.]

NONSTANDARD Choosing a college, Rosa sent her application. [The college had to be chosen *before* she could send an application.]

STANDARD **Having chosen** a college, Rosa **sent** her application. [This idea may also be properly expressed by using the word *after* before the present participle: *After* choosing a college, Rosa sent her application.]

The Present and the Perfect Infinitives

7g. Use the present infinitive (*to go, to see,* etc.) to express action following another action.

NONSTANDARD The dancers were upset because they had planned to have performed for us. [What had the dancers planned, *to have performed* or *to perform?* The present infinitive *to perform* should be used because the action it expresses follows the action of the verb *had planned.*]

STANDARD The dancers were upset because they **had planned to perform** for us.

NONSTANDARD He wanted to have invited all the seniors. [Did he want *to have invited* or *to invite?*]

STANDARD He **wanted to invite** all the seniors.

7h. Use the perfect infinitive (*to have gone, to have seen,* etc.) to express action before another action.

EXAMPLE We **are** happy **to have met** you. [The action expressed by the perfect infinitive *to have met* came before the time of the other verb, *are.*]

EXERCISE 17. Using Verbs Correctly. The sentences in this exercise contain errors in the use of verbs. Correct the sentences according to the rules you have just studied. You will not need to change more than one verb or verbal for each sentence.

1. Spending three hours on a review of chemistry, we then worked on irregular French verbs.
2. I should have liked to have met them.
3. I rewrote the book review that I already typed.
4. We gained two hours when we flew from Missouri to California because the sun rose in the east.
5. We wanted to have avoided any controversy.
6. Sometime before the bus leaves, I will finish packing.

7. They already ate dinner when I stopped by.
8. We were hoping to have had a short-answer test in history instead of an essay exam.
9. If you told me you were going shopping, I would have gone too.
10. By the time dinner was ready, I did all my math homework.

WRITING APPLICATION B:
Using Verb Tenses Consistently for Clarity

A time machine is an intriguing idea. However, do not make your writing a time machine which tosses your readers from past to present to future without reason. Use verb tenses consistently and logically. Otherwise you may lose your readers in your confused world of time.

Writing Assignment

Choose an especially memorable event that has taken place in your senior year. Recreate the event in writing. You might use narration, description, or exposition. Read your writing carefully to make sure that all verb tenses are consistent.

ACTIVE AND PASSIVE VOICE

A verb is in the *active* voice when it expresses an action performed *by* its subject. A verb is in the *passive* voice when it expresses an action performed *upon* its subject or when the subject is the result of the action.

ACTIVE VOICE The car hit a tree. [subject acting]

PASSIVE VOICE The tree was hit by a car. [subject acted upon]

All transitive verbs (those that take objects) can be used in the passive voice. Instead of the usual situation in which the verb expresses an action performed by the subject and affecting the object, a passive construction has the subject receiving the action. Compare the following sentences.

ACTIVE VOICE In the novel the spy (S) stole (V) the secrets (O).

S V
PASSIVE VOICE In the novel the secrets were stolen by the spy.

S V
In the novel the secrets were stolen.

To form the passive construction, the object of the active sentence is moved ahead of the verb and becomes the subject. A form of *be* is added to the verb, and the subject of the active sentence is either expressed in a prepositional phrase or dropped.

Notice that in the passive voice the main verb is always a past participle, and the tense is expressed by an appropriate form of *be*.

ACTIVE The plumber **fixed** the leaky pipe.
PASSIVE The leaky pipe **was fixed** by the plumber.

ACTIVE The captain usually **reads** the lineup.
PASSIVE The lineup **is** usually **read** by the captain.

The Retained Object

Active sentences that have direct objects often have indirect objects as well. When they do, either the direct or indirect object can become the subject in a passive construction:

S V IO DO
ACTIVE The company sent us a letter.

S V
PASSIVE We were sent a **letter** (by the company).

S V
PASSIVE A letter was sent **us** (by the company).

In both of the passive sentences above, one of the objects has been made the subject and the other continues to function as a complement of the verb. In the first sentence the direct object is retained as a complement; in the second it is the indirect object that is retained. The object that continues to function as a complement in a passive construction is called a *retained object.*

Use of Passive Voice

The choice between the active or passive voice is usually a matter of taste, not of correctness. However, it is important to remember that a passive verb is usually less forceful than an active one and that a long succession of passive verbs usually produces an awkward effect.

WEAK PASSIVE The event was completed when a triple somersault was done by Mario.

ACTIVE Mario completed the event by doing a triple somersault.

WEAK PASSIVE Steady rains were hoped for by all of us, but a hurricane was wanted by none of us.

ACTIVE All of us hoped for steady rains, but none of us wanted a hurricane.

SUCCESSION OF PASSIVES I *was asked* by Ms. Long to visit her animal shelter for unwanted pets. Rows of cages *had been placed* along both sides of a room. First a large parrot *was shown* to me. Elsewhere, a scrawny puppy *was being comforted* by an assistant. Ms. Long said that so many unwanted pets *had been brought* to her, it was difficult for all of them to *be housed* there. It *was agreed* by us that the responsibility of owning a pet *should be understood* by people before a pet *is bought.*

7I. Use the passive voice sparingly. Avoid weak and awkward passives. In the interest of variety, avoid long passages in which all the verbs are passive.

There are, however, some qualifications of this general rule which should be mentioned. The passive voice is particularly useful in two common situations.

(1) Use the passive voice to express an action in which the actor is unknown.

EXAMPLE All the tickets **had been sold** many days ago.

(2) Use the passive voice to express an action in which it is desirable not to disclose the actor.

EXAMPLE Poor judgment **was used** in making this decision.

In some instances the passive voice is more convenient and just as effective as the active voice. The following passive sentences are entirely acceptable.

The laser **was invented** by an American.
The space travelers **were cheered** by the crowds and **praised** by the press.
Ivy Swan, who **is known** by all for her songs, **has been emulated** by many young, hopeful singers.

Remember, however, that the active voice is generally stronger than the passive and less likely to get you into stylistic difficulties.

EXERCISE 18. Revising Sentences in the Passive Voice. Revise the following sentences by changing the passive verbs to active verbs wherever you think the change is desirable. If you think the passive is preferable, copy the sentence unchanged.

1. After the computers had been installed by the service reps, a training session was held for us by them.
2. If the children had been enchanted by Mr. Wright's stories before, they would be even more enthralled by his new tale of a fantasy kingdom.
3. A community meeting was held by the area homeowners to discuss the landfill project, which had been proposed by the City Council.
4. The team's code of fair play was agreed to and observed by all the players.
5. While the decorations are being made by Calvin, the buffet will be prepared by Edna.
6. Potatoes had been cultivated by the Incas more than twenty centuries before they were grown by the Europeans.
7. Her ten-speed bike was ridden by her through the country.
8. The lesson on constitutional amendments, which had been assigned to us last week by the teacher, was reviewed by us before the test.
9. Shinae Chun is admired and respected by her colleagues.
10. If the practicality of home robots had been demonstrated by Mike Smith, his request for funding would not have been rejected by the committee.

THE SUBJUNCTIVE MOOD

Verbs may be in one of three moods: *indicative, imperative,* or *subjunctive*. Almost all the verbs you use are in the *indicative mood.* The *imperative mood* is used to express a request or a command.

IMPERATIVE **Draw** a circle around the verb phrase.
Turn off the radio immediately.

The only common uses of the subjunctive mood in modern English are to express a condition contrary to fact and to express a wish. These uses occur mainly in formal standard English and usually apply to only two verb forms—*be* and *were*. The following partial conjugation of *be* will show how the subjunctive mood differs from the indicative.

Present Indicative		*Present Subjunctive*	
Singular	*Plural*	*Singular*	*Plural*
I am	we are	(if) I be	(if) we be
you are	you are	(if) you be	(if) you be
he is	they are	(if) he be	(if) they be

The present subjunctive is used only in certain rather formal situations.

EXAMPLES We recommended that she **be** invited to speak.
They urged that Thad **be** reinstated.
We move that Alma **be** nominated.

7j. The subjunctive *were* is usually used in contrary-to-fact statements (after *if* or *as though*) and in statements expressing a wish.

CONTRARY TO FACT If I **were** [not *was*] you, I would be very nervous. [I am not you.]
If Rex **were** [not *was*] thinner, he'd disappear. [He is not thinner.]
Doris teased me as though she **were** [not *was*] my sister. [She is not my sister.]

WISH I wish I **were** [not *was*] fabulously rich.
I wish Ms. Perkins **were** [not *was*] our coach.

Past Indicative		*Past Subjunctive*	
Singular	*Plural*	*Singular*	*Plural*
I was	we were	(if) I were	(if) we were
you were	you were	(if) you were	(if) you were
he was	they were	(if) he were	(if) they were

EXERCISE 19. Using the Subjunctive Mood Correctly. Some of the following sentences contain errors in the use of the subjunctive mood. Others are correct. Number your paper 1–10. If the verbs in the sentence are correct, write a + after the appropriate number. If a verb is incorrect, copy it and write the correct form of the verb next to it.

EXAMPLE 1. If I was you, I would apply for the scholarship.
1. *was—were*

1. Willis insisted that every employee is invited to the company picnic.
2. I'd be a lobster fisherman if I was living on Cape Cod.

USAGE

3. Gloria was confused all day because it seemed as though it was Friday, but it was only Thursday.
4. Striking out again, Katie moaned, "I wish I was a better hitter!"
5. Vernon lost many of his friends because he acted as if he were better than they.
6. If boxing was less violent, many people would respect it more.
7. "I wish this book was shorter," sighed Sabrena as she turned to page 378.
8. We often complain about working too many hours; but if we were to work fewer, we would be complaining about smaller paychecks.
9. I wish I was able to go to the concert, but I have to work.
10. "I wish it was next year already so that I would be in college," Takala said.

REVIEW EXERCISE B. Using Verbs Correctly. Some of the following sentences contain errors in the use of verbs. Others are correct. Number your paper 1–20. If the verbs in a sentence are correct, place a + after the corresponding number on your paper. If a verb is incorrect, write the correct form after the proper number.

EXAMPLE 1. I drunk more than a gallon of lemonade.
1. *drank*

1. If I was Joan's coach, I'd tell her to relax more.
2. For the holidays they planned to have gone fishing.
3. We swum to shore when we spotted the shark.
4. If you would have written the report yesterday, you could have gone to the concert with us.
5. When the temperature rises, Sid becomes grouchy.
6. As the climbers ascended the mountain, they noticed a shiny object laying on the ledge beneath them.
7. If they weren't too proud to ask, I'd have been glad to help them paint the house.
8. Why don't you ask if they already seen that exhibit?
9. They had forgotten that yesterday was my birthday.
10. As soon as we returned to the campsite, we discovered that someone took our food and gear.
11. If I had begun my chores this morning, I would have finished in time to go to the show.

12. When the news of the explosion come over the radio, Dr. Trimble had already rushed to the site.
13. He swept the floor and then lay the linoleum flooring.
14. If I was more confident, I could try out for the play.
15. If we would have had the engine tuned, I'm sure we would not be stranded on the highway now.
16. We have counted the money and have lain it in the safe.
17. As Ms. Hall interviewed the professor, she realized that the batteries went dead in the tape recorder.
18. In her report Clara explained that shock waves from earthquakes were recorded on seismographs.
19. They wished they were going to the music festival instead of the annual family reunion.
20. Jake, our new supervisor, worked for this company for the past 20 years.

CHAPTER 7 REVIEW: POSTTEST

Using Verbs Correctly. Some of the following sentences contain errors in the use of verbs. Others are correct. Number your paper 1–25. If the verbs in a sentence are correct, write a + after the proper number. If a verb is incorrect or awkward, write the correct form after the proper number.

EXAMPLE 1. If she was he, she'd have spoken up.
1. *were*

1. The choir had not sung so well in years.
2. She thought the runners had broke the world record.
3. If we would have checked, we'd have known the store was closed.
4. They were setting on the bench and feeding the ducks.
5. She laid another log on the fire to ward off the cold.
6. We would have preferred to have eaten Chinese food.
7. Mrs. Ames was pleased that when the driver's test was taken by her son, he passed easily.
8. The shoppers laid down their purchases carefully.
9. Cindy retraced her steps and found the café at which she left her credit card.

10. If I was Luis, I would have argued with the umpire.
11. We cheered when the movie finally begun.
12. You should never have lain your radio near the edge.
13. They would have liked to interview the astronauts.
14. I had just laid down on the beach when it started to rain.
15. The ice cubes had not froze in time for the party.
16. Yesterday I swum in the Millers' new pool.
17. Dan worked for this company for eighteen years, longer than any other current employee.
18. The rate of inflation has raised steadily.
19. When they returned to the scene, they discovered that the weapon was taken.
20. I never realized that hurricanes and typhoons were really the same thing.
21. When I enter college, my parents will be married thirty years.
22. The movie was especially liked by Kira and her brother because of the beautiful nature photography.
23. When we saw the group perform, Julia, the lead vocalist, just broke her contract with a big recording company.
24. If we had the chance, we would have stopped by your house.
25. They found the cat laying on the closet shelf.

USAGE

CHAPTER 8

Correct Use of Modifiers

FORMS OF ADJECTIVES AND ADVERBS; COMPARISON

An adjective modifies a noun or a pronoun. An adverb may modify a verb, an adjective, or another adverb. These are familiar statements, but applying them to usage is sometimes difficult. Should you say "tastes strong" or "tastes strongly," "played good" or "played well"? These and other usage problems are discussed in this chapter.

DIAGNOSTIC TEST

Selecting the Correct Modifier. Number your paper 1–20. Select the correct word in parentheses in each sentence.

EXAMPLE: 1. The hurricane hit the town very (sudden, suddenly).
1. *suddenly*

1. Some of these plums taste (bitter, bitterly) to me.
2. I didn't do as (good, well) on the test as I thought I had.
3. Have you seen a (friendlier, more friendlier) spaniel than mine?
4. Those imitation diamonds look (real, really) valuable.
5. The weather this afternoon is (pleasanter, more pleasant) than it was this morning.
6. Jan is younger than (anyone, anyone else) in her class.
7. Having tried both brands of glue, I found that Macrogrip is (stronger, strongest).
8. When you get to the stop sign, turn (sharp, sharply) to the left.

9. This is the (baddest, worst) storm this town has ever seen.
10. The room won't look so (bad, badly) after it has been painted.
11. The close of the letter read, "With our (most sincerest, sincerest) thanks."
12. The coast road is more scenic, but Route 180 is (quicker, quickest).
13. The landscape looks (strange, strangely) in this eerie light.
14. The turbostream engine will give better gasoline mileage than (any, any other) engine ever made.
15. We build cars (sturdy, sturdily) enough to last one hundred thousand miles.
16. Rehearsals are going as (good, well) as can be expected.
17. Did you feel (sad, sadly) when you lost your watch?
18. Learning to dance (good, well) takes practice.
19. The lizard turned its head so (slow, slowly) that it looked as if it weren't moving at all.
20. Jeanne looked (casual, casually) in my direction.

USAGE

ADJECTIVE AND ADVERB FORMS

Before reviewing the usage of adjectives and adverbs, you should make sure that you are able to tell which is the adjective form of a word and which is the adverb form. Most adverbs end in -ly (*clearly*, *happily*, *eagerly*), but not *all* adverbs. Moreover, a few common adjectives end in -*ly*. Some words do have the same form whether used as an adjective or as an adverb.

The following list includes some common adjectives and adverbs with identical forms. It also includes some adjectives ending in -*ly*.

ADJECTIVES	ADVERBS	ADJECTIVES ENDING IN -LY
a *short* race	She stopped *short*.	*nightly* walk
a *close* call	Stand *close* to me.	*bodily* harm
a *high* shelf	She jumped *high*.	*hourly* pay
a *right* answer	Do it *right*.	*unfriendly* man
a *first* time	She left *first*.	*lively* beat
a *hard* problem	He tried *hard*.	*seemly* choice
a *straight* path	Drive *straight*.	*early* class
a *last* chance	We play *last*.	*likely* area
a *fast* start	Walk *fast*.	*weekly* meeting

8a. Linking verbs, especially the verbs of sense (*taste, smell, feel,* etc.), are often followed by an adjective. Action verbs are often followed by an adverb.

EXAMPLES The cider tasted **sweet.** [The adjective *sweet* is correct after the linking verb *tasted.* It modifies the subject *cider.*]
The voices sounded **angry.** [The adjective *angry* is correct after the linking verb *sounded.* It modifies the subject *voices.*]
The man shouted **angrily.** [The adverb *angrily* is correct after the action verb *shouted.* It modifies the verb *shouted.*]

Some verbs may be used as either linking or action verbs. *Look* is one example.

EXAMPLES Chris looked **happy.** [After the linking verb *looked,* the adjective *happy* is correct. It modifies *Chris.*]
Chris looked **happily** out the window. [After the action verb *looked,* the adverb *happily* is correct. It modifies *looked.*]

When you are not sure whether a verb is a linking verb, try substituting a form of *seem,* which is always a linking verb. If the substitution does not greatly change the meaning of the sentence, the verb is a linking verb and should be followed by an adjective.

EXAMPLES Chris looked happy. [*Chris seemed happy* has about the same meaning; hence *looked* is a linking verb.]
Chris looked happily out the window. [*Chris seemed happily out the window* does not make sense; hence *looked* is not a linking verb in this sentence.]

8b. In making a choice between an adjective and an adverb, ask yourself what the word modifies. If it modifies a noun or pronoun, choose the adjective. If it modifies a verb, choose the adverb.

PROBLEM They dug a hole (deep, deeply) enough to plant the tree.
SOLUTION They dug a hole **deep** enough to plant the tree. [The adjective *deep* modifies the noun *hole.*]

PROBLEM Has he been studying math (regular, regularly)?
SOLUTION Has he been studying math **regularly?** [The adverb **regularly** modifies the action verb *has been studying.*]

EXERCISE 1. Selecting Adjectives and Adverbs. Number your paper 1–20. Select the correct word in parentheses in each sentence. If the word modifies the subject, select the adjective; if it modifies the

USAGE

verb, select the adverb. Remember that a linking verb is followed by an adjective.

1. The sled's runners slid (smooth, smoothly) over the ice.
2. The weather outside looks (miserable, miserably).
3. Plan your outline as (careful, carefully) as possible.
4. The official explanation of the budget cut sounds (incredible, incredibly).
5. Why was she looking at me (suspicious, suspiciously)?
6. This apple tastes (peculiar, peculiarly) to me.
7. Don't feel (glum, glumly) about missing the game.
8. You can watch (contented, contentedly) from the sidelines.
9. Dawn goes jogging (regular, regularly).
10. He disappeared (quiet, quietly) behind the curtain.
11. The conference room smelled (stuffy, stuffily).
12. After the first act, we all applauded (enthusiastic, enthusiastically).
13. The stage manager appeared (sudden, suddenly).
14. She spoke (serious, seriously) to the audience.
15. "The leading lady in the play," she said, "is feeling (sick, sickly)."
16. "She is resting (comfortable, comfortably) backstage."
17. "Her understudy will take over the lead (temporary, temporarily)."
18. The understudy seemed (nervous, nervously) to the audience.
19. After a while she was saying her lines (easy, easily).
20. The audience felt (happy, happily) for the understudy.

Bad and *Badly*

Bad is an adjective modifying nouns and pronouns. *Badly* is an adverb, modifying verbs, adjectives, and adverbs. Since the verbs of sense —*feel, smell, taste, sound*—are followed by an adjective, it is standard English to say *feel bad, smell bad,* etc.

Joan feels bad about the broken vase.

The warped record sounds bad.

The common expression *feel badly,* however, has, through usage, become acceptable English, although ungrammatical. Used with other verbs of sense, *badly* is not yet standard. Do not say *smell badly, taste badly,* etc.

Well and Good

Well may be used as either an adjective or an adverb. As an adjective, *well* has three meanings.

1. *To be in good health:*

   He feels **well.**[1] He seems **well.**

2. *To appear well-dressed or well-groomed:*

   She looks **well** in that dress.

3. *To be satisfactory:*

   All is **well.**

As an adverb, *well* means to perform an action capably.

She wrote very **well.**

Good is always an adjective. It should never be used to modify a verb.

NONSTANDARD The choir sang good at the concert.
STANDARD The choir sang **well** at the concert.

NONSTANDARD We bowled very good as a team.
STANDARD We bowled very **well** as a team.

USAGE

Real and Really

Real is an adjective meaning "actual" or "true." *Really* is an adverb and should be used to modify an adjective or another adverb, even though *real* is commonly used in everyday speech.

INFORMAL Your new car is real nice.
FORMAL Your new car is **really** nice.

INFORMAL He played real well in the tryouts.
FORMAL He played **really** well in the tryouts.

Slow and Slowly

Slow is an adjective except in the expressions *Drive slow* and *Go slow,* which have become acceptable because of their wide use on highway signs. *Slowly* is an adverb.

[1] *He feels good* is also correct, though its meaning is not limited to health. Example: He feels *good* about the new job offer.

EXERCISE 2. Correcting Errors in the Use of Modifiers. Number your paper 1–10. Some of the sentences contain errors in the use of *bad* and *badly, well* and *good, real* and *really,* and *slow* and *slowly.* If a sentence is correct, write + next to the appropriate number. If a word is used incorrectly, copy it on your paper and next to it write the correct form.

EXAMPLE: 1. After a long rehearsal, the dance troupe performed good.
1. *good—well*

1. After she had lost the election, Bernadette felt very bad.
2. Charlotte was real happy about getting an *A* on her history test.
3. Ms. Stein is a good teacher who prepares her lessons well.
4. Some shades of blue and green go good together.
5. Let's hope the rest of the day doesn't go this bad.
6. "I'm sure I did good on that test," Anzu confidently remarked.
7. Eating slowly aids digestion.
8. Everyone wondered whether the stone in his ring was a real diamond.
9. "Please speak slow when you give your election speech," Mr. Schmidt advised the nervous candidates.
10. "Life can't be treating you all that bad," I told Walker.

USAGE

EXERCISE 3. Analyzing the Use of Modifiers. Number your paper 1–20. If the *italicized* modifier in a sentence is correct, write a + after the proper number. If it is incorrect, write the correct form, and after the correct form write the word it modifies.

EXAMPLE 1. Something sounds *strangely* next door.
1. *strange—something*

1. The players did *good* in the fourth quarter.
2. The bread dough rose too *quick.*
3. I am glad to see you looking *well* after the operation.
4. Limburger cheese smells very *bad.*
5. We walked *slow* on the icy sidewalk.
6. Liz seemed *sad* to hear the news.
7. Sam feels *bad* about forgetting your birthday.
8. Anita is afraid she did *poor* on the test.
9. She sounded very *angrily* on the phone.

10. These new jeans do not fit me *good* at all.
11. Rita answered the questions *precisely.*
12. Fortunately, no one was hurt *bad* in the accident.
13. I could not see the game very *good* from my seat.
14. This old watch has been running fairly *good.*
15. Ms. Tate's company can do the job *efficiently.*
16. The judge rapped the gavel *sharp* to restore order.
17. We didn't win, but we played *well.*
18. My tennis shoes do not look *well* anymore.
19. Jen works *slow* but she is accurate.
20. The whole day has gone *bad* for me.

WRITING APPLICATION A: Expressing Emotion Through the Use of Linking Verbs Followed by Adjectives

People often have a hard time expressing emotion, perhaps because they are shy or very private, perhaps because they have never had any practice. Emotions are real and important, however; they indicate that a person is human instead of mechanical, like a robot. The verb *feel* is usually used for expressing emotions. Linking verbs such as *feel* are often followed by adjectives instead of adverbs.

EXAMPLE Incorrect: I feel *badly* about not making the varsity team. [The adverb *badly* is incorrect after the linking verb *feel.*]

Correct: I feel *bad* about not making the varsity team. [The adjective *bad* is correct after the linking verb *feel.*]

Writing Assignment

The writer E. M. Forster said about the English that they are "afraid to feel." He went on to say that he had been taught at school that the expression of feeling is bad form. How do you view the subject of feelings? Do you express them openly or "bottle" them up? Which feelings do you most often show? Write a paragraph on this subject. At some point, use the verb *feel* followed by an adjective or several adjectives.

USAGE

COMPARISON OF ADJECTIVES AND ADVERBS

8c. *Comparison* refers to the change in the form of adjectives and adverbs when they indicate the degree of the qualities they express. There are three degrees of comparison: *positive, comparative,* and *superlative.*

POSITIVE	COMPARATIVE	SUPERLATIVE
big	bigger	biggest
eager	more eager	most eager
gladly	more gladly	most gladly

Comparative and Superlative Forms

(1) Most adjectives and adverbs of one syllable form their comparative and superlative degrees by adding *-er* and *-est.*

POSITIVE	COMPARATIVE	SUPERLATIVE
neat	neater	neatest
warm	warmer	warmest
fast	faster	fastest

(2) Some adjectives of two syllables form their comparative and superlative degrees by adding *-er* or *-est*; other adjectives of two syllables form their comparative and superlative degrees by means of *more* and *most.* (Sometimes, either method is correct.)

When you are in doubt as to how a word is compared, consult an unabridged dictionary.

POSITIVE	COMPARATIVE	SUPERLATIVE
lively	livelier	liveliest
agile	more agile	most agile

(3) Adjectives of more than two syllables and adverbs ending in *-ly* usually form their comparative and superlative degrees by means of *more* and *most.*

POSITIVE	COMPARATIVE	SUPERLATIVE
delightful	more delightful	most delightful
quietly	more quietly	most quietly

(4) Comparison to indicate less or least of a quality is accomplished by using the words *less* and *least* before the adjective or adverb.

USAGE

POSITIVE	COMPARATIVE	SUPERLATIVE
weak	less weak	least weak
contented	less contented	least contented
urgently	less urgently	least urgently

Irregular Comparison

Adjectives and adverbs that do not follow the regular methods of forming their comparative and superlative degrees are said to be compared irregularly.

POSITIVE	COMPARATIVE	SUPERLATIVE
bad	worse	worst
good, well	better	best
many, much	more	most

EXERCISE 4. Using Comparative and Superlative Forms. Write the comparative and superlative forms of the following words. Use a dictionary.

EXAMPLE 1. flat
1. *flatter, flattest*

1. tiny
2. wistful
3. ill
4. modest
5. curious
6. proudly
7. abruptly
8. good
9. gently
10. thin

Use of Comparatives and Superlatives

8d. Use the comparative degree when comparing two things; use the superlative degree when comparing more than two.

COMPARISON OF TWO THINGS

Although both Laura and Ted wrote on the same topic, Laura's paper was **longer** [not *longest*].
The pitcher threw curveballs and sliders; the curveball was the **more** [not *most*] **successful** pitch.

COMPARISON OF MORE THAN TWO THINGS

Of the **three** routes, the expressway is usually the **most** [not *more*] **congested**.
Which of the **ten** photos is the **most** attractive?

> **USAGE NOTE** Rule 8d is generally observed by writers of formal English. In informal speech and writing, however, the superlative is often used for emphasis, even though only two things are being compared:

INFORMAL Which park did you like best, Yellowstone or Hot Springs? [formal: *better*]
Of the two operas, Mozart's *The Marriage of Figaro* is the most amusing to me. [formal: *more*]

8e. Include the word *other* or *else* when comparing one thing with a group of which it is a part.

NONSTANDARD Diamond, a crystalline form of carbon, is harder than any mineral in the world. [Since diamond is also one of the minerals of the world, this sentence says illogically that diamond is harder than itself.]
STANDARD Diamond, a crystalline form of carbon, is harder than any **other** mineral in the world.

NONSTANDARD He ran more races than anyone in his club. [He is a member of the club; he cannot run more races than himself.]
STANDARD He ran more races than anyone **else** in his club.

8f. Avoid double comparisons.

A double comparison is one in which the degree is formed incorrectly by adding *-er* or *-est* in addition to using *more* or *most*.

NONSTANDARD Alice is a more faster swimmer than I.
STANDARD Alice is a **faster** swimmer than I.

NONSTANDARD She is the most friendliest girl in school.
STANDARD She is the **friendliest** girl in school.

EXERCISE 5. Using Comparatives and Superlatives Correctly. Number your paper 1–10. Some of the sentences contain errors in the use of the comparative and superlative degrees of adjectives. If a sentence is correct, write + next to the appropriate number. If a comparison is used incorrectly, copy it on your paper and next to it write the correct form.

EXAMPLE 1. That was the most highest grade Oscar ever earned on a Spanish test.
1. *most highest—highest*

USAGE

1. Colleen thought nothing could be as bad as the snow; but when the ice storm arrived, she said, "This weather is even worser!"
2. Both twins, Holly and Julie, have brown eyes, but Holly's are darkest.
3. In each graduating class, the valedictorian is the student whose average is higher than that of any senior.
4. Because he wrote the Declaration of Independence, Thomas Jefferson is regarded as one of the most important Americans in United States history.
5. People need to develop a more clear sense of self-worth.
6. Sue made the mistake of buying a darker shade of paint than she needed for the small room.
7. Performing better than all the gymnasts, Mary Lou Retton was the first American to win an Olympic gold medal in her sport.
8. Myles is taking more classes than I.
9. Dividing the pie in two, Felicia took the least and gave me the larger portion.
10. According to my friend Juan, Houston, Texas, is more interesting and more exciting than any city in that state.

EXERCISE 6. Using Modifiers Correctly. Number your paper 1–20. For each correct sentence, write a + after the proper number; revise each incorrect sentence and write it correctly.

EXAMPLE 1. I am least prepared to take the test than you.
1. *I am less prepared to take the test than you.*

1. I tried to sing as good as she sang.
2. Josh studied more than anyone in his physics class.
3. I have narrowed my choices to two colleges, and I want to visit them to see which I like best.
4. The shoppers looked oddly at the street musicians.
5. If the dough smells badly, don't bake it.
6. Monica seems good enough to leave the hospital.
7. Mr. Brown is many pounds more heavier than I.
8. The pedestrian stared defiantly at the motorists.
9. He inched very gradual toward the doorway.
10. After a hot day, a cold glass of water tastes good.
11. How did you finish your assignment so prompt?

12. The picture on this television set is much more clearer than on that one.
13. Thunderclouds loomed threateningly overhead.
14. We thought Patti was the most talented of all the actors in the community play.
15. They all did well on the test.
16. I read the shorter of the three books for my report.
17. You cheered more often than anyone at the concert.
18. She was less determined to win than her sister.
19. He thought she seemed gracefuller than the other model.
20. Why is she walking so slow toward the house?

USAGE

WRITING APPLICATION B: Using Comparison to Express Critical Judgment

It is important for readers and viewers to develop critical skills before they attempt to make judgments. You are often asked to compare two or more people, places, or things. In order to express the comparison, you must use adjectives or adverbs in a comparative form.

EXAMPLE Of the three bird prints by Ray Harm, the one entitled *Cardinal* is the *richest* in bright color contrasts. [The superlative form is used because more than two things are being compared.]

Donatello's statue of David is *more realistic* than Michelangelo's *David.* [The comparative form is used because two things are being compared.]

Writing Assignment

Immature readers or viewers are often interested mainly in plot. They value violent action, dangerous missions, close escapes, and so on. More mature critics look for action that is significant. That is, they value action that reveals something meaningful about life or people. Write a comparison of several books or television shows. Judge whether the action is an end in itself or, rather, a means to reveal something significant. Use comparatives and superlatives correctly.

CHAPTER 8 REVIEW: POSTTEST

Identifying the Correct Use of Modifiers. Number your paper 1–25. Some of the following sentences contain errors in the use of modifiers. If a sentence is correct, write + next to the appropriate number on your paper. If the sentence is incorrect, write the incorrect word or words and then write the proper word(s).

EXAMPLE 1. Among my three brothers and sisters, my sister Giselle has the better sense of humor.
1. *better—best*

1. "This is the most drab outfit I have ever had," said Louise. "Why did I buy it?"
2. Which is widest, the Mississippi River or the Colorado River?
3. My English teacher thinks that Shakespeare is better than any writer who ever lived.
4. My parents read both a morning and an evening newspaper, but I think the morning paper is best.
5. As Mr. Connolly explained the procedure for the experiment, Lisa said to me, "This is going to be real difficult."
6. When the temperature reached 103° in August, the Board of Health warned people to walk slowly when they were outdoors.
7. That paint is the most palest shade of blue I have ever seen.
8. Because the drummer played bad, the band's melody line was drowned out.
9. Pointing to two glasses partially filled with water, the magician asked, "Which glass has the least water?"
10. In preparing for a job interview, you should wear styles and colors of clothing that look attractively on you.
11. Mr. Martinez asked, "Is Donna still feeling badly?"
12. If Mark pedals his bike that slow, he'll never get home.
13. Philadelphia and Atlantic City are the largest cities near my home, but Philadelphia is actually the closest of the two.
14. We found it hard to understand why Randy had spoken as rude as he did in response to a simple question.
15. Has Pete been saving money regular for the trip he wants to take to Alaska?
16. He can't play the guitar too good, but his records sell well.

17. Tommy Lee thinks a vacation in the mountains is peacefuller than any other kind of vacation.
18. The economist said that interest rates would be going up steady for the next five years.
19. Among the Tong triplets, Chi Wan has always been the more industrious one.
20. "Sharon has been working harder than anyone here," I said.
21. My sister's bedroom looked messily this morning.
22. The iced tea tasted too sweetly for me.
23. "Nurse Lopez, I feel remarkably well today, better than I have ever felt before," said Mr. Parker.
24. There is a control on the television set for making the picture a little less brighter.
25. The cheese smells badly but tastes good.

CHAPTER 9

Glossary of Usage

COMMON USAGE PROBLEMS

USAGE

DIAGNOSTIC TEST

Selecting Standard Words and Expressions. The sentences in this exercise contain usage problems discussed in this chapter. Number your paper 1–20. After the proper number, write the standard choice of the two given in parentheses.

EXAMPLE: 1. We were (kind of, rather) disappointed with the results.
1. *rather*

1. After Shirley had starred in our spring play, she acted (like, as if) she were an important and famous movie star.
2. Lionel gave a (credible, credulous) account of how he had spent so much money on his vacation.
3. When we need the tape, we never know where (it's at, it is).
4. At the restaurant where I work, all four of us divide the tips evenly (between, among) ourselves.
5. Neither my parents (or, nor) their friends ever miss watching the Super Bowl game.
6. As I was about to pay for my new jeans, I suddenly realized I (had, hadn't) scarcely any money in my wallet.
7. Because it was (liable, likely) to rain, Lorraine canceled her plans to go swimming.
8. Will you please take your package (off, off of) the table?
9. (Accept, Except) for Carlos and Glenn, everyone went to the fair.

10. The reason we are moving is (because, that) my parents have always wanted to live in Oregon.
11. Whenever I'm not doing (something, nothing) challenging, I grow bored easily.
12. Fairbanks, Alaska, is a long (way, ways) away from Orlando, Florida.
13. Although we do the same type of work, Hasina and I are (affected, effected) differently by it.
14. Whenever we go (anywhere, anywheres), Judy always seems to meet someone she knows.
15. (Bring, Take) the dog with you when you go out for a walk.
16. When I first went (in, into) the principal's office, I felt a little nervous.
17. Marie admitted that if she (had, would have) checked the oil, the engine wouldn't have given her a problem.
18. Looking at the crisp green beans, Rosa said, "(This, Those) kind of beans has always been my favorite."
19. It's an (allusion, illusion) to think you can become successful without hard work.
20. Emily's grandparents (immigrated, emigrated) here from Poland.

THE VARIETIES OF ENGLISH

The English of today is a rich and complex language which exhibits great variety among its native speakers. In general, we can distinguish two broad categories of English usage: *standard* and *nonstandard.*

Standard English

Standard English, which has evolved over many centuries, is the form used most widely. It is the language of most educational, legal, governmental, and professional documents. It is used in newspapers, magazines, and books. It is the English we hear from radio and television announcers and persons making formal speeches.

Standard English can vary in different situations, but certain conventions or rules within it are fairly constant, and well-educated people deem them worthy of being observed. That is why we apply the name *standard* to this variety.

Nonstandard English

Standard and *nonstandard* English are not, of course, different languages. Some words appear only in one or the other form, but most words can appear in either. The main differences are in the use of pronouns and certain verb forms. A user of standard English would say *brought,* for instance, where a user of nonstandard English might say *brung*. Some other examples:

STANDARD	NONSTANDARD
He did it **himself**.	He did it **hisself.**
You and **she** fight all the time.	You and **her** fight all the time.
He **doesn't** trust me.	He **don't** trust me.
She **ran** right into me.	She **run** right into me.
They **could have** helped us.	They **could of** helped us.

Sentences like those in the right-hand column are used by perhaps millions of English speakers. Our fiction is full of characters who use recognizably nonstandard speech. Eudora Welty and William Faulkner are among writers admired for their ability to capture the special lilt of certain dialects of nonstandard English. Occasionally someone makes nonstandard English his trademark. Dizzy Dean, a famous pitcher for the St. Louis Cardinals and later a radio and television announcer, turned his nonstandard speech into an asset. The following excerpt is from a *New York Times* interview with Dean:

> And I reckon that's why that now I come up with *ain't* once in a while, and have the Missouri teachers all stirred up. They don't like it because I say that Marty Marion or Vern Stephens *slud* into second base. What do they want me to say—*slidded?*
>
> Me and Paul [Dizzy's brother, also a pitcher for the Cards] didn't have to worry about that sort of stuff when we were winning games for the old Gas House Gang. And I don't know why I should get a sweat up now.
>
> Paul, he'd win one game and I'd win the next.
>
> Didn't nobody come around after the game and ask whether we'd throwed or threw the ball in there to make a play.
>
> We won 'em, no questions asked.

There are so many varieties of nonstandard English—as there are standard and nonstandard varieties of all living languages—that it seems best to describe that form as simply scattered sets of conventions that are recognizably different from those of the standard language. But the audience for each set is relatively small. In contrast, standard English is the medium of communication certain to reach the broadest audience of speakers of English and find a hearing.

TWO KINDS OF STANDARD ENGLISH

Standard English is used in so many different situations—ranging from telephone conversations to formal speeches—that it would be impossible to name a particular kind appropriate for each situation. But we can distinguish two domains of standard English: *formal* and *informal*.

Formal English

For the most part, formal English, like formal dress and formal manners, is appropriate for special occasions. It is also the language of serious writing. It is used in formal essays, essay answers to examination questions, formal reports, research papers, literary criticism, scholarly writings, and addresses on serious or solemn occasions.

Formal English is likely to include words that rarely come up in ordinary conversation. The sentences are likely to be more elaborately constructed and longer than those of ordinary writing. Contractions are rarely used. Formal English pays close attention to refinements in usage and avoids slang.

Note the long and carefully constructed sentences in the following example of formal English. Notice also the formal vocabulary:

> Formidable and grand on a hilltop in Picardy, the five-towered castle of Coucy dominated the approach to Paris from the north, but whether as guardian or as challenger of the monarchy in the capital was an open question. Thrusting up from the castle's center, a gigantic cylinder rose to twice the height of the four corner towers. This was the *donjon* or central citadel, the largest in Europe, the mightiest of its kind ever built in the Middle Ages or thereafter. Ninety feet in diameter, 180 feet high, capable of housing a thousand men in a siege, it dwarfed and protected the castle at its base, the clustered roofs of the town, the bell tower of the church, and the thirty turrets of the massive wall enclosing the whole complex on the hill. Travelers coming from any direction could see this colossus of baronial power from miles away and, on approaching it, feel the awe of the traveler in infidel lands at first sight of the pyramids.
>
> Seized by grandeur, the builders had carried out the scale of the *donjon* in interior features of more than mortal size: risers of steps were fifteen to sixteen inches, window seats three and a half feet from the ground, as if for use by a race of titans. Stone lintels measuring two cubic yards were no less heroic. For more than four hundred years the dynasty reflected by these arrangements had exhibited the same quality of excess. Ambitious, dangerous, not infrequently ferocious, the Coucys had planted themselves on a promontory of land which was formed by nature for command.
>
> BARBARA TUCHMAN

USAGE

Informal English

Informal English is the language most people use most of the time. It is the language of most magazines, newspapers, books, and talks intended for general audiences. It is also generally used in most contemporary short stories, novels, and plays.

The conventions of informal English are less rigid than those of formal English. Sentences may be long or short, and they are likely to sound more like conversation, in contrast to the stately rhythms of formal English. Contractions often appear in informal English, and slang is sometimes used.

In the following example of written informal English, notice that the speech patterns are the familiar everyday ones, the words are generally simple, and the sentences, for the most part, are shorter and less varied than most formal sentences.

> If you enjoy shaking hands, take the initiative. Formerly the man was supposed to wait for the woman to offer her hand, but that rule went out with the one-horse shay.
>
> But know when to stop. I have seen two people shaking hands on and on, neither knowing how to let go. Their problem was like that of the two pedestrians, approaching each other, who keep sidestepping in the same direction until they finally bump into each other.
>
> Don't be a knuckle crusher, and don't go to the other extreme, extending your hand like a limp mackerel. Instead, give the other hand a light pressure or squeeze, a sort of hand-hug. Let your hand, as well as your eyes and your voice, register, "I'm glad to meet you."[1]

EXERCISE 1. Distinguishing Different Kinds of English. Read each of the following passages carefully and identify the type of English to which it belongs—formal, informal, or nonstandard. Note the particular words and constructions that cause you to label the passage as you do.

1

In a few weeks, you will each receive a copy of the treasurer's report. Anyone who wants to gripe about the way we're spending the club's money will get a chance at next Saturday's business meeting.

2

If I'd of known they was goin' to let you feed the elephants, I'd of went with you.

[1] Excerpt from *Speech Can Change Your Life* by Dorothy Sarnoff. Copyright © 1970 by Dorothy Sarnoff. Reprinted by permission of Doubleday & Company, Inc.

3

Those actions of his former subordinates that the General was now powerless to oppose, he elected to support. In his eagerness to anticipate any new mischief that might occur to the junta, he promulgated a series of new laws, each more harshly repressive than the last, which even the most rabid of the young officers would not have dared to propose.

4

One thing is, she don't take long walks like she used to. Every morning we used to see her out there, takin' those brisk steps. Just as fast! You'd of thought there was something after her. And if you was to meet her, she'd never stop to say nothing to you. Just bob her head at you and go right on. Now that she ain't comin' by anymore, we sort of miss it.

EXERCISE 2. Revising Passages for Specific Circumstances. Revise each of the following passages as directed.

1. *Change this nonstandard English, used in an oral summary of an article, into standard informal English.*

   The President finally got his dander up and told them Russians to get their stuff out of Cuba fast or else! He said the Navy would search ships headed for Cuba and if they didn't stop they'd be sorry.

2. *A student tells her friends of a conversation she has had with the school principal. Put her sentence into the language she would use in reporting the same conversation to her class.*

   Yeah, old Sherlock Holmes told me that any kids caught sneaking out of assembly would get kicked out of school.

3. *A youngster used this nonstandard English to tell about an incident. Change it into standard informal English.*

   When Mom and me come home, we seen right away they'd been somebody messing around with the car.

4. *A mayor made these informal comments to the City Commission. Rewrite them, using the kind of English the mayor probably would choose to explain the same thing to an audience of citizens.*

   In a couple of weeks you'll all receive the report recommending a new high school. You can bet that there'll be plenty of moaning from those people up on the Hill.

WRITING APPLICATION:
Acquiring Flexibility in Levels of Usage

Examine these two ways of conveying the same information:

EXAMPLES 1. In cinema, an extraordinary new genre called scientific fantasy has been developed. Using formality of language and vividness of imagery, this genre portrays the universal theme of benevolence pitted against malevolence. Through the heroic and often macabre intergalactic confrontations, the struggle is waged for the ultimate purpose of establishing moral equilibrium.

2. There's a new kind of movie called science fantasy. The characters use big, scientific words. Some of the scenes are incredible. The theme is usually good versus evil. There are a lot of bloody battles out in space. In the end, good wins out.

Writing Assignment

Now write two paragraphs of your own, using a subject of your own choosing, to illustrate your ability to use both informal and formal English. As in the example above, use formal English in the first paragraph and informal English in the second.

IMPROVING YOUR USAGE

While we can speak generally about three kinds of English—formal standard, informal standard, and nonstandard—the lines between them are not always easy to draw. One kind of usage shades into another. An expression we think of as being informal may turn up in a formal address. A slang word that originates in nonstandard English may become an acceptable part of the informal vocabulary; many words and constructions that we think of as belonging to standard speech may come into use among speakers of nonstandard English. The great majority of our words and our ways of putting them together are common to all three.

Sources of Usage Information

If your language conforms to the conventions of standard English, your main concern will be to vary your specific word choices to meet a particular need. The need will be determined by the nature of the audience, whether you are speaking or writing.

There will be times, of course, when you cannot be sure whether a particular word or expression is suitable for the occasion. You can get help with your decision by turning to a textbook like this one, by referring to a dictionary, or by consulting a special book on usage, such as one of those listed on page 175. Most important of all, you can pay closer attention to the preferences of people who speak the language with obvious care.

You will find the rules of grammar a useful but not invariably reliable guide to usage. Remember, grammar describes the system of a language; usage is concerned with appropriate forms of expression. The two are not always the same, for language is a living and growing thing, and life and growth are not always logical. The people who use a language are constantly changing it. Since the rules of grammar describe the way the language works, when the system changes, the rules change.

The Importance of Standard English

Effective speaking and writing goes beyond mere acceptance of the most appropriate grammatical rules. It embraces such qualities as clarity, forcefulness of expression, honesty, originality, freshness, and—often—brevity. Yet the conventions of standard English should never be underestimated as the essential foundation of good speaking and writing. If you deviate from the conventions of standard English, people will think more about how you are expressing yourself than about what you are saying.

Any language that calls attention to itself or strikes listeners as unsuitable to the situation gets in the way of communication. If you speak as casually with a prospective employer as you do when talking with close friends, you may ruin your chances of getting the job. If you jokingly use nonstandard language around strangers, they may get the impression that you do not know standard English. It is important to know the different forms of English and to make wise choices from them.

Guides to Usage

The following books contain accurate information about English usage problems. (Other dictionaries are listed on page 444.) None of them can tell you exactly what to say or write, but they can help you make up your mind.

American Heritage Dictionary of the English Language: New College Edition. Boston: Houghton Mifflin Company, 1978.

Bernstein, Theodore M. *The Careful Writer: A Modern Guide to English Usage*. New York: Atheneum, 1979.

Copperud, Roy H. *American Usage and Style: The Consensus*. New York: Van Nostrand Reinhold, 1980.

Strunk, William, Jr., and E. B. White. *Elements of Style*. NewYork: Macmillan Pub. Co., Inc., 1979.

The items in this glossary are arranged in alphabetical order, with exercises interspersed. Problems in spelling, such as the difference between *already* and *all ready* and similar words often confused, are taken up on pages 264–270 in the chapter on spelling.

USAGE

a, an These short words are called *indefinite articles*. They refer to one of a general group.

A woman bought Larry's car.
The pioneers came upon **a** herd of buffalo.
Maria was in **an** accident in her father's car.
Jonathan fished for **an** hour before he caught that bass.

Use *a* before words beginning with a consonant sound; use *an* before words beginning with a vowel sound. In the examples above, *a* is used before *herd* because *herd* begins with a consonant sound. *An* is used before *hour* because *hour* begins with a vowel sound.

accept, except *Accept* is a verb; it means "to receive." *Except* as a verb means "to leave out"; as a preposition it means "excluding."

I **accepted** the gift gratefully.
Debbie has a perfect attendance record, if you **except** the day she stayed home with the flu.
We were busy every evening this week **except** Tuesday.

adapt, adopt *Adapt* means "to change in order to fit or be more suitable; to adjust." *Adopt* means "to take something and make it one's own."

When it rained on the day of the senior class picnic, we **adapted** our plans.
The Broadway play was **adapted** from a popular television miniseries.
The couple who **adopted** the baby read many books and **adopted** some suggestions for infant care.

affect, effect *Affect* is usually a verb; it means "to impress" or "to influence (frequently the mind or feelings)." *Effect* as a verb means "to accomplish, to bring about." *Effect* as a noun means "the result of some action."

Try not to let careless remarks **affect** you.
The school board **effected** [brought about] drastic changes in the budget.
The **effects** [results] of the hurricane were shown on the evening news.

all the farther, all the faster Used informally in some parts of the country to mean "as far as, as fast as."

DIALECT Thirty miles per hour was all the faster the first airplane could travel.
STANDARD Thirty miles per hour was **as fast as** the first airplane could travel.

allusion, illusion An *allusion* is a reference to something. An *illusion* is a mistaken idea.

In her essay she made many **allusions** to the American pioneers.
The behind-the-scenes report destroyed her **illusions** of Hollywood.

alumni, alumnae *Alumni (pronounced* ə·lum′nī) is the plural of *alumnus* (male graduate). *Alumnae* (pronounced ə·lum′nē) is the plural of *alumna* (female graduate). The graduates of a coeducational school are referred to (as a group) as *alumni.*

All of my sisters are **alumnae** of Adams High School.
Both men are **alumni** of Harvard.
My parents went to their college **alumni** reunion.

amount, number Use *amount* to refer to a singular word; use *number* to refer to a plural word. (See also **number,** page 187.)

The **amount** of research (singular) on stress is overwhelming.
A **number** of reports (plural) on stress are available.

and etc. Since *etc.* is an abbreviation of the Latin *et cetera*, which means "and other things," you are using *and* twice when you write "and etc." The *etc.* is sufficient.

The new store in the mall sells videotapes, audio cassettes, cameras, radios, electronic games, **etc.** [not *and etc.*]

and which, but which The expressions *and which, but which* (*and who, but who*) should be used only when a *which* (or *who*) clause precedes them in the sentence.

NONSTANDARD Our jazz band was pleased with the audience's enthusiastic response and which we had not expected before the concert.

STANDARD Our jazz band was pleased with the audience's response, **which** was enthusiastic **and which** we had not expected before the concert.

STANDARD Our jazz band was pleased with the audience's enthusiastic response, **which** we had not expected before the concert.

anywheres, everywheres, nowheres Use these words and others like them *without* the final *s.*

I could not find my keys **anywhere;** I looked **everywhere,** but they were **nowhere** in the house.

at Do not use *at* after *where.*

NONSTANDARD Where are they living at now?

STANDARD **Where** are they living now?

EXERCISE 3. Selecting Standard Words and Expressions. The sentences in this exercise contain usage problems presented on the preceding pages in the glossary. Number your paper 1–20. Write the standard choice of the words in parentheses.

1. Some pets find it hard to (adapt, adopt) to city life.
2. This new product has had a harmful (affect, effect) on some people.
3. Does this poem contain any (allusions, illusions) to Homer's *Odyssey*?
4. Jane and Nina are (alumni, alumnae) of our school.
5. I own a large (number, amount) of campaign buttons.
6. During my travels in Europe, I met Americans (everywheres, everywhere).
7. Everyone likes peanut butter (accept, except) you.
8. One line looks longer because of an optical (allusion, illusion).
9. We all (adapted, adopted) the resolution to have a class picnic.
10. A letter went out to all (alumni, alumnae) of the state university.
11. This is (all the farther, as far as) I can run.
12. How does humidity (affect, effect) the speed of sound?
13. Everyone (accept, except) Janet and me applied there.
14. I hope that at least one college will (accept, except) me for admission next year.
15. Ms. Benchley is an (alumna, alumnus) of Reed College.
16. Were any crops (affected, effected) by this year's dry spell?

17. The quiz-show contestant won a large (amount, number) of points by correctly answering questions about geography.
18. The expression "lock, stock, and barrel" is an (allusion, illusion) to the parts of a flintlock rifle.
19. Please (accept, except) my congratulations.
20. The end of the film had a great emotional (affect, effect) on us.

bad, badly See page 156.

because The use of *because* after *reason is* ("The reason is because . . .") is common in informal English, but it is generally avoided in formal writing. In a sentence beginning "The reason is . . . ," the clause following the verb is a noun clause used as a predicate nominative. A noun clause may begin with *that* but not with *because,* which usually introduces an adverb clause.

ACCEPTABLE The reason she arrived late was **that** [not *because*] her car had a flat tire.

BETTER She arrived late **because** her car had a flat tire.

WRITING APPLICATION A:
Learning to State Reasons Correctly

In both speaking and writing, you are often asked to defend a position and to give the reasons behind your opinion. Sooner or later, you will be faced with the construction *the reason is. The reason is because* may be acceptable in informal writing, but in formal writing it is not. Instead, you should think of the clause following the verb *is* as a predicate nominative.

EXAMPLE The *reason* I object to capital punishment *is* **that it is cruel and unusual punishment.** (In this example, the noun clause following the verb *is* begins correctly with *that,* not *because.*)

Writing Assignment

Take a position on a controversial subject. Be prepared to defend your position with sound and logical reasons. In your topic sentence use either *the reason is* or *the reasons are.* Be sure to follow this construction with a noun clause or several noun clauses beginning with *that.*

being as, being that Nonstandard English when used for *since* or *because*.

NONSTANDARD Being as Emily had lived in Montreal for five years, she could speak both French and English.

STANDARD **Because** Emily had lived in Montreal for five years, she could speak both French and English.

beside, besides *Beside* means "by the side of" someone or something. *Besides* means "in addition to."

Who sits **beside** you in English class?
Besides my homework, I have an errand to run.

between, among The distinction between these words is usually observed in formal English. Use *between* when you are thinking of two items at a time, whether or not they are part of a larger group.

We have to choose **between** Anne and Lisa.
I cannot remember the difference **between** a polka, a two-step, and a mazurka. [*Between* is correct because the speaker is thinking of one dance and another dance—*two at a time.*]
They would know the difference **between** the four teams.

Use *among* when you are thinking of a group rather than of separate individuals.

She is respected **among** her peers.
I hated to decide **among** so many qualified applicants.

bring, take Use *bring* when the meaning is to convey something *to the person speaking.* Use *take* when the meaning is to convey something *away from the person speaking. Bring* is related to *come; take* is related to *go.*

Remember to **bring** your new albums when you *come* to my house.
Take [not *bring*] your warm jacket when you **go** to the game this afternoon.

can't hardly, can't scarcely See *The Double Negative* (page 191).

could of Sometimes carelessly written for *could have*. Do not write *of* for *have*. Similar expressions frequently written incorrectly are *ought to of, might of, must of.*

NONSTANDARD Wanda could of told us it wasn't a costume party before we rented these chicken suits.

STANDARD Wanda could **have** told us it wasn't a costume party before we rented these chicken suits.

USAGE

credible, creditable, credulous Sometimes confused because of their similarity, these words have quite different meanings.

Credible means "believable."

The child gave a **credible** excuse for breaking the window in the kitchen.

Creditable means "praiseworthy."

Her quick thinking and competent action were **creditable.**

Credulous means "inclined to believe just about anything."

The **credulous** woman and her neighbors signed up for the trip to Mars.

data The plural form of the Latin *datum.* In standard informal English, *data* is frequently used, like a collective noun, with a singular pronoun and verb.

INFORMAL The census data was finally published.

However since *data* has only recently become acceptable as a singular word, you will be safer if, in your writing, you use the word as a plural. See **phenomena.**

FORMAL The census **data were** finally published.

discover, invent Do not use *invent* to mean "discover." *Invent* means "to make something not known before, to bring something into existence." *Discover* means "to find something that has been in existence but was unknown."

Elias Howe **invented** the sewing machine.
The engineers **discovered** new oil deposits in Michigan.

done Not the past form of *do. Done* always needs a helping verb: *has done, was done, will be done,* etc. The past form of *do* is *did.*

NONSTANDARD We done all our chores in an hour.
STANDARD We **did** all our chores in an hour.
STANDARD We **had done** all our chores in an hour.

don't A contraction of *do not, don't* should not be used with a singular noun or the third person of singular pronouns (*it, he, she*). Use *doesn't.* See pages 90–91.

NONSTANDARD It don't worry us.
STANDARD It **doesn't** worry us.

USAGE

effect, affect See **affect, effect.**

emigrate, immigrate *Emigrate* means "to go from a country" to settle elsewhere. *Immigrate* means "to come into a country" to settle.

The war has forced thousands of people to **emigrate** from their homeland to other, more peaceful countries.
Marie's grandparents **immigrated** here in 1950.

etc. See **and etc.**

except, accept See **accept, except.**

famous, notorious *Famous* means "well and widely known." *Notorious* means "widely known" but in an unfavorable sense.

Gloria Steinem and Betty Friedan are **famous** leaders of the women's movement in the United States.
Al Capone was a **notorious** gangster in the 1920's.

farther See **all the farther.**

fewer, less In standard formal English *fewer* (not *less*) is used before a plural noun. *Less* is used before a singular noun.

We printed **fewer** [not *less*] prom tickets this year.
I spent **less** time in the library this morning.

good, well See page 157.

EXERCISE 4. Identifying Correct Expressions. The sentences in this exercise contain usage problems explained on pages 178–181. Double negatives and the listed items explained elsewhere in this text are not covered. Number your paper 1–20. Write after the proper number the correct choice of the words in parentheses.

EXAMPLE 1. We could (of, have) taken the bus.
1. *have*

1. (Being that, Because) Eric is shy, he doesn't say much.
2. When the car broke down, we had only five dollars (between, among) the six of us.

USAGE

3. (Beside, Besides) our volunteer work, our club sponsors an annual ski trip.
4. Please (bring, take) your guitar when you come to my party.
5. Jon is so (credulous, credible) that he believed your crazy story.
6. They sold (fewer, less) new cars than used cars.
7. In what year was the transistor (invented, discovered)?
8. My reason for missing the rehearsal was not (credulous, credible).
9. Did you (bring, take) your gift back to the store?
10. Basketball is his favorite sport (beside, besides) tennis.
11. I had (fewer, less) cavities than my sister.
12. They (done, did) their best to win the play-offs.
13. Cold weather (don't, doesn't) bother him very much.
14. (Among, Between) the four of us, we can paint the house.
15. If I had known you weren't busy, I would (of, have) asked you to help me.
16. Many people (emigrated, immigrated) to the United States in the nineteenth century.
17. All the critics wrote about Gene Wilder's (creditable, credulous) performance in his most recent movie.
18. Alan Shepard, Jr., became (famous, notorious) as the first American in space.
19. I want to (invent, discover) a fabric that never gets dirty.
20. Angie forgot to (bring, take) her homework assignment when she went to school this morning.

USAGE

EXERCISE 5. Identifying Correct Expressions. This exercise covers all usage items explained in the glossary to this point. Number your paper 1–20. If a sentence does not contain a usage error, write a + after the proper number. If it does contain an error, write the correct form.

EXAMPLE 1. We excepted the telegram nervously.
1. *accepted*

1. Frank has less hobbies than his friend.
2. Dr. Nash stopped by to check on my progress, being as she was in the neighborhood anyway.
3. Will the thunderstorms affect the graduation ceremonies?
4. Would you please take this monstrosity out of here?
5. Anyone as credible as you would buy a refrigerator in the Antarctic.

6. Sue Ellen plays and enjoys many sports: baseball, tennis, bowling, field hockey, volleyball, and etc.
7. The reason for the widespread concern for eagles is because many are dying from lead poisoning.
8. The story contains too many allusions to Marie Antoinette.
9. Margie couldn't find her bus pass anywheres.
10. Where will we be staying at on vacation?
11. Six laps of the pool is all the farther I can swim.
12. The manager divided the work evenly between the four of us.
13. We were grateful to our knowledgeable coach and who guided us patiently throughout the year.
14. My aunts, who are identical twins, are both alumnae of Smith.
15. The foreign exchange student has found it difficult to adapt to life in the United States.
16. If I had known you were ill, I could of let you read my notes from physics class.
17. The Russian ballet dancer immigrated from his homeland to find creative freedom.
18. The amount of push-ups that he can do is incredible.
19. To prepare her report, Judy used data that were published by the Department of the Treasury.
20. Even though Roy said it don't matter, I can see that he is angry.

had of The *of* is superfluous.

NONSTANDARD If we had of asked permission, we could have used the auditorium for our meeting.
STANDARD If we **had asked** permission, we could have used the auditorium for our meeting.

had ought, hadn't ought Do not use *had* with *ought.*

NONSTANDARD They had ought to be more patient.
STANDARD They **ought** to be more patient.
NONSTANDARD I hadn't ought to go to the movies again.
STANDARD I **ought not** to go to the movies again.

he, she, they, etc. Do not use unnecessary pronouns after a noun. This error is sometimes called the *double subject.*

NONSTANDARD My cousin she designs her own clothes.
STANDARD My cousin designs her own clothes.

hisself, theirselves These words are sometimes incorrectly used for *himself, themselves.*

NONSTANDARD Lou built the shed hisself.
STANDARD Lou built the shed **himself.**

illusion, allusion See **allusion, illusion.**

immigrate, emigrate See **emigrate, immigrate.**

imply, infer *Imply* means "to suggest something." *Infer* means "to interpret, to get a certain meaning from a remark or an action."

Mrs. Hanson **implied** during her lecture that we needed more practice.
We **inferred** from her comments that we need to practice more.

USAGE

in, into In standard formal usage, observe the difference in meaning between these words. *In* means "within"; *into* suggests movement from the outside to the inside.

FORMAL Feeling nervous, I walked **into** [not *in*] the personnel office.
INFORMAL We threw some pennies **in** the well and made a wish.
FORMAL We threw some pennies **into** the well and made a wish.

invent, discover See **discover, invent.**

kind, sort, type In standard formal usage the adjectives *this, these, that, those* are made to agree in number with the words *kind, sort, type; this kind, these kinds; that sort, those sorts.*

We prefer **this kind** of magazines.
We prefer **these kinds** of magazines.

kind of, sort of In standard formal usage, avoid using these expressions to mean "rather" or "somewhat."

INFORMAL I feel kind of depressed today.
FORMAL I feel **rather** [somewhat] depressed today.

kind of a, sort of a The *a* is superfluous.

What **kind of** [not *kind of a*] sports car is this?

lay, lie See pages 129–30.

learn, teach *Learn* means "to acquire knowledge." *Teach* means "to dispense knowledge."

If Ms. Green **teaches** [not *learns*] us, we will **learn** more.

leave, let *Leave* (*left*) means "to go away." *Let* means "to allow, to permit."

NONSTANDARD Leave us finish our dinner.
STANDARD **Let** us finish our dinner.
NONSTANDARD He shouldn't have left us borrow his car.
STANDARD He shouldn't have **let** us borrow his car.

The expressions "Leave me alone" and "Let me alone" are both correct and are commonly used interchangeably. Strictly speaking, "Leave me alone" suggests that you want somebody to go away, leaving you by yourself. "Let me alone" suggests that you want somebody to stop bothering you.

less, fewer See **fewer, less.**

liable See **likely, liable.**

lie, lay See pages 129–30.

like, as *Like* is a preposition and introduces a prepositional phrase. *As* is usually a conjunction and introduces a subordinate clause.

Jo sings **like her sister.** [prepositional phrase]
Jo sings **as her sister does.** [subordinate clause]

Like as a conjunction is commonly heard in informal speech, but it is unacceptable in formal English.

INFORMAL She plays golf like the pros do.
FORMAL She plays golf **as** the pros do.

like, as if *Like* should not be used for *as if* or *as though,* which are conjunctions used to introduce clauses.

INFORMAL She looks like she studied all night.
FORMAL She looks **as if** [as though] she studied all night.

likely, liable These words are often used interchangeably, but some writers of standard formal English prefer to observe the following distinctions: *Likely* is used to express simple probability.

Ginny is **likely** to arrive any minute.

Liable is used to express probability with a suggestion of harm or misfortune; it is also used to mean "responsible" or "answerable."

The children playing near the gravel pit are **liable** to get hurt.
Mrs. Lee is **liable** for the damages her daughter caused.

myself, ourselves Most careful writers of English avoid using pronouns ending in *-self*, *-selves* to replace personal pronouns as subjects or objects. See page 113.

Amy and **I** [not *myself*] are in charge of decorations.
Could you do a favor for Wanda and **me?** [not *myself*]

WRITING APPLICATION B:
Using the Conjunction *As* in a Topic Sentence

Whether you are reading or watching a movie or a television show, you generally want characters who are *credible*. This means that they are believable. A character who is thoroughly evil, for example, is not believable if he suddenly does something kind and unselfish. When you judge whether or not characters are *credible*, you are a literary critic. In a topic sentence about a character's credibility, you might also use the conjunction *as*. This construction, which introduces a subordinate clause, arises as you tell *why* a character is or is not credible. (*Like* is commonly substituted for *as* in this construction, but it is unacceptable in formal English.)

EXAMPLE In *The Red Badge of Courage*, Henry Fleming is *credible* because he reacts *as* a young new recruit would in his first battle. [The word *credible* is used correctly. The conjunction *as* is used—not *like*—to introduce the subordinate clause.]

Writing Assignment

Select a character from fiction, the movies, or television who has made an impression on you. Ask yourself if this character is *credible*. Why or why not? Frame a topic sentence similar to the example above. Then write at least one paragraph explaining why the character is or is not believable.

EXERCISE 6. Identifying Usage Errors. The sentences in this exercise cover usage problems explained in the part of the glossary that follows Exercise 3. Number your paper 1–20. If the usage is correct, write a + after the proper number; if it is incorrect, write a 0.

1. In his address to Congress, the President implied that an economic reversal might occur soon.
2. Without any warning, the cat jumped from the chair and leaped in my arms.
3. The children helped themselves to more turkey.
4. When you have time, will you learn me to sew?
5. Leave me figure this problem out by myself.
6. We had ought to have been more considerate.
7. Your room looks as if a tornado had been through it.
8. What am I to imply from your sarcastic remarks?
9. Ben did all the work himself.
10. If you had of asked me, I would have told you.
11. What can you infer from the closing couplet of this sonnet?
12. You hadn't ought to complain so much.
13. Why doesn't he get his work done like he's supposed to?
14. Jane and myself are the editors of our yearbook.
15. We implied from the principal's announcement that our school's administration is becoming stricter.
16. I asked my boss if he would let me have Saturday afternoon off.
17. Some people they're always making a fuss about nothing.
18. Are you implying that I can't read music?
19. Leave them stay if they don't want to join us.
20. We cheered like we never cheered before.

nauseated, nauseous These words do not mean the same thing. *Nauseated* means "sick." *Nauseous* means "disgusting, sickening."

After riding on the roller coaster, the child became **nauseated.**
The chemical reaction gave off a **nauseous** odor.

none *None* may be either singular or plural. See pages 83–84.

notorious, famous See **famous, notorious.**

number The expression *the number of* takes a singular verb. The expression *a number of* takes a plural verb. (See page 91, Rule 5s.)

USAGE

The number of candidates **was** surprising.
A number of candidates **were** nominated by the committee.

number, amount See **amount, number.**

of Do not use *of* unnecessarily. See **could of** and **had of.**

off of The *of* is unnecessary.

They pushed us **off** [not *off of*] the raft as a joke.

Do not use *off* or *off of* for *from.*

NONSTANDARD I got some free advice off of the mechanic.
STANDARD I got some free advice **from** the mechanic.

or, nor Use *or* with *either;* use *nor* with *neither.*

Either Gwen **or** Lily will lead the discussion.
Neither Gwen **nor** Lily will lead the discussion.

ought See **had ought, hadn't ought.**

persecute, prosecute Distinguish between these words, which have quite different meanings. *Persecute* means "to attack or annoy someone," often for a person's beliefs. *Prosecute* means "to bring legal action against someone for unlawful behavior."

The old regime **persecuted** those who held opposing views.
The district attorney **will prosecute** anyone caught looting.

phenomena *Phenomena* is the plural form of the word *phenomenon.* Do not use it as a singular noun.

We studied **these** [not *this*] **phenomena** of nature, which **are** [not *is*] rare indeed.
We studied **this phenomenon** of nature, which **is** rare indeed.

politics, mathematics, athletics For the number of these words and other similar words, see page 90.

reason is because See **because.**

respectfully, respectively *Respectfully* means "with respect" or "full of respect." *Respectively* means "each in the order given."

USAGE

Even though I disagreed, I listened **respectfully** to their side.
Jane Eyre, Emma, and *Adam Bede* were written by Charlotte Brontë, Jane Austen, and George Eliot, **respectively.**

Reverend, Honorable These titles should never be used with a person's last name alone. In addition, the word *the* commonly precedes the titles.

NONSTANDARD Reverend Becker, the Reverend Becker, Honorable Lugar
STANDARD the Reverend Mark Becker, the Reverend M. L. Becker, the Reverend Mr. Becker, the Reverend Dr. Becker, the Honorable Richard Lugar.

rise, raise See page 132.

same, said, such Avoid such artificial uses of these words as the following:

We worked hard on the props and had **same** guarded against pranksters.
Josie complains about taking care of her young cousin, but she is really fond of **said** cousin.
Steve suggested we skip classes, but I don't approve of **such.**

says Commonly used incorrectly for *said.*

NONSTANDARD Doris argued and says, "We should have come earlier."
STANDARD Doris argued and **said,** "We should have come earlier."

scarcely See *The Double Negative* (page 191).

shall, will The old distinction between these words is no longer observed by most people. *Shall,* which was once considered the only correct form for the simple future in the first person, has been replaced by *will* in most speech and writing.

STANDARD I **shall** be glad to mail your package.
I **will** be glad to mail your package.

In a few expressions *shall* is the only form ever used and so presents no usage problem: *Shall we go? Shall I help you?* To use *will* in these expressions would change the meaning. With the exception of these special uses, *will* is as correct as *shall.*

sit, set See page 131.

USAGE

slow, slowly See page 157.

so Avoid using this overworked word too frequently.

POOR The car ran out of gas, so we walked two miles to the nearest service station.
BETTER When the car ran out of gas, we walked two miles to the nearest service station.
BETTER Because the car had run out of gas, we walked two miles to the nearest service station.

some, somewhat Use *somewhat* rather than *some* as an adverb.

FORMAL The rate of inflation in Europe has slowed **somewhat** [not *some*].

take, bring See **bring, take.**

this here, that there The *here* and the *there* are unnecessary.

NONSTANDARD This here shop has the best bargains.
STANDARD **This** shop has the best bargains.

these kind, those kind See **kind, sort, type.**

ways Sometimes used informally for *way* in referring to distance.

INFORMAL At dusk they were still a long ways from the campsite.
FORMAL At dusk they were still a long **way** from the campsite.

well, good See page 157.

when, where Do not use *when* or *where* in writing a definition.

NONSTANDARD A hurricane is when a tropical cyclone has winds faster than 75 miles per hour.
STANDARD A hurricane is a tropical cyclone that has winds faster than 75 miles per hour.
NONSTANDARD An implosion is where something bursts inward.
STANDARD An implosion is a bursting that is focused inward.

where . . . at See **at.**

which, that, who *Which* should be used to refer to things only. *That* may be used to refer to either things or people. *Who* should be used to refer to people only.

USAGE

I like movies **which** [that] have happy endings.
Debra is an actress **who** [not *which*] inspires admiration.
Debra is an actress **that** inspires admiration.

The Double Negative

A double negative is a construction in which two negative words are used where one is sufficient. Formerly, double negatives were quite acceptable, but now they are considered nonstandard.

can't hardly, can't scarcely The words *hardly* and *scarcely* are negatives. They should never be used with *not.*

NONSTANDARD It is so dark in here I can't hardly see where I'm going.
STANDARD It is so dark in here I **can hardly** see where I'm going.
NONSTANDARD There isn't scarcely enough time to eat lunch.
STANDARD There **is scarcely** enough time to eat lunch.

can't help but In standard formal English, avoid this double negative.

FORMAL We **can't help applauding** [not *can't help but applaud*] Ron's positive attitude.

haven't but, haven't only In certain uses *but* and *only* are negatives. Avoid using them with *not.*

FORMAL They **had** [not *hadn't*] **but** two tickets left.
They **had** [not *hadn't*] **only** two tickets left.

no, nothing, none Not to be used with another negative word.

NONSTANDARD Haven't you no money?
STANDARD **Haven't** you **any** money?
STANDARD **Have** you **no** money?

NONSTANDARD Carol hasn't said nothing about the picnic.
STANDARD Carol **has said nothing** about the picnic.
STANDARD Carol **hasn't said anything** about the picnic.

NONSTANDARD Joel didn't sell none today.
STANDARD Joel **sold none** today.
STANDARD Joel **didn't sell any** today.

EXERCISE 7. Identifying Correct Expressions. The sentences in this exercise cover usage problems explained in the section of the

USAGE

glossary that follows Exercise 4. Number your paper 1–20. Write after the proper number the correct word in parentheses.

EXAMPLE 1. I don't have (any, none) left.
1. *any*

1. They only had a little (ways, way) left to run in the marathon.
2. Neither the freshman class (or, nor) the sophomore class will have the problems we faced.
3. We were taught to treat our elders (respectively, respectfully).
4. Luis (can, can't) hardly keep from being proud of you.
5. We studied the Mayans, (who, which) had developed a system of writing, as well as an accurate calendar.
6. Ms. Peters explained the (phenomenon, phenomena) of a supernova.
7. Our enthusiasm has dampened (some, somewhat).
8. Many ancient rulers (persecuted, prosecuted) the people they conquered and made them slaves.
9. I was so sleepy that I (could, couldn't) hardly keep my eyes open.
10. The detectives (haven't, have) no clues in the case.
11. I (had, hadn't) no good reason for being late.
12. In her speech she (says, said) we were at fault.
13. We (had, hadn't) learned anything from the film.
14. The candidates (have, haven't) only three minutes each to state their platforms.
15. She would neither let me tell her the right answer (or, nor) let me give her any other help.
16. We (had, hadn't) but one choice to make.
17. The jazz band and the symphony orchestra will rehearse in rooms 115 and 135, (respectively, respectfully).
18. The manager insisted that there wasn't (any, no) reason for making the customers wait so long.
19. Before we moved, I lived only a little (ways, way) from school.
20. I'm probably getting the flu, because I have felt (nauseous, nauseated) all day long.

USAGE

REVIEW EXERCISE A. Selecting Appropriate Expressions. The sentences in this exercise contain usage problems presented in the glossary. Number your paper 1–20. If a sentence does not contain a usage error, write a + on your paper. If a sentence does contain a usage error, write a 0. Your teacher may ask you to write the correct form after each 0.

EXAMPLE 1. The amount of voters has grown.
1. 0 (*number*)

1. Leave us explain our arguments.
2. Eugenia can't hardly wait for vacation to start.
3. Who first discovered the laser?
4. We worked hard to effect a change in the school's policy on flexible lunch hours.
5. Beside your loyalty as a friend, I appreciate your sense of humor.
6. I resent their allusions to my mistakes.
7. The library has a large amount of new books.
8. You would of had trouble driving in Syracuse without snow tires.
9. Being that I'm short, please let me stand in front.
10. Her talk implied that she favored the honor system.
11. The reason you are tired is because we watched the late show.
12. The principal has no patience with those type of behavior.
13. At the supermarket I bought kiwi fruit, papayas, mangoes, and etc.
14. Since Dan started his part-time job, he has had less chances to be with his friends.
15. My parents are members of the alumni association.
16. Bring your riding boots when you go to the stable.
17. Backlighting is when the main source of light is placed behind the subject being photographed.
18. Jody dances as if his feet hurt.
19. Why don't you get some advice off of Rhoda?
20. Thirty feet is all the farther I can throw a football.

REVIEW EXERCISE B. Selecting Appropriate Expressions. The sentences in this exercise contain usage problems presented in the glossary. Number your paper 1–20. If a sentence does not contain a usage error, write a + on your paper. If a sentence does contain a usage error, write a 0.

1. We had to adapt the stage lighting for the rock concert.
2. The mayor made an illusion to our outstanding safety record.
3. A large amount of nails are in the toolbox.
4. Where did you stay at over Thanksgiving?
5. Everyone except Tim has accepted the invitation.

6. Among the two choices, I like the first one better.
7. The data on acid rain are not complete.
8. My mother emigrated to the United States before I was born.
9. Do you know about Bluebeard, who was famous for his cruelty?
10. You are credulous enough to believe the fortuneteller.
11. My sister she attends Iowa State University.
12. We inferred from Rudy's comments that the movie was dull.
13. The Whites grew all the vegetables theirselves.
14. I had ought to spend more time with my friends.
15. He has been the catcher for every game this year, and he is beginning to look kind of tired.
16. Ms. Robinson learned me all I know about public speaking.
17. What kind of a car is that?
18. We spoke respectfully to the Honorable Frank Murphy when he visited our class.
19. There were four freshmen which made the basketball team.
20. A number of suggestions have been submitted to the committee.

CHAPTER 9 REVIEW: POSTTEST

Revising Expressions by Correcting Errors in Usage. The sentences in this exercise cover problems explained in the entire glossary. Number your paper 1–25. If a sentence does not contain a usage error, write a + on your paper. If a sentence does contain a usage error, revise the incorrect portion of the sentence.

EXAMPLE: 1. I was surprised to learn that Robert's parents are wealthy, because he doesn't act like he's rich.
1. *doesn't act as if he's rich.*

1. The form said, "Please enclose a copy of your birth certificate, and we will return said document at a later date."
2. We couldn't help but admire the way the snow lay upon the hills.
3. You hadn't ought to be so careless about your new watch.
4. In a collision the guilty driver is liable for damage to the other car.
5. The weather was kind of muggy as we began to weed the garden.
6. The door scraped loudly because it was off of its hinges.

7. Members of the Student Council tried to effect the faculty's attitude toward the new dress code for school dances.
8. The picture of the notorious discoverer of the cure appeared on the front page of every major newspaper.
9. Theo don't care what others think; he has the courage to say what he believes.
10. Reverend Timothy Butler performed the wedding ceremony.
11. Esperanza and Patrick, respectfully valedictorian and salutatorian, delivered excellent commencement addresses.
12. When our teacher became ill and was replaced by a substitute, we found it difficult at first to adopt to a new routine.
13. Whenever I feel sad, I can't hardly wait to be with my best friend.
14. Arthur Fiedler he made the Boston Pops concerts popular with millions of people all over America.
15. The reason we're so late is because our car wouldn't start.
16. Scientists are still unable to explain fully the phenomena referred to as UFO's.
17. Then Tom says, "Maybe I'll go and maybe I won't."
18. Because Eula made a mistake when she put the film into the camera, none of her pictures could be developed.
19. Three players came off of the bench and ran out onto the field.
20. Even when he is reading difficult material, Mato is very skillful in inferring the main idea of a passage.
21. We plan to visit Tim at Christmas being as we haven't seen him in three years.
22. I have never seen this kind of insect before.
23. Where was Beth at last night when all of us went to the game?
24. Neil is an expert on jazz trumpeters and who are famous.
25. Our teacher said we had done a credible job on our project.

PART 3 MECHANICS

CHAPTER 10

Capitalization

STANDARD USES OF CAPITAL LETTERS

Capital letters serve as an important signal to the reader. They indicate the beginnings of sentences, and they distinguish names and titles. Confusion can easily result if capital letters are not used according to the conventions of standard English.

DIAGNOSTIC TEST

Identifying Standard Uses of Capital Letters. Number your paper 1–20. In each of the following pairs of items, either item a or item b is correctly capitalized according to standard usage. After the proper number, write the letter of the version containing the standard usage.

EXAMPLE 1. a. a Movie starring Lena Horne
b. a movie starring Lena Horne
1. *b*

1. a. Resolved: That the dress code should be reinstated.
   b. Resolved: that the dress code should be reinstated.
2. a. a nation in the middle east
   b. a nation in the Middle East
3. a. took courses in English, Spanish, and chemistry
   b. took courses in English, Spanish, and Chemistry
4. a. the crew of the Space Shuttle *Columbia*
   b. the crew of the space shuttle *Columbia*

MECHANICS

5. a. at the intersection of Seventh avenue and Market street
   b. at the intersection of Seventh Avenue and Market Street
6. a. a letter of inquiry addressed to American airlines
   b. a letter of inquiry addressed to American Airlines
7. a. a trip to Yosemite National Park
   b. a trip to Yosemite national park
8. a. chief justice Rehnquist
   b. Chief Justice Rehnquist
9. a. fought the Battle of Saratoga during the Revolutionary war
   b. fought the Battle of Saratoga during the Revolutionary War
10. a. enjoyed Hemingway's *the Sun also Rises*
    b. enjoyed Hemingway's *The Sun Also Rises*
11. a. made copies on the xerox machine
    b. made copies on the Xerox machine
12. a. a biography of the American novelist Edith Wharton
    b. a biography of the american novelist Edith Wharton
13. a. a visit to the West Coast of Oregon
    b. a visit to the west coast of Oregon
14. a. a birthday gift from Aunt Madge
    b. a birthday gift from aunt Madge
15. a. freedom to worship god according to personal beliefs
    b. freedom to worship God according to personal beliefs
16. a. Prime Minister Margaret Thatcher of England
    b. prime Minister Margaret Thatcher of England
17. a. a course in World History at Roosevelt high school
    b. a course in world history at Roosevelt High School
18. a. celebrating the fourth of July
    b. celebrating the Fourth of July
19. a. a delicious chinese dinner at Wong's Restaurant
    b. a delicious Chinese dinner at Wong's Restaurant
20. a. birds migrating across the strait of Gibraltar
    b. birds migrating across the Strait of Gibraltar

In the use of capital letters, as in all matters pertaining to language usage, variations are common. In standard usage, for instance, the names of the seasons are not capitalized, but some newspapers do capitalize them. Newspapers may also adopt what they call the "down style" of capitalization, in which words like *avenue, university,* and *library* are not capitalized as they are in standard usage when used with a particular name.

STANDARD USAGE	"DOWN STYLE"
Fifth **A**venue	Fifth **a**venue
Brandeis **U**niversity	Brandeis **u**niversity
Detroit **L**ibrary	Detroit **l**ibrary

The usage described in this book is standard ("up style") usage, which is generally followed in books and magazines.

10a. Capitalize the first word in a sentence.

If you do not always use a capital letter at the beginning of a sentence, refer to Chapter 14 to make sure that you can recognize the end of one sentence and the beginning of the next.

(1) Capitalize the first word of a formal statement following a colon.

EXAMPLE The committee included the following statement: **I**n light of these statistics, we recommend that four-way stop signs be installed.

(2) Capitalize the first word of a resolution following the word *Resolved*.

EXAMPLE Resolved: **T**hat government support of the arts be increased.

(3) Capitalize the first word of a direct quotation.

EXAMPLE Ms. Simpson said, "**Y**our sister is a born leader."

Do not capitalize the first word of a quoted sentence fragment.

EXAMPLE I agree with Ms. Simpson's comment that my sister is a "**b**orn leader."

(4) Capitalize the first word of a statement or question inserted in a sentence without quotation marks.

EXAMPLE My question is, **W**ill this action solve the problem?

> ☞ **NOTE** Traditionally, poets capitalize the first word in a line of poetry. This use of capitals, although by no means as common today as it once was, is still often found.

10b. Capitalize the pronoun *I* and the interjection *O*.

You will probably have little use for the interjection *O,* which is used only in such rare expressions as "O happy day, come soon!" The common interjection *oh* ("Oh, what a beautiful morning!") is capitalized only when it appears at the beginning of a sentence. *Oh* is usually followed by a mark of punctuation, but *O* is rarely followed by punctuation.

EXAMPLES Rejoice in the Lord, **O** ye righteous!
He was doing, **oh**, about 35 miles an hour.

10c. Capitalize proper nouns and proper adjectives.

A proper noun is the name of a particular person, place, or thing. A common noun names a kind or type. Words that name a kind or a type *(poodle, sloop, sonnet)* are not capitalized. Names given to individuals within the type are proper nouns and are capitalized (**F**ifi, **W**anderer, "**S**onnet on **C**hillon").

PROPER NOUNS	COMMON NOUNS
Denise **T**seng	woman
Mexico	country
Suwannee **R**iver	river

A proper adjective is an adjective formed from a proper noun.

PROPER NOUNS	PROPER ADJECTIVES
France	**F**rench
Asia	**A**sian
Shakespeare	**S**hakespearean

Study the following classifications of proper nouns.

MECHANICS

(1) Capitalize the names of persons.

Before writing names beginning with *Mc* or *Mac* (meaning "son of"), find out whether or not the person spells the name with two capitals. Custom varies: **M**c**D**uff, **M**ac**N**eill, **M**acdonald, **M**ackenzie, etc. Names beginning with *O'* (meaning "of the family of") usually contain two capitals: **O'C**asey, **O'C**onner. Also ask about surnames of other origins than Scots or Irish: **L**afitte, **L**a**F**arge, **L**a **G**uardia, **L**as **C**asas, **de la R**enta, **D**e **L**a **R**ey, **de K**ooning, **D**e **K**ruif, von **G**oethe, etc.

The abbreviations *Sr.* and *Jr.* following a name are capitalized: John D. Rockefeller, **S**r.; Martin Luther King, **J**r.

(2) Capitalize geographical names.

Cities, townships, counties, states, countries, continents New York City, Concord Township, Dade County, New Mexico, United States of America, North America

Islands, peninsulas, beaches Coney Island, Keweenaw Peninsula, Turtle Beach

Bodies of water Silver Lake, Lake Michigan, Delaware River, Pacific Ocean, Dead Sea, Willow Pond, Biscayne Bay, Straits of Florida

Mountains Appalachian Mountains, Mount St. Helens

Streets Park Avenue, Gulf Boulevard, Lincoln Parkway, Coast Highway, Interstate 80, Thirty-fourth Street [In a hyphenated street number, the second word begins with a small letter.]

Parks, forests, canyons, dams Central Park, Redwood National Park, Palo Duro Canyon, Grand Coulee Dam

Recognized sections of the country or the world the South, the Northwest, the Far East

> ☞ **NOTE** Do not capitalize *east, west, north*, and *south* when they indicate direction. Do capitalize them when they refer to recognized sections of the country.

EXAMPLES At the corner, turn west, and you will see the museum on the south side of the street.
Is the Midwest the "heart" of the country?

The modern tendency is to write nouns and adjectives derived from *East, West, North*, and *South* without capital letters (a *southerner, southern* hospitality, *midwestern* customs), but the capitalization of such words is also correct.

Adjectives specifying direction are not capitalized unless they are part of the name of a country: northern Utah, western United States, but East Germany, Western Samoa.

> ☞ **NOTE** Some nouns and adjectives derived from proper names are no longer capitalized: mackintosh, macadam, morocco leather, china dishes. Most such words may be written with or without capital letters, however: roman (Roman) numerals, plaster of paris (Paris), venetian (Venetian) blinds, turkish (Turkish) towel, gothic (Gothic) style, etc. When you are in doubt about the capitalization of words of this kind, refer to your dictionary.

EXERCISE 1. Identifying Standard Uses of Capitalization. Number your paper 1–20. After the proper number, write the letter of the standard form (*a* or *b*).

1. a. the Nile river
   b. the Nile River
2. a. She said, "Tell me, too."
   b. She said, "tell me, too."
3. a. an American Citizen
   b. an American citizen
4. a. Los Angeles County highways
   b. Los Angeles County Highways
5. a. east of the river
   b. East of the river
6. a. Fifty-Second Street
   b. Fifty-second Street
7. a. Hoover Dam
   b. Hoover dam
8. a. Charles Adams, Jr.
   b. Charles Adams, jr.
9. a. We heard him say he was "pleased to be here."
   b. We heard him say he was "Pleased to be here."
10. a. people of the Far East
    b. people of the far east

EXERCISE 2. Using Standard Capitalization. Write the following names, terms, and phrases, using capital letters wherever they are required in standard usage.

1. cook county
2. an african village
3. four miles south
4. ranching in the south
5. forty-ninth street
6. olympic national park
7. a city like new orleans
8. a popular spanish singer
9. an arabian stallion
10. james o'toole, jr.

MECHANICS

(3) Capitalize names of organizations, business firms, institutions, and government bodies.

Organizations Spanish Club, League of Women Voters, Humane Society

Business firms Delta Airlines, Procter and Gamble Company, Control Data Corporation, International Business Machines, Grand Hotel, Fox Theater

Institutions Loyola University, First Baptist Church, Biology Department

Government bodies Congress, House of Representatives, Federal Aviation Administration, Department of Commerce, Internal Revenue Service

☞ **NOTE** The names of government bodies are capitalized when they are exact names. Do not capitalize such general names as the following: *the state legislature, the latest department meeting, commission agenda.*

> ☞ **NOTE** Do not capitalize words such as *hotel, theater, church, high school, college,* and *university* unless they are part of a proper name.

EXAMPLES		
	Chelsea Hotel	a hotel in New York
	Webster High School	a nearby high school
	United States Postal Service	the local post office

(4) Capitalize the names of historical events and periods, special events, and calendar items.

Historical events American Revolution, Renaissance, Civil War, Vietnam War

Special events Special Olympics, Conference on World Hunger, Kentucky Derby, Senior Prom

Calendar items Monday, June, Halloween, Professional Secretaries' Week

> ☞ **NOTE** The names of the seasons are not capitalized unless the seasons are personified.

EXAMPLES an early winter
Summer's royal progress

(5) Capitalize the names of nationalities, races, and religions.

EXAMPLES Caucasian, Semitic, Roman Catholic, Baptist, Congregationalist, Korean, Romanian, Afro-American

(6) Capitalize the brand names of business products.

EXAMPLES Mazola, Xerox, Polaroid, Atari

> ☞ **NOTE** A common noun that often follows a brand name is not capitalized except in advertising displays.

EXAMPLES Phillips screwdriver, Campbell's soup, Waring blender

(7) Capitalize the names of ships, planes, monuments, awards, and any other particular places, things, or events.

EXAMPLES the *Merrimac* (ship), Vietnam Memorial, Nobel Prize, Academy Award, Statue of Liberty

> ☞ **NOTE** Do not capitalize the names of school subjects, except for the names of languages and for course names followed by a number.

EXAMPLES English, Latin, Italian, math, art, chemistry, Chemistry II, Art 102

> ☞ **NOTE** Rooms and some other nouns identified by a numeral or letter are capitalized.

EXAMPLES Room 31, Parlor B, School District 18, Chapter 4

> ☞ **NOTE** Names of school classes may or may not be capitalized, but the modern tendency is to capitalize them; however, the words *senior, junior, sophomore, freshman* are not capitalized when used to refer to a student.

EXAMPLE The senior agreed to speak before the Sophomore Class. [or sophomore class]

MECHANICS

EXERCISE 3. Using Standard Capitalization. Number your paper 1–20. Rewrite each item using correct capitalization. Write *C* after the number of a correct item.

1. itawamba junior college
2. a hotel across town
3. central high school
4. She is a junior.
5. the swiss people
6. a royal typewriter
7. winter blizzard
8. the barclay hotel
9. trigonometry
10. physics I
11. labor day
12. history department
13. apple computer
14. two high-school seniors
15. bureau of the census
16. *zephyr* (train)
17. the crusades
18. the world series
19. newport athletic club
20. an italian restaurant

EXERCISE 4. Using Standard Capitalization. List the words that should be capitalized in each sentence. When the words make up a phrase, write them as a phrase: *Sunshine Skyway, National Gallery of Art.* Indicate the number of the sentence in which each word or word group appears.

EXAMPLE 1. When my family lived in mexico city, we often had picnics in chapultepec park.
1. *Mexico City*
Chapultepec Park

1. One of our science teachers, ms. stephens, took her biology II classes to winslow marsh to study snails and collect water samples for testing in the high-school laboratory.
2. The massachusetts institute of technology campus in cambridge extends for more than a mile along the charles river.
3. Iowa department of education planners agreed with franklin county leaders that the new community college should be built in an urban location to make it accessible to many residents.
4. The explorers' club from my high school in bond, kansas, visited the jones fire science training center, where they watched a demonstration of rappelling, the skill of descending a sheer wall with the aid of a double rope.
5. In 1754 columbia college, then called king's college, stood next to trinity college, near the corner of broadway and wall street.
6. Mr. samuel reynolds, jr., my history teacher, captivated his audience of high-school seniors as he vividly described the battle of britain during world war II.
7. Just west of fernandina beach, highway a1a crosses the amelia river and then curves by the entrance to fort clinch state park.
8. The denson hotel and the star theater, at the corner of river avenue and twenty-first street, are being renovated as part of the city's efforts to improve the area tourists first see when they enter the city.
9. Kathleen o'brien, who still has her native irish accent, read some of william butler yeats's poems to our english class on wednesday.
10. Sara turner, owner of turner's nutrition now, a chain of health food stores known for the development of ultravita yogurt, endowed memorial hospital's new wing, which was built this spring on the block between the hospital and finley mall.

10d. Capitalize titles.

(1) Capitalize the title of a person when it comes before a name.

EXAMPLES Superintendent Davis, Dean Williams, President Robinson, Prime Minister Shamir

(2) Capitalize a title used alone or following a person's name only if it refers to a high government official or someone else to whom you want to show special respect.

EXAMPLES Dr. Glenda Davis, superintendent of schools; Ms. Williams, dean of women; Marie Robinson, class president; *but* Neil Goldschmidt, Governor of Oregon; Thurgood Marshall, Justice of the Supreme Court [titles of high government officials]
the Senator, *but* the work of a senator; the General's orders, *but* the insignia of a general; the Chief Justice, the Secretary of State, the Prince of Wales.

> ☞ NOTE When used to refer to the head of a nation, the word *president* is usually capitalized. Two capitals are required in *vice-president* when it refers to the vice-president of a nation. The words *ex-* and *-elect* used with a title are not capitalized: *ex*-President, Governor-*elect*.

> ☞ NOTE When a title is used in place of a person's name, it is usually capitalized.

EXAMPLES Goodbye, Professor.
Yes, Senator, please ask about it.

(3) Capitalize a word showing family relationship when the word is used with a person's name but *not* when it is preceded by a possessive (unless the possessive is part of the name).

EXAMPLES Uncle Juan, Cousin Nora, my cousin Nora, your mother, *but* my Aunt Sandy (when "Aunt Sandy" is considered her name)

> ☞ NOTE Words of family relationship are usually, but not always, capitalized when used in place of a person's name.

EXAMPLE I think someone told Grandma.

(4) Capitalize the first word and all important words in titles of books, periodicals, poems, stories, articles, documents, movies, paintings, and other works of art, etc. [The important words are the first word and all other words except articles (*a, an, the*), coordinating conjunctions, and prepositions of fewer than five letters.]

EXAMPLES *Great Expectations*, *Fortune*, "The Force That Through the Green Fuse Drives the Flower," Bill of Rights, *Bird in Space* [sculpture]

> ☞ NOTE The words *a, an, the* written before a title are capitalized only when they are part of the title. Before the names of magazines and newspapers, they are not capitalized.

EXAMPLES *The Count of Monte Cristo, A Farewell to Arms* [*The* and *A* are parts of the titles.]
Have you read the *Collected Stories* by Jean Stafford? [*The* is not part of the title.]
the *Science Digest*, the *St. Louis Dispatch*

(5) Capitalize words referring to the Deity.

EXAMPLES God, the Almighty, Lord

Pronouns referring to God (*he*, *him*, and rarely, *who*, *whom*) are often capitalized.

EXAMPLE Grace asked God to bring peace to His earth.

The word *god* when used to refer to the gods of ancient mythology is not capitalized.

EXAMPLE Cassandra could foretell the future but was condemned by the god Apollo never to be believed.

MECHANICS

EXERCISE 5. Using Standard Capitalization. Number your paper 1–20. After the proper number, rewrite each item using standard capitalization. Write *C* after the number of a correct item.

1. captain Ahab
2. *guërnica* [painting]
3. Ms. Solomon, the center director
4. the club president
5. aunt Betty
6. senator Dole
7. mayor Fulton of Nashville
8. *down and out in paris and london* [book title]

9. the speaker of the House of Representatives
10. Rabbi Klein, a military chaplain
11. ex-president Carter
12. the leader of a brass band
13. a sergeant in an army
14. the lord in his wisdom
15. the magna carta
16. your aunt
17. the *Los Angeles times*
18. duties of a legislator
19. Mildred Zaharias, former national golf champion
20. "the world is too much with us" [poem]

WRITING APPLICATION B:
Using Capitalization Correctly to Make Your Writing Clear

By using capitalization correctly, you enable your reader to understand your meaning. Compare the following examples:

EXAMPLES I concocted my formula for white peanut butter while I was living in west Virginia.
I concocted my formula for White peanut butter while I was living in West Virginia.

In the first example, the reader would naturally think that the writer had developed peanut butter that is white while living in the west part of the state of Virginia. The second example makes it clear that the writer is using a brand name and referring to a different state.

Writing Assignment

After an absence of ten years, you have returned to town to attend the tenth reunion of your graduating class. The organizers of the reunion have asked everyone in the class to write a personal sketch for inclusion in a booklet to be distributed at the banquet. Write the sketch, using capitalization correctly; tell where you have been during the last ten years and what you have done.

REVIEW EXERCISE. Using Standard Capitalization. This exercise covers all of the capitalization rules in the chapter. List in order the words that should be capitalized in each sentence.

1. The civitan club of midland township meets once a month in the restaurant next to the plaza theater.

2. As I started to laugh, aunt Dora and uncle John simultaneously asked, "you did what?"
3. In their english classes this term, the juniors have read *o pioneers!,* a novel by willa cather about swedish immigrants in nebraska.
4. A report from the secretary of labor included this statement: most of the new jobs in the next decade will be in service fields.
5. According to professor De La Rey, Tennyson's *idylls of the king* was published in 1859, the same year that saw the publication of Darwin's *origin of species,* FitzGerald's translation of omar khayyam's *rubaiyat,* and Dickens' *a tale of two cities.*
6. In "canto I" the poet Ezra Pound describes an ominous sea voyage to the same mythical land of the dead visited by the hero Odysseus in the *Odyssey,* an epic by the greek poet Homer.
7. The president joined the secretary of state at Dulles international airport for their trip to south america for a conference.
8. Speaking to a reporter from the *County Clarion,* coach Sheila Kim explained the drafting of a team resolution, which read, in part, "Resolved: that we will win all of our games next year."
9. After high school, my cousin Joe completed additional courses at Thompson vocational center and took a job with the Boone electronics company, which makes the electrowhiz circuit board.
10. When one student at Sunrise preschool woefully remarked that he was "tired of resting," the other children quickly agreed.
11. My grandparents lived for many years in the middle west, but when they retired they moved to southern California, finally settling in mecca, a town between palm springs and the salton sea.
12. In ancient egypt the people worshiped many gods equally until the sun god Ra became the principal deity.
13. The Raffles hotel in singapore, a base for many explorers' adventures in the far east, is named after sir Thomas Raffles, who founded the island country as a british colony in 1819.
14. Dr. Bruce Jackson, jr., principal of the high school, formerly taught mathematics I classes and an introductory class in computer science offered to freshmen and sophomores.
15. From the St. Croix island national monument in Maine to the Huleia wildlife refuge in Hawaii, public lands managed by the federal government, including the military, equal a third of the nation's total acreage.

16. Susan o'Rourke, president of the jogging club, has an exercise route that takes her three times a week through Myers park, down Carriage street, and then back west to Dean avenue.
17. The vice-president of the United States automatically takes over if the president dies in office.
18. Shea stadium, near the site of the New York world's fair, is the home of the mets, the national league baseball team in New York.
19. My aunt, who spent some years in the south when she was younger, likes spicy Texas chili.
20. The will of the swedish industrialist and inventor of dynamite, Alfred Nobel, established the Nobel prize to honor those who have benefited the world in the areas of literature, medicine, physics, chemistry, and peace; a prize in economics was added in 1969.

CHAPTER 10 REVIEW: POSTTEST

Identifying Standard Uses of Capital Letters. Number your paper 1–20. Many of the following sentences contain errors in standard capitalization. If a sentence contains an error, write the corrected word, term, or phrase after the proper number. If the sentence is correct as written, write *C* after the proper number.

EXAMPLE 1. Manolo Cruz will be attending Stanford university in the Fall.
1. *University fall*

1. I am studying russian, English, and Art this Semester.
2. Go north for two Streets and then turn east on Central Avenue.
3. The Mountain Ranges in the Western states offer a variety of hiking and hunting experiences for those who love the outdoors.
4. For most Americans, Thanksgiving day is one for family gatherings.
5. Last summer I enjoyed reading *To Kill A Mockingbird* by Harper Lee, a southern writer.
6. HOMES is an acronym for the great lakes: Huron, Ontario, Michigan, Erie, and Superior.
7. Salt Lake City, Utah, is the headquarters of the Church of Jesus Christ of Latter-Day Saints, commonly called the mormon church.
8. Despite their political differences, my mother, a Democrat, and my father, a Republican, work together to increase voter registration.

9. Born in Mississippi, William Faulkner won the Nobel prize in 1949.
10. In the History of the United States, only one person, Gerald R. Ford, has held the nation's highest office without being elected either president or Vice-President.
11. Among the items on display at the Smithsonian institution in Washington, D.C., is the armchair used by Archie Bunker in the comedy series *All in the Family*.
12. The senior class will hold its Prom on Friday, May 14.
13. George Strum, Mayor for two terms, has announced that he will be a candidate again next November.
14. The first American woman in space, Sally Ride, was a member of the crew aboard the space shuttle *challenger* launched from cape Canaveral, Florida, on June 18, 1983.
15. Aldous Huxley's novel *Brave new World,* published in the 1930's, foreshadowed many of the moral dilemmas that would accompany the development of Genetic Engineering in the 1970's and 1980's.
16. My sister Eartha attends Boston University, and my brother Bayard attends the university of Notre Dame.
17. Henry David Thoreau, the New England writer, immortalized a small Massachusetts Pond in *Walden,* an autobiographical account of his two years alone at Walden Pond.
18. Because Mike's letter was addressed to 730 Lexington Place instead of to 730 Lexington Court, it was delayed for six days.
19. America's political and economic interests are closely tied to those of its northern neighbor, Canada, and to those of its southern neighbors, the central American countries.
20. When she came to Washington High School earlier this year, Ms. Morales, our new Principal, quickly earned a reputation as a good Administrator and a caring person.

SUMMARY STYLE SHEET

Kansas **C**ity	a **c**ity in Kansas
Frederick Douglass **N**ational **P**ark	our **n**ational **p**arks
Thirty-first **S**treet	across the **s**treet
Shell **L**ake	a shallow **l**ake
North America	**n**orthern Wisconsin
the Toastmasters' **C**lub	a public-speaking **c**lub
Boeing **C**ompany	an aircraft **c**ompany
Lakeland **H**igh **S**chool	a new **h**igh **s**chool
Black Hawk **C**ollege	
the American **R**evolution	a successful **r**evolution
the Chrysler **B**uilding	a New York City **b**uilding
the **F**ourth of July	the **f**ifth of July
the **S**enior **P**rom	a **p**rom given by **s**eniors
the **J**unior **C**lass	**j**unior **c**lasses
English, **F**rench, **L**atin	**s**ocial **s**tudies, **a**rt, **b**iology
History II	a course in world **h**istory
Fall's coat of many colors	**s**pring, **s**ummer, **w**inter, **f**all
Dean Marsh	Mrs. Marsh, the **d**ean
the **P**resident (U.S.)	the **p**resident of our club
Mayor Smith	a **m**ayor's duties
May **G**od go with you.	tribal **g**ods of the Cherokees
the **S**outh	a mile **s**outh (**n**orth, **e**ast, **w**est)
Tell **M**other (or **m**other).	Tell my **m**other.
Uncle Joe	my **u**ncle
Prell **s**hampoo	
a **M**ethodist, an **A**rab	
*The **P**ickwick **P**apers*	
the ***S**aturday **E**vening **P**ost*	

CHAPTER 11

Punctuation

END MARKS AND COMMAS

Punctuation helps make the meaning of a sentence clear to the reader. Some marks of punctuation indicate in writing the pauses and stops that the voice makes in speaking. They indicate not only where a pause should come but also how long the pause should be—the comma standing for a slight hesitation, the period for a longer one. Other vocal inflections are conveyed by the question mark and the exclamation point.

MECHANICS

DIAGNOSTIC TEST

Correcting Sentences by Adding or Deleting End Marks and Commas. Number your paper 1–20. After the proper number, write all words that are followed by incorrect punctuation, and add or delete end marks and commas in accordance with the standards of written English. If a sentence is correct as written, write C.

EXAMPLES
1. We went to the mall, to the movies, and to our favorite restaurant, this afternoon.
1. *restaurant*
2. Well I think it's a good idea.
2. *Well,*

1. Mr. Stanton will you please give me a reference?
2. The students the teachers and the administrators are looking forward to the long Memorial Day weekend.

3. Jenny Ho will be valedictorian, and Abe Gehrke will be salutatorian.
4. On the first day of the second semester of the school year Botow Okamoto drove up in a sleek red car.
5. Students who do well in academic subjects should in my opinion be commended by their school administrators.
6. When she took her first ride in a hot-air balloon she experienced the amazing silence half a mile above the surface of the earth.
7. Lisa and Conrad arrived on time but everyone else was late.
8. No Sandy will not leave until the fifth of August.
9. Because I need exercise I ride my bicycle six miles each day.
10. Although Alan had worked very hard on his essay Mr. Burar felt it needed more revision.
11. Dolores Garcia a former Olympic swimmer is going to coach at our school next year.
12. Look at the size of the fish I caught.
13. On January 1 2000 my niece will celebrate her twenty-first birthday.
14. Mom or Dad or Uncle Paul will cook dinner tonight.
15. Tomorrow morning before school, the juniors will prepare juice, toast, and ham, and eggs for the seniors.
16. As I looked at the traffic which was backed up as far as I could see I decided to leave the highway and drive along local streets.
17. Please address all complaints to Joseph Redwing Jr Department of Consumer Affairs 4749 Cole Street Eugene OR 97401.
18. In San Francisco the summer temperatures often go no higher than sixty-eight degrees but in nearby San Jose the thermometer often climbs above eighty degrees in the summer.
19. Having suffered from headaches for ten days Mida decided to consult her family physician.
20. My grandmother a maid all her life saved her money and put both of her children through college.

This chapter and the one that follows describe the conventions for punctuating sentences according to the standards of written English and provide exercises to help you fix these uses in your mind. Punctuating exercises is at best an artificial activity, however, and you must be very careful to carry these punctuation principles over into your writing.

Do not overpunctuate. Use a mark for punctuation for only two reasons: (1) because meaning demands it, or (2) because conventional usage requires it.

END MARKS

11a. A statement is followed by a period.

EXAMPLE Spring break begins April 10.

11b. An abbreviation is followed by a period.[1]

EXAMPLES Blvd. Oct. B.C. Messrs.

> ☞ **NOTE** Abbreviations in the metric system are often written without periods.

11c. A question is followed by a question mark.

(1) Distinguish between a statement containing an indirect question and a sentence that asks a question directly.

EXAMPLES Susan wants to know when the first match starts. [a statement containing an indirect question—followed by a period]

Do you know when the first match starts? [a direct question —followed by a question mark]

(2) Polite requests in question form (frequently used in business letters) may be followed by a period; a question mark is also correct.

EXAMPLES Would you please correct my account in this amount.

Would you please correct my account in this amount?

(3) A question mark should be placed inside quotation marks when the quotation is a question. Otherwise, it should be placed outside the quotation marks.

EXAMPLES Harold asked, "Have you heard from Dolores?" [The quotation is a question.]

Could I say, "I just don't want to go"? [The quotation is not a question. The sentence as a whole, however, is a question.]

[1] For a fuller discussion of abbreviations see page 378.

11d. An exclamation is followed by an exclamation point.

EXAMPLES What a wonderful idea**!** You're joking**!**
How lovely**!** Congratulations**!**

(1) Many exclamations begin with either "What a . . ." or "How . . ." as in two of the preceding examples. When you begin a sentence with these words, check the end mark carefully.

(2) An interjection at the beginning of a sentence is usually followed by a comma.

CUSTOMARY Ah**,** there you are!
RARE Ah! There you are!

(3) An exclamation point should be placed inside quotation marks when the quotation is an exclamation. Otherwise, it should be placed outside the quotation marks.

EXAMPLES "What a good movie**!**" exclaimed Mary as she left the theater.
Don't say "It can't be done"**!**

11e. An imperative sentence may be followed by either a period or an exclamation point, depending upon the force intended.

EXAMPLES Please write me a letter**.**
Hold that line**!**

EXERCISE 1. Correcting a Passage by Adding End Marks. Many periods and all exclamation points and question marks have been omitted from the following passage. Copy in a column on your paper all words that should be followed by end marks. After each word, write the end mark required. If a new sentence should begin after the end mark, write the first word of the sentence, giving it a capital letter. Before each word, write the number of the line in which it appears.

EXAMPLE 1. How glad I was to see him alas, he seemed not so glad, but did
2. greet me with, "What a surprise" and asked, "How are you" it
3. had been a long time . . .
1. *him! Alas*
2. *surprise! you?" It*

Lynn Block, Ph D, Director of Research for the Hubert F Langston Soap Company, looked at her calendar. "Oh, no" she groaned. Today she must conduct interviews to hire a new secretary. "How nerve-racking it is when an applicant is unprepared" Nonetheless, she was ready for the 9:00 A.M. interview when 9:00 came, however, the applicant had not arrived.

At 9:35 A.M., the receptionist ushered in the late arrival. "Oh, dear" thought Dr Block as she surveyed the young man's torn jeans, unironed T-shirt, and shaggy hair. To questions about his qualifications, the young man answered only yes or no, and he did not apologize for his lateness when asked about it, he mumbled something about oversleeping. "Gee," Dr. Block puzzled, "this person has good experience and typing skills, but he certainly doesn't seem to want the job."

The next applicant, Ms Smith, was early. In walked a young woman wearing a professional tool belt with well-cared-for carpentry tools around her waist. She said, "I'm so sorry to disturb you I must have taken a wrong turn when I got off the elevator I'm interested in the maintenance position being advertised."

"I'll say" exclaimed Dr. Block. She directed the woman to the maintenance office on the Sixth St side of the building and wished her luck. To herself, she mused, "Whew at this rate, I may never get a secretary." By then the next interviewee had arrived—on time. "Now what" wondered Dr. Block. Looking up to see a neatly dressed young man, she asked, "Are *you* sure you're in the right place it's been a highly unusual morning so far."

He replied, "Oh, yes I'm applying for the secretarial position. I'm very much interested in it" Dr. Block smiled, and the interview proceeded. He gave brief, helpful explanations and asked appropriate questions about the job. About his future career plans, he said "I would someday like to be an office manager I like office work and believe good management is vital to a smooth operation."

"You're right about that" exclaimed Dr. Block. After the interview ended, Dr. Block pondered her choices. She thought, "Well, he doesn't have as much experience or quite as high a typing rate as the first interviewee, but I know whom I'm going to hire"

THE COMMA

The comma—the most frequently used mark of punctuation—is used mainly to group words that belong together and to separate those that do not. Certain other uses have little to do with meaning but are standard ways of punctuating sentences.

Items in a Series

11f. Use commas to separate items in a series.

EXAMPLES She had been a correspondent for the wire service in London, Paris, Rome, and Madrid.

There were books on the desk, posters on the wall, and clothing on the floor.

> ☞ **NOTE** Do not place a comma before the first item or after the last item in a series.

INCORRECT The students in the auto mechanics class learned, to replace the spark plugs, adjust the points, and change the oil, in three different makes of automobiles.

CORRECT The students in the auto mechanics class learned to replace the spark plugs, adjust the points, and change the oil in three different makes of automobiles.

It is permissible to omit the comma before the *and* joining the last two items in a series if the comma is not needed to make the meaning clear. There are some constructions in which the inclusion or omission of this comma affects the meaning of the sentence.

Timepieces may be classified in the following categories: sundials, hourglasses, clocks, watches and chronometers. [four categories]

Timepieces may be classified in the following categories: sundials, hourglasses, clocks, watches, and chronometers. [five categories]

> ☞ **NOTE** Words customarily used in pairs are set off as one item in a series: *bag and baggage, pen and ink, hat and coat, pork and beans,* etc.

For supper they served a tossed salad, spaghetti and meatballs, garlic bread, milk, and fruit.

(1) If all items in a series are joined by *and* or *or*, do not use commas to separate them.

EXAMPLE We can go under or over or around it.

MECHANICS

(2) Independent clauses in a series are usually separated by a semicolon; however, short independent clauses may be separated by commas.

EXAMPLE We talked, we walked, we laughed, and we sang.

11g. Use a comma to separate two or more adjectives preceding a noun.

EXAMPLES She is a creative, intelligent executive.

How can you watch that boring, silly, worthless program?

(1) Do not use a comma before the final adjective in a series if the adjective is thought of as part of the noun.

INCORRECT It was a crisp, clear, invigorating, fall day.
CORRECT It was a crisp, clear, invigorating fall day. [*Fall day* is considered one item. The adjectives modify *fall day,* not *day.*]
CORRECT She hung small, round, delicate Chinese lanterns. [*Chinese lanterns* is thought of as one word.]

(2) If one of the words in a series modifies another word in the series, do not separate them by a comma.

EXAMPLE Why did he wear a bright red cap?

Comma Between Independent Clauses

11h. Use a comma before *and, but, or, nor, for, so,* and *yet* when they join independent clauses, unless the clauses are very short.

EXAMPLES Monday's meeting had gone smoothly, yet I felt a controversy brewing.

I'll go this way and you go that way. [independent clauses too short to require punctuation]

When the conjunction joins two verbs, not two main clauses, a comma is not used.

EXAMPLES Geraldo gave me some good advice and got some from me in return. [The conjunction joins the verbs *gave* and *got.*]

Geraldo gave me some good advice, and I gave him some in return. [The conjunction joins two independent clauses.]

> ☞ **NOTE** Many writers use the comma before these conjunctions only when necessary to keep the meaning clear.

NOT CLEAR We didn't know whether to stay for the weather forecaster had predicted rain.

CLEAR We didn't know whether to stay**,** for the weather forecaster had predicted rain.

As you can see from this example, a reader may easily be confused if the comma is omitted. This is especially true of the comma before the conjunction *for,* which should always be preceded by a comma when it means *because.*

EXERCISE 2. Correcting Sentences by Adding Commas. The following sentences cover rules 30f–h. Number your paper 1–10. For each sentence, write the words that should be followed by a comma, placing the comma after the word. Be prepared to explain the punctuation you use.

1. The police searched everywhere but there were no fingerprints.
2. Albert Levin ordered salad juice and macaroni and cheese.
3. States along the Continental Divide include New Mexico Colorado Wyoming Idaho and Montana.
4. I played the melody on the guitar and the electric bass provided the rhythm.
5. She is a bright charming young woman.
6. We are learning more and more about space through our new and stronger telescopes our huge radar installations and our instrument-packed space probes.
7. At the airport I lost my luggage hat and coat and briefcase.
8. They are responsible for the confusion arose because of statements they made.
9. Young children do not use capital letters consistently and their punctuation is frequently unconventional.
10. The smoke choked us the odor sickened us and the wind chilled us.

MECHANICS

Nonessential Elements

11i. Use commas to set off nonessential clauses and nonessential participial phrases.

A nonessential (nonrestrictive) clause is a subordinate clause that is not essential to the meaning of the sentence but merely adds an idea.

NONESSENTIAL Carla Harris, **who was offered scholarships to three colleges,** will go to Vassar in the fall.

The basic meaning of this sentence is *Carla Harris will go to Vassar in the fall.* The subordinate clause does not affect this basic meaning; it merely adds an idea to the sentence. It is a nonessential clause because it does not limit in any way the word it modifies—*Carla Harris.* Clauses that modify proper nouns are nearly always nonessential.

The opposite of a nonessential clause is an essential (restrictive) clause.

ESSENTIAL Carla Harris is the only senior **who won scholarships to three colleges.**

Here the subordinate clause is essential to the sentence, for without it the sentence would mean something else: *Carla Harris is the only senior.* The subordinate clause limits the meaning of *senior* to [*that*] *senior who won scholarships to three colleges.*

Study the following examples of essential and nonessential clauses until you understand the terms. Note the punctuation: *essential—no punctuation; nonessential—set off by commas.*

ESSENTIAL New Orleans is the city **that interests me the most.**
NONESSENTIAL Pierre, **which is the capital of South Dakota,** is on Lake Sharpe in the center of the state.

ESSENTIAL The man **who said that** is my English teacher.
NONESSENTIAL Mr. Gerz, **who is my English teacher,** said that.

> ☞ **NOTE** Many writers prefer to use *that* rather than *which* to introduce an essential clause that modifies a thing; *which* is acceptable, however.

Sometimes a clause may be interpreted as either essential or nonessential. In such instances the writer must decide which interpretation to give the clause and punctuate it accordingly.

EXAMPLES Dave took his problem to the librarian who is an authority on reference books. [interpreted as essential]

Dave took his problem to the librarian, who is an authority on reference books. [interpreted as nonessential]

Since the punctuation of the first sentence indicates that the clause is essential, the reader assumes that there is more than one librarian. Dave chose the one who is an authority on reference books. From the punctuation of the second sentence, the reader assumes that there is only one librarian and that the librarian is an authority on reference books.

EXERCISE 3. Identifying Essential and Nonessential Clauses. Some of the sentences in this exercise contain essential clauses; others contain nonessential clauses. Number your paper 1–10. If the italicized clause is essential, write *E* after the proper number; if it is nonessential, write *C* to indicate that you would use commas in the sentence.

1. Employees *who always have a ready smile* make the job seem easier.
2. She is wearing the shirt *that she received for her birthday.*
3. Her new shirt *which was a birthday gift* is in her favorite color.
4. People *who are overly nervous* may not make good drivers.
5. Adults *whose development has been studied and recorded* continue to mature, usually in predictable stages, after the age of eighteen.
6. Cities *that seem alike* bear a closer look.
7. School boards *that need to build new facilities* often ask voters to pass a bond issue.
8. The Suez Canal *which is 103 miles long* connects the Mediterranean Sea and the Red Sea.
9. That law *which may have met a real need one hundred years ago* should be repealed or rewritten to deal with today's situation.
10. The Federal Reserve System *which is the central bank of the United States* monitors money and credit growth.

A participial phrase is a group of related words containing a participle (see page 41). Present participles end in *-ing;* past participles of regular verbs end in *-ed* or *-d.*

Like a nonessential clause, a nonessential participial phrase is set off by commas.

NONESSENTIAL My baby brother**, frightened by thunder,** climbed into my lap.
ESSENTIAL A child **frightened by thunder** often needs reassurance.

NONESSENTIAL The scattered band members came together suddenly**, quickly arranging themselves into the first formation.**
ESSENTIAL I watched the scattered band members **quickly arranging themselves into the first formation.**

EXERCISE 4. Correcting Sentences by Adding Commas. This exercise covers all comma rules given up to this point in the chapter.

MECHANICS

After the proper number, write all words in the sentence that should be followed by a comma. Add the comma after each word. Be prepared to explain your answers.

1. Any student who wishes to join the gymnastics team will have to excel in floor exercises on the balance beam and on the uneven parallel bars.
2. The sophomores decorated the gym the juniors provided the refreshments and the seniors took care of the tickets.
3. Anyone taking the basic photography course will learn how to shoot close-ups portraits and still lifes.
4. The judge leaving her chambers stopped to talk to some court reporters who had gathered around her.
5. We got encouragement from everyone but our parents helped us most of all.
6. Careful writers distinguish between *uninterested* which means "indifferent" and *disinterested* which means "unbiased."
7. Any student wishing to sing or act or perform on Class Day should sign up before tomorrow which is the deadline.
8. Governor Quigley whose speeches are filled with clichés appeared on television last night asking people to "tighten their belts bite the bullet pull their own weight and give till it hurts."
9. A mongrel which had followed me halfway home suddenly trotted up to me and staring at me soulfully started to lick my hand.
10. A story that appeared in yesterday's newspaper was about the Toronto Maple Leafs which is my favorite hockey team.

Introductory Elements

11j. Use a comma after certain introductory elements.

(1) Use a comma after words such as *well, yes, no,* and *why* when they begin a sentence.

EXAMPLES Well, what do you think?

Yes, you are welcome to join us.

Why, the whole story sounds suspicious!

(2) Use a comma after an introductory participial phrase.

EXAMPLE **Giggling like a child,** he wrapped the last present.

> ☞ **NOTE** Do not confuse a gerund ending in *-ing* and used as the subject of the sentence with an introductory participial phrase.

EXAMPLES **Cleaning and painting my room** was hard but fun. [gerunds used as compound subject—not followed by a comma]
Cleaning and painting my room, I ran across a favorite ring of mine. [introductory participial phrase—followed by a comma]

(3) Use a comma after a succession of introductory prepositional phrases.

EXAMPLE **At the end of the block next to the old railroad station in Mill Heights,** my grandparents own a small house.

> ☞ **NOTE** A single introductory prepositional phrase need not be followed by a comma unless it is parenthetical (*by the way, on the contrary,* etc.) or the comma is necessary to prevent confusion.

EXAMPLES **By the way,** I heard from Grace Lee yesterday.
With athletes, injuries can end careers.
In the evening I like to visit friends.

MECHANICS

(4) Use a comma after an introductory adverb clause.

EXAMPLE **While Sal put on his tuxedo,** the flute player checked the sheet music.
As soon as we left the house, we heard the phone ring.

EXERCISE 5. Correcting Sentences by Adding Commas. This exercise covers all comma rules to this point in the chapter. Number your paper 1–10. Write the words in each sentence that should be followed by a comma, placing a comma after each word.

1. One draft is not enough for most writers can improve their work by revising it.
2. When they finished playing the drums were moved offstage to make room for the dancers.

3. By the end of the second day of school all students seemed to have found their correct classrooms teachers and lockers.
4. Oh if it's all right with you I'll ask Gloria and Agnes or Leo.
5. In the second half of the third period Johnson evaded the defense caught a twenty-yard pass and raced into the end zone.
6. Speaking at the forum Kay Stone described her experience as head of a household civic fund-raiser and business owner.
7. After a lengthy discussion the committee whose members were not satisfied voted to reject both of the two themes proposed for the prom and seek fresh ideas.
8. Many of those in the long winding ticket line had arrived just within the past hour but we having arrived before dawn held places near the sales window.
9. Regional theaters are prospering in many cities but the Broadway stage is still the goal of most young actors dancers and musicians.
10. As Phil began climbing the ladder began to slip out at the bottom and I immediately grabbed it to keep it in place.

WRITING APPLICATION A:
Using Commas Correctly to Make Your Writing Clear

Introductory participial phrases and adverb clauses lend variety to sentences, helping you avoid a monotonous tone. Unless these introductory elements are punctuated correctly, however, your reader may misread the sentence. Compare the following examples:

EXAMPLES We finished eating. The table was cleared. We played *Monopoly.*
When we finished eating the table was cleared for a game of *Monopoly.*
When we finished eating, the table was cleared for a game of *Monopoly.*

Writing Assignment

Select a famous person who particularly interests you. Write an account of this person's life, including material that is lively and interesting as well as factual. Use introductory participial phrases and adverb clauses to add variety to your writing. Proofread your paper to make sure you have used commas correctly.

Interrupters

11k. Use commas to set off an expression that interrupts a sentence.

Use two commas to set off an expression unless the expression comes first or last in the sentence.

(1) Appositives and appositive phrases are usually set off by commas.

An appositive is a word—with or without modifiers—that is set beside a noun or pronoun and identifies or explains it. An appositive phrase consists of an appositive and its modifiers.

EXAMPLE An interview with Florence Cohen**, the noted landscape architect,** will appear Sunday in the *Herald***, our local paper.**

When an appositive is so closely related to the word it modifies that it appears to be part of that word, no comma is necessary. An appositive of this kind is called a restrictive appositive. Usually it is one word.

EXAMPLES Her cousin **Rita**

The novel ***Arrowsmith***

The preposition ***with***

(2) Words used in direct address are set off by commas.

EXAMPLES Do you know**, Lena,** where your brother is?

Jerry, please see about this.

You seem upset**, my friend.**

(3) Parenthetical expressions are set off by commas.

The following expressions are commonly used parenthetically: *I believe* (*think, know, hope,* etc.), *I am sure, on the contrary, on the other hand, after all, by the way, incidentally, in fact, indeed, naturally, of course, in my opinion, for example, however, nevertheless,* and *to tell the truth.*

EXAMPLES The train will**, I am sure,** be on time.

On the contrary, exercise is relaxing.

That clever Jameson was the first to solve the puzzle**, naturally.**

Knowledge of this rule and of the expressions commonly used parenthetically is helpful in punctuating, but in many instances your intention is what determines the punctuation that you use. If you want the reader to pause, to regard an expression as parenthetical, set it off; if not, leave it unpunctuated. Sometimes, however, the placement of the expression in the sentence determines the punctuation.

EXAMPLES That is **indeed** startling news. [no pause]

That is**, indeed,** startling news. [pause]

Indeed, that is startling news. [comma required by placement]

I hope this report will help clarify the situation for you. [no comma because of placement]

This report will**, I hope,** help clarify the situation for you. [comma required by placement]

EXERCISE 6. Correcting Sentences by Adding Commas. The following exercise covers all comma rules to this point in the chapter. Number your paper 1–10. After the proper number, write the words in each sentence that should be followed by a comma, placing a comma after each word. Write *C* if the item is correct.

1. The plot of that book a murder mystery is in my opinion far too complicated.
2. Polish workers however did not seem to agree with government labor policies for many tried to organize their own trade unions.
3. The nineteenth-century book *El Jíbaro* which was written by Manuel A. Alonso is considered the first Puerto Rican classic.
4. If you quickly get your application in our office will be able to process it before the deadline which is this afternoon.
5. Please understand friends that as much as I would like to I cannot be at the picnic the game and the track meet at the same time.
6. The people riding in the front of the roller coaster were the ones who screamed the most loudly.
7. Looking for economical transportation Harry who had never bought a car before nervously scouted the possibilities at Country Motors which sells used sedans station wagons and pickup trucks.
8. In spite of an initial lack of support Armanda and Julie who were very determined continued their campaign to clean up the vacant lots a task they admitted would take some time.
9. Before you start putting that jigsaw puzzle together Rosa I hope you are sure that it will when completed fit on the table.
10. When Jamie had finished the chicken and potatoes were all gone and the beans carrots and salad had been left untouched.

WRITING APPLICATION B:
Using Commas to Make Your Writing Clear

Like blinking yellow lights at an intersection, the commas before and after certain parenthetical expressions signal the reader to prepare for a change—in this case, a change in the direction of the writer's presentation. Notice in the following example how the commas that set off the parenthetical expression *however* prepare you for the information in the second sentence.

EXAMPLE Leontyne Price's world-famous soprano voice was still powerful and still drew capacity crowds. In 1985, however, she decided to end her operatic career.

Writing Assignment

Write a composition discussing the advantages and disadvantages of the college you will attend or the job you will look for after you graduate from high school. Proofread your paper carefully to make sure you have used commas correctly with parenthetical expressions.

Conventional Uses

MECHANICS

11l. Use a comma in certain conventional situations.

(1) Use a comma to separate items in dates and addresses.

EXAMPLES Hawaii achieved statehood on August 21, 1959, becoming the fiftieth state.

Write to me at 423 Twentieth Street, Salt Lake City, UT 84101, after the first of May. [*Two-letter postal abbreviation used with ZIP code. There is no comma between the state and ZIP code.*]

EXAMPLES Their twins were born on Saturday, March 6, 1982, in Detroit, Michigan.

☞ **NOTE** When only the month and day or only the month and year are given, no punctuation is necessary.

EXAMPLES It was on June 20 that we began rehearsals.
A severe storm hit much of western Europe in January 1985.

When the items are joined by a preposition, do not use commas.

EXAMPLE Joanna lives at 301 Green Street in San Diego, California.

(2) Use a comma after the salutation of a friendly letter and after the closing of any letter.

EXAMPLES Dear Angela, Sincerely yours,

(3) Use a comma after a name followed by *Jr., Sr., Ph.D., etc.*

EXAMPLES Peter Grundel, Jr. Lorraine Henson, Ph.D.

> **NOTE** If these abbreviations are used within a sentence, they are followed by a comma as well:
>
> Hazel Sellers, M.D., will be the guest speaker.

Unnecessary Commas

11m. Do not use unnecessary commas.

The tendency of modern writers is to use commas sparingly. You should be able to show either that the commas you use help the reader to understand what you have written or that they are required by standard usage—as in a date or address, for example. Unnecessary commas are just as confusing to the reader as the absence of necessary ones.

REVIEW EXERCISE. Correcting Sentences by Adding End Marks and Commas. This exercise covers end marks and all comma uses. Rewrite the sentences so that they are punctuated correctly.

1. Stalled in the traffic jam the motorcyclists Carl and Lou who were on their way home settled in to wait.
2. According to that book the history of fine arts is divided into the following periods: classical medieval renaissance baroque neoclassical and modern.
3. Our apartment at 310 Columbia Avenue Fort Wayne Indiana was cozy but I also enjoyed living at 2125 West Third Street in Omaha Nebraska.

4. Jay Carson Jr a senior with good organizational skills arranged for the benefit concert setting the date and ticket sales hiring the musical talent and handling the publicity.
5. In 1936 the library staff at the *Tribune* began recording the newspaper on microfilm and now the library has microfilm copies of every issue from October 14 1858 up to the most recent one.
6. When Jolene who was taking her road test got behind the wheel her mother smiling proudly looked on attentively.
7. On the spur of the moment Lily who was known for her thoughtfulness decided against going to the party and went instead to see Jan her friend who had been hospitalized with appendicitis.
8. As the students watched Dr. Stanford an expert in distillation and a widely published author was demonstrating how to set up the special separation process explaining each step carefully.
9. Our company which we started as high-school seniors can provide all types of home office and factory cleaning services.
10. How disappointed we were to find that our research papers on which we had worked for weeks had been destroyed in the school fire, and Ms Harper had not even had a chance to read them
11. When the doctor informed me that on the one hand only a very small percentage of people suffer a bad reaction to the vaccine and that on the other hand the disease it prevents is nearly always fatal what could I do but agree to have the shot
12. In an address delivered on Tuesday August 3 in Phoenix Arizona she said that the way to peace is through international economic cooperation political understanding and disarmament.
13. Having found a good home the scrawny undernourished kitten had grown into a cat that was small but glossy and beautiful.
14. At the edge of the deep woods along the shore of Goose Lake they made camp for the night.
15. Well if I had wanted to go I would have said so.
16. Surprisingly the secondhand clothes were not torn or dirty or out of style.
17. Why I think it's remarkable that you have already completed the project for the others started before you did
18. The island of Tierra del Fuego named the Land of Fire by the explorer Ferdinand Magellan because of its many Indian bonfires lies off the southern tip of South America in a cold windy climate.

19. Benjamin Banneker a noted inventor astronomer and mathematician served on the commission that surveyed and laid out Washington DC
20. I beg your pardon sir but do I know you

CHAPTER 11 REVIEW: POSTTEST

Correcting Sentences by Adding or Deleting End Marks and Commas. Number your paper 1–25. Most of the following sentences contain errors in the use of end marks or commas. After the proper number, write all words that are followed by incorrect punctuation, adding or deleting end marks and commas in accordance with the standards of written English. If a sentence is correct, write *C*.

EXAMPLE 1. My best friend has moved to 712, Mills Avenue, Orlando, FL 32806.
1. 712

1. Marilyn and Antonio who work at a local child care center greatly enjoy inventing, and playing games with the children.
2. Unfolding solar panels placing satellites into orbit and conducting medical experiments kept the space shuttle crew busy and interested throughout their space flight.
3. Because we had to rekindle the fire our cookout was delayed.
4. Well if you want to apply for admission to eight colleges you will surely have to pay a large sum in application fees.
5. On the beaches of Louisiana Florida and Georgia this has been a summer of boating fishing and swimming.
6. "It is my pleasure to introduce Cranston Fellows Jr. who has recently returned from a visit to Sydney Australia," said Adele Peters president of the Students' Foreign Exchange League.
7. The diplomats both educated at American University in Washington DC received posts in Athens Greece and Nicosia Cyprus.
8. "The house is on fire" shouted my father. "Everyone out."
9. On the far wall to the right of the main entrance you will see a striking oil painting done in matte black, neutral gray and ash white.
10. "November 30 will be the deadline for submitting outlines note cards and thesis paragraphs for your papers," said Ms. Walsh.

MECHANICS

11. Coming home from the football game we were delighted to be greeted by the fragrant spicy aroma of Ned's spaghetti sauce.
12. Studying *Beowulf* for the first time the class enjoyed Grendel the grim gruesome monster.
13. The treasurer's report did I believe make it clear that the Senior Class has been very successful in its fund-raising activities this year.
14. Interrupting his friends Philip asked, "Are you ready to leave"?
15. My aunt and uncle who have been married for twenty-five years plan to visit Egypt Kenya and Sierra Leone next October.
16. Joanne moaned, "Oh this weather is terrible"!
17. We spent the morning cleaning the basement and sorting boxes but in the afternoon we rode our bicycles along lovely country roads.
18. This is an emergency; I need to see a doctor immediately.
19. Naturally the seafood that I like best lobster is also the most expensive.
20. "Mr. President" said the Secretary of State "here is the preliminary draft of the treaty"
21. We have already decided to hold our class reunion on July 4 2008 at the Hyatt Regency Hotel in San Francisco California.
22. Professor Dimitri Pantermalis a Greek archaeologist recently announced the excavation of a rare mosaic dating from the second century AD when Greece was under Roman rule.
23. Much to my delight the festival offered jazz country rock and classical music.
24. Using hyperbole the store took out a full-page newspaper ad reading "World's Most Spectacular Labor Day Sale"!
25. When they went to the prom Martha wore a white lace gown and George wore a light blue tuxedo.

MECHANICS

SUMMARY OF USES OF END MARKS AND COMMAS

11 a. Use a period at the end of a statement.

11 b. Use periods with abbreviations.

11 c. Use a question mark at the end of a question.

11 d. Use an exclamation point at the end of an exclamatory sentence.

11 e. Use either a period or an exclamation point at the end of an imperative sentence, depending on the force intended.

11 f. Use commas to separate items in a series.

11 g. Use a comma to separate two or more adjectives preceding a noun.

11 h. Use a comma before *and, but, or, nor, for, so,* and *yet* when they join independent clauses, unless they are very short.

11 i. Use commas to set off nonessential clauses and nonessential participial phrases.

11 j. Use a comma after certain introductory elements.
(1) After words such as *well, yes, no, why,* etc., when they begin a sentence
(2) After an introductory participial phrase
(3) After a succession of introductory prepositional phrases
(4) After an introductory adverb clause

11 k. Use commas to set off expressions that interrupt the sentence.
(1) Appositives
(2) Words in direct address
(3) Parenthetical expressions

11 l. Use a comma in certain conventional situations.
(1) To separate items in dates and addresses
(2) After the salutation of a friendly letter
(3) After a name followed by *Jr., Sr., Ph.D.,* etc.

11m. Do not use unnecessary commas.

CHAPTER 12

Punctuation

OTHER MARKS OF PUNCTUATION

Although the marks of punctuation treated in this chapter are used less frequently than the period and comma, they are often important. Just as you have learned to follow certain conventions in grammar and usage and spelling, you should observe the conventional uses of the punctuation marks described in this chapter.

DIAGNOSTIC TEST

Correctly Using Punctuation Marks Other Than End Marks and Commas. Number your paper 1–20. Each of the following sentences contains an error in punctuation. Proofread each sentence, and, after the proper number, write as much of the sentence as is necessary to correct the punctuation.

EXAMPLE 1. Looking at Paulas pictures of our Senior Class trip, we felt as though we were back in Washington, D.C.
1. *Paula's*

1. Labor Day traffic was rerouted from the washed-out bridge consequently, a massive backup of cars developed.
2. Who is your favorite mystery writer on the following list, Agatha Christie, P. D. James, Wilkie Collins, or Edgar Allan Poe?

3. One of my favorite Biblical passages is the story of Jesus and the Samaritan woman in John 4-5.
4. Since Lydia visited Europe last summer, she has been using foreign expressions such as bonjour and ciao constantly.
5. The class judged the commercials to have little appeal for teenagers or adults, that is, they considered the ads suitable only for children younger than thirteen.
6. "How long will it take for the pictures of the class play to be developed"? I asked.
7. Our English class agreed that Richard Connell's short story The Most Dangerous Game is one of the best we have ever read.
8. The confusion occurred because I thought the gift was your's instead of Dorothy's.
9. "Because we have recorded a twenty three percent increase in productivity," stated the factory owner to his employees, "each of you will receive a bonus in your next paycheck."
10. Its anyone's guess who will win the election for student council officers next week.
11. Please turn down the radio I'm getting a headache from the vibrations.
12. Outstandingly successful people, whether they excel in politics, sports, or the arts, share a common trait: they are self motivated.
13. We might and according to the tour schedule should have a free afternoon in Rome.
14. Juanita asked the librarian for: the *Readers' Guide to Periodical Literature* and the latest *World Almanac.*
15. According to my sister, a college sophomore, her sociology professor expects his students to read "The New York Times" each day before attending class.
16. When we finish school at 2-15, I'll drive you home.
17. "You may not realize that auto mechanics are skilled specialists", said Mr. Busch on our first day in Auto Mechanics I.
18. Because I have spent so many happy times there, I love to visit my grandmother's and grandfather's house.
19. "The second string team will begin practice as soon as the varsity players have left the field," announced Coach Carberry.
20. Since I am on a tight budget, I was glad to see the ad announcing a special sale on mens' jeans.

THE SEMICOLON

12a. Use a semicolon between independent clauses not joined by *and, but, or, nor, for, yet,* or *so.*

EXAMPLES Three candidates have filed for the new commission seat**;** none of them have any previous experience in public office.

Read all the choices**;** don't write the first answer that seems correct.

You must have some basis for deciding whether to express two independent clauses with a semicolon between them, or two sentences with a period (and capital letter). In most writing, the division into sentences is preferable. A semicolon is used only when the ideas in the two clauses are so closely related that a period would make too distinct a break between them.

12b. Use a semicolon between independent clauses joined by such words as *for example, for instance, that is, besides, accordingly, moreover, nevertheless, furthermore, otherwise, therefore, however, consequently, instead,* or *hence.*

EXAMPLES Everyone in this area takes visitors to our local tourist attraction**; for instance,** I went there just last Sunday with my visiting aunt.

The speech was long and repetitious**; consequently,** listeners fidgeted in their seats and whispered among themselves.

When the connectives mentioned in this rule are placed at the beginning of a clause, the use of a comma after them is frequently a matter of taste. When they are clearly parenthetical (interrupters), they are followed by a comma. The words *for example, for instance,* and *that is* are always followed by a comma. The word *however* is almost always followed by a comma.

EXAMPLES Leaders of the two countries saw no hope for a settlement**; that is,** each claimed the other was stubborn and unwilling to compromise.

Leaders of the two countries saw no hope for a settlement**; however,** they were willing to meet again. [. . . they were willing, *however,* to meet again.]

Most of the words listed in this rule, however, are rarely used at the beginning of a clause. They are usually placed later in the clause.

EXAMPLE The situation is intolerable**;** we **therefore** need to take immediate action.

12c. A semicolon (rather than a comma) may be needed to separate independent clauses joined by a coordinating conjunction when there are commas within the clauses.

EXAMPLE Super Stop, the store on Falk Avenue, sells not only groceries but also prescription drugs, cosmetics, hardware, garden supplies, and sportswear; and its first shoppers, interviewed on the news last week, seemed very pleased with the convenience the store offers.

> ☞ **NOTE** As suggested in Rule 12c by the words "may be needed," you are allowed considerable leeway in applying this rule. When there are only one or two commas in the independent clauses, the semicolon is not needed. It is required when there are so many commas, as in the example above, that the sentence would be confusing without the semicolon.

12d. Use a semicolon between items in a series if the items contain commas.

EXAMPLE Winners in the competition were Alene Murphy, first place; Jeff Bates, second place; Ed Davis, third place; and Nancy Green, who, as a member of the Student Council, had proposed the contest.

WRITING APPLICATION A: Using Semicolons to Make Your Writing Clear

Determining the amount of information to include in a single sentence is an important part of writing clearly. You can help your reader understand that ideas are closely related by using semicolons to join independent clauses. In the following example the semicolon links two independent clauses, signaling the reader that the ideas are closely related:

EXAMPLE I am much more tolerant than I used to be; for example, my little brother's teasing no longer bothers me.

Writing Assignment

Write a composition comparing and contrasting yourself as you are now—not just physically, but intellectually and emotionally—and as you were three years ago. Proofread it carefully to make sure you have used semicolons correctly to join independent clauses expressing closely related ideas.

THE COLON

12e. Use a colon to mean "note what follows."

(1) Use a colon before a list of items, especially after expressions like *as follows* and *the following*.

EXAMPLES Amazingly enough, the small bag held everything**:** shirts, pants, sweaters, a jacket, shoes, underwear, nightclothes, toiletries, and a present for my hosts.

Be prepared to answer the following questions**:** What was your last job? Why did you leave it? What other experience have you had? [list introduced by "the following"]

> ☞ **NOTE** When a list constitutes the direct object of a verb or the object of a preposition, do not use a colon.

EXAMPLES We **collected** blankets, canned goods, medical supplies, and clothing for the flood victims. [list is direct object]

Dan has always been interested **in** snakes, frogs, lizards, and other reptiles. [list is object of preposition *in*]

(2) Use a colon before a long, formal statement or quotation.

EXAMPLE Dr. Stafford made the following observation**:** Cooperation between the leading nations of the world is essential to the survival of the planet. [Note that a formal statement of this kind need not be enclosed in quotation marks.]

MECHANICS

(3) Use a colon between independent clauses when the second clause explains or restates the idea in the first.

EXAMPLE Those hanging lamps are the most popular kind**:** they are inexpensive, come in many colors, and are easy to install.

12f. Use a colon in certain conventional situations.

(1) Use a colon between the hour and the minute when you write the time.

EXAMPLE 8**:**00 A.M.

(2) Use a colon between chapter and verse in referring to passages from the Bible.

EXAMPLE Proverbs 3:3

(3) Use a colon between volume and number or between volume and page number of a periodical.

EXAMPLES *Harper's* 203:16 [volume and number]
Harper's 203:16-19 [volume and page numbers]

(4) Use a colon after the salutation of a business letter.

EXAMPLES Dear Ms. Ayala: Gentlemen: Dear Sir or Madam:

WRITING APPLICATION B:
Using Colons Correctly to Make Your Writing Clear

Since the semicolon and the colon serve completely different purposes, it is important to distinguish between them in your writing. Your reader relies on these marks to know whether to expect, for example, an independent clause closely related to the preceding one (after a semicolon) or a list (after a colon). In the first example, below, the misuse of a semicolon for a colon is misleading.

EXAMPLES Three committees were set up for the banquet; awards, decorations, and food.
Three committees were set up for the banquet: awards, decorations, and food.

Writing Assignment

You are serving on the awards committee for a banquet to honor outstanding writers in the senior class. Decide what kind of awards to present and how many, and write a letter ordering the items. Proofread it carefully to make sure that you have used colons correctly.

UNDERLINING (ITALICS)

12g. Use underlining (italics) for titles of books, films, plays, television programs, periodicals, works of art, ships, etc.

EXAMPLES The Old Man and the Sea
the San Diego Tribune, or the San Diego Tribune
the Senior Scholastic
the View of Toledo, Appalachian Spring, The Thinker
the Norway, the Garden State Special, the Columbia

The use of quotation marks for titles is now generally limited to short compositions such as short stories, short poems, parts of publications and episodes of television programs; the titles of the publications and television programs themselves are underlined. (Compare page 246.)

EXAMPLE Read Chapter 39, "Americans in the Second World War (1941–1945)," from Rise of the American Nation.

> ☞ **NOTE** When set in type, underlined words are italicized.
> *The Old Man and the Sea* the *Senior Scholastic*

The words *a, an, the,* written before a title, are underlined only when they are part of the title. Before the names of magazines and newspapers, they are not underlined.

EXAMPLE I found some good ideas for my paper in my text, The History of the Americas, and in several back issues of the New York Times.

12h. Use underlining (italics) for words, letters, and figures referred to as such and for foreign words not yet adopted into English.

EXAMPLES The most common English word is the; the letters used most frequently are e and t; and numbers often confused are 7 and 9.

I know the Latin phrase ab initio—it reminds me of all the setbacks I've ever had—but the saying ad astra per aspera gives me hope.

EXERCISE 1. Using Colons, Semicolons, and Italics Correctly. Number your paper 1–10. After the proper number, write the words and numbers that should be followed by a semicolon or a colon, and write the appropriate punctuation after each. Write and underline all words that should be italicized.

1. From 1970 to 1981, one-parent families doubled in number however, two-parent families in 1981 still comprised nearly 80 percent of families with children.

2. Performers in the show included the following band members playing two instruments apiece Tony Fleming, trumpet and trombone Donna Bryant, clarinet and saxophone and Phyllis Ward, drums and steel guitar.
3. Our local paper, the Morning Ledger, always carries these features comics, advice columns, and a crossword puzzle.
4. Interesting stories are plentiful in the Bible two of my favorites are the battle between David and Goliath in I Samuel 17 4–57 and the story of the good Samaritan in Luke 10 25–37.
5. Groups of art students, all going to see Egyptian, Assyrian, and Greek exhibits, boarded the buses at 8 30 but the buses did not leave until 9 00, when the parking lot was finally cleared and the last stragglers had boarded.
6. Ms. Bell often assigns reading in current magazines for instance, our latest one runs as follows The Atlantic, 218 33–44 U.S. News and World Report, 26 5 Changing Times, 8 62–67.
7. According to historians, Michelangelo always thought of himself first as a sculptor his sculpture the Pietà is the only work he ever signed.
8. She revised her report three times first, for content second, for organization and third, for style.
9. Legislators were in a difficult position they had to finance demand for increased services without calling for increased taxes.
10. While downtown, I bought several gifts a cookbook for my father a print of Rousseau's The Jungle for my mother and for my sister, the album featuring the soundtrack of Annie.

MECHANICS

QUOTATION MARKS

12l. Use quotation marks to enclose a direct quotation—a person's exact words.

DIRECT QUOTATION My sister said, "My favorite singer is Lena Horne."

Do not use quotation marks to enclose an indirect quotation—one that does not give a person's exact words.

INDIRECT QUOTATION My sister said her favorite singer is Lena Horne.

Enclose means to place quotation marks at both the beginning and the end of a quotation. Omission of quotation marks at the end of a quotation is a common error.

(1) A direct quotation begins with a capital letter.

EXAMPLE She told me, "Finish this assignment first."

Exception: If the quotation is only a fragment of a sentence, do not begin it with a capital letter:

EXAMPLE A reviewer called the movie "**a** futile attempt to trade on his reputation as a maker of blockbusters."

(2) When a quoted sentence is divided into two parts by an interrupting expression such as *he said* or *Mother asked,* the second part begins with a small letter.

EXAMPLE "Take care," he warned, "that you don't spill anything."

If the second part of a divided quotation is a new sentence, it begins with a capital letter.

EXAMPLE "Don't open the door," he pleaded. "**W**e're developing the film."

(3) A direct quotation is set off from the rest of the sentence by commas or by a question mark or an exclamation point.

EXAMPLES Flo said**,** **"**We could send them a telegram."
"What would you say to that**?"** she asked.

> ☞ **NOTE** If the quotation is only a phrase, do not set it off by commas.

EXAMPLE For him, **"**one for all and all for one**"** is the key to a successful club.

(4) Other marks of punctuation, when used with quotation marks, are placed according to the following rules:

1. *Commas and periods are always placed inside the closing quotation marks.*

EXAMPLE **"**I'm sure**,"** said Joe, **"**that we'll be finished by Friday**."**

MECHANICS

2. *Semicolons and colons are always placed outside the closing quotation marks.*

EXAMPLES "Eva," my grandmother said, "you should keep up with your chores"; then she reminded me that it was my turn to wash the dishes.

Gail Sloan describes the following as "deserted-island reading": *An Encyclopedia of World History,* the complete works of Shakespeare, and *Robinson Crusoe.*

3. *Question marks and exclamation points are placed inside the closing quotation marks if the quotation itself is a question or an exclamation; otherwise they are placed outside.*

EXAMPLES "Is everyone present?" asked the teacher.

"How perceptive you are sometimes!" she exclaimed.

Were you surprised when he said, "You win"?

Stop saying "You know"!

No more than one comma or one end mark is used at the end of a quotation.

INCORRECT Who said, "No one can make you feel inferior without your consent."? [two end marks, period and question mark]

CORRECT Who said, "No one can make you feel inferior without your consent"?

INCORRECT Did you ever ask yourself, "Where will I be ten years from now?"?

CORRECT Did you ever ask yourself, "Where will I be ten years from now?"

(5) When you write dialogue, begin a new paragraph every time the speaker changes.

EXAMPLE "Hi, guys. Look what I just got!" said Jessie as she came up to her friends Mark and Sue. She was cradling a sophisticated new 35mm camera in her hands.

"That's beautiful!" said Sue.

Raising his eyebrows, Mark said, "Where did you get it?"

"Oh, I got a great deal at the camera shop—and a loan from my mother."

"How," they both asked at once, "will you pay her back?"

"Well, I have my part-time job," said Jessie. "I'm also going to take pictures for people—at a modest price, of course. Say," she added, "wouldn't you two like to have your pictures taken?"

(6) When a quoted passage consists of more than one paragraph, place quotation marks at the beginning of each paragraph and at the end of the entire passage, not at the end of each paragraph.

> ☞ **NOTE** Usually such a long quotation is set off from the rest of the paper by indentation and single spacing. In such a case, no quotation marks are necessary.

(7) Use single quotation marks to enclose a quotation within a quotation.

EXAMPLE What she said was, "For Tuesday read Masefield's poem 'Sea Fever.' "

12j. Use quotation marks to enclose titles of short works such as poems, short stories, articles, songs, and individual episodes of television programs; and of chapters and other parts of books.

EXAMPLE Read Chapter 19, "The Progressive Movement."
My favorite episode of *Star Trek* is "The Trouble with Tribbles."

> ☞ **NOTE** Book titles and names of magazines are indicated by underlining (italics) (see page 241).

12k. Use quotation marks to enclose slang words, technical terms, and other expressions that are unusual in standard English.

Use this device sparingly.

EXAMPLES I don't think he is a "nerd."

The names Kansas and Arkansas are derived from the Sioux Indian word for "downstream people."

EXERCISE 2. Using Punctuation Marks Correctly. Rewrite the following sentences, inserting quotation marks, other required punctuation, and capitalization.

1. How many of you Mrs. Martinez asked have studied a foreign language for more than two years.
2. Nice try Donna was what the coach said.
3. We should have started our homework earlier said Beth we have answered only three questions so far.

4. Where have you been she asked.
5. Someone once asked George Bernard Shaw how old he was, and he answered I'm as old as my tongue and a few years older than my teeth.
6. To whom was Stendhal referring asked Mrs. Ross when he dedicated his novels to the happy few.
7. Was it Elizabeth Browning asked Sandra who wrote the poem Shall I Compare Thee to a Summer's Day?
8. Cast off shouted the captain we're bound for Rio.
9. Would you let us hand in our research papers next week Ms. Lewis we asked none of the books we need are in the library.
10. Alice whispered thank you for lending me the article Is There Life on Other Planets?

THE APOSTROPHE

12l. To form the possessive case of a singular noun, add an apostrophe and an *s*.

EXAMPLES Dora's choice Kelly's coat Ross's sleeve

In words of more than one syllable that end in an *s*-sound, it is permissible to form the singular possessive by adding the apostrophe without the *s*. This is done to avoid too many *s*-sounds.

EXAMPLES the seamstress' work Odysseus' travels

> ☞ **NOTE** Since the use of the apostrophe varies among writers, it is not possible to make a hard and fast rule about the apostrophe in singular words ending in *s*. Thus *Hughes' poetry* and *Hughes's poetry* are equally acceptable. Punctuate according to pronunciation. If you say a word as "Hugheses" or "McCullerses," write "Hughes's" and "McCullers's." If you say "Hughes" poems or "McCullers" novels, write "Hughes'" and "McCullers'."

(1) To form the possessive case of a plural noun ending in *s*, add only the apostrophe.

EXAMPLES girls' team the Millses' back yard

> **NOTE** The few plural nouns that do not end in *s* form the possessive by adding the apostrophe and an *s* just as singular nouns do.

EXAMPLES women's tournament
children's playground

(2) Personal pronouns in the possessive case (*his, hers, its, ours, yours, theirs,* and the relative pronoun *whose*) do not require an apostrophe.

INCORRECT We thought the top score was her's.
CORRECT We thought the top score was **hers.**

INCORRECT I have witnessed democracy at it's best.
CORRECT I have witnessed democracy at **its** best.

INCORRECT Who's notebook is this?
CORRECT **Whose** notebook is this?

(3) Indefinite pronouns (*one, everyone, everybody,* etc.) in the possessive case require an apostrophe and an *s*.[1]

EXAMPLES **Everyone's** vote counts equally.
She consented to **everybody's** request for a class meeting.

EXERCISE 3. Proofreading Possessives. Number your paper 1–20. If the possessive case for each item in the list has been correctly formed, write *C* after the proper number. If it has been incorrectly formed, write the correct form.

1. everyone's share
2. bus' windows
3. children's books
4. this school's reputation
5. pants' cuffs
6. Is this your's?
7. a girl's or a boy's bike
8. opened it's covers
9. flower's bud
10. The loss is our's.
11. a street of lawyer's offices
12. at the Gibb's home
13. that nation's debts
14. women's objections
15. found it's way home
16. travelers' briefcases
17. soldiers knapsacks
18. did its best
19. babie's toys
20. the poets' works

MECHANICS

[1] Note the correct form of such words used with *else:* everyone *else's;* somebody *else's*. Note that there is no apostrophe in *oneself.*

(4) In hyphenated words, names of organizations and business firms, and words showing joint possession, only the last word is possessive in form.

HYPHENATED **father-in-law's** hobby

ORGANIZATIONS The **Economic and Social Council's** members
Black and Decker's tools

JOINT POSSESSION **Dotty and Fay's** report

Exception: When the second word is a possessive pronoun, the first word is also possessive.

INCORRECT Dotty and my report
CORRECT **Dotty's and my** report

(5) When two or more persons possess something individually, each of their names is possessive in form.

EXAMPLE **Tom's** and **Bill's** jackets

(6) The words *minute, hour, day, week, month, year,* etc., when used as possessive adjectives, require an apostrophe. Words indicating an amount in cents or dollars, when used as possessive adjectives, require apostrophes.

EXAMPLES a minute's work, five minutes' work
a day's rest, three days' rest[1]
one cent's worth, five cents' worth

EXERCISE 4. Revising Phrases by Forming Possessives. In the following list, the possessive relationship is expressed by means of a phrase. Revise each item so that the possessive case of the noun or pronoun is used to express the same relationship.

EXAMPLE 1. a vacation of two weeks
1. *a two weeks' vacation*

1. hats of Carol and Pat
2. dressing room of the men
3. job of my sister-in-law
4. character of a person
5. business of Jorge and Ralph
6. speech of the governor-elect
7. a pause of a moment
8. worth of two cents
9. highlights of the film
10. shoes of the women
11. insignia of the sergeant-at-arms

[1] Also correct: a three-day rest, etc.

MECHANICS

12. worth of four dollars
13. catalog of Lord and Taylor
14. prize of Ralph Bunche
15. sides of it
16. remarks of the judges
17. trip of Maria and Alma
18. a wait of an hour
19. heat of the sun
20. albums of Simon and Garfunkel

12m. Use an apostrophe to show where letters have been omitted in a contraction.

A contraction is a word made up of two words combined into one by the omission of one or more letters.

EXAMPLES For *do not,* the contraction is *don't.* [The letter *o* is omitted.]
For *it is,* the contraction is *it's.* [The letter *i* is omitted.]
For *they are,* the contraction is *they're.* [The letter *a* is omitted.]

> ☞ **NOTE** The most common error in the use of the apostrophe comes from the confusion of *it's,* which means *it is,* with the possessive form *its* (*its* appearance). Another common error is the insertion of the apostrophe in the wrong place: *does'nt* for *doesn't,* etc. Also note that *let's* in an expression such as "Let's go!" is a contraction of *let us* and requires an apostrophe.

12n. Use the apostrophe and *s* to form the plurals of letters, numbers, and signs, and of words referred to as words.

EXAMPLES *Hawaii* is spelled with two *i*'s.
He correctly placed the decimal before the two *6*'s.
Don't you need +'s in that equation?
Try not to use so many *very*'s in your writing.

MECHANICS

EXERCISE 5. Proofreading Possessives and Contractions and Revising Phrases by Forming Possessives. Number your paper 1–20. Write the following phrases and sentences, inserting apostrophes where they are needed and changing the phrases to possessive forms. If an item is correct, write *C.*

1. womens sports
2. statements of a mayor-elect
3. Its great, isn't it?
4. sand in its gears
5. Its still early, Im sure.
6. If he lets us, well go too.
7. Her cousins choices were the same as hers.
8. Lets see whats going on.
9. I've found its no help.

10. firm of Dun and Bradstreet
11. Whats its title?
12. on a minutes notice
13. locker of Frank and Carlos
14. Whos on Vickys bicycle?
15. this pianos keys
16. How many *i*s are there in *Mississippi*?
17. childrens magazine
18. Her scores were a 9.0 and two 8.5s in the freestyle event.
19. books of Woodward and Bernstein
20. office of the principal

THE HYPHEN

12o. Use a hyphen to divide a word at the end of a line.

Try to avoid dividing words at the end of a line in order to maintain an even margin unless it is necessary. For rules that will help you in deciding where to place the hyphen, see page 379.

12p. Use a hyphen with compound numbers from *twenty-one* to *ninety-nine* and with fractions used as adjectives.

EXAMPLES **forty-two** applicants
a **two-thirds** majority, *but* **two thirds** of the voters

12q. Use a hyphen with the prefixes *ex-*, *self-*, *all-*; with the suffix *-elect*; and with all prefixes before a proper noun or proper adjective.

EXAMPLES

ex-mayor	non-European
self-controlled	anti-Fascist
all-star	pro-Canadian
president-elect	Pan-American

Variant spellings exist (*reelect, re-elect, reëlect*), but the modern tendency is to close up most other prefixes (*reelect*).

12r. Hyphenate a compound adjective when it precedes the word it modifies.

EXAMPLE well-liked author The author is well liked.

> ☞ NOTE Do not use a hyphen if one of the modifiers is an adverb ending in *-ly*.

EXAMPLES highly polished surface quickly done task

12s. Use a hyphen to prevent confusion or awkwardness.

EXAMPLES re-collect [prevents confusion with *recollect*]
anti-icer [avoids the awkwardness of *antiicer*]

THE DASH

12t. Use a dash to indicate an abrupt break in thought.

EXAMPLES He might—if I have anything to say about it—change his mind.

The truth is—and you probably already know it—we can't do it without you.

12u. Use a dash to mean *namely, in other words,* or *that is* before an explanation.

EXAMPLE It was a close call—the sudden gust of wind pushed the helicopter to within inches of the power line. [The dash means *that is*.]

In this use, the colon and the dash are frequently interchangeable.

EXAMPLE It was a close call: the sudden gust of wind pushed the helicopter to within inches of the power line.

PARENTHESES

12v. Use parentheses to enclose incidental explanatory matter that is added to a sentence but is not considered of major importance.

EXAMPLE Former Representative Jordan (Texas) was on that committee.

The population of the United States is shifting (see Chart B) to the South and the Southwest.

NOTE Commas, dashes, and parentheses are frequently used interchangeably to set off incidental matter.

(1) Be sure that any material within parentheses can be omitted without changing the basic meaning or structure of the sentence.

IMPROPER USE OF PARENTHESES Tina had been shopping (in that store) most of her life. [The idea in parentheses is too important to the meaning of the sentence to be placed in parentheses.]

(2) Punctuation marks are used within parentheses when they belong with the parenthetical matter. Punctuation marks that belong with the main part of the sentence are placed after a closing parenthesis.

EXAMPLES Fred Bates asked us (What a silly question**!**) if we really thought we could do it.

If the committee is headed by Alison (Is she here**?**)**,** the student council will probably support it.

BRACKETS

You will seldom have a use for brackets. Commas, dashes, and parentheses are preferable as means of setting off parenthetical matter.

12w. Use brackets to enclose explanations within parentheses or in quoted material when the explanation is not part of the quotation.

EXAMPLES Ms. Gray was quoted as saying in her acceptance speech: "I am honored by it **[**the award**]**, but I would like to share the recognition with those who made my work possible."

By a vote of 5–4, the Supreme Court overturned the lower court's ruling. (See page 149 **[**Diagram A**]** for a chronology of the case.)

REVIEW EXERCISE. Proofreading Passages for Punctuation and Capitalization. Most of the necessary punctuation and capitalization has been omitted from the following passages. Rewrite the passage, proofreading it carefully and preparing a version that uses the conventions of standard English. The only changes you need to make in paragraphing are those required by dialogue. Some of the existing punctuation is incorrect, but in most instances you need only *add* punctuation and capitals.

1

No discussion of Americas outstanding sports figures would be complete without reference to Jim Thorpe who was voted in 1950 the greatest athlete of the centurys first half. His feats in football track and baseball remain unique and his strength and speed are legendary born of irish french and indian heritage and reared in prague oklahoma Thorpe began earning

honors early in his life he was an all american halfback for two years while playing for the local indian school and broke all previous records in winning the gold medals for the pentathlon and the decathlon at the 1912 olympic games where he was hailed as the greatest athlete in the world. Because hed already begun playing professional baseball however he was forced to return his medals a year later (They were restored posthumously in 1982) Thorpe spent six outstanding years in professional baseball but he became best known as a football player who could do everything well run pass catch punt and more. He played professional football for over ten years with great ability in 1969 sixteen years after his death and on the national football leagues fiftieth birthday Thorpe was named to footballs all time all professional team.

2

Roger Morton sat back for a moment feeling slightly proud of himself. Have you finished those sample business letters yet asked Ms Zimsky the typing teacher. Yes Roger replied quickly. I think Ive improved on the format too. Look how much space ive saved on each page Ms Zimsky glanced down These arent done the way they are in the book. Just do them that way for now though you need to finish this chapter today or youll be way behind. Theres no time to talk about format. Embarrassed and tired Roger later told his friend Annette about the incident. Your problem she mused isnt that you improved the letters its the same one I had once on my job at bartons shop. I learned that any time you want to change a procedure no matter how great an improvement it is you should first talk it over with the person who will need to approve it. Try discussing your idea again when Ms Zimsky has more time. Roger went back to the typing classroom after school and Ms Zimsky listened thoughtfully to all his suggestions Oh I see what youre doing here she said. Its really a very good idea in fact I think Ill share it with the whole class. See you tomorrow then Roger Yes said Roger with a smile and thanks for listening Ms Zimsky.

CHAPTER 12 REVIEW: POSTTEST

Using Punctuation Correctly. Number your paper 1–25. Each of the following sentences contains at least one error in the use of punctuation or italics. Rewrite the sentence correctly.

EXAMPLE 1. Why did you let your work go until the last minute asked my friend Tanya when I told her my problem?

1. *"Why did you let your work go until the last minute?" asked my friend Tanya when I told her my problem.*

1. When I read The Hobbit, my favorite chapter was the one in which Bilbo meets Gollum.
2. Among the members of the Fine Arts Commission meeting in New York City were several talented people Diane Keaton actress Paul McCartney musician Paul Taylor choreographer and Lee Krasner artist.
3. My brothers and sisters and I have been encouraged to be self reliant since we were children.
4. The origin of the bacterial infection see note below and its cure posed a grave puzzle to the medical experts.
5. Shakespeares Hamlet is a popular play because it involves a ghost murder and romance.
6. I believe we will win this game, said the soccer coach to the newspaper sportswriter.
7. Paulette sent in my application before the deadline however she neglected to put a stamp on the envelope.
8. After we had returned from our class trip to Houston, our teacher Ms Ryan said "we were the most well behaved group she had ever chaperoned."
9. When a graduate of our high school appeared on television playing Scott Joplin's Maple Leaf Rag, a new interest in ragtime music blossomed at Franklin High School.
10. "These packages are your's arent they" asked Tamala as she nearly tripped.
11. Although the oil contract had not been renewed, the oil company made a delivery the customers complained when they received the bill.
12. The mayor elect met today with members of the Allentown Youth Council see picture on page 40.
13. When asked her opinion, the president of the brokerage firm said I favor purchasing blue chips those with a history of steady earnings and stable prices.
14. Monicas noisy muffler makes it impossible for her to drive down the street without attracting attention.
15. Suspending students from school for cutting classes creates a Catch-22 situation, said education consultant Cho Yin Lum.
16. In a stunning upset, said the radio announcer the Liberals have defeated the Conservatives!

17. At Book Lore the bookstore where I work sale's have increased twenty seven percent since last month.
18. Do you know that Europeans write their 7s differently from the way Americans do asked Estrella?
19. Ill never forget the first time I read Walt Whitmans poem When Lilacs Last in the Dooryard Bloom'd said Megan it made me feel the tragedy of Abraham Lincolns death.
20. Have you read this months issue of Seventeen?
21. During the pep rally and even after it had ended the cheerleading captain, Teresa Suarez, led the students in enthusiastic cheering.
22. Within the next three weeks, new television stations will begin broadcasting from the following cities Salinas California Kalamazoo Michigan and Fairbanks Alaska.
23. George Gershwins Rhapsody in Blue is probably the best-known American composition in the world.
24. January 3 is the birthday shared by two world famous writers Cicero and J. R. R. Tolkien.
25. Helena knew it would be a less than perfect day when she heard herself saying Don't forget to dot your ts and cross your is.

CHAPTER 13

Spelling

IMPROVING YOUR SPELLING

This chapter suggests a number of things you can do to improve your spelling:

1. Be careful.
2. Use the dictionary.
3. Keep a list of your own spelling errors.
4. Learn to spell words by syllables.
5. Learn a few helpful spelling rules.
6. Learn to distinguish between words that sound alike.
7. Learn lists of commonly misspelled words.

MECHANICS

GOOD SPELLING HABITS

1. *Be careful.* Care in writing and in proofreading your compositions will eliminate errors in the spelling of simple words like *to, there,* and *its,* which account for so many of teachers' corrections on students' themes.

2. *Use the dictionary.* Some students would rather take a chance on guessing than expose themselves to the truth. But the only sure way to find out how to spell a word is to look it up.

3. *Keep a list of your own spelling errors.* We do not all misspell the same words. The habit of recording in your notebook the words you misspell in your compositions will pay you a large return on the investment of a little time and patience.

4. *Learn to spell words by syllables.* This is the "divide and conquer" technique used with success by invading armies. It is equally effective in attacking a long and troublesome word. Dividing a long word into

syllables gives a number of short parts; hence you can simplify your spelling problem by acquiring the habit of dividing words into syllables and spelling them part by part.

Two common causes of spelling mistakes are the omission of a letter or syllable and the addition of an extra letter or syllable. A student who spells *probably* as though it were *probaly* has made the first kind of mistake. If you spell *lightning* as though it were *lightening*, you have made the second kind. Errors like these stem from errors in pronunciation, which, in turn, are the result of not knowing the exact syllables in the word.

EXERCISE 1. Spelling Words by Syllables. Write each of the following words in syllables—place a hyphen between syllables. When you have completed the exercise and studied the words, take a test on them from dictation. Whether your divisions correspond exactly with the dictionary syllabication is not important, provided the words are divided into pronounceable parts and all letters are included and no letters are added.

1. modern
2. similar
3. library
4. surprise
5. athletics
6. disastrous
7. government
8. privilege
9. perspiration
10. boundary
11. candidate
12. equipment
13. recognize
14. business
15. representative
16. entrance
17. accidentally
18. sophomore
19. quiet
20. mischievous

SPELLING RULES

5. *Learn a few helpful spelling rules.* Although some spelling rules are hopelessly complicated, a few are simple enough and important enough to justify the effort required to master them. Study the following rules and apply them whenever possible in your writing.

ie and *ei*

13a. Write *ie* when the sound is *ē*, except after *c*.

EXAMPLES believe, thief, fierce ceiling, receive, deceive
EXCEPTIONS seize, either, weird, leisure, neither

Write *ei* when the sound is not *e*, especially when the sound is *a*.

EXAMPLES freight, neighbor, weigh, height
EXCEPTIONS friend, mischief

EXERCISE 2. Spelling *ie* and *ei* Words. Write the following words, supplying the missing letters (*e* and *i*) in the correct order. Be able to explain how the rule applies to each.

1. for...gn
2. br...f
3. rel...ve
4. conc...ve
5. v...l
6. n...ce
7. c...ling
8. gr...f
9. p...ce
10. retr...ve
11. sl...gh
12. ach...ve
13. handkerch...f
14. perc...ve
15. s...ge
16. w...rd
17. rec...pt
18. bel...f
19. f...nd
20. l...sure

–cede, –ceed, and –sede

13b. Only one English word ends in *–sede: supersede;* only three words end in *–ceed: exceed, proceed, succeed;* all other words of similar sound end in *–cede*.

EXAMPLES precede, recede, secede, accede, concede

Adding Prefixes

A *prefix* is one or more than one letter or syllable added to the beginning of a word to change its meaning.

13c. When a prefix is added to a word, the spelling of the word itself remains the same.

il + legal = **illegal**
in + elegant = **inelegant**
im + movable = **immovable**
un + necessary = **unnecessary**
a + moral = **amoral**
mis + spell = **misspell**
re + commend = **recommend**
over + run = **overrun**

Adding Suffixes

A *suffix* is one or more than one letter or syllable added to the end of a word to change its meaning.

13d. When the suffixes *–ness* and *–ly* are added to a word, the spelling of the word itself is not changed.

MECHANICS

EXAMPLES mean + ness = mean**ness**
final + ly = final**ly**

EXCEPTIONS Words ending in *y* usually change the *y* to *i* before *–ness* and *–ly:* ready—read**ily**; heavy—heav**iness**; happy—happ**iness**. One-syllable adjectives ending in *y*, however, generally follow Rule 13d: dry—dry**ness;** shy—shy**ly**.

EXERCISE 3. Spelling Words with Prefixes and Suffixes. Spell correctly the words indicated.

1. *rate* with the prefix *over*
2. *habitual* with the suffix *ly*
3. *green* with the suffix *ness*
4. *material* with the prefix *im*
5. *appoint* with the prefix *dis*
6. *apprehend* with the prefix *mis*
7. *practical* with the suffix *ly*
8. *abated* with the prefix *un*
9. *natural* with the prefix *un*
10. *stubborn* with the suffix *ness*
11. *legible* with the prefix *il*
12. *appropriate* with the prefix *in*
13. *appear* with the prefix *dis*
14. *movable* with the prefix *im*
15. *construct* with the prefix *re*
16. *animate* with the prefix *in*
17. *similar* with the prefix *dis*
18. *keen* with the suffix *ness*
19. *avoidable* with the prefix *un*
20. *merry* with the suffix *ly*

13e. Drop the final *e* before a suffix beginning with a vowel.

EXAMPLES care + ing = car**ing** use + able = us**able**

EXCEPTIONS Keep the final *e* before *a* or *o* if necessary to retain the soft sound of *c* or *g* preceding the *e:* noticeable, courageous

MECHANICS

13f. Keep the final *e* before a suffix beginning with a consonant.

EXAMPLES care + ful = care**ful** care + less = care**less**

EXCEPTIONS true + ly = truly argue + ment = argu**ment**
acknowledge + ment = acknowledg**ment** [more usual spelling]

13g. With words ending in *y* preceded by a consonant, change the *y* to *i* before any suffix not beginning with *i*.

EXAMPLES funny—funnier; hurry—hurried; hurry—hurrying

13h. Double the final consonant before a suffix that begins with a vowel if both of the following conditions exist: (1) the word has only one syllable or is accented on the last syllable; (2) the word ends in a single consonant preceded by a single vowel.

EXAMPLES plan + ing = planning [one-syllable word]
forget + ing = forgetting [accent on last syllable; single consonant and single vowel]
cancel + ed = canceled [accent not on last syllable]
prefer + able = pref′erable [accent shifts; not on last syllable]

EXERCISE 4. Spelling Words with Suffixes. Write correctly the words formed as follows:

1. defer + ed
2. defer + ence
3. hope + ing
4. approve + al
5. benefit + ed
6. nine + ty
7. prepare + ing
8. profit + ing
9. write + ing
10. propel + ing
11. desire + able
12. control + ed
13. hope + less
14. move + ing
15. true + ly
16. run + ing
17. singe + ing
18. fame + ous
19. name + less
20. red + est

The Plural of Nouns

13i. Observe the rules for spelling the plural of nouns.

(1) The regular way to form the plural of a noun is to add *s*.

EXAMPLES chair, chairs book, books

(2) The plural of some nouns is formed by adding *es*.

The *e* represents the extra sound heard when *-s* is added to words ending in *s, sh, ch,* and *x*.

EXAMPLES dress, dresses birch, birches
box, boxes bush, bushes

(3) The plural of nouns ending in *y preceded by a consonant* is formed by changing the *y* to *i* and adding *es*.

EXAMPLES fly, flies enemy, enemies lady, ladies

(4) The plural of nouns ending in *y preceded by a vowel* is formed by adding an *s*.

EXAMPLES monkey, monkeys donkey, donkeys

(5) The plural of most nouns ending in *f* or *fe* is formed by adding *s*. The plural of some nouns ending in *f* or *fe* is formed by changing the *f* to *v* and adding *s* or *es*.

EXAMPLES Add *s*: roof, roofs   dwarf, dwarfs   chief, chiefs

Change *f* to *v* and add *s* or *es*:
knife, knives   calf, calves
loaf, loaves   wharf, wharves

(6) The plural of nouns ending in *o preceded by a vowel* is formed by adding *s*. The plural of nouns ending in *o preceded by a consonant* is formed by adding either *s* or *es*.

EXAMPLES *o* following a vowel:
rodeo, rodeos   radio, radios

o following a consonant:
hero, heroes   potato, potatoes
mosquito, mosquitoes

EXCEPTIONS Words of Italian origin ending in *o* that refer to music form the plural by adding *s*: piano, pianos; soprano, sopranos; solo, solos.

(7) The plural of a few nouns is formed by irregular methods.

EXAMPLES child, children   mouse, mice   ox, oxen
woman, women   tooth, teeth   goose, geese

(8) The plural of compound nouns written as one word is formed by adding *s* or *es*.

EXAMPLES cupful, cupfuls
leftover, leftovers
strongbox, strongboxes

(9) The plural of compound nouns consisting of a noun plus a modifier is formed by making the noun plural.

In the following examples, the phrases *in-law* and *of-war* and the adjectives *martial, general,* and *by* are all modifiers. It is the nouns modified by them that are made plural.

EXAMPLES mother-in-law, mothers-in-law
man-of-war, men-of-war
court martial, courts martial
secretary-general, secretaries-general
passer-by, passers-by

(10) The plural of a few compound nouns is formed irregularly.

EXAMPLES drive-in, drive-ins
tie-up, tie-ups
six-year-old, six-year-olds

(11) Some nouns are the same in the singular and the plural.

EXAMPLES sheep, deer, trout, species, Chinese

(12) The plural of some foreign words is formed as in the original language.

EXAMPLES alumnus (*man*), alumni (*men*)
alumna (*woman*), alumnae (*women*)
datum, data
crisis, crises

(13) The plural of other foreign words may be formed either as in the foreign language or by adding *s* or *es*.

EXAMPLES index, indices *or* indexes
appendix, appendices *or* appendixes

> ☞ **NOTE** In certain words the English plural is the preferred one; for example, *formulas* not *formulae*. Whenever there is any doubt about which plural to use, consult the dictionary.

MECHANICS

(14) The plural of numbers, letters, signs, and words considered as words is formed by adding an apostrophe and an *s*.

EXAMPLES If you think there are ten 5's in that column, you'd better count again.
There are two *s*'s in *necessary*.
My last paper was full of 0's, not +'s.
Don't use too many *I*'s in writing your paper.

EXERCISE 5. Writing the Plural Form of Nouns. Write the plural form of each of the following nouns. Be able to explain your spelling on the basis of the rules.

1. candy
2. sheep
3. piano
4. valley
5. alumnus
6. cameo
7. torch
8. chief
9. tomato
10. gas
11. fly
12. alto
13. brother-in-law
14. shelf
15. bench
16. editor in chief
17. spoonful
18. hero
19. knife
20. goose

EXERCISE 6. Explaining the Spellings of Words. By referring to the rules on the preceding pages, explain the spelling of each of the following:

1. misstate
2. stubbornness
3. peaceable
4. ladies
5. alumnae
6. leisure
7. occurred
8. writing (*e* dropped)
9. roofs
10. weigh

WORDS THAT SOUND ALIKE

6. *Learn to distinguish between homonyms, words that sound alike.* These words present problems because they sound alike but have different meanings and different spellings. You probably have had trouble distinguishing between *principle* and *principal, capital* and *capitol,* and other such pairs. Most of the paired words in the following lists sound alike. Some pairs, however, are confused even though they are not pronounced exactly alike.

---

already — *previously*
I had *already* seen the movie twice.

all ready — *all are ready* (or *wholly ready*)
Give the signal when you are *all ready.*

all right — [This word really does not belong in this list, but it is included here because many persons think there is a word spelled *alright,* as though *all right* did have a homonym. There is no word *alright.* The correct spelling is always *all right.*]

---

altar — *a table or stand in a church or a place for outdoor offerings*
The priest was standing beside the *altar.*

alter — *to change*
If we are late, we will *alter* our plans.

MECHANICS

---

altogether *entirely*
She doesn't *altogether* approve of me.

all together *everyone in the same place*
We were *all together* at Christmas.

---

born *given birth*
When were you *born*?

borne *carried*
He has *borne* his hardships bravely.

---

brake *device to stop a machine*
A defective *brake* caused the accident.

break *to fracture, shatter*
Try not to *break* any dishes.

---

capital *city; money or property;* also, as an adjective, *punishable by death* or *of major importance*
Washington is the *capital* of this country.
Killing a police officer is a *capital* offense.
That is a *capital* idea.

capitol *building*
The *capitol* faces a park.

---

cloths *pieces of cloth*
Try the new cleaning *cloths*.

clothes *wearing apparel*
Her *clothes* are expensive.

EXERCISE 7. Selecting Correct Spelling Words to Complete Sentences. Number your paper 1–10. Write after the proper number the correct one of the words given in parentheses in the sentences below.

1. Mother was (all together, altogether) too surprised to protest.
2. Events have (born, borne) out my predictions.
3. If you (brake, break) a window, you will pay for it.
4. When you are (already, all ready) I will help you.
5. Was her work (alright, all right)?
6. We polished the car with (cloths, clothes).
7. We will (altar, alter) the building to suit tenants.

8. The dome on the (capital, capitol) is illuminated at night.
9. The club members were (all together, altogether) only once.
10. When did the Supreme Court rule on (capital, capitol) punishment?

---

coarse *rough, crude*
He wore a suit of *coarse* cloth and used *coarse* language.

course *path of action; part of a meal; a series of studies*
The golf *course* is outside of town.
Soup was the first *course.*
I am taking a *course* in cooking.

---

complement *something that completes or makes perfect*
The *complement* of 50° is 40°. [*completes* a 90° angle]
His part of the job *complements* mine. [Together they *complete* the job.]

compliment *a remark that says something good about a person; to say something good*
I am pleased by your *compliment.*
She *complimented* me on my backhand.

---

consul *representative of a foreign country*
The American *consul* in Quito helped us during our visit.

council, councilor *a group called together to accomplish a job;* a member of such a group is a *councilor*
The *council* met to welcome a new *councilor.*

counsel, counselor *advice; the giving of advice;* one who gives advice is a *counselor*
I accepted the wise *counsel* of my *counselor.*

---

des′ert *a dry region*
We flew across the *desert.*

desert′ *to leave*
She *deserted* her friends in their time of need.

dessert′ *the final course of a meal*
The *dessert* was ice cream.

---

formally *conventionally or properly, according to strict rules*
She spoke *formally* and with great dignity.

formerly *in the past, previously*
I was *formerly* a member of that club.

MECHANICS

---

its [possessive]
The village is proud of *its* school.

it's *it is*
It's a long way.

---

later *more late*
We will arrive *later.*

latter *the second of two*
When given the choice of an apple or an orange I chose the *latter.*

---

lead [present tense] *to go first*
You *lead* and we will follow.

led [past tense]
She *led* the team to victory.

lead [pronounced **led**] *a heavy metal*, also *graphite in a pencil*
The industrial uses of *lead* are many.

EXERCISE 8. Selecting Correct Spelling Words to Complete Sentences. Number your paper 1–10. Write after the proper number the correct one of the words given in parentheses in the sentences.

1. Our (consul, counsel) in Romania has returned to Washington.
2. I enjoyed the dinner but not the (dessert, desert).
3. Avoid (course, coarse) language.
4. I do not enjoy parties conducted as (formally, formerly) as this one.
5. We are not sure which (course, coarse) to follow.
6. Are you sure (its, it's) not too late?
7. I spent five summers working as a camp (councilor, counselor).
8. I spoke to the mayor and the superintendent; the (later, latter) was more helpful.
9. Albert (lead, led) the team to a championship.
10. These shoes (complement, compliment) my blue dress.

---

loose *free, not close together*
The animals broke *loose.*
They stumbled in the *loose* sand.

lose [pronounced **lo͞oz**] *to suffer loss*
When did you *lose* your books?

---

miner — *worker in a mine*
A *miner's* job is sometimes dangerous.

minor — *under legal age; less important*
A *minor* cannot marry without a parent's or guardian's consent.
They raised only *minor* objections.

---

moral — *good;* also *a lesson of conduct*
His good conduct showed him to be a *moral* person.
The class understood the *moral* of the story.

morale — *mental condition, spirit*
The *morale* in our school is excellent.

---

passed — *verb*
The Fiat *passed* me at the finish line.

past — *noun* or *adjective* or *preposition*
Some persons prefer to live in the *past* (n.) because *past* (adj.) events seem more interesting than present ones.
I went *past* (prep.) your house without realizing it.

---

peace — *opposite of strife*
Everyone prefers *peace* to war.

piece — *a part of something*
They ate every *piece* of cake.

---

personal — *individual*
He gave his *personal* opinion.

personnel — *a group of people employed in the same place*
The *personnel* of the company ranged in age from 16 to 64.

---

plain — *not fancy;* also *a flat area of land;* also *clear*
She lives in a very *plain* home.
We crossed the *plains* in two days.
Our problem is *plain*.

plane — *a flat surface;* also *a tool;* also *an airplane*
Plane geometry is a study of imaginary flat surfaces.
The carpenter used a *plane*.
A *plane* circled the airport.

---

principal — *head of a school;* also *the main one of several things*
They went to the *principal's* office.
The *principal* cause of accidents is carelessness.

principle *a rule of conduct;* also a *main fact* or *law*
The judge accused the criminal of having no *principles.*
She understands the *principles* of mathematics.

---

quiet *still, silent*
A study hall should be *quiet.*

quite *completely, wholly;* also *to a great extent or degree*
I had *quite* forgotten her advice.
Angela is *quite* tall.

EXERCISE 9. Selecting Correct Spelling Words to Complete Sentences. Number your paper 1–10. Write after the proper number the correct one of the words given in parentheses in the sentences that follow.

1. All three nations signed a (peace, piece) treaty.
2. Do these printed instructions seem (plain, plane) to you?
3. This store's sales (personal, personnel) are very helpful.
4. The (principal, principle) of solar energy is easy to understand.
5. If you (loose, lose) your concentration, you might (loose, lose) the tennis match.
6. Can you tell the (principal, principle) parts of the verb "to shrink"?
7. Students should remain (quiet, quite) during a study period.
8. Does every fable have a (moral, morale)?
9. On my way to school I always walk (passed, past) the bakery.
10. If you can vote, you are officially no longer a (miner, minor).

---

stationary *in a fixed position*
The classroom desks are *stationary.*

stationery *writing paper*
I received three boxes of *stationery* at Christmas.

---

than conjunction
I am stronger *than* she.

then adverb meaning *at the time*
Wear a green hat; *then* I'll recognize you.

---

there *a place;* also used as an expletive (see pages 26–27)
We were *there* at two o'clock.
There were four of us.

their [possessive]
The pupils bring *their* own lunches.

they're *they are*
They're going with us.

---

to a preposition or part of the infinitive form of a verb
Give the book *to* me, please.
We will have *to* leave early.

too adverb meaning *also* or *too much*
George is a sophomore, *too*.
It is *too* late to go now.

two *one plus one*
We had only *two* dollars.

---

waist *middle part of the body*
She wore a wide belt around her *waist*.

waste *unused material;* also *to squander*
Pollution can be caused by industrial *wastes*.
Don't *waste* your time.

---

who's *who is, who has*
Who's coming?
Who's been here?

whose [possessive]
Whose coat is this?

---

your [possessive]
Is this *your* coat?

you're *you are*
You're a true friend.

MECHANICS

EXERCISE 10. Selecting Correct Spelling Words to Complete Sentences. Number your paper 1–10. Write after the proper number the correct one of the words given in parentheses in the following sentences:

1. They had neglected to lock (there, their) lockers.
2. I wanted to go to camp, (to, two, too).
3. Tie the rope around your (waist, waste).
4. The platform, we discovered when we tried to move it, was (stationary, stationery).

5. No one could remember (whose, who's) name had been drawn first.
6. As soon as (their, they're) printed, we will ship the books.
7. Write your letters on business (stationary, stationery).
8. (Your, You're) lucky to have such a good job.
9. I cannot do any more (then, than) I have done.
10. I was surpised at (you're, your) taking that attitude.

REVIEW EXERCISE. Selecting Correct Spelling Words to Complete Sentences. Number your paper 1–25. After the proper number, write the correct one of the words in parentheses in the following sentences:

1. Columbia is the (capital, capitol) of South Carolina.
2. Have you discussed this problem with your guidance (councilor, counselor)?
3. The vegetation in the (dessert, desert) surprised us.
4. Mrs. Crane (formally, formerly) taught here.
5. Every nation must conserve (its, it's) resources.
6. My companion (lead, led) me down a dark passage.
7. We were (all ready, already) to start before dawn.
8. Try not to (lose, loose) your keys.
9. Success is the best (moral, morale) builder.
10. The new (altar, alter) is made of white marble.
11. I have read Murdoch and Spark, and I prefer the (later, latter).
12. (Its, It's) time to think about getting a job.
13. There was (all together, altogether) no truth in the report.
14. Members of the (counsel, council) are elected annually.
15. (Course, Coarse) wood absorbs more paint than fine-grained wood.
16. My red tie (complements, compliments) my blue suit.
17. Jack (past, passed) the ball to Joe.
18. When you are (all together, altogether), I'll take a group picture.
19. The mission was completed with no loss of (personal, personnel).
20. We prefer (stationary, stationery) seats in our classrooms.
21. There's a student (whose, who's) going to succeed.
22. His act was not outstanding, but it was (alright, all right).
23. The (principals, principles) of democracy are admired.
24. Do you know (they're, their, there) new address?
25. Mrs. Starkey gave our play (complimentary, complementary) reviews.

COMMONLY MISSPELLED WORDS

7. *Learn lists of commonly misspelled words.* Frequent short spelling tests are an effective means of fixing correct spellings in your mind. On the following pages you will find a list of 300 commonly misspelled words. Taking no more than twenty at a time, have these words dictated to you. Study the ones you miss and record them in your list of spelling errors. When you have studied them (divided them into syllables and practiced writing each word several times), write them again from dictation. Spelling tests should be written, not oral.

Three Hundred Spelling Words[1]

abundant
academically
accelerator
accessible
accidentally
acclimated
accommodation
accompaniment
accomplishment
accuracy

acknowledge
acquaintance
adequately
admission
admittance
adolescent
advantageous
aerial
allege
allegiance

alliance
allotting
annihilate
anonymous
apologetically

apparatus
apparent
arousing
arrangement
atheistic

attendance
awfully
ballet
bankruptcy
barbarian
basketball
beggar
behavior
beneficial
bibliography

biscuit
blasphemy
boulevard
bracelet
buffet
bureaucrat
burial
calculation
camouflage
capitalism

carburetor
caricature
catalog
catastrophe
cellar
cemetery
changeable
chassis
Christianity
circumstantial

colossal
communist
comparative
competition
complexion
conceivable
connoisseur
conscientious
consciousness
consistency

controlling
controversy
cruelty
curriculum
debacle

[1] The list does not include the homonyms listed on pages 264–270.

decadent
deceitful
deference
descendant
desirable

despair
detrimental
devastation
devise
dilemma
diligence
disastrous
disciple
discrimination
diseased

dissatisfied
division
ecstasy
efficiency
embarrassment
emperor
emphasize
endeavor
enormous
entertainment

enthusiastically
entrance
environment
espionage
exhaustion
exhibition
exhilaration
expensive
exuberant
familiarize

fascination
fascism
feminine
financier
fission

forfeit
fulfill
fundamentally
gaiety
galaxy

gauge
grammatically
guidance
harassment
hereditary
hindrance
horizontal
hospital
hygiene
hypocrisy

ideally
idiomatic
incidentally
independent
indispensable
inevitable
influential
ingenious
initiative
innocent

inoculate
institution
intellectual
interference
irrelevant
irresistible
kerosene
laborious
larynx
leisurely

license
liquor
livelihood
luxurious
magistrate

magnificence
maintenance
malicious
manageable
maneuver

marriageable
martyrdom
materialism
meadow
mediocre
melancholy
melodious
metaphor
miniature
mischievous

misspelled
mortgage
mosquito
municipal
mysterious
naive
necessity
neurotic
noticeable
novelist

nucleus
nuisance
nutritious
obedience
occasionally
occurrence
omitting
opportunity
orchestra
outrageous

pageant
pamphlet
paralysis
parliament
pastime

peasant
pedestal
penicillin
perceive
permanent

permissible
persistent
perspiration
phenomenon
physician
picnicking
playwright
pneumonia
politician
precede

presence
prestige
presumption
prevalent
privilege
procedure
propaganda
propagate
prophesy
prove

psychoanalysis
pursue
quietly
rebellion
receive
recommendation
reference
referred
rehearsal
relieve

reminiscent
remittance
representative
resources
responsibility
reveal
safety
seize
separation
sergeant

siege
significance
souvenir
specimen
sponsor
statistics
strategic
stubbornness
succeed
succession

summed
superintendent
supersede
suppress
surroundings
susceptible
symbolic
symmetrical
symphonic
synonymous

tariff
temperament
temperature
tendency
theoretical

tolerance
tomorrow
tortoise
traffic
tragedy

transcend
transparent
tried
twelfth
tyranny
undoubtedly
universal
unmistakable
unnatural
unnecessary

unscrupulous
vaccine
vacuum
valedictory
variation
vaudeville
vehicle
vengeance
versatile
vigilance

villain
vinegar
visage
welcome
whisper
whistle
withhold
yacht
yawn
yield

SENTENCE STRUCTURE

CHAPTER 14

Sentence Completeness

FRAGMENTS AND RUN-ON SENTENCES

Two kinds of sentence errors are all too common: fragments and run-on sentences. The first is the writing of only part of a sentence, a *fragment,* as though it were a whole sentence, with a capital letter and a period. The second is the writing of two or more sentences as though they were one sentence. The writer mistakenly uses a comma, or no punctuation at all, between the sentences. You may think of these two sentence errors as opposites. The fragment is not complete; the run-on sentence is more than complete.

SENTENCE FRAGMENTS

A group of words is a complete sentence when it has a subject and a verb and expresses a complete thought.

COMPLETE After the flood the barn roof lay in the yard.
INCOMPLETE After the flood the barn roof in the yard
INCOMPLETE After the flood the barn roof lying in the yard

Because they lack a verb, the last two examples do not express a complete thought. Words ending in *-ing,* like *lying,* are not verbs when they are used alone. To serve as the verb in a sentence, such words need a *helping verb* to form a verb phrase (see page 13).

NO VERB	After the flood the barn roof lying in the yard
VERB PHRASE	After the flood the barn roof **was lying** in the yard.

14a. A *sentence fragment* is a group of words that does not express a complete thought. Since it is part of a sentence, it should not be allowed to stand by itself.

The Phrase Fragment

A phrase is a group of words acting as a single part of speech and not containing a verb and its subject.

There are many kinds of phrases (participial, gerund, appositive, prepositional, infinitive), but regardless of their kind, they all have one important characteristic—they are parts of a sentence and must never be separated from the sentence in which they belong. When a phrase is incorrectly allowed to stand by itself, it is a fragment.

Study the ways in which the unattached phrase fragments in the following examples are corrected.

FRAGMENT	Last Saturday I saw Gloria. Riding her new ten-speed bicycle. [This participial phrase fragment modifies the word *Gloria.* It should be included in the sentence with the word it modifies.]
FRAGMENT CORRECTED	Last Saturday I saw Gloria **riding her new ten-speed bicycle.**
FRAGMENT	We pitched our tent on the north side of the lake. At the edge of a grove of pine trees. [This prepositional phrase fragment modifies the verb *pitched* and belongs in the sentence.]
FRAGMENT CORRECTED	We pitched our tent on the north side of the lake **at the edge of a grove of pine trees.**
FRAGMENT	My parents finally gave me permission. To go with Gail to the game at West Point. [Here, an infinitive phrase fragment has been separated from the word *permission,* which it explains.]
FRAGMENT CORRECTED	My parents finally gave me permission **to go with Gail to the game at West Point.**
FRAGMENT	Aunt Deborah came bearing gifts. A wristwatch for Jean and a ring for me. [This appositive phrase fragment belongs in the sentence preceding it, separated by a comma from *gifts,* the word to which it refers.]

FRAGMENT CORRECTED Aunt Deborah came bearing gifts, **a wristwatch for Jean and a ring for me.**

The Subordinate Clause Fragment

Another type of fragment is the subordinate clause that is incorrectly separated from the sentence in which it belongs. A clause is a group of words containing a subject and predicate and used as a part of a sentence. A subordinate clause does not express a complete thought and should not stand alone.

FRAGMENT The orchestra played "A Night in the Tropics." Which Louis Gottschalk wrote in 1859.

FRAGMENT CORRECTED The orchestra played "A Night in the Tropics," which Louis Gottschalk wrote in 1859.

14b. Do not separate a phrase or a subordinate clause from the sentence of which it is a part.

EXERCISE 1. Revising to Eliminate Fragments. Some of the items in this exercise consist of one or two completed sentences; others contain sentence fragments. Number your paper 1–10. If all the parts of an item are complete sentences, write *C.* If an item contains a fragment, revise it to include the fragment in the sentence.

1. Elizabeth Blackwell was born in 1821. And died in 1910.
2. When, in 1832, her parents could no longer tolerate the social and political situation in Bristol, England. They immigrated with their eight children to New York.
3. A few years later Elizabeth established a school for girls. Feeling depressed by the economic plight of her family.
4. A woman friend, dying of cancer, suggested that Elizabeth, who loved to study, become a doctor. At first, Elizabeth totally rejected this suggestion.
5. In spite of herself, the idea of being a doctor plagued Elizabeth. Leading her to inquire into the possibility of a woman studying medicine.
6. When told that it would be impossible for a woman to become a doctor, she became determined to follow her friend's advice. Not certain how she should proceed against the forces of prejudice.

7. Finally, in 1847 and after many rejections, the Medical Institution of Geneva College in northern New York State accepted Elizabeth Blackwell. Now known as Hobart College.
8. She graduated in 1849 at the head of her class. A young woman convinced that she was right and determined to change ideas about education.
9. She was not content with being the first woman in the United States to gain an M.D. degree from a medical school. Elizabeth Blackwell spent the next two years of her life doing graduate work in Europe.
10. In 1857 Elizabeth Blackwell established the New York Infirmary for Indigent Women and Children, a hospital staffed by women. She decided to open the hospital on May 12, the birthday of her friend Florence Nightingale.

RUN-ON SENTENCES

When a comma (instead of a period, a semicolon, or a conjunction) is used between two complete sentences, the result is a *run-on sentence.* One sentence is permitted to "run on" into the next.

Inexperienced writers make this type of sentence error more often than the fragment error. Usually it results from carelessness in punctuation rather than from lack of understanding. Because the error involves misusing a comma—to separate sentences—it is sometimes referred to as a "comma fault." A worse, but less common, kind of run-on sentence results from omitting all punctuation between sentences.

14c. Avoid the run-on sentence. Do not use a comma between sentences. Do not omit punctuation at the end of a sentence.

RUN-ON SENTENCE Choosing a camera is difficult, there are many on the market.

These two sentences should be either separated by a period or joined into one sentence by a conjunction or a semicolon. There are four ways of correcting the error:

1. Choosing a camera is difficult. There are many on the market.
2. Choosing a camera is difficult, **for** there are many on the market.
3. Choosing a camera is difficult **because** there are many on the market.
4. Choosing a camera is difficult; there are many on the market.

> ☞ **NOTE** Do not be surprised, now that you know to avoid using sentence fragments and run-on sentences, if you occasionally find them in the best newspapers and magazines. To create a particular effect, professional writers do at times write fragments and use the comma between sentences. Leave this use of the comma and the fragment to the experienced judgment of the professional.

EXERCISE 2. Revising Run-on Sentences. The items in this exercise are run-on sentences. Write the final word in the first sentence in each item and follow it with the first few words of the second sentence. Indicate how you would eliminate the faulty comma: for example, a semicolon, a conjunction, a period and a capital letter. Do not be satisfied with using a period and a capital letter in every case; to clarify the relationship between ideas, some of the items should be corrected in other ways.

EXAMPLE 1. Flo didn't hear about the party until Thursday, she had to change her plans.
1. *Thursday; therefore she had . . .*

1. In social studies this year we are studying about ways to solve our major national problems, so far we have covered poverty, unemployment, inflation, and pollution.
2. We have a pet lovebird at home, its call is as harsh and shrill as the screech of chalk on the chalkboard.
3. Lovebirds are comical creatures, they are always busy rearranging objects in their cage.
4. Ynes Mexia, the botanical explorer, discovered rare tropical plants on her expeditions to Mexico and South America, these discoveries were of great value to science.
5. Juan took an art elective and discovered he had talent, now he spends his afternoons in the art room.
6. At an advanced age she began to write the story of her colorful life, at least she thought her life had been colorful.
7. The astounding scientific developments of one generation are accepted commonplaces in the next generation, the computer and the cassette recorder, for instance, are taken for granted today.
8. A new club is being formed for the study of social behavior, instead of just reading, students will do research and conduct interviews.

9. A large suggestion box has been placed in the hall just outside the principal's office, students can, by this means, express their pet peeves about the school, they should not sign their names.
10. First try to do the work by yourself, if you can't do it, ask for help.

EXERCISE 3. Revising to Eliminate Sentence Fragments and Run-on Sentences. The following exercise contains sentence fragments and run-on sentences. Prepare to explain to the class how you would eliminate the sentence errors.

1. I have never known anyone who was a better worker than Paula. Who always did her homework in half the time I took, she usually had it done twice as well, too.
2. I asked Paula to help me with my math once. When I was particularly desperate, I hadn't been getting good grades for several weeks.
3. Mr. Rehman urges all musicians to continue to study their instruments in high school. Because he knows that as they get busier and busier, many students stop taking lessons, sports and other activities cut in on their practice time.
4. A mammoth crane was brought here to lift into place the steel girders. Huge orange-colored beams that were easily set into place. Almost as though they were matchsticks.
5. Everyone was asking me about Stacey. Where she was and what she was doing, wild rumors had been circulating.
6. The city's water supply has been threatened. Very little rain or snow having fallen during the past weeks.
7. I learned to like poetry when I read Kipling, his poems appealed to me. Because of their strong rhythm and their rhyme.
8. I have learned to recognize several kinds of customers. Especially the kind that likes to argue about the merchandise, when I see one of these coming, I duck out of sight.
9. Women's colleges were established in America in the nineteenth century. During the Victorian period. When girls were considered frail flowers to be kept safe and separate.
10. Audiences appeared to enjoy the play, the reviews in the papers, however, were unfavorable.

CHAPTER 15

Coordination and Subordination

RELATIONSHIPS BETWEEN IDEAS IN A SENTENCE

COORDINATE IDEAS

When a sentence contains more than one idea, the ideas may be equal in rank or unequal in rank. Ideas that are equal in rank are *coordinate.* (*Co-* means "equal"; *-ordinate* means "ordered" or "ranked.")

COORDINATE IDEAS Mrs. Carter is an architect, **and** Mrs. Murphy is a lawyer.
We tried everything we could, **but** nothing worked.

The writer of the preceding sentences considered the two ideas in each sentence of equal rank; he gave them equal emphasis by expressing them in independent clauses. The clauses are coordinate clauses.

Clear Relationship Between Coordinate Ideas

The relationship between coordinate ideas is made clear by the word used to connect the two ideas. Different connectives express different relationships. The common kinds of relationship between coordinate clauses are *addition, contrast, choice,* and *result.*

Addition

The following connectives indicate that what follows is supplementary to what precedes.

EXAMPLES I wrote to her, **and** she wrote to me.
I like to get letters; **besides,** hers are amusing.

also	furthermore	besides	moreover
and	likewise	both . . . and	then

Contrast

The following connectives introduce an idea that in some way conflicts or contrasts with what has gone before.

EXAMPLES I wrote to her, **but** she did not write to me.
We are close friends; **nevertheless,** I am angry with her.

but	still	nevertheless
however	yet	

Choice

The following connectives introduce an alternate possibility.

EXAMPLES You write to her, **or** I will write to her.
You write to her; **otherwise,** I will not write to you.

either . . . or	or, nor
neither . . . nor	otherwise

Result

The following connectives state a result or consequence of the preceding statement.

EXAMPLE I wrote to her; **therefore** she wrote to me.

accordingly	hence
consequently	therefore

15a. Make clear the relationship between the ideas in coordinate clauses by using connectives that express the relationship exactly.

A good writer chooses connectives carefully, making certain that they will express exactly the relationship intended between the ideas in the sentence.

If the wrong connective is used, the relationship between the ideas will not be clear. The connectives in the following *not-clear* sentences were poorly chosen.

NOT CLEAR Mr. Bothwell took a vacation, and his health did not improve.
CLEAR Mr. Bothwell took a vacation, **but** his health did not improve. [contrast]

NOT CLEAR The veterans spent a year in the hospital, but they emerged entirely well.

CLEAR The veterans spent a year in the hospital; **consequently,** they emerged entirely well. [result]

> ☞ **NOTE** When used to join coordinate clauses, the words *and, but, yet, or,* and *nor* are usually preceded by a comma.

When used to join coordinate clauses, the words *besides, likewise, furthermore, moreover, however, nevertheless, otherwise, consequently, therefore, hence,* and *accordingly* are usually preceded by a semicolon.

EXERCISE 1. Using Appropriate Connectives. Number your paper 1–10. Determine the logical relationship between the two clauses in each sentence, and write after the proper number what this relationship is: *addition, contrast, choice,* or *result.* Then write an appropriate connective from the preceding lists—the word which will make unmistakably clear the relationship between clauses. Give the correct punctuation mark with each connective.

EXAMPLE 1. The demand exceeded the supply prices remained the same.
1. *contrast ; nevertheless*

1. The students were dismissed at one o'clock nobody went home.
2. Bea was seriously injured in yesterday's practice she will not be able to play in the game today.
3. Jimmy played right end I played left end on the varsity.
4. Deliver the shipment by Friday I will cancel my order!
5. Math is my hardest subject I have never failed a math test.
6. In an auditorium of this size, you must speak louder your audience will not be able to hear you.
7. This magazine publishes the best literary criticism it is a financial failure.
8. The American economy has long depended on a high level of military spending some people fear the economic consequences of ending the arms race.
9. The oil burner had stopped during the night the house was cold when we awoke.
10. We had heard the assignment we hadn't understood it.

SUBORDINATE IDEAS

When ideas in a sentence are unequal in rank, the ideas of lower rank are subordinate. (*Sub-* means "under" or "lower.") If the idea of lower rank is expressed in a clause, the clause is a *subordinate* clause.[1] The main idea of the sentence is expressed in an *independent* clause.

EXAMPLES The pilot, who was a veteran flyer, brought her crippled plane down safely. [Independent clause—greater emphasis: *The pilot brought her crippled plane down safely;* subordinate clause—lesser emphasis: *who was a veteran flyer.*]

Because each of them was politically ambitious, the council members rarely supported one another's proposals. [Independent clause—greater emphasis: *the council members rarely supported one another's proposals;* subordinate clause—lesser emphasis: *Because each of them was politically ambitious.*]

Adverb Clauses

15b. Make clear the relationship between subordinate adverb clauses and independent clauses by selecting subordinating conjunctions that express the relationship exactly.

The relationship between the idea in a subordinate adverb clause and the idea in an independent clause is made clear by the subordinating conjunction that introduces the subordinate clause. The common kinds of relationships between subordinate adverb clauses and independent clauses are *time, cause* or *reason, purpose* or *result,* and *condition.*

Some of the subordinating conjunctions can be used in more than one way and therefore appear in more than one list.

Time

The following subordinating conjunctions introduce clauses expressing a time relationship between the idea in the subordinate clause and the idea in the independent clause.

EXAMPLE Several guests arrived **before** *we were ready.*

after	before	until	whenever
as	since	when	while

[1] For a more detailed explanation of subordinate clauses see pages 56–68.

Cause or Reason

The following subordinating conjunctions introduce clauses expressing the cause or reason for the idea expressed in the independent clause. The subordinate clause tells *why*.

EXAMPLE We stopped **because** *the light was red.*

as since because whereas

Purpose or Result

The following subordinating conjunctions introduce clauses expressing the purpose or the result of the idea in the independent clause.

EXAMPLES Astronauts undergo the most rigorous training **so that** *they will be able to handle any emergency.* [The subordinate clause states the purpose of training described in the independent clause.]

Extreme differences of opinion developed in the committee **so that** *agreement seemed unlikely.* [The subordinate clause states a result of the committee's differences of opinion.]

that in order that so that

Condition

The following subordinating conjunctions state the condition or conditions under which the idea in the independent clause is true. Think of *although, even though, though,* and *while* as meaning "in spite of the fact that." They introduce a condition in spite of which the idea in the independent clause is true.

EXAMPLES **Although** (in spite of the fact that) *it was raining,* we went to the game. [The clause states the *condition* under which we went to the game.]

If *you pass the examination,* you will pass the course. [The clause states under what condition you will pass the course.]

although though provided that if
even though while unless

EXERCISE 2. Using Appropriate Subordinating Conjunctions. Number your paper 1–10. From the preceding lists, choose a subordinating conjunction to fill the blank in each sentence, and write it after the proper number. Make sure the conjunction you choose fits the meaning of the sentence. After the conjunction, tell what relationship it expresses: *cause* or *reason, condition, purpose* or *result,* or *time.*

1. —— you buy a rare manuscript, make certain of its authenticity.
2. William Henry Ireland was one of the most successful forgers —— he was only a teen-ager at the height of his exploits.
3. Ireland began forging Shakespeare manuscripts —— his father had a keen interest in them.
4. —— he forged a document, Ireland had to do careful research on the proper details such a document would require.
5. Special blends of ink were required —— the age would be properly deceptive.
6. Ireland's father published a collection of his son's forgeries —— he considered his son worthy of complete confidence.
7. The skepticism of scholars increased enormously —— it became impossible to answer their objections.
8. Ireland published a confession —— the documents were proved to be fraudulent, and his father's health declined.
9. —— he tried to ease his father's disappointment, the older man died in disgrace at the height of the furor.
10. —— Ireland himself died in 1835, the art of forgery obviously did not die with him.

EXERCISE 3. Using Appropriate Subordinating Conjunctions. Number your paper 1–10. From the lists on pages 286–87, choose an appropriate subordinating conjunction to fill the blank in each sentence. Notice that when an adverb clause begins a sentence, it is followed by a comma.

1. —— we had eaten, we sat by the fireplace and told ghost stories.
2. —— she had not slept well the night before, Melissa did not run as well as her coach had expected.
3. You will solve this problem —— you take one step at a time.
4. —— Van Gogh is now considered a great painter, his work was not appreciated in his lifetime.
5. I bandaged my cut —— it would not become infected.
6. —— you arrived so late, you will have to sit at the back.
7. —— I had ordered two pairs of gloves, the mail-order company sent me two pairs of pants instead.
8. —— the defense attorney made her final plea, the prisoner sat stiffly in a chair.
9. The doctor administered the new antibiotic —— no further complications would arise.

10. Many people fail to enjoy music —— they do not know how to listen properly.

EXERCISE 4. Revising Sentences by Inserting Subordinate Adverb Clauses. Revise each of the following sentences by adding a subordinate clause at the beginning or at the end of each sentence. Vary your choice of subordinating conjunctions.

EXAMPLE 1. The fans filed out of the stadium.
1. *After the game was over, the fans filed out of the stadium.*

1. The heat became unbearable.
2. We started jogging in the afternoons.
3. Arturo agreed to come with us.
4. Lauren began clapping enthusiastically.
5. You will not have enough time to finish the composition.

Adjective Clauses

The subordinate clauses in the preceding exercises are *adverb* clauses. Subordinate *adjective* clauses are also helpful in clarifying the relationship between ideas because they permit a writer to emphasize one idea above another.[1] A writer may, for instance, wish to express the following ideas in one sentence: *Sacajawea acted as interpreter for explorers of the West. She was a Lemhi Indian.* To emphasize that Sacajawea acted as interpreter, the writer places this information in an independent clause and subordinates the other idea by placing it in an adjective clause.

> **Sacajawea,** who was a Lemhi Indian, **acted as interpreter for the explorers of the West.**

On the other hand, for a different purpose, the writer may wish to change emphasis by reversing the positions of the ideas.

> **Sacajawea,** who acted as interpreter for explorers of the West, **was a Lemhi Indian.**

15c. Make clear the relative emphasis to be given ideas in a complex sentence by placing the idea you wish to emphasize in the independent clause and by placing subordinate ideas in subordinate clauses.

EXERCISE 5. Revising Complex Sentences with Adjective Clauses. Change the emphasis in each of the following sentences by

[1] Adjective clauses may begin with *who, whom, whose, which, that* and *where.*

placing in the independent clause the idea that is now in the subordinate clause and by placing in the subordinate clause the idea that is now in the independent clause.

1. *Z,* which is a voiced palatal fricative, is the last letter of the English alphabet.
2. Dictionary listings, which end with words beginning with *z,* proceed alphabetically.
3. *Zeal,* which comes from an ancient Greek word meaning "jealousy," is one of the more familiar words found there.
4. Animal lovers, who may not welcome the name, can be called *zoophiles.*
5. *Zymurgy,* which means "the chemistry of fermentation," results in good wine and ends at least one dictionary.

CORRECTING FAULTY COORDINATION

Faulty coordination occurs when two unequal ideas are placed in coordinate clauses as though they deserved equal emphasis.

FAULTY COORDINATION The Governor was a native of Ohio, and she was elected for a third term. [ideas of unequal rank]

The two ideas in this sentence are vastly different. It is unlikely that a writer would wish to give them equal rank. The faulty coordination can be corrected by placing one of the ideas in a subordinate position. Which idea the writer puts in the subordinate clause will depend on the purpose.

FAULTY COORDINATION CORRECTED **The Governor,** who was a native of Ohio, **was elected for a third term.**

or **The Governor,** who was elected for a third term, **was a native of Ohio.**

15d. Faulty coordination may be corrected by placing ideas of lesser emphasis in a subordinate position. An idea may be given less emphasis by being expressed in a subordinate clause or a modifying phrase or an appositive.[1]

(1) Subordination may be accomplished by a subordinate clause.

FAULTY COORDINATION The books are on the new-book shelf, and they may be borrowed for a week.

CORRECTED BY AN ADJECTIVE CLAUSE The books **that are on the new-book shelf** may be borrowed for a week.

[1] For the use of subordination in eliminating choppy sentences and in achieving sentence variety, see pages 324–29. For the use of subordination in correcting stringy sentences, see pages 337–38.

CORRECTED BY AN ADVERB CLAUSE **If the books are on the new-book shelf,** they may be borrowed for a week.

EXERCISE 6. Revising Sentences by Correcting Faulty Coordination. Clarify the relationship between ideas in the following examples of faulty coordination by placing one of the ideas in a subordinate clause, either an adverb clause or an adjective clause. Choose carefully the subordinating conjunctions that introduce your adverb clauses.

1. I am taking a course in bookkeeping this year, and I will have a better chance of getting an office job this summer.
2. Mr. and Mrs. Davis have donated a hundred books to our school's library, and they own a large bookstore in town.
3. Columbia College was originally named King's College, and it was established by King George III of England.
4. Mosquitoes and gnats buzzed around our heads, and we still had an enjoyable picnic in the park.
5. Nora and I heard that a course in photography would be given in the spring, and we signed up for it.

(2) Subordination may be accomplished by a modifying phrase.

FAULTY COORDINATION The house is at the end of the street, and it is very modern in design.

CORRECTED BY A MODIFYING PHRASE The house **at the end of the street** is very modern in design.

(3) Subordination may be accomplished by an appositive.

An appositive is a word, with or without modifiers, which follows a noun or pronoun and helps to explain it.

FAULTY COORDINATION Ms. Fitch is the manager of the store, and she is tall and attractive.

CORRECTED BY AN APPOSITIVE Ms. Fitch, **the manager of the store,** is tall and attractive.

EXERCISE 7. Revising Sentences by Correcting Faulty Coordination. Revise the following sentences by correcting the faulty coordination in the ways prescribed.

Revise by inserting a modifying phrase:

1. The call was to abandon ship, and it came from the captain.
2. I need to find a recent magazine article, and it should be about the process of digital recording.
3. The woman was playing the accordion, and she had a repertoire of hundreds of folk songs.
4. Neal hit a line drive to left field, and it happened with two out and runners on first and third.
5. The bottle contained ammonia, and it fell onto the floor and spilled.

Revise by inserting an appositive:

6. Mr. Miller is the custodian of our building, and he came to this country only three years ago.
7. The new ruler is a woman of great experience in government, and she should be able to reconcile the factions in the country.
8. The violin was an instrument with a beautiful tone, and it belonged to my grandfather.
9. This passenger plane is the fastest one in the world, and it will take you to Europe in record time.
10. Her new book is a volume of poetry, and it got very good reviews.

SUMMARY

(1) Make clear the relationship between ideas in a sentence by using connectives that express the relationship exactly.

(2) Correct faulty coordination by placing ideas of lesser emphasis in a subordinate position. Use a subordinate clause or a modifying phrase or an appositive.

EXERCISE 8. Revising Sentences. The relationship between ideas in the following sentences is not clear: the conjunctions used are not exact, or the sentences contain faulty coordination. Revise the sentences. Some may be revised in more than one way.

1. The Bay Challenge Cup represents the highest achievement in sailing, and it was first put up for competition in 1903.
2. The principle that government employees shall not strike has been challenged, and it applies to both federal and state employees.

3. High school graduates are better educated today than ever before, and they have a hard time finding jobs.
4. The final chapters of this book outline a constructive program dealing with the problem, and they are the most important.
5. Every business has several ambitious competitors, and no business can afford to stand still.
6. The new regulations call for the opening of school at 7:30 every morning, and they are unpopular with both students and teachers.
7. Mr. Greenberg was a high-school coach for many years, and he is now coaching college teams in Ohio.
8. Representatives came from more than fifty countries, and they met in the United Nations Building in New York City.
9. The title of the book was interesting, and the book itself was dull.
10. The potato season was poor, and the potato farmers managed to avoid going into debt.
11. Miss Lang had not directed many plays, and she knew how to manage an inexperienced cast.
12. Helen may go to Wellesley next year, and she may go to Barnard.
13. Carl has taken piano lessons for only three years, and he is already a good pianist.
14. Mr. Stark has never paid back the money he borrowed, and he wants me to lend him more.
15. We waited on the corner for an hour, and the bus didn't come.
16. The Commercial High School is a large stone building on Market Street, and it is attended by students from all over the city.
17. Stewart Harrison was a famous detective, and he could not solve the arsenic murder case.
18. Miss Armstrong has been selling advertising for many years, and she has been made advertising director of the *Herald*.
19. I am going to the airport to meet a friend, and she is from Ohio.
20. Professor Drake had been head of the chemistry department for twenty years, and she died yesterday.

CHAPTER 16

Clear Reference

PRONOUNS AND ANTECEDENTS

The meaning of a pronoun is clear only when you know what it refers to. The word to which a pronoun refers is its *antecedent*. For example, the sentence "He was talking with them" has little meaning unless you know to whom the pronouns *he* and *them* refer.

In the following sentences, arrows connect the pronouns and their antecedents.

I asked Mr. Jordan for the answer, but he didn't know it.

The Potters have a new sailboat on which they intend to cruise.

Handing George the coat, the salesclerk said, "Try this on for size."

16a. A pronoun must refer clearly to the right antecedent. Avoid *ambiguous* reference, *general* reference, and *weak* reference.

Charlie is always thinking about cars. *It* [*cars?*] is his only interest. [The antecedent cannot be substituted; the reference is faulty.]

One simple way of testing pronoun reference is to substitute the antecedent for the pronoun.

Charlie is always thinking about cars. *They* [*cars*] are his only interest. [The antecedent fits.]

AMBIGUOUS REFERENCE

(1) Avoid *ambiguous reference.* Ambiguous reference occurs when a pronoun refers confusingly to two antecedents so that the reader does not know at once which antecedent is meant.

AMBIGUOUS The President appointed Senator Moore as chairman because he was convinced of the importance of the committee's work.

Here the pronoun *he* can refer to either the President or Senator Moore. The context in which such a sentence appears will ordinarily provide readers with the clues they need to identify the antecedent. Occasionally, however, the use of a pronoun that can refer to more than one antecedent causes momentary confusion. Such ambiguous reference can usually be avoided by rephrasing the sentence.

CLEAR The President, convinced of the importance of the committee's work, appointed Senator Moore as chairman.

CLEAR Because Senator Moore was convinced of the importance of the committee's work, the President appointed him as chairman.

Occasionally, the only way to avoid ambiguity is to replace the pronoun with the appropriate noun:

AMBIGUOUS The partnership between Jones and Potter ended when he drew the firm's money from the bank and flew to Brazil.

CLEAR The partnership between Jones and Potter ended when Jones drew the firm's money from the bank and flew to Brazil.

EXERCISE 1. Revising Sentences by Correcting Ambiguous Pronouns. Find the ambiguous pronoun in each of the following sentences. Make the sentence clear either by revising it or by replacing the pronoun with a noun.

1. Fay was arguing with Jane, and she looked unhappy.
2. One of the passengers told the bus driver that she didn't know the route very well.
3. Right after the accountant sent in a report to the treasurer, she became very much alarmed.
4. Raise the viewfinder to your eye, turning it slowly to the right until it is focused.
5. Our job was to remove the labels from the old bottles and wash them.

GENERAL REFERENCE

(2) Avoid *general reference.* General reference occurs when a pronoun refers confusingly to a general idea that is only vaguely expressed.

The pronouns *which, this, that,* and *it* are commonly used in a general way.

GENERAL The boys wore ski boots to their classes which the principal disapproved of.

In this sentence the pronoun *which* refers to the general idea, *the wearing of ski boots to class;* however, the pronoun is placed so that it appears to refer to *classes.*

CLEAR The principal disapproved of **the boys' wearing** ski boots to class.

In the next example, the pronoun *it* does not have a clear antecedent. A definite noun makes the meaning clear.

GENERAL Great ships were moving slowly up the harbor; tugs and ferryboats scurried in and out among them; here and there a white cabin cruiser sliced sharply through the blue water under the suspension bridge. It was thrilling to a young farmer.

CLEAR The **sight** was thrilling to a young farmer.

Although you can sometimes correct general reference by merely substituting a noun for the unclear pronoun, you will often find it necessary to revise the entire sentence.

GENERAL In her act Maria told jokes, did impersonations, and sang comic songs. This amused her audience.

CLEAR Maria amused her audience by telling jokes, doing impersonations, and singing comic songs.

EXERCISE 2. Revising Sentences by Correcting General References. The following sentences contain examples of general, or vague, reference. Revise the sentences or replace the unclear pronouns with nouns.

1. The Chinese were bitter when Russia withdrew its technical assistance; they said it would harm the Chinese economy.
2. Macbeth's mind was constantly imagining horrible things, and that frightened him.
3. I enjoyed the author's style and the type of characters she wrote about. It made me want to read her other books.

4. Rabbi Meyer came to the house daily, from which a sturdy friendship grew.
5. A great deal of effort went into planning the expedition, hiring the right sort of men, and anticipating every emergency, which accounts for the success of the undertaking.

WEAK REFERENCE

(3) Avoid *weak reference.* Weak reference occurs when the antecedent has not been expressed but exists only in the writer's mind.

WEAK We spent the day on a fishing boat, but we didn't catch a single one.

In this sentence there is no antecedent of the pronoun *one*. The adjective *fishing* is not the antecedent, since it is fish, not fishing, that *one* refers to. The writer meant the pronoun to stand for the noun *fish*.

CLEAR We spent the day on a fishing boat, but we didn't catch a single **fish.**
CLEAR We spent the day on a fishing boat trying to catch some **fish,** but we didn't catch a single **one.**

In other words, the antecedent of a pronoun should be a noun. When the antecedent is "hidden" in a modifier or a verb form, the reference is weak.

WEAK The people want honest public servants, but that has not always been a virtue of politicians.

In this sentence the antecedent should be the noun *honesty,* but the noun is "hidden" in the adjective *honest.* Correct the sentence by replacing the weak pronoun with a noun.

CLEAR The people want honest public servants, but **honesty** has not always been a virtue of politicians.

In the next sentence, the antecedent of *it* should be the noun *writing,* which is "hidden" in the verb *wrote.*

WEAK Lois wrote whenever she could find the time, but none of it was ever published.
CLEAR Lois wrote whenever she could find the time, but none of **her writing** was ever published.
CLEAR Lois found time for her **writing** whenever she could, but none of **it** was ever published.

Correct weak references by replacing the weak pronoun with a noun or by giving the pronoun a clear antecedent.

EXERCISE 3. Revising Sentences by Correcting Weak References. The following sentences contain examples of weak references. Revise the sentences by correcting the weak references.

1. I take many pictures with my camera and consider it an enjoyable hobby.
2. Being neighborly is important because you may need their help someday in an emergency.
3. She was a virtuoso violinist, but she never owned a valuable one.
4. She is highly intelligent, but she hides it from people she doesn't know well.
5. Our guide said the Pueblo village was well worth seeing, but it would take three hours.

INDEFINITE USE OF PRONOUNS

16b. In writing, avoid indefinite use of the pronouns *it, they,* and *you.*

The indefinite use of *it, they,* and *you* occurs in ordinary conversation but is not acceptable in writing.

INDEFINITE In the final chapter it implies that the hero died a martyr's death.
BETTER **The final chapter** implies that the hero died a martyr's death.

INDEFINITE On this flight to California, they serve meals without charge.
BETTER On this flight to California, **meals** are served without charge.

INDEFINITE In some countries, you don't dare express political views openly.
BETTER In some countries, **the people** don't dare express political views openly.

> NOTE The expressions *it is raining, it seems, it is late* are, of course, entirely correct.

EXERCISE 4. Revising Sentences by Correcting Faulty References. The sentences in this exercise contain examples of ambiguous, general, and weak references. There are some examples of the indefinite use of *it, they,* and *you.* Revise the sentences either by replacing a faulty pronoun with a noun, or by revising the entire sentence. Make the meaning unmistakably clear.

1. Golf wouldn't cost me so much if I didn't lose so many in the rough.
2. The radiator was leaking badly; it ran all over the garage floor.
3. In the cabin he checked the fuel. In those days this might mean the difference between life and death.
4. She overcame her hip injury which doctors had said was impossible.
5. Her spelling and sentence structure are not good, but most of it is due to carelessness.
6. Ruth saw Julie when she was in town last week.
7. In yesterday's editorial, it says the mayor has failed to live up to his campaign promises.
8. The witness testified that she had seen the accused when she was eating dinner in the dining car, which convinced the jury of her presence on the train.
9. The library does not have enough copies of some of the books in greatest demand by students writing research papers, which makes it hard for you.
10. In Washington they are skeptical about the success of the new farm program.

CHAPTER 17

Placement of Modifiers

MISPLACED AND DANGLING MODIFIERS

A modifier should clarify or make more definite the meaning of the word it modifies. If the modifier is placed too far from this word, the effect of the modifier may be either lost or diverted to some other word.

MISPLACED MODIFIERS

17a. Place phrase and clause modifiers as near as possible to the words they modify.

A misplaced modifier may mislead the reader or force him to reread the sentence in order to understand its meaning.

CONFUSING Two meetings have been held to make arrangements for a return bout in the office of the State Athletic Commission.

Although most readers know that the return bout is not likely to be held *in the office of the State Athletic Commission*, they may be momentarily distracted by this interesting thought. Placing the phrase next to *held*, the word it modifies, makes the sentence clear.

CLEAR Two meetings have been held in the office of the State Athletic Commission to make arrangements for a return bout.

CONFUSING I bought a small computer for the accounting staff, which gave everyone a great deal of trouble.

The computer, not the staff, gave everyone trouble. The clause *which gave everyone a great deal of trouble* should be next to *computer*.

CLEAR I bought the accounting staff a small computer, which gave everyone a great deal of trouble.

CONFUSING The thief decided to make a run for it when he saw the police officer, abandoning the stolen car and dashing into the woods.

This sentence would be clearer if, on first reading, it did not give the impression that the police officer was abandoning the stolen car and dashing into the woods. Moving the adverb clause *when he saw the police officer* to the beginning of the sentence makes it clear that the thief, not the police officer, ran away.

CLEAR When he saw the police officer, the thief decided to make a run for it, abandoning the stolen car and dashing into the woods.

The usual way to clarify a sentence containing a misplaced modifier is to move the modifier next to the word it modifies. In the sentence above, however, moving the participial phrases next to *thief* changes the meaning of the sentence: *The thief, abandoning the stolen car and dashing into the woods, decided to make a run for it when he saw the police officer.* Often, you can improve a sentence by moving an adverbial modifier (in this instance *when he saw the police officer*) to the beginning of the sentence.

The important factor in the placement of modifiers is that you make yourself clear at first reading. Do not try to hide behind the weak explanation, "You know what I mean."

EXERCISE 1. Revising Sentences by Correcting Misplaced Modifiers. The following sentences may be confusing on first reading because of a misplaced phrase or clause. Revise the sentences by placing modifiers near the words they modify. You may find that placing an adverbial modifier first often improves the sentence.

1. Major Evans was decorated for his action but was haunted by the memory of the men who had died in the battle years later.
2. The company now runs a late bus for skiers leaving at 6:15.
3. One of our observers sighted a plane through binoculars that she could not identify.

4. The causeway has a drawbridge to permit the passage of fishing boats from which all fishing is prohibited.
5. The community center was built by Mrs. Borden, who later became Mrs. Gruber, at a cost of $800,000.
6. At Tuesday's meeting, the mayor discussed the enormous cost of filling in the Buskill Swamp with city council members.
7. Father bought a gadget for his new car from a fast-talking salesclerk that was guaranteed to reduce gas consumption.
8. She wore a straw hat on the back of her head which was obviously too small.
9. Ms. Steinberg, the explorer, described her trips through the jungle in our social studies class.
10. Uncle Jim bought a new carriage for the baby that was named "Boodle Buggy."

DANGLING MODIFIERS

17b. A modifying phrase or clause must clearly and sensibly modify a word in the sentence. When there is no word that the phrase or clause can sensibly modify, the modifier is said to dangle.

DANGLING MODIFIER Carrying a heavy pile of books, her foot caught on the step.

An introductory participial phrase (see pages 41–43) modifies the noun or pronoun following it. In this example, the phrase *carrying a heavy pile of books* appears to modify *foot.* Since a foot could not carry a pile of books, the phrase cannot modify it sensibly. The phrase, therefore, is a dangling modifier. You can correct the sentence in two ways:

1. By adding a word that the phrase can sensibly modify.

   Carrying a heavy pile of books, **she** caught her foot on the step.

2. By changing the phrase to an adverb clause.

   While she was carrying a heavy pile of books, her foot caught on the steps.

Study the following examples of dangling modifiers and the ways in which they have been corrected.

DANGLING MODIFIER Representing the conservative point of view, the liberals rebutted her.

CORRECTED Representing the conservative point of view, she was rebutted by the liberals.

CORRECTED Since she represented the conservative point of view, the liberals rebutted her.

DANGLING MODIFIER To win the baseball championship this year, Luis and Oscar should join our team.

CORRECTED If we are to win the baseball championship this year, Luis and Oscar should join our team.

CORRECTED To win the baseball championship this year, we should get Luis and Oscar to join our team.

A few dangling modifiers are either so idiomatic as to be entirely acceptable or so clear that no possible confusion can result. The following examples are not objectionable:

> Relatively speaking, the cost of living has remained static for several years.
> To be perfectly frank, the rate of inflation is still too high.

EXERCISE 2. Revising Sentences by Correcting Dangling Modifiers. Each of the following sentences contains a dangling modifier. Revise the sentences by correctly placing the modifiers.

1. Left alone in the house, the thunderstorm terrified him.
2. Enormous and architecturally striking, everyone is impressed by the new building.
3. When selecting a college, the social life seems to interest some students more than education.
4. While talking with friends, the topic of dentistry came up.
5. After flying in darkness for two hours, the moon rose, and navigation became less difficult.
6. To keep the guacamole dip from turning brown, its surface should be covered with a thin layer of mayonnaise.
7. After working in the fields all day, little strength was left for social activities.
8. To understand many of the allusions in modern literature, a knowledge of Greek and Roman myths is essential.
9. Having promised to be home by midnight, the family was annoyed when I came in at two o'clock.
10. Riding in the glass-bottomed boat, hundreds of beautiful tropical fish could be seen.

TWO-WAY MODIFIERS

A third way in which a careless writer sometimes causes confusion is by placing a modifier in such a way that it may be taken to modify two words. As a result, the reader cannot be sure which of the two possible meanings is intended. Such a modifier is called a *two-way*, or a *squinting*, modifier.

EXAMPLE Mary said *during the meeting* Jo acted like a fool.

Since the phrase *during the meeting* may be taken to modify either *said* or *acted*, this sentence is not clear. Did Mary say this during the meeting, or did Jo act like a fool during the meeting? The sentence should be revised to make it say one thing or the other.

CLEAR **During the meeting** Mary said Jo acted like a fool.

CLEAR Mary said Jo acted like a fool **during the meeting**.

Here is another example of a two-way modifier:

NOT CLEAR Tell Fred *when he comes home* I want to see him.

CLEAR **When he comes home,** tell Fred I want to see him.

CLEAR Tell Fred I want to see him **when he comes home**.

EXERCISE 3. Revising Sentences by Correcting Faulty Modifiers. The sentences in this exercise contain misplaced, dangling, and squinting modifiers. Revise each sentence so that its meaning will be clear on first reading.

1. The Simpsons gave a toy robot to one of their children with a bullet-shaped glass head and flashing red eyes.
2. Pounding the piano keys with all her might, the chords of the prelude resounded through the concert hall.
3. We saw a herd of sheep on the way to our hotel.
4. To succeed in college, a great deal of time must be spent studying.
5. When only five years old, Dad took me to see my first baseball game.
6. Topped with yogurt, many people love fresh strawberries.
7. While trying to get ready for school, the doorbell suddenly rang.
8. Elaine told Joanne after the first act the drama gets more exciting.

9. By practicing a foreign language daily, great fluency can be gained.
10. A tarantula was shown to me by the museum's curator that had eight legs and a huge, hairy body.
11. Preferring the mountains to the seashore, the Great Smokies were chosen as our vacation spot.
12. After working in Washington for twenty years, the methods of lobbyists were familiar.
13. This bank approves loans to reliable individuals of any size.
14. Being completely untamed, Anita warned us that the animals were dangerous.
15. One can see more than a hundred lakes, flying at an altitude of several thousand feet.
16. Jack bought a book of shorthand lessons along with his new typewriter, which he read and studied diligently.
17. Living constantly under the eyes of the police, her nervousness increased.
18. Plans for a new road have finally been approved after three years of red tape to stretch across the valley.
19. Ramón wanted to know before the game began what the referees said to the two captains.
20. Rounding a sharp curve, a detour sign warned us of danger.

CHAPTER 18

Parallel Structure

STRUCTURES OF EQUAL RANK; FAULTY PARALLELISM

Parallelism in sentence structure exists when two or more sentence elements of equal rank are similarly expressed. Stating equal and closely related ideas in parallel constructions often adds clarity and smoothness to writing.

KINDS OF PARALLEL STRUCTURE

18a. Express parallel ideas in the same grammatical form.

There are three sentence elements which commonly require parallel treatment; coordinated ideas, compared and contrasted ideas; and correlative constructions.

Coordinate Ideas

Coordinate ideas are equal in rank. They are joined by coordinate connectives. The coordinate connectives most often used in parallel structure are *and*, *but*, *or*, and *nor*.

To express parallel ideas in the same grammatical form, pair one part of speech with the same part of speech, a verbal with the same kind of verbal, a phrase with a phrase, a clause with a clause. Do not pair unlike grammatical forms.

FAULTY The committee studied all aspects of the problem—humane, political, and cost. [The adjectives *humane* and *political* are paired with the noun *cost.*]

PARALLEL The committee studied all aspects of the problem—**humane, political**, and **financial**. [All three coordinate elements are adjectives.]

FAULTY According to my teacher, my composition revealed exceptional creative ability but that I make too many spelling errors. [noun paired with clause]

PARALLEL According to my teacher, my composition revealed exceptional creative **ability** but too many spelling **errors**. [noun paired with noun]

PARALLEL According to my teacher, my composition revealed **that I have exceptional creative ability** but **that I make too many spelling errors**. [clause paired with clause]

Compared or Contrasted Ideas

FAULTY Water-skiing no longer interests me as much as to go scuba diving. [gerund *water-skiing* paired with infinitive *to go*]

PARALLEL **Water-skiing** no longer interests me as much as **scuba diving.** [gerund paired with gerund]

PARALLEL **To water-ski** no longer interests me as much as **to scuba dive.** [infinitive paired with infinitive]

FAULTY Her novel was praised more for its style than for what it had to say. [noun paired with clause]

PARALLEL Her novel was praised more for its **style** than for its **ideas.** [noun paired with noun]

Correlative Constructions

Correlative constructions are formed with the correlative conjunctions *both . . . and, either . . . or, neither . . . nor, not only . . . but* (*also*).

FAULTY At the gate they tried both persuasion and to force their way in. [noun paired with infinitive]

PARALLEL At the gate they tried both **persuasion** and **force.** [noun paired with noun]

FAULTY The new clerk soon proved herself to be not only capable but also a woman who could be trusted. [adjective paired with noun]

PARALLEL The new clerk soon proved herself to be not only **capable** but also **trustworthy**. [adjective paired with adjective]

COMPLETED PARALLELISM

18b. Place correlative conjunctions immediately before the parallel terms.

NONSTANDARD Mrs. Sayers is not only president of the National Bank but also of the Chamber of Commerce. [*Not only* precedes a noun, *president,* whereas *but also* precedes a prepositional phrase, *of the Chamber of Commerce.*]

STANDARD Mrs. Sayers is president **not only** *of the National Bank* **but also** *of the Chamber of Commerce.*

NONSTANDARD The team both felt the satisfaction of victory and the disappointment of defeat.

STANDARD The team felt **both** *the satisfaction* of victory **and** *the disappointment* of defeat.

18c. In parallel constructions, repeat an article, a preposition, or a pronoun whenever necessary to make the meaning clear.

Note that the omission or inclusion of a word in the paired sentences below changes the meaning.

> Before the meeting I talked with the secretary and treasurer. [The sentence may mean that I talked with one person who holds both offices.]
> Before the meeting I talked with the secretary and **the** treasurer. [This sentence indicates that I talked with two persons.]

> The weather was a greater handicap to the invading army than their enemy. [This sentence may mean that the invaders were handicapped more by the weather than by their enemy.]
> The weather was a greater handicap to the invading army than **to** their enemy. [This sentence means that the invaders had the greater handicap.]

> We feel certain that she is capable, she will succeed, and you will be proud of her. [In a series of parallel *that* clauses, the meaning is usually clearer if the introductory word is repeated in each clause.]
> We feel certain **that** she is capable, **that** she will succeed, and **that** you will be proud of her.

EXERCISE 1. Revising Sentences by Correcting Faulty Parallelism. Revise the following sentences by putting parallel ideas into the same grammatical form. Correct any errors in the placement of correlative conjunctions and in the omission of necessary articles, prepositions, or pronouns.

1. Its large size, simple structure, and how readily available it is, make the common cockroach convenient to study.
2. Cockroaches have smooth, leathery skin; long, thin antennae; and they have a body that is thick and flat.
3. They are not only found in urban areas but also in the tropics.
4. Cockroaches may be dark brown, pale brown, or of a green color that is delicate.
5. Cockroach eggs are laid in small cases, carried on the female body, and then they deposit them in hidden crevices.
6. A typical cockroach lives as a nymph for about a year, and as an adult its life lasts about half a year.
7. Cockroaches will eat anything, but they especially like sweet foods and foods that are starchy.
8. We might not only view the cockroach with disgust but also interest.
9. The cockroach both is the most primitive living winged insect and the most ancient fossil insect.
10. We have as much to learn from the cockroach's evolution as there is to gain from extinguishing it.

18d. Include in the second part of a parallel construction all words necessary to make the construction complete.

Occasionally you may fail to include in one part of a parallel construction all the words necessary to make the construction complete.

INCOMPLETE Linda always chose topics that were more difficult than the other students.

COMPLETE Linda always chose topics that were more difficult than **those of** the other students.

In the first of these sentences you feel that something has been omitted because the sentence compares *topics* with *students*.

EXERCISE 2. Revising Sentences by Using Correct Parallelism. Correct the parallelism in each of the following sentences by inserting the words that have been omitted.

1. Ms. Connor's lectures are easier to comprehend than Ms. Moore.
2. A modern director's interpretation of *Hamlet* is very different from a nineteenth-century director.
3. A dog's ability to hear high-pitched sounds is much keener than humans.

4. How do your grades in English compare with science?
5. The biographical information in the encyclopedia is more detailed than the dictionary.
6. People have been more interested in reading the book than the movie version.
7. The view from the World Trade Center is even more spectacular than the Empire State Building.
8. The strength in my left hand is greater than my right hand.
9. Some birds like to eat fruit as much as insects.
10. This month the price of gold has risen more sharply than silver.

EXERCISE 3. Revising Sentences by Correcting Faulty Parallelism. The following sentences contain faulty parallelism. Rephrase the sentences so that the parallelism will be correctly and logically expressed.

1. One of the accident victims suffered a broken arm, several broken ribs, and one of her lungs was punctured.
2. She not only was industrious, but she could be depended on.
3. As we left the harbor, the radio weather report predicted gale-force winds, heavy rain, and that tides would be abnormally high.
4. A cloudy day is better for a game than sunshine.
5. She spoke about her experience in Australia and several predictions about the country's future.
6. To the unthinking person, war may be a romantic adventure, but a foolish and dirty business is the way the wise person regards it.
7. The unexpected cooperation of China was a greater surprise to Russia than the United States.
8. The skipper had a harsh voice, a weatherbeaten face, and was very stocky in build.
9. We were not sure that our request for a raise was fair or it would be granted.
10. The speech of cultivated Britishers is not so different as it used to be from Americans.
11. Attention has been centered on the need for more teachers, adequate classrooms, and there isn't enough new equipment.
12. This was a much harder assignment for me than Luis.
13. The ambassador did not know whether the President had sent for him or the Secretary of State.

14. Her friends not only were shocked by her failure but they felt a great disappointment.
15. The players were annoyed not so much by the decisions of the officials as the hostile crowd.
16. The company announced a bonus for all five-year employees and that deserving new employees would be given additional benefits.
17. The headmaster insisted that all of us return by ten o'clock and the housemasters must check us in.
18. High-school programs have been accused of being too closely tied in with college education and that they neglect the average teen-ager.
19. Pioneers came with hopes of being happy and free and to make their fortunes in the new world.
20. All delegates to the convention were advised that on their return they would both have to make a written and oral report.

CHAPTER 19

Unnecessary Shifts in Sentences

AWKWARD CHANGES IN SUBJECT AND VERB FORMS

Within a sentence a shift is a change from one subject to another or from one verb to another. Often shifts are acceptable because they are necessary to express the meaning the writer intends.

ACCEPTABLE SHIFT The trials of peace are great, but the dangers of war are greater. [The shift in subject from *trials* to *dangers* is a natural one.]

The smoothness of a sentence is sometimes seriously affected, however, by an unnecessary and awkward shift.

AWKWARD A student should choose books from the reading list so that you can be sure they are acceptable to the teacher. [The unnecessary shift from *student* to *you* is awkward and confusing.]

ACCEPTABLE A **student** should choose books from the reading list so that **he or she** can be sure they are acceptable to the teacher.

AWKWARD Pam did her math homework, and then her theme was written. [The shift from active to passive voice and the resulting shift in subject is unnecessary and awkward.]

ACCEPTABLE Pam **did** her math homework, and then she **wrote** her theme.

19a. Avoid unnecessary shifts from one subject to another.

UNNECESSARY SHIFTS

Fishers from many states visit the Ontario lakes where *fish* are found in abundance and, in the cool, crisp air of the North woods, a welcome *relief* from summer heat is enjoyed. *Planes, trains,* or *automobiles* bring the fishers to the edge of the wilderness. From there *boats* are used to penetrate the remoter waters where *trout, bass, pickerel, perch,* and freshwater *salmon* are caught.

SHIFTS AVOIDED

Fishers from many states visit the Ontario lakes where *they* find fish in abundance and, in the cool, crisp air of the North woods, enjoy a welcome relief from summer heat. After coming by plane, train, or automobile to the edge of the wilderness, the *fishers* use boats to penetrate the remoter waters, where *they* catch trout, bass, pickerel, perch, and freshwater salmon.

19b. Avoid unnecessary shifts from one verb form to another within one sentence.

(1) Avoid unnecessary shifts in the voice of verbs.

Unnecessary shifts from one subject to another are often the result of a shift from active to passive voice.

When the subject of a verb is acting, the verb is in the *active voice.* When the subject of a verb is acted upon, the verb is in the *passive voice.*[1]

S ⟶ V
ACTIVE VOICE Jane **won** both events. [subject acting]

S ⟵ V
PASSIVE VOICE Both events **were won** by Jane. [subject acted upon]

Note that a shift in voice results in a shift in subject.

UNNECESSARY SHIFT Volunteers made [active verb] the dangerous journey after dark, but no wolves were encountered [passive verb].

SHIFT AVOIDED Volunteers **made** [active verb] the dangerous journey after dark but **encountered** [active verb] no wolves.

(2) Avoid unnecessary shifts in the tense of verbs.

Changing without reason from one tense to another within a sentence creates an awkward and confusing effect. Stick to the tense you start with unless there is an excellent reason for changing.

[1] A fuller treatment of voice will be found on pages 145–48.

UNNECESSARY SHIFT At this point the President reads [present tense] a prepared statement but refused [past tense] to answer any questions.

SHIFT AVOIDED At this point the President **read** [past tense] a prepared statement but **refused** [past tense] to answer any questions.

SHIFT AVOIDED At this point the President **reads** [present tense] a prepared statement but **refuses** [present tense] to answer any questions.

In correcting unnecessary shifts in subject and verb, you will often find the best method is to omit the second subject. This can usually be done by using the second verb in the same voice as the first and making the verb compound.

UNNECESSARY SHIFT A good driver has complete control of the car at all times, and allowance is made for the carelessness of other drivers.

SHIFT AVOIDED A good **driver has** complete control of the car at all times **and makes** allowances for the carelessness of other drivers. [The use of the compound active voice for both verbs corrects the awkward shift.]

EXERCISE 1. Revising Sentences to Eliminate Unnecessary Shifts in the Subject and in the Verb. Most of the following sentences contain unnecessary shifts from one subject to another or from one verb form to another. By revising these sentences orally in class, show how these shifts may be avoided. Two of the sentences are acceptable. Identify them.

1. If one wants to try a delicious recipe from Puerto Rico, you should make rice with pigeon peas.
2. To start, sauté three tablespoons of diced salt pork until the fat has melted.
3. A chopped onion and two minced cloves of garlic should be added to the skillet, and then add two chopped green peppers.
4. After you have peeled two tomatoes, chopping them comes next.
5. The tomatoes, too, should be placed into the skillet, and you should cook the entire mixture for five minutes.
6. A tablespoon of capers goes in next, and you should follow this with a teaspoon of salt, two cups of uncooked long-grain rice, and three cups of water.
7. After you stir the rice, a pound of cooked pigeon peas needs to be added.
8. A tablespoon of achiote should not be forgotten to be included, since this spice imparts a lovely golden color to the food.

9. When the liquid comes to a boil, cover the skillet, the flame should be reduced, and simmer the mixture until the water has been absorbed.
10. Stir the mixture occasionally to keep the rice from sticking, and continue cooking until the rice is dry and fluffy.

EXERCISE 2. Revising Sentences to Eliminate Shifts in the Subject and in the Verb. The sentences in this exercise are awkward because of unnecessary shifts in the subject and in the verb. Revise the sentences to eliminate these shifts.

1. Adolescents naturally rebel against authority, but the authority of the law must be respected by them.
2. Lonely students might participate in an extracurricular activity so that new friendships can be made.
3. A senior must not only pass all courses and graduate, but also plans for your future must be made quickly.
4. My brother frequently procrastinates, and a tendency toward laziness is occasionally shown.
5. My father has some amusing peculiarities which are not recognized by him.
6. The union's demands were unacceptable even though some concessions were contained in them.
7. If a teacher wants to be liked, you must treat students impartially.
8. Coach Martin always insisted on long practice sessions and strict training, but her winning teams justify her methods.
9. The Vice-President flew to the Paris Conference, but few concrete results were accomplished by him.
10. A good student can win a college scholarship, and thus his parents are relieved of part of the cost of a college education.
11. When you buy a car, a person should be sure he can afford the upkeep.
12. In the end Robert stays with his mother, and the girl he loves is lost to him forever.
13. The cement and sand are first mixed thoroughly; then add the water.
14. The experienced boat operator is aware of the danger of fire, and when filling the gas tank, great precautions are taken not to spill gasoline in the bottom of the boat.

15. As a young district attorney he handled the Tammany Hall case, and the backing of the Republican Party was won.
16. As the bus careens toward the edge of the road, we thought our time had come, and we grab our seats in desperation.
17. Many doctors recognize the value of health insurance, but the kind we should have is something they could not agree on.
18. Searching for the right words, Livia composed her closing sentence, and another essay was brought to its logical conclusion.
19. Sammy had just finished his bitter denunciation of all teachers and of one chemistry teacher in particular, when he turns around and Ms. Lerner was seen in the laboratory doorway.
20. An explorer must study maps very carefully so that you will be able to plan your trip efficiently.

CHAPTER 20

Sentence Conciseness

AVOIDING WORDINESS AND OVERWRITING

It is a mistake to believe that wordiness is a virtue. Most good writing is effective because it is not cluttered with unnecessary words.

Moreover, do not think that wordiness appears only in long compositions. A long piece of writing may contain no superfluous words, whereas a short piece may be full of them. Studying the principles and doing the exercises in this section will make you aware of wordiness in writing and help you to avoid it.

SUPERFLUOUS WORDS AND UNNECESSARY REPETITION

The following example of wordiness was the opening paragraph of a high-school student's composition about an overnight hike. Lines have been drawn through the superfluous words.

> When ~~in the course of human events, when~~ a woman finds it necessary to rest her weary bones, she packs up and goes on what is inappropriately called a vacation. Last summer I had the good fortune to go ~~during the summer~~ to a mountain camp in ~~the mountains of~~ eastern Pennsylvania. On the day that I arrived, ~~when I got to camp~~ I found that the camp had been quarantined because of the measles that one of the younger campers had brought in, ~~and no one who was in the camp could leave.~~ After we had spent

a week in camp, the prospect of an overnight hike in the mountainous wilds looked especially good to us campers who had been so long confined to camp by the quarantine.

20a. Avoid wordiness by eliminating superfluous words and the unnecessary repetition of ideas.

WORDY The game is played with tiny, little round balls, which, in my opinion, I think, are made of steel.

BETTER The game is played with tiny balls which, I think, are made of steel.

WORDY After descending down to the edge of the river, we boarded a small raft that was floating there on the surface of the water.

BETTER After descending to the edge of the river, we boarded a small raft.

EXERCISE 1. Revising Sentences to Eliminate Superfluous Words. Revise the following sentences, eliminating superfluous words.

1. We watched the big, massive black cloud rising up from the level prairie and covering up the sun.
2. Far away in the distance, as far as anything was visible to the eye, the small, diminutive shapes of the campers' tents were outlined in silhouette against the dark sky.
3. When what the speaker was saying was not audible to our ears, I asked her to repeat again what she had said.
4. During this year's current baseball season, all home games and many away games in other cities may be watched at home on your television screen as they are brought to you over station WPIX.
5. During the hours in the morning before noon, there is a variety of radio programs of different kinds to which you may listen to.
6. As you continue on in the book a little further, you will be surprised and amazed by the clever skill of the writer of the book in weaving in together the many previously unrelated threads of his story.
7. She was firmly determined to combine together both of the two divisions of the firm in order to achieve a stronger company eventually in the long run.
8. Circling around his adversary with a menacing look on his face, Broadhurst bided his time and waited for an opening through which he could connect up with his mighty right.
9. The President's struggle with Congress ended up in a victory for the

President when the public voted at the November election to reelect him again to the Presidency for another term of four years.

10. The final conclusion of the novel on which she had been working on for more than five years was disappointing to everyone who read the manuscript, and she decided to revise and change the story.

EXERCISE 2. Revising Sentences by Eliminating Unnecessary Words. Revise the following wordy paragraph. Eliminate all unnecessary words, but keep the ideas clear.

When we were two hundred yards away from our objective, which was a small little grove of pine trees on the sloping side of a hill, we were confronted by a vast, wet swamp. I remembered that during the last two weeks we had had, out of fourteen days, ten days of rain, and decided in my own mind to send out a few scouts who might discover a way by means of which we could reach the grove without getting our feet wet. Then, when the scouts reported back that their efforts to try to find a dry path through the swamp had been unsuccessful, we gave up and resigned ourselves to sloshing knee-deep through the muddy water.

CONCISENESS THROUGH REDUCTION

The opposite of wordiness is conciseness. In your effort to write well, you will profit from studying some ways to make your writing more concise. Of course, there is a danger in being too economical in your use of words; writing that is too concise will not be clear and will not achieve its intended effect. Nevertheless, the following rule will call to your attention some helpful methods of avoiding wordiness.

20b. Avoid wordiness by reducing clauses to phrases, and phrases to single words. This process is known as *reduction*.

1. ***Clauses reduced to participial, gerund, or infinitive phrases***

CLAUSE	**When they were trapped by a cave-in,** the miners waited for rescuers.
PARTICIPIAL PHRASE	**Trapped by a cave-in,** the miners waited for rescuers.
CLAUSE	**Because we had found no one home,** we left a note.
PARTICIPIAL PHRASE	**Having found no one home,** we left a note.
CLAUSE	**If you leave at noon,** you can get to Chicago at three o'clock.
GERUND PHRASE	**Leaving at noon** will get you to Chicago at three o'clock.

CLAUSE We decided **that we would get an early start.**
INFINITIVE PHRASE We decided **to get an early start.**

2. ***Clauses reduced to prepositional phrases***

CLAUSE The teams **that had come from Missouri** were not scheduled to play the first day of the tournament.
PHRASE The teams **from Missouri** were not scheduled to play the first day of the tournament.

CLAUSE **When the sun sets,** the streetlights come on.
PHRASE **At sunset** the streetlights come on.

3. ***Clauses reduced to appositives***

CLAUSE Dr. Brown, **who is the chief surgeon,** will operate.
APPOSITIVE Dr. Brown, **the chief surgeon,** will operate.

CLAUSE Her two dogs, **one of which is a collie and the other a spaniel,** perform different duties on the farm.
APPOSITIVE Her two dogs, **a collie and a spaniel,** perform different duties on the farm.

4. ***Clauses and phrases reduced to single words***

CLAUSE The dance classes **that have been canceled** will be rescheduled.
WORD The **canceled** dance classes will be rescheduled.

CLAUSE Laura is a runner **who never tires.**
WORD Laura is a **tireless** runner.

PHRASE Her career **in the movies** was brief.
WORD Her **movie** career was brief.

PHRASE She greeted everyone **in a cordial manner.**
WORD She greeted everyone **cordially.**

Usually the time for reduction is during revision of your papers. Revising the sentences in the following exercises will give you practice in writing more concisely.

EXERCISE 3. Revising Sentences Through Reduction. Revise the following sentences by reducing the italicized clauses to phrases or appositives or single words, and the italicized phrases to single words. Omit any unnecessary words, and, if needed, occasionally change the word order.

1. We decided to wait for the bus *in order that we might save money.*
2. After I had finished the assigned reading, I read three novels *that were written by Virginia Woolf.*

3. This small hotel, *which is situated in Connecticut,* is patronized mainly by *people from Boston.*
4. *After he lost a leg in an accident which occurred while he was hunting*, Monty Stratton, *who was a pitcher for the White Sox*, made a comeback in baseball *that was amazing.*
5. Our seats *in which we sat at the Michigan-Ohio State football game* were almost on the forty-yard line, *and they were at the top of the stadium.*
6. The poetry *of Blake* had an influence *that is notable* on the poetry *of Yeats.*
7. *While he was inspecting his new house, which is in the suburbs*, Mr. Doyle stumbled over a piece of flooring and fell down the stairs *leading to the cellar.*
8. Our days *that we spent in the north woods* last summer would have been perfect if it had not been for the mosquitoes *that were enormous and hungry.*
9. Inez, *who is an ambitious young actress*, found that the acting *that she did in a stock company in the summer* gave her the experience *that she needed.*
10. The most common complaint *that is made by students* is that every teacher chooses Friday *on which to give examinations.*

EXERCISE 4. Revising Sentences by Eliminating Unnecessary Words and by Using Reduction. Revise the following wordy paragraph. Eliminate all unnecessary words and reduce clauses to phrases or appositives or single words. You may change the word order, but you must keep the ideas clear.

Needless to say, I am not one of those who are members of the senior class who believe that the senior lounge should be closed during the week of exams. It goes without saying that seniors need a place that is quiet and relaxing in order for them to escape the pressures which accompany exam week. If the lounge is closed during this time, it would mean that seniors would be forced to use the cafeteria, which is crowded, or the auditorium, which is noisy, for the purpose of relaxation. Furthermore, the use of the senior lounge during exam week is by this time one of the few privileges that seniors are still able to enjoy here at East High; not long ago the right of seniors to park cars in the parking area reserved for members of the faculty was recently taken away by the Student-Teacher Council. If more privileges are taken away, the morale of seniors will weaken.

THE OVERWRITTEN STYLE

In their efforts to write impressively, high-school students sometimes produce writing that is so artificial, flowery, and cumbersome as to be absurd. Such a style results from the mistaken notion that big words, unusual words, and figures of speech, no matter how commonplace, are "literary." A mistake of this kind is made by trying too hard to sound like a great writer. The resulting style is said to be "overwritten."

20c. Avoid an overwritten style. Write naturally without straining after a "literary" effect.

Avoid the kind of overwriting exhibited by the following paragraphs.

HARBOR FOG

The fog slowly crept in and covered the metropolis with its sinister cloak of impressive quietude. An entire day of heavy rain had drenched the surrounding municipality, forming puddles in the thoroughfares which reflected the shimmering images of the gleaming street lights and the illumination emanating from multitudes of office windows.

As I stood on the magnificent span that arched above the swirling waters, the mournful warnings of the anchored ships pierced the dense fog. The constant beat of the harbor bell buoys and the gentle lapping of the murky water on the pilings of this bridge combined to permeate the night air with a mystic tenseness.

Although it was late, the never-ceasing rumble of activity from the nearby city could still be apprehended. The penetrating night air was heavy with moisture and with each soft puff of breeze the salt of the sea could be detected.

During World War II, Representative Maury Maverick of Texas became impatient with the overwritten style of some government writing and branded it "gobbledygook." Here is an example of the gobbledygook that troubled Mr. Maverick: "Illumination is required to be extinguished upon vacating these premises." You can see how much more effective "Turn out the lights when you leave" would be.

EXERCISE 5. Revising Sentences to Correct an Overwritten Style. Each of the following sentences is an example of overwriting. Using simpler words, revise the idea that is here expressed in a forced and unnatural style.

1. In a vast explosion of frozen precipitation, Jan shot through the feathery drift, maintaining without apparent effort her equilibrium upon the fragile strips of ash strapped to the pedal extremities.

2. The bitterest irony of our fevered time is the oft-repeated concept that only by creating more magnificent and more deadly instruments of explosive destruction can human beings bring to this whirling planet the era of tranquility for which it has longed since the beginning of time.
3. Following our educational endeavors of the day, several of us conscientious seekers after knowledge relaxed our weary cerebrums by lending our ears to the latest discs at Kent's music emporium.
4. Bent upon a week's exploration of our nation's vast regions of tranquil pristine wilderness, I bade a fond farewell to my anxious mater and, with my earthly possessions ensconced in a commodious rucksack, embarked upon my great adventure via public omnibus.
5. Lifting the pigskin from the water-soaked gridiron with his trusty toe, Harvey booted it with mathematical precision directly between the white uprights silhouetted against the setting sun.

CHAPTER 21

Sentence Combining and Revising

VARIETY, INTEREST, EMPHASIS

SENTENCE COMBINING

Good writers avoid the choppy style caused by using too many short, subject-first sentences. Study how the following paragraph, written in a choppy style, has been revised to achieve a more fluent, more mature style. The revised version uses subordination, coordination, apposition, and other devices to indicate clearly the relationship between ideas.

The sinking of the *Titanic* was a great disaster. The *Titanic* weighed 42,000 metric tons. It was the largest ship of its time. It was the most luxurious ship of its time. The sinking was one of the worst maritime disasters in history. The *Titanic* was on its maiden voyage. The ship struck an iceberg off the Grand Banks of Newfoundland. The accident happened on the night of April 14, 1912. The night was clear and cold. The captain had received iceberg warnings. He had chosen to pass through a perilous ice field. The rate of speed was 42 kilometers per hour. He wished to reach New York ahead of schedule. The *Titanic*'s hull had sixteen watertight compartments. The iceberg punctured five compartments. The ship's designers thought no accident could puncture more than four compartments. The ship sank in less than three hours. Over 1,500 of the 2,220 passengers and crew drowned. Another ship, the *Californian*, lay stopped in the water. It was less than eighteen kilometers away. It did not respond to the distress signal. The radio operator was off duty. The *Carpathia* was ninety kilometers away. It reversed course. It sped through the ice floes. It picked up survivors. By the time it arrived, many lives had been lost. The *Titanic* disaster quickly led to the reform of maritime safety laws.

The sinking of the 42,000-metric-ton *Titanic*, the largest and most luxurious ship of its time, was one of the worst maritime disasters in history. On the clear, cold night of April 14, 1912, the ship, on its maiden voyage, struck an iceberg off the Grand Banks of Newfoundland. Although the captain had received iceberg warnings, he had chosen to pass through a perilous ice field at 42 kilometers per hour in order to reach New York ahead of schedule. The iceberg punctured five of sixteen watertight compartments in the ship's hull, one more than the ship's designers had thought possible in any accident, and the ship sank in less than three hours, with the loss of over 1,500 of the 2,220 passengers and crew. Another ship, the *Californian*, lay stopped in the water less than eighteen kilometers away, but it did not respond to the distress signal because its radio operator was off duty. The *Carpathia*, which was ninety kilometers away, sped through the ice floes and picked up the survivors, but by then many lives had been lost. The *Titanic* disaster led to the reform of maritime safety laws.

As you combine short, choppy sentences in the exercises that follow, you will be learning to achieve a more fluent style, richer in variety and interest.

21a. Combine short, related sentences by inserting adjectives, adverbs, and prepositional phrases.[1]

Note how the following three sentences have been rewritten as one sentence by eliminating unnecessary words.

THREE SENTENCES The Prime Minister closed the session.
The Prime Minister felt weary.
He closed the session with the Cabinet.

ONE SENTENCE The **weary** Prime Minister closed the session **with the Cabinet**.

There may be more than one correct way to combine short sentences.

THREE SENTENCES The plane moved slowly.
The plane moved along the runway.
The plane moved toward the hangar.

ONE SENTENCE The plane moved **slowly along the runway toward the hangar**.

or

Along the runway, the plane moved **slowly toward the hangar**.

[1] See pages 37–40 for information on prepositional phrases.

There are other correct ways in which these sentences could have been combined. Although you often have some degree of choice in combining short, related sentences, you may find that some combinations do not read smoothly, such as, *Along the runway toward the hangar slowly the plane moved.* You should avoid these combinations as well as those that change the meaning of the original short sentences.

EXERCISE 1. Combining Sentences by Inserting Adjectives, Adverbs, or Prepositional Phrases. Combine each group of short, related sentences by inserting adjectives, adverbs, or prepositional phrases into the first sentence and by eliminating unnecessary words. Add commas and conjunctions where they are necessary.

EXAMPLE 1. Peregrine falcons soar.
They soar gracefully.
They soar near their nests.
1. *Peregrine falcons soar gracefully near their nests.*

1. Peregrine falcons became scarce.
They became scarce in the United States.
They became scarce because of the pesticide DDT.
2. No breeding pairs remained.
No pairs remained east of the Mississippi.
No pairs remained by 1970.
No pairs of falcons remained.
3. Scientists are reintroducing falcons.
The scientists are from Cornell University.
The falcons are wild.
The scientists reintroduce falcons under controlled conditions.
The scientists reintroduce falcons to the eastern United States.
4. The ban on DDT has helped the falcons.
The ban was effective.
The ban has helped considerably.
The falcons have been endangered.
5. Peregrines are hatching eggs.
These peregrines are in the Eastern wilderness.
They are hatching eggs for the first time.
It is the first time since the 1950's.

21b. Combine closely related sentences by using participial phrases.

Participial phrases—phrases containing a participle with its complements or modifiers—help you add concrete details to nouns and pronouns. In the following example, the participial phrases describe the subject of the sentence, the noun *ship*.

> **Badly damaged by high winds** and **deserted by half its crew**, the ship finally reached a safe harbor.

Participial phrases are a useful way to combine sentences.

TWO SENTENCES The colors were orange, red, and blue.
The colors were painted on the ceiling.
ONE SENTENCE The colors **painted on the ceiling** were orange, red, and blue.

The second sentence has been turned into a participial phrase, *painted on the ceiling,* and inserted in the first sentence. Unnecessary words have been deleted.

A participle or participial phrase must always be close to the noun or pronoun it modifies. Otherwise the sentence may be confusing.

MISPLACED Wrapped in silver paper, the bride accepted the wedding present.
IMPROVED The bride accepted the wedding present **wrapped in silver paper**.

EXERCISE 2. Combining Sentences by Using Participial Phrases. Combine each of the following pairs of sentences into one sentence by turning either the first sentence or the second sentence into a participial phrase and inserting it into the remaining sentence. Punctuate the combined sentences correctly.

EXAMPLE 1. The employee asked for a raise.
The employee found out about the boss's temper.
1. *Asking for a raise, the employee found out about the boss's temper.*

1. Tomb robbers searched inside a crypt.
   Tomb robbers found gold.
2. The pitcher concentrated on the batter.
   The pitcher forgot about the base runner.
3. The index in this book is very long.
   It contains every topic found on every page.
4. The student did not hand in her paper.
   The student realized that two pages were missing.
5. We held back our cheers.
   We waited for the speech to end.
6. The van failed to stop at the red light.
   It narrowly missed another car.

7. I left the bread in the oven too long.
   I burned the crust.
8. Our counselor was stung by a bee.
   Our counselor yelled angrily.
9. The teacher was pleased with the test results.
   The teacher congratulated the class.
10. The hurricane swept across the ocean.
    The hurricane demolished every boat in its path.

21c. Combine short, related sentences by using appositives or appositive phrases.

Appositives and appositive phrases add detail to nouns and pronouns by helping to identify or explain them. The appositive phrase in the following sentence helps identify the noun *captain.*

> The captain of the swim team, **holder of six school records,** won a full athletic scholarship.

Two sentences can often be combined through the use of an appositive or an appositive phrase.

TWO SENTENCES Many students in the school play lacrosse.
Lacrosse is the national summer sport of Canada.

ONE SENTENCE Many students in the school play lacrosse, **the national summer sport of Canada.**

EXERCISE 3. Combining Sentences by Using Appositives or Appositive Phrases. Combine the following pairs of sentences by turning one of the sentences into an appositive or an appositive phrase. Punctuate the combined sentence correctly. Answers may vary.

EXAMPLE 1. Elizabeth Bowen was born in Ireland. She is one of the leading fiction writers in England since World War I.
1. *Elizabeth Bowen, one of the leading fiction writers in England since World War I, was born in Ireland.*

1. In *The Death of the Heart* the protagonist is a sensitive person, ill at ease with the world.
   The Death of the Heart is one of Bowen's best-known novels.
2. Bowen was a nurse and an air-raid warden during World War II.
   Bowen wrote about the psychological effects of war on civilians.
3. In *Going Home*, Doris Lessing writes about a return visit to Rhodesia.

Going Home is an autobiographical narrative.

4. Doris Lessing is a sensitive observer of social and political struggles.
   She describes people attempting to find meaning in life.
5. Katherine Mansfield is a modern master of the short story.
   She died of tuberculosis at the age of thirty-four.

21d. Combine short, related sentences by using compound subjects or verbs or by writing a compound sentence.

Compound subjects and verbs, as well as compound sentences, are common. Writers, however, often overuse compound constructions by loosely stringing together ideas that belong in separate sentences (see pages 337–38). You should not only learn the appropriate function of various connectives but should also avoid the overuse of *and* or *so*.

Compound subjects and verbs are joined by coordinating conjunctions such as *and, but,* and *or* and by correlative conjunctions such as *either—or, neither—nor,* and *both—and.*

EXAMPLES **Either** Mr. Sands **or** one of his students will bring the radio.
We watched the game **and** cheered our team to victory.

Independent clauses are joined into a compound sentence by conjunctions such as *and, but,* and *for* or by other connectives such as *furthermore, yet, however, therefore, either—or*, and *neither—nor*. The relationship of the independent clauses determines which connective works best.

EXAMPLES Two cats were stranded in the tree, **and** no one could rescue them.
The police officer questioned him; **however**, he refused to answer.
[Note the use of the semicolon.]

Ideas in separate sentences can be combined by using the appropriate connecting words. See pages 283–87 for a complete list of connecting words.

TWO SENTENCES Rain had soaked the playing field.
Practice was not canceled.

ONE SENTENCE **Although** rain had soaked the playing field, practice was not canceled.

EXERCISE 4. Combining Simple Sentences into a Compound Sentence. The following items consist of two closely related ideas. Combine these ideas into a single sentence, using the appropriate connectives.

EXAMPLE 1. The Congress will approve this bill.
The President will veto it.
1. *The Congress will approve this bill, but the President will veto it.*

1. The basketball team has played well all season.
   It will probably win the championship.
2. Frank worked hard on his homework.
   His friend had given him the wrong assignment.
3. America must learn to use less energy.
   There will be a more severe energy shortage in a few years.
4. The prospects are bleak for new gym equipment.
   The student council will recommend this important purchase.
5. School spirit sometimes wanes during the winter months.
   The seniors have organized a carnival in December.

21e. Combine short, related sentences into a complex sentence by putting one idea into a subordinate clause.

Subordination allows you to express the relationship between two unequal ideas within a single sentence. Methods for subordinating ideas include the use of an adjective clause, an adverb clause, and a noun clause. Mastering these methods of subordination will improve the variety and clarity of your writing.

(1) Use an adjective clause to combine sentences.

Adjective clauses, like adjectives, modify nouns or pronouns. In the following sentence, the adjective clause is printed in boldfaced type.

The detective **who solved the case** was a master at logical thinking.

To combine sentences by using an adjective clause, you must first decide which idea to emphasize (see page 289). Then you must choose the correct relative pronoun to join the sentences.

RELATIVE PRONOUNS who, whom, whose, which, that

The adjective clause must always be placed close to the word or words it modifies.

TWO SENTENCES The story has an intricate plot.
I found the plot hard to follow.
ONE SENTENCE The story has an intricate plot **that I found hard to follow.**

EXERCISE 5. Using Adjective Clauses to Combine Sentences.

Combine the following pairs of sentences by subordinating one idea in an adjective clause. Punctuate your sentences correctly.

EXAMPLE 1. Martin Luther King, Jr., married Coretta Scott.
He met her while studying at Boston University.
1. *Martin Luther King, Jr., married Coretta Scott, whom he met while studying at Boston University.*

1. My uncle is an experienced traveler.
He has recently returned from the Grand Canyon.
2. Richard prefers trout fishing.
It requires more patience than deep-sea fishing.
3. Pedro drove the truck.
Pedro has just received his driver's license.
4. Melissa is about to begin her project.
You can reach her after eight this evening.
5. I forgot the notebook.
It was lying on the sofa.

(2) Use an adverb clause to combine sentences.

Adverb clauses can express a relationship of time, cause, purpose, or condition between two ideas within a single sentence.[1]

EXAMPLE **Although you present a convincing argument,** I will not change my mind.

To combine sentences by using an adverb clause, you must first decide which idea should become subordinate. You must then decide which subordinating conjunction best expresses the relationship between the two ideas.

TWO SENTENCES Elsie received the reply in the mail.
She tore open the envelope impatiently.

ONE SENTENCE **When Elsie received the reply in the mail,** she tore open the envelope impatiently.

EXERCISE 6. Using Adverb Clauses to Combine Sentences. Combine each pair of sentences by subordinating one idea in an adverb clause. Punctuate the combined sentences correctly.

EXAMPLE 1. Sally did her best.
She was unable to win the prize.
1. *Although Sally did her best, she was unable to win the prize.*

[1] See pages 286–87 for a list of common subordinating conjunctions.

1. The committee members could not agree.
   The whole matter was referred to the president.
2. The president took the responsibility.
   She wanted to settle the matter herself.
3. She decided to bring the issue before the entire club.
   Everyone could express an opinion.
4. There was a great deal of talk.
   Nothing was decided.
5. A decision is reached today.
   The donors will not give us the money.
6. The city council offered to give us money for a clubhouse.
   We would let the public use it.
7. We had never admitted the public to our meetings.
   We didn't want to admit them to our clubhouse.
8. We would not lose the chance for a new clubhouse.
   Some of us favored admitting the public.
9. I agreed with those in favor of admitting the public.
   I sympathized with the others.
10. No agreement was reached.
    The money went to another club.

(3) Use a noun clause to combine sentences.

A noun clause is a subordinate clause used as a noun. Read the following examples of noun clauses and note how they are used.

> **Whoever buys that car** will be sorry. [noun clause as subject]
> Yesterday we learned **what Napoleon had accomplished.** [noun clause as direct object]
> We can spend the money for **whatever we like**. [noun clause as object of preposition]

A noun clause can also be used as a predicate nominative and as an indirect object. Noun clauses are usually introduced by *that, what, whatever, why, whether, how, who, whom, whoever,* or *whomever.*

Noun clauses are sometimes used without the introductory word *that.*

EXAMPLE My sister said the trip would take three days.

EXERCISE 7. Using Noun Clauses to Combine Sentences. Combine each of the following pairs of sentences by turning the italicized sentence into a noun clause. Use one of the introductory words listed above.

EXAMPLE 1. *They thought that they did not need help.*
This was a very foolish idea.
1. *That they did not need help was a very foolish idea.*

1. The new senator promised.
The state would get more aid.
2. *Could they endure the debate?*
That was uncertain.
3. *They might succeed.*
This was the incentive that kept them working.
4. The odor of smoke convinced the family.
They should call the fire department.
5. The attorney asked a question.
He asked how the defendant had found the money.

REVIEW EXERCISE A. Using Sentence-Combining Methods. Using the sentence-combining methods you have practiced thus far, combine each group of sentences into one smooth, well-written sentence. You may omit unnecessary words and change the word order, but you may not change the meaning of the original sentences. Punctuate your combined sentences correctly.

EXAMPLE 1. Hugo Gernsback began publishing *Amazing Stories.*
He began in 1926.
Amazing Stories was the first science-fiction magazine.
1. *In 1926 Hugo Gernsback began publishing* Amazing Stories, *the first science-fiction magazine.*

1. Science fiction ranges from projection to speculation.
The projection is careful.
The speculation is outlandish.
Science fiction usually requires the appearance of credibility.
2. *Frankenstein* is an early example of science fiction.
Frankenstein is a novel by Mary Shelley.
Frankenstein describes the scientific creation of human life.
3. There is another early example of science fiction.
The example is H. G. Wells's *The Time Machine.*
The Time Machine entertains.
The Time Machine offers social criticism.
The Time Machine predicts the future.

4. Some critics did not accept science fiction as serious literature.
   These critics did not accept it easily.
   Writers often included science fiction in their works.
   These writers were major twentieth-century authors.
5. Today science fiction has supporters.
   Science fiction has many active supporters.
   They hold annual conventions.
   They present Hugo and Nebula awards.
   These awards are for the year's best writing.

REVIEW EXERCISE B. Combining Sentences to Add Variety to a Paragraph. Combine the short, choppy sentences in the following paragraph into longer, smoother sentences. Be sure that the sentences you write add variety to the paragraph. Use correct punctuation.

> Mount St. Helens erupted in May 1980. It is near Vancouver, Washington. The eruption was sudden. The force was over five hundred times that of an atomic bomb. The explosion was caused by pressure from gas and molten rock. It tore the top off the mountain. It threw ash high into the air. The explosion and subsequent mudslides caused many deaths. More than thirty people died. The destruction left many homeless. The force of the blast leveled huge trees. The area was wide. The mud killed hundreds of deer and elk. The mud turned Spirit Lake into a mudhole. The lake was formerly picturesque. Much of the ash fell to earth within a few days. A cloud of dust remained in the stratosphere. This cloud was over much of the Northern Hemisphere. People saw spectacular sunrises and sunsets. This continued for two years. The sunrises and sunsets were rose-colored. The sunsets were due to solar rays. They struck microscopic particles of ash. Scientists suspect that intermittent showers will continue. The showers will consist of volcanic ash. They will continue for the next two decades.

AVOIDING MONOTONY

21f. Experiment with the length and structure of your sentences to achieve greater interest and variety.

Sentences in English—both spoken and written—usually begin with the subject. Any piece of writing in which most of the sentences needlessly depart from this normal order will strike a reader as artificial. However, an unbroken sequence of subject-predicate sentences may result in another stylistic fault—monotony. Such a sequence of sentences is monotonous because it lacks the logical connections and special emphasis that variations in sentence structure can provide. For example, the following sentences are perfectly clear:

> The two friends quarreled violently over a matter of slight importance. They never spoke from that time on.

But a closer connection can be made between these two sentences by moving the adverb phrase, which refers to the quarrel, up to the beginning of the second sentence:

> The two friends quarreled violently over a matter of slight importance. **From that time on** they never spoke.

Similarly, an important idea expressed by a modifier can be emphasized:

> Sue was not impressive in the classroom.
> **On the tennis court**, however, she came into her own.

The contrast is less striking when the second sentence begins with its subject:

> Sue was not impressive in the classroom.
> She came into her own, however, on the tennis court.

The normal order of sentences should not be shunned merely for the sake of variety. However, beginning a sentence with an important modifier can increase the force and clarity of your thought as well as provide a pleasing variation.

The exercises that follow are intended to give you practice in using different kinds of sentence openers. Used sparingly, these devices will improve your writing.

(1) Begin some of your sentences with a transposed appositive or with one of these modifiers: single-word modifier, phrase modifier, clause modifier.

Appositives

> The human brain, an enormously complex mechanism, contains about ten billion nerve cells. [subject first]
> **An enormously complex mechanism,** the human brain contains about ten billion nerve cells. [transposed appositive first]

Single-Word Modifiers

> The book is long and badly written, and it failed to hold my interest. [subject first]

Long and badly written, the book failed to hold my interest. [single-word modifiers first]
A number of changes have been made recently. [subject first]
Recently, a number of changes have been made. [single-word modifier first]

Phrase Modifiers

She was almost unbeatable on the tennis court. [subject first]
On the tennis court, she was almost unbeatable. [prepositional phrase first]
Joe tired rapidly during the second set and decided to save his strength for the third set. [subject first]
Tiring rapidly during the second set, Joe decided to save his strength for the third set. [participial phrase first]
Kim worked late every night to win the essay prize. [subject first]
To win the essay prize, Kim worked late every night. [infinitive phrase first]

Clause Modifiers

Investigators of the cause of the crash had to depend on evidence found in the wreckage because there were no survivors or witnesses. [subject first]
Because there were no survivors or witnesses, investigators of the crash had to depend on evidence found in the wreckage. [clause first]

EXERCISE 8. Revising Sentences by Varying Sentence Beginnings. Revise each sentence so that it will begin with an appositive or a single-word, phrase, or clause modifier.

1. A bowling team was formed this winter for the first time in the history of the school.
2. A sinister figure stepped cautiously into the dark room.
3. Candidates for a driver's license must take a written examination to prove their knowledge of traffic regulations.
4. The children, when both parents are working, are cared for in nursery schools.
5. The audience, tired and hot, soon became impatient.
6. We were frightened by the explosion and dared not move.
7. More than half of the 90,000 acres under cultivation had been ruined by the recent drought.
8. Jim, a merchant sailor for ten years, knew every important port in the world.
9. The new houses, although they look exactly alike from the outside, have very different interiors.
10. A small boy, sobbing bitterly, ran toward me.

(2) Vary the structure of your sentences by means of subordination. Avoid the exclusive use of simple and compound sentences.[1] Skillful use of the complex sentence is an indication of maturity in style.

REVIEW EXERCISE C. Using Subordination to Combine Sentences. Using subordination, combine the short sentences in each group into one long, smooth sentence.

1. Amelia Earhart made her first solo crossing of the Atlantic in 1932.
   Five years later she attempted a round-the-world flight.
   She became a major figure of concern when her plane lost radio contact on the second of July.
2. Gwendolyn Brooks is a poet, the author of *A Street in Bronzeville.*
   She has won the Pulitzer Prize.
   She has taught poetry in several Chicago colleges.
3. Eleanor Roosevelt was both versatile and talented.
   She wrote some very important books.
   One of them was *On My Own.*
   She was twice a delegate to the United Nations.
4. The Shakespeare Memorial at Stratford-on-Avon houses a theater.
   Stratford-on-Avon is the birthplace of Shakespeare.
   The Memorial also contains a gallery and a library.
5. On March 10, 1876, Alexander Graham Bell spoke through the first electromagnetic telephone.
   He spoke to Watson, his assistant.
   He said, "Mr. Watson, come here; I want you."

AVOIDING "STRINGY" STYLE

21g. Give variety to your writing by avoiding the "stringy" style which results from the overuse of *and* and *so.*

In everyday conversation we tend to string our ideas out, one after another, by means of the simple conjunctions *and* and *so.* In writing, however, this sort of thing appears childish and monotonous.

(1) Correct a stringy sentence by subordination of ideas.

STRINGY SENTENCE College admission standards continue to rise, *and* tension and anxiety build to a ridiculous point in college-preparatory seniors, *and* this spoils their final year in high school.

[1] For a review of subordination, see pages 286–92. For an explanation of the kinds of sentences, see pages 68–70.

IMPROVED As college admission standards continue to rise, tension and anxiety build to a ridiculous point in college-preparatory seniors, spoiling their final year in high school. [One *and* has been removed by means of the beginning subordinate clause. The other has been removed by means of the participial phrase, *spoiling their final year in high school.*]

The use of *so* as a conjunction is considered poor form. Its use can usually be avoided by using a subordinate clause or a phrase expressing cause or reason.

POOR USE OF *SO* Maria Martinez believed in tradition, *so* she experimented with ancient Pueblo pottery techniques.

IMPROVED Believing in tradition, Maria Martinez experimented with ancient Pueblo pottery techniques. *or*
Because she believed in tradition, Maria Martinez experimented with ancient Pueblo pottery techniques.

STRINGY USE OF *SO* We heard the static on the radio, *so* we were afraid of a thunderstorm, *so* we decided not to go out in the boat.

IMPROVED Fearing a thunderstorm when we heard the static on the radio, we decided not to go out in the boat.

(2) Correct a stringy sentence by dividing it into two sentences.

STRINGY SENTENCE I am very fond of foreign films, and so I go to the Celtic Theater more than to the other theaters, and we get only the best foreign films, so I not only learn a lot, but I see better pictures.

IMPROVED Being very fond of foreign films, I go to the Celtic Theater more than to the other theaters. Since we get only the best foreign films, I not only learn a lot, but I see better pictures. [stringiness corrected by subordination and by division into two sentences]

EXERCISE 9. Revising Sentences. Revise the sentences by one or more of the following methods: subordination, division into more than one sentence, and reduction. Get rid of the monotonous use of *and* and *so*. You may add a few words of your own if the words will help you to improve the sentences.

1. Tom Sawyer made Becky Thatcher jealous by talking to Amy Lawrence, and then Becky became very upset, so she invited everyone except Tom and Amy to her picnic, and then spent recess with Alfred, and she pretended not to notice Tom.
2. Tom and Becky continued to be angry with each other for a while, and then eventually they made up, and Tom looked forward to going to Becky's picnic.

3. Mrs. Thatcher set the day for the picnic and Tom and Becky visited the cave called "McDougal's Cave" with the rest of the company, and played hide-and-seek after exploring the wonders of the cave.
4. They followed a little stream of water, and Tom played the role of a discoverer, and Becky thought that was fun and followed him.
5. They wound down through the cave this way and that and crept from cavern to cavern and found a spring-fed pool.
6. In one cavern the ceiling was completely lined with bats, and the bats swarmed down when Tom and Becky entered the cavern with their candles, and one of them almost snuffed Becky's candle out.
7. Soon the stillness of the caves dampened Tom and Becky's spirits, and they realized that they had gone some distance from the others, and suddenly they were afraid they might be unable to get back.
8. They started back, and indeed they had become lost, and there was no way Tom could remember which route they had followed, and they had only one piece of cake and a few candle-stumps.
9. After several false starts through the various tunnels their candles gave out, and they were left in total darkness, and Becky wept, and they both thought they were certain to die in the pitch-black cave.
10. Leaving Becky alone, Tom took a length of rope and traced his way through the tunnels looking for an exit and soon saw a candle, so he shouted at the top of his voice, and the next thing he knew a familiar face was there in front of him.

CHAPTER 22

Sentence Revision

PRACTICE EXERCISES

This chapter contains exercises only. The exercises will test your understanding of sentence correctness, clearness, and smoothness, and they will give you practice in revising faulty sentence structure.

REVISING SENTENCES BY CORRECTING ERRORS IN SENTENCE STRUCTURE

EXERCISE 1. Revising Sentences by Correcting Errors in Sentence Structure. You will find below a list of errors in sentence structure. Each faulty sentence in the exercise illustrates one of these errors. You are to do two things: (1) write *before* the number of the sentence the letter of the error illustrated, and (2) write *after* the number of the sentence a revision which eliminates the error. Make sure that your revision is correct, clear, and smooth. If the sentence is correct as it stands, write a + before its number.

A Lack of agreement (subject and verb, or pronoun and antecedent)
B Incorrect case of pronoun
C Dangling modifier
D Lack of parallelism or faulty parallelism
E Unclear reference of pronoun (ambiguous, general, weak)

EXAMPLE 1. Do you know whom it was?
B 1. Do you know who it was?

1. People may disapprove of laws, but that doesn't prove they are good or bad.

2. Human behavior is complicated and difficult, not only to analyze but for evaluation.
3. The law is society's tested system of behavior, and they would have even worse problems without it.
4. Unless two individuals observe the same laws, the more powerful can always take advantage of the weaker.
5. Any wise judge, as well as the more experienced citizens, can appreciate that.
6. The fundamental principle behind all laws are the same.
7. It is that the rights of others limit the rights of any individual.
8. The law has many arms touching all of us, and to prescribe the proper limits in all our different roles.
9. It governs you as a student and I as a writer.
10. Hoping for order in our social dealings with one another, the fact that legality requires judicial decision often makes us impatient.
11. The complexity of judicial decisions reflects how complex is law itself.
12. When a law is carelessly formulated or improperly applied, a judge can cut them down to size.
13. The presiding judge in an American court of law is a person whom scholars agree has no counterpart in other nations.
14. Making every effort to avoid the "tyranny" of politics, the Constitution was written by men who knew how the law can be twisted to the selfish interests of those in power.
15. In the Constitution, legislative and executive power is restricted more than they are in other national systems of government.
16. Facing one practical question after another, this restriction was less a matter of design than it was the result of many difficult decisions individually reached.
17. If the writers of the Constitution had not given the powers they did to the courts, they would have been subject to one of the other branches of government.
18. The mood of an executive and the whim of a legislator consequently does not determine one's fate in a court of law.
19. Instead, the acts of executives and the laws of legislatures all become subject, when necessary, to the judgment of a judge.
20. Abuse and violation of the existing law was the last resort of the colonists.

EXERCISE 2. Revising Sentences by Correcting Errors in Sentence Structure. Follow the directions for Exercise 1.

A Sentence fragment
B Run-on sentence
C Incorrect tense or verb form
D Misplaced modifier
E Unclear relationship between sentence ideas (lack of subordination, faulty coordination)

1. Our camp, which lays at the north end of the lake, is overshadowed by the cliffs that raise steeply above it.
2. Team teaching offers teachers at least one important advantage, it enables each teacher on the team to teach his specialty.
3. Since it has a full squad of seasoned players, this year's football team should win the championship.
4. The car was driven by a stunning girl with whitewall tires.
5. The band in its new uniforms and the high-stepping majorette with her twirling baton as well as the stirring music.
6. A compromise is a settlement of differences reached by mutual concessions between two parties.
7. Secret police with hidden cameras that were trying to take pictures at the meeting were physically ejected by angry students.
8. She had intended to have gone to the dance with her brother.
9. At home we suffer the constant interference of our parents, at college we will be free to make our own decisions.
10. Tickets for matinees will cost $3.50, and matinees will be given on Wednesdays and Saturdays.
11. These experiences will be valuable in my career as a social worker, and it is a career in which I shall work with all kinds of people.
12. At the beginning of my junior-level Spanish course, the teacher reviewed the material I had the year before.
13. During negotiations between labor and management, work in the factory continued as usual.
14. The five junior-high-school buildings will cost eight million dollars, and they were approved by the taxpayers in yesterday's balloting.
15. We found several of the students in the shop very busy. Learning how to take a motor apart and put it together again.
16. The senator denied the many charges that had been made against her briefly and categorically.

17. In high school I have been unable to take some courses I wanted and have been required to take others I did not want.
18. Twenty percent of the students said they were satisfied with their own study habits, fifty-four percent said they wished they knew how to study more effectively.
19. If you would have come earlier, you could have seen the first act.
20. The demand for good television material exceeds the supply, and some of the best material, important news events, is not being fully used, and the reason is that news telecasts are not profitable.

REVISING SENTENCES BY SELECTING THE BEST EXPRESSIONS

EXERCISE 3. Revising Sentences by Selecting the Best Expressions. Number your paper 1–20. The italicized part of each sentence below is revised in two ways. If you consider one of these revisions an improvement, write the letter of the better one (*a* or *b*). If you consider the sentence correct as it stands, write +.

1. Behind one of the doors waits a tiger, *and the other has a beautiful lady behind it.*
   a. . . . and behind the other waits a beautiful lady.
   b. . . . and a beautiful lady waits behind the other.
2. If you go on a trip, *it will give you an excellent chance to practice your camera technique.*
   a. . . . you will have an excellent chance to practice your camera technique.
   b. . . . an excellent chance to practice your camera technique will be yours.
3. When developing films, *a darkroom will be needed.*
   a. . . . one thing you will need is a darkroom.
   b. . . . you will need a darkroom.
4. A deep-sea fisher needs an outboard motor much larger *than a fisher who fishes in sheltered waters.*
   a. . . . than that used by a fisher in sheltered waters.
   b. . . . than one fishing in sheltered waters.
5. Although they listen to several news broadcasts each day, *most people continue to buy a daily paper.*
   a. . . . a daily paper continues to be bought by most people.

b. . . . the buying of a daily paper by most people continues.

6. During the winter *Angela both developed her skill in skiing and ice-skating.*
   a. . . . Angela developed her skill in both skiing and ice-skating.
   b. . . . Angela developed both her skill in skiing and in ice-skating.
7. *Pat and him told Mike and I* the answers to the homework problems.
   a. . . . Pat and him told Mike and me . . .
   b. . . . Pat and he told Mike and me . . .
8. Ever since the accident, *driving past that spot*, the whole experience has returned.
   a. . . . while driving past that spot, . . .
   b. . . . as I have driven past that spot, . . .
9. *Was it he who* you thought stole the money?
   a. Was it he whom . . .
   b. Was it him whom . . .
10. When one of the girls *have completed their report, ask them* to bring it to me.
    a. . . . has completed their report, ask them . . .
    b. . . . has completed her report, ask her . . .
11. Don't expect *Jane and I to be as good as her* in English.
    a. . . . Jane and me to be as good as she . . .
    b. . . . Jane and I to be as good as she . . .
12. Plans for the P.T.A. party *include not only dancing but also* a floor show and a buffet supper.
    a. . . . not only include dancing but also . . .
    b. . . . include not only dancing, but also the guests will enjoy . . .
13. To my complete surprise the students *accepted the new type of examination which the teachers had prepared without a complaint.*
    a. . . . accepted the new type of examination without a complaint, which the teachers had prepared.
    b. . . . accepted without a complaint the new type of examination which the teachers had prepared.
14. The mayor's economy committee *has been investigating street-cleaning costs, and it has published a report on its findings.*
    a. . . . , which has been investigating street-cleaning costs, has published a report on its findings.
    b. . . . has been investigating street-cleaning costs, and a report has been published on its findings.

15. The two causes of "college neurosis" are trying to get into college *and then you try to stay there.*
    a. . . . and then to try to stay there.
    b. . . . and then trying to stay there.
16. *The students received the new yearbook*, which came out on the last day of school, *with enthusiasm.*
    a. The students received with enthusiasm the new yearbook . . .
    b. The students with enthusiasm received the new yearbook . . .
17. *The telegram reached me too late advising against going to Chicago.*
    a. Too late the telegram advising against going to Chicago reached me.
    b. The telegram advising against going to Chicago reached me too late.
18. *It is not the cost of a gift but its appropriateness that matters.*
    a. The cost of a gift does not matter, but the appropriateness of it does.
    b. It is not the cost that matters of a gift, but its appropriateness.
19. After being reprimanded twice, *the teacher, for further punishment, sent Ann to the principal.*
    a. . . . by the teacher, Ann was sent to the principal for further punishment.
    b. . . . the teacher sent Ann to the principal for further punishment.
20. *Driving through the mountains, we were impressed by the engineering achievements of road builders.*
    a. We were impressed by the engineering achievements of road-builders, driving through the mountains.
    b. We were impressed by the engineering achievements, driving through the mountains, of road builders.

REVISING AWKWARD SENTENCES

EXERCISE 4. Revising Awkward Sentences. This exercise is composed of awkward sentences which you are to revise in any way that will make them clearer and smoother. Your purpose is to express the same idea in a better way. Sentences may contain specific errors or they may be simply clumsy. You may add words or omit words wherever you wish, provided you do not alter the meaning. Each problem can be handled in a single sentence, but your teacher may allow you to divide some of the problems into two sentences.

1. She tried to find out the boy's name that she was to invite.
2. Featherbedding is one result of automation, which is the practice of keeping workers on the job, which is unnecessary, because the job has been made obsolete by machines.
3. The dean was more impressed by the candidate's scholastic record than his athletic record impressed him.
4. There are many persons who have jobs part of the year, and a job is not held by them the rest of the year, being among the unemployed.
5. There is a great deal of Franklin's philosophy which certainly everyone who reads it can benefit from in his *Autobiography*.
6. Soon families will have helicopters just like cars today and will be able to go from place to place much more easier than by car since there will be a direct route and the traffic will be much less.
7. Since we hadn't no tire repair kit, the motorcycle was pushed to the nearest gas station where we had a patch put on it.
8. Tammy was an optimist, easygoing, and nothing ever seemed to trouble her no matter what happened.
9. Opening the curtain, an empty stage was revealed, but the stage crew arrived a moment later and, busily working and talking, the set was soon up for the first act.
10. In a child a negative attitude may come from the natural desire for recognition and independence, but when an adult shows a negative attitude, it may be a symptom of neurosis.

COMPOSITION

CHAPTER 23

Writing and Thinking

THE WRITING PROCESS

Writing is not a single activity; it is not something that you can or should do in a single sitting, all at one time. Whenever you write, whether a paragraph or a composition, you are involved in an ongoing process of thinking, decision making, and rethinking. In this chapter, you will learn and practice the stages of the writing process and the many steps that make up each stage.

THE WRITING PROCESS

PREWRITING—Identifying your purpose and audience; choosing and limiting a subject; considering attitude and tone; gathering information; classifying and ordering information

WRITING A FIRST DRAFT—Expressing your ideas in sentences and paragraphs

EVALUATING—Judging the content, organization, and style of a draft

REVISING—Improving the content, organization, and style

PROOFREADING—Checking the revised version to correct errors in grammar, usage, and mechanics

WRITING THE FINAL VERSION—Preparing a final version and proofreading it

PREWRITING

During prewriting, the first stage in the writing process, you answer five important questions: Why am I writing? For whom am I writing? What will I write about? What will I say? How will I say it?

THE WRITER'S PURPOSE

23a. Have in mind a clear purpose for writing.

Every piece of writing has a purpose—sometimes more than one. Even when multiple purposes exist, however, a single purpose usually guides the writing. In an essay about what happened during your driving test, you may explain the test, but your main purpose is to tell a story about your experience.

Techniques for Prewriting. As you begin to plan your paper, remember the four basic purposes for writing:

• *Narrative* writing tells a story or relates a series of events.	A letter describing your first day at a new job
• *Expository* writing gives information or explains.	A definition of a water table for an essay question
• *Descriptive* writing describes a person, place or thing.	An essay describing the Grand Canyon
• *Persuasive* writing attempts to persuade or convince.	A brochure encouraging eighteen-year-olds to vote

EXERCISE 1. Identifying Purposes for Writing. Identify the purpose (to narrate, to explain, to describe, or to persuade) for writing about each of the following topics. (Some items could have more than one purpose.)

1. What a penguin looks like
2. The history of the founding of Pennsylvania

3. A funny incident during a shopping trip
4. How to tune a guitar
5. Why high-school students should volunteer to help elderly people in the community

EXERCISE 2. Identifying Purpose in Writing. Identify the writer's purpose in the following paragraph.

> David Gordon's new ballet, *Field, Chair, and Mountain,* uses ordinary folding chairs in a unique way. The dancers enter the stage carrying their own chairs. In the first section of the "chair" part of this ballet, the chair is each dancer's partner, giving support and balance as the dancers move in unison in a long series of graceful, intricate movements. Even in a romantic duet between the lead male and female dancers, a chair is central to the movements. Finally, the whole troupe dances in pairs, each pair with a chair. The graceful, innovative, sometimes humorous movements are danced to a nineteenth-century piano concerto by the Irish composer John Field.

CRITICAL THINKING: Analyzing How Purpose Affects Writing

Analysis is a critical thinking skill that you use in two ways when writing: to break a whole into its smaller parts and to determine how the parts are related. During prewriting, you are examining the separate elements of your paper and their effects on each other. For example, you analyze how purpose affects both the content of your writing and the particular words you use.

Consider the differences in two paragraphs about the danger of ultraviolet light; one paragraph explains and one tells a story. The explanation includes scientific facts and uses fairly formal language. The narration includes interesting details and uses less formal language.

> Natural sunlight and some artificial sources of illumination can cause a host of visual difficulties. Ultraviolet light from the sun and from lamps can cause cataracts and retinal damage. Even during winter, when the amount of ultraviolet radiation reaching the earth's surface is greatly reduced, those such as skiers and skaters exposed to intense direct or reflected light can suffer harm. Dr. Morris Waxler of the Food and Drug Administration says that they should wear sunglasses that filter out ultraviolet light during exposure to the midday sun and to other strong sources.
>
> JANE E. BRODY

> When I was seven and my brother thirteen, my parents took us for a vacation to Florida. We drove from the freezing January of Cleveland, Ohio, to the tropical sunshine of sunny Miami, making the trip in three days. The warmth and the ocean were unbelievable to us, straight from a gray, cold winter. My brother and I hurried to the beach and spent all of our first afternoon swimming, building sand castles, and—worst of all—lying on our stomachs at the shoreline while the waves washed delightfully over our legs. Of course, I didn't realize it, but I was absorbing enough ultraviolet rays to burn my legs badly. By evening, I was in considerable pain; by morning I could not walk. I spent the next three days in bed, recovering from that painful sunburn. And that's the last bad sunburn I've ever had. Now I always cover my fair, freckled skin with sunscreen, and I always limit my time in the sun. Nothing is worth the pain of a bad sunburn.

Persuasion and description also combine different details and language. Persuasive writing presents opinions, reasons, and evidence in formal, concise, clear language. Descriptive writing uses concrete and sensory details to create vivid images with less formal language and a freer writing style.

EXERCISE 3. Analyzing How Purpose Affects Writing. Two purposes for writing are given for each topic below. Consider how each purpose would affect a piece of writing in two ways. First, decide what aspect of the topic you would write about. Then list at least three details you would include to develop the topic for each purpose. Be prepared to explain your answers.

1. *Topic:* The worst natural disaster you have experienced
   Purpose: a. To inform b. To describe
2. *Topic:* The problem of adult illiteracy
   Purpose: a. To persuade b. To tell a story

THE WRITER'S AUDIENCE

23b. Identify the audience for whom you are writing.

Audiences for your writing may vary widely in age and background; therefore, you cannot write in the same way for all audiences. Like purpose, audience affects both content and language. If your topic is a new type of word processing software, you will write about it differently for members of your computer club than for your other classmates.

EXERCISE 4. Identifying Purpose and Audience. Go to the library and find six different samples of writing. You may include magazine and newspaper articles, novels, and short stories. For each piece of writing, identify what you think is the writer's main purpose and who you think is the intended audience.

CRITICAL THINKING:
Analyzing How Audience Affects Writing

The following paragraphs were written for adults interested in the birds of the northern states:

> Until recently most students of migration focused on its mechanics, such as energetics, or navigation and orientation. Little was known about what happens to "our" birds during the months they are away from their breeding grounds. Where do they go? What dangers do they face? How do they live in their winter homes? Nature's grandest theatrical event remained largely mysterious.
>
> Now ornithologists who followed the birds into the tropics are able to answer some of those questions. One point, though it may ruffle our proprietary instincts, ought to be cleared up at once. A good many of the most familiar birds in our gardens and forests are not "ours" at all. Families such as the wood warblers, vireos, flycatchers, and tanagers are, for the most part, not northern birds that happen to fly south for a while to escape the wintry blasts. They are tropical birds that come north for a few months every year to raise a family and then return to their ancestral homes.
>
> FRANK GRAHAM, JR.

If you rewrote this information for fifth-graders, you would have to explain or omit some unfamiliar terms, such as *energetics, navigation, orientation,* and *ornithologists.* You might provide a brief background about migration, and you would omit the references to "our" birds and "proprietary instincts." You might also replace the rather flowery phrases *grandest theatrical event* and *ancestral homes.* Finally, you would generally simplify vocabulary and shorten sentences to make the information easier to understand.

Also be aware of purpose when analyzing audience, because the two are closely related. In persuasive writing, for example, you must carefully consider readers' beliefs and prejudices. Your answers to the questions on the following page will help you understand your audience and adapt your writing to that audience.

Techniques for Prewriting. Ask yourself the following questions about your audience:

- What information does the audience already know about the topic?
- What background or technical information might this audience need to understand the topic? What terms might be defined for them?
- What language and style are most appropriate for the audience: simple or complex words and sentences, casual or formal presentation?
- Does the audience have any bias (strong feelings either for or against) about the topic that could affect the writing? If so, what is the bias?

EXERCISE 5. Analyzing the Effects of Audience. Read the following item, in which four different audiences are given for one topic and purpose. Then write out answers to the questions that follow.

Topic: Why all high-school students should be required to take four years of a foreign language

Purpose: To persuade

Audiences: (a) twelfth-graders, (b) high-school foreign language teachers, (c) members of the local board of education, (d) local businesspeople

1. Which audiences would have greater knowledge of the topic? Less knowledge?
2. For which audiences would terms need to be defined? What terms might be defined for the audience(s)?
3. Which audiences would need background information? What kind of background information might be supplied for them?
4. Which audiences might have strong feelings for or against the subject? What might the feelings be? How would the feelings affect your writing?
5. For which audience would you choose to write? Why?

EXERCISE 6. Rewriting a Paragraph for Different Audiences. Select one paragraph from a high-school or college textbook or a reference book. Choose a topic that interests you—one you already have some background knowledge of or experience with. Then rewrite the paragraph for two of the following audiences. At the beginning of each version, be sure to identify the audience.

a. Fourth-grade students
b. Adults who have no previous knowledge of the topic
c. Exchange students from the Soviet Union

CHOOSING AND LIMITING A SUBJECT

23c. Choose a subject that is appropriate to your audience.

When choosing a subject, always consider your readers' knowledge and interests. While you could explain the concept of probability to third-graders—by giving extensive, simplified definitions—that subject is better for an older audience. The subject of probability, however, is not appropriate for every audience that can understand the concepts. You might choose it for a science-essay contest, but you would not choose it for your first contribution to the school newspaper. Make sure that your readers will be interested in your subject and that it is neither too complex nor too simple for them.

EXERCISE 7. Choosing a Subject Appropriate for an Audience. Consider the following subjects in relation to the five audiences listed below. Determine the audiences for which each subject would be appropriate. Be prepared to explain your answers.

Audiences: (a) readers of the local newspaper, (b) business owners, (c) parents, (d) your classmates, (e) senior citizens

1. How to make money in the stock market
2. How to get along with teen-agers
3. Planning a Thanksgiving dinner for thirty
4. The most valuable postage stamps in the world
5. How to do batik (a method of dyeing cloth)

23d. Limit your subject so that it can be adequately covered in the form of writing you have chosen.

A *subject* is a broad, general area of knowledge, such as "robots" or "art." A *topic* is a limited subject, such as "the use of robots in the home" and "Vincent Van Gogh's landscapes at Arles." A topic for a paragraph is necessarily more limited than one for a composition because a paragraph allows less space for developing the main idea. If you choose a topic too extensive for your form of writing, you cannot present it adequately to your audience.

EXERCISE 8. Distinguishing Between Subjects and Topics. Identify each item as either a general subject (*S*) or a limited topic (*T*) for a short composition.

1. How to prepare tacos
2. William Shakespeare
3. Efforts to save the endangered manatee
4. Better television programs
5. How to create a crossword puzzle

CRITICAL THINKING:
Analyzing a Subject

To find limited topics for writing, you may analyze a subject by dividing and subdividing it into smaller parts. Depending on the subject, the basis for your analysis may be time periods, examples, features, uses, causes, or types.

EXAMPLES 1. *Subject divided into examples*

Subject: Dogs that are bred for hunting
Main divisions: Retrievers
Hounds
Setters
Pointers
Spaniels

2. *Subject divided into features or aspects*

Subject: Dreams
Main divisions: Why people dream
Types of dreams
Interpretation of dreams
Scientific study of dreaming

EXERCISE 9. Analyzing Subjects to Develop Topics. From the following list, choose three subjects and divide each one into at least five smaller parts. (Note: For each subject, different analyses are possible and correct.)

1. Congress
2. Team sports
3. Personality
4. American literature
5. Exploration
6. Pollution
7. Alcoholism
8. Popular music
9. Medicine
10. Precious metals

EXERCISE 10. Limiting a Subject to Develop Topics Suitable for Paragraphs. Choose one of the subjects that you analyzed for Exercise 9. Could each of these topics be covered adequately in a paragraph of about 150 words? If not, divide the topics further until you have at least three that can be adequately covered in a paragraph. List them, and save your paper.

TONE

23e. Consider your attitude toward your topic and its expression through tone.

Your attitude, or point of view, toward your topic is important because it affects both the details you include and the language you use in your writing. The expression of your attitude—whether approving, angry, humorous, or fearful—is called *tone.*

Consider the tone of the following movie review. Clearly the writer's attitude is negative, but what particular words and details convey her attitude and create the sarcastic tone? If you wanted to write a favorable review of the film, what changes in words and details would you make to alter the tone?

> "Cross Creek," an account of a woman's struggle to become a writer, is given a supernal glow by the director Martin Ritt. The picture seems to be suffering from earthshine: everything is lighted to look holy, and whenever the score isn't shimmering and burnishing, nature is twittering. It's all pearly and languid, and more than a little twerpy—it's one long cue for "Oh, What a Beautiful Mornin'." Loosely based on Marjorie Kinnan Rawlings' semi-autobiographical tales about what she learned during her years in an orange grove in the Florida swamps, the movie opens in 1928. We're meant to admire Mrs. Rawlings (Mary Steenburgen), a Northerner, for her courage in leaving her home and husband and going down to Florida to write. But the script doesn't give even a hint of why she bought the grove (sight unseen), or why she thinks she'll find more propitious conditions for writing gothic romances in the subtropical marshland than she had in her bedroom or her study in New York. The filmmakers view her as a feminist

ahead of her time—a heroine who gives up a social life and goes out on her own to face hardships. Yet the way they tell the story, she's almost immediately equipped with everything she has cast aside. When her jalopy gives out before she arrives at her property, it's said to be in hopeless condition, but the courtly and handsome hotelkeeper Norton Baskin (Peter Coyote), who drives her to her tumbledown shack, shows up again a day or two later bringing the car, which has been repaired so that it looks sparkling and new. Meanwhile, friendly neighbors have been dropping in, and Mrs. Rawlings has hired a young black woman, Geechee (Alfre Woodard), to clean and cook, and field hands to take care of the crops. The house is already transformed; it's gracious and orderly, and she's at her typewriter, with a potted gloxinia blooming nearby. She's ladylike, and the local people do everything for her. So what's so heroic about her—beyond her managerial skills?

PAULINE KAEL—*The New Yorker*

EXERCISE 11. Identifying Tone. Bring to class five paragraphs from different sources, such as magazines, short stories, novels, and nonfiction books. Identify the tone of each paragraph and the author's attitude toward the topic.

GATHERING INFORMATION

23f. Gather information appropriate to your purpose.

Your purpose for writing largely determines the kinds of information you must gather. For example, to *describe* your grandparents' kitchen, you would need to provide vivid details for your readers: the utensils, the furniture and appliances, even the smells in the room. To *give information* about Haleakala National Park on Maui Island, you would provide facts about the park and about sightseeing within it.

No matter what kinds of details you need, however, you can learn techniques to make your information gathering easier. The methods discussed in the following pages show you both how to tap your own creativity and how to analyze a topic.

Direct and Indirect Observation

(1) Use your powers of observation to note specific details.

Whenever your observations are made through your own senses of sight, smell, sound, taste, or touch, they are called *direct observations.* In the following paragraph, Harry Crews's firsthand observation provides interesting details that create a vivid picture of a room.

> I went on down the hallway and out onto the back porch and finally into the kitchen that was built at the very rear of the house. The entire room was dominated by a huge black cast-iron stove with six eyes on its cooking surface. Directly across the room from the stove was the safe, a tall square cabinet with wide doors covered with screen wire that was used to keep biscuits and fried meat and rice or almost any other kind of food that had been recently cooked. Between the stove and the safe sat the table we ate off of, a table almost ten feet long, with benches on each side instead of chairs, so that when we put in tobacco, there would be enough room for the hired hands to eat.
>
> HARRY CREWS

Indirect observations are all those not made directly through your own senses. When you listen to other people telling about their experiences or read about other people's observations, you are making an indirect observation. Much of the information that you gather for writing comes through indirect observations.

CRITICAL THINKING:
Observing Specific Details

You cannot possibly remember every sensory detail of an experience, but you can improve your powers of observation. Concentrate on paying attention to specifics, and you will discover many interesting details for your writing.

EXERCISE 12. Improving Your Powers of Observation. Choose one of the following places, take a pencil and paper with you, sit (or stand) in one place for ten minutes, and list as many sensory details (sight, sound, smell, touch, and taste) as you can.

1. A shopping mall
2. The school cafeteria during lunch hour
3. The street outside your home at 6:00 A.M.
4. An empty field (or woods or vacant lot)
5. A bus stop or subway station

A Writer's Journal

(2) Keep a writer's journal to record your thoughts and feelings about your experiences.

A writer's journal can be a rich source of ideas for writing as well as a record of specific experiences. You may record any number of things in a journal: sudden insights, considered opinions, striking sights, overheard conversations, quotations from favorite books, and reactions to other people. A writer's journal should contain only what you want to share with others; however, you might also keep a private journal for your own use.

EXERCISE 13. Using a Journal Entry to Gather Ideas for Writing. Read the following journal entries and then answer the questions that follow them.

> January 22. Not too often that frost hits southern Florida—sometimes the central part of the state, but not here. Temperature going down to 30 degrees tonight after two days of "Arctic" weather. Rest of the country having weird weather, too: -27° in Chicago with a wind-chill factor that makes it -80°. I'm glad I'm missing that. (Poor Uncle Bernie in Chicago.) Trying to save my vegetable garden. Draped all of the vegetables with black plastic. Mom helped me water the ground well without getting leaves wet. I feel sorry for the farmers with acres and acres. Can't use smudge pots here; don't even know where I'd find one. We've moved my two zebra finches to the kitchen, the warmest room in the house. They're so delicate they'd never survive the chill in the rest of the house. Hoping for the best tonight.
>
> January 23. Temperature went down to 29! A record for southern Florida. Vegetable plants are all frozen, but I tried my best. When the weather warms, I'll start again with tomato seedlings, eggplants, peppers. Farmers here lost most of their crops, and upstate citrus crops are badly damaged.

1. The journal writer decided to write a composition explaining how to plant a small vegetable garden. List at least three other topics, suggested by the entry, that the writer might have chosen.
2. Where would you look for information about the topics you listed in item 1?

Brainstorming and Clustering

(3) Use brainstorming and clustering to find writing ideas.

Both brainstorming and clustering are techniques that generate a free flow of ideas. You may use these techniques either to think of topics for writing or to generate specific details to develop a topic you have already chosen.

When you brainstorm you think of one specific subject or topic, and then write down every idea, word, or phrase that comes to mind as you concentrate on that subject or topic. The end result is a long list of words or phrases—the longer, the better—written under the subject or topic you started with. Relax, but work quickly, jotting down every idea that occurs to you, and do not stop until you have run out of ideas. Only then should you evaluate the items you have listed. Circle those that seem usable, and write down any others suggested by your evaluation.

One writer created the following list during a five-minute brainstorming on the subject "deer."

DEER

hunting deer
kinds of deer—tiny Key deer; white-tailed deer
deer endangered?
what happens to deer in winter—food supply?
deer need salt
Bambi and other deer stories
gentle, peaceful creatures
what do they harm? eat gardens, crops
relatives of antelopes? many African species?
sayings associated with deer—shy as a deer, run like a deer
social structure of deer—travel in groups? stay in families? how many born each year?
where are most deer living—what parts of the U.S.?
many road signs about deer crossing; urban areas?
life cycle of deer
males called bucks; females—does; babies—fawns

Clustering, or *making connections,* is like brainstorming, but the result is a diagram of related ideas, not an unordered list. The end result is a diagram (instead of a list, as in brainstorming) with ideas grouped together around the subject or topic you started with. Begin by writing your subject or topic in the center of the paper and circling it. As ideas come to mind, write them down, circle them, and draw lines connecting them either to the central idea or to each other.

Here is the subject "deer" as a clustering diagram. Notice that some of the ideas are related only to the subject "deer," not to other ideas.

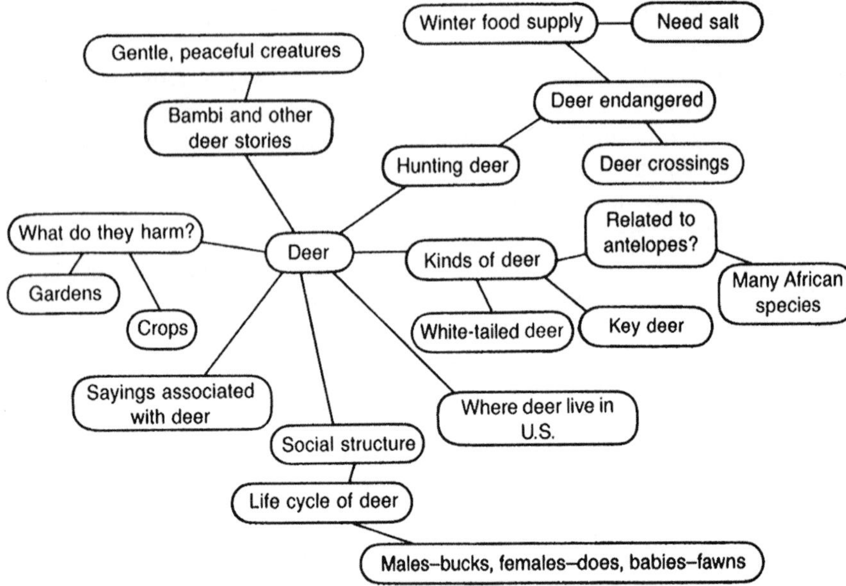

EXERCISE 14. Using Brainstorming or Clustering to Gather Information. Use either brainstorming or clustering to gather information about a topic you developed for Exercise 10 or for another topic.

Asking the 5 *W-How?* Questions

(4) Ask the *5 W-How?* questions to gather information.

The *5 W-How?* questions—*Who? What? Where? When? Why?* and *How?*—can help you gather specific details to use in your writing. Not every question will apply to every topic.

EXAMPLE *Topic:* The founding of this city (community)
Who? Who founded this city?
What? What was here before the city was founded?
Where? Where was the first settlement built?
Where is the oldest part of the city?
When? When was the city founded?
Why? Why was the city founded at this particular place?
Why did the first people come here?
How? How was the city founded?

EXERCISE 15. Gathering Information by Asking the 5 *W-How?* Questions. Use the *5 W-How?* questions to gather information about one of the following topics or a topic of your own. Write both your questions and the answers. (You may need to do research to find some answers.)

1. The records set by an outstanding athlete
2. An important change in your life
3. A solution to a problem in your community
4. The Civil War's major battle
5. An accident

Asking Point-of-View Questions

(5) Use different points of view to gather information.

Considering your topic from different points of view is another way to gather information. Three basic questions—What is it? How does it change or vary? What are its relationships?—will generate other questions specific to a topic.[1]

1. *What is it?* This first point of view focuses on the topic itself: what it looks like, what it does, and how it differs from others of its kind. The question *What is it?*—because it defines—is useful even for abstract ideas.

EXAMPLES *Topic:* My favorite place to be alone and think
[Where is the place? What does it look like? Why have I chosen it as my favorite place? What are my feelings when I am there?]

Topic: What is a democracy?
[How does a democracy work? What are its unique characteristics? What nations today are democracies?]

2. *How does it change or vary?* The second point of view focuses on how a topic changes over time. Its questions help you discover information about a topic's history and future, as well as how a topic keeps its identity even when it varies.

[1] This technique is based on ideas in *Rhetoric: Discovery and Change* by Richard E. Young, Alton L. Becker, and Kenneth E. Pike (New York: Harcourt Brace Jovanovich, 1971).

EXAMPLE *Topic:* What is a sonnet?
[When was a sonnet first defined? Are there different types of sonnets? How do they differ? What characteristics distinguish all sonnets from other poems? What are some famous early sonnets? What are some modern sonnets?]

3. *What are its relationships?* Using the third point of view, you analyze the topic's elements or aspects, considering how they are related to each other and to the topic as a whole. You may also consider how the topic is related to similar topics.

EXAMPLE *Topic:* Requirements for a successful speech
[What are the indispensable elements of a successful speech: content, organization, humor, presentation? Which element is most important? Least important? Or are they all equally important? How is a good speech like a good performance in a play?]

EXERCISE 16. Gathering Information by Asking Point-of-View Questions. Use the three point-of-view questions (What is it? How does it change or vary? What are its relationships?) to generate questions for two writing topics. You may use any topics in this chapter or choose new ones. Write all of the questions you think of as well as your answers.

CLASSIFYING INFORMATION

23g. Classify your ideas and information by grouping related ideas.

The next step in the writing process is to organize the ideas and details you have gathered. You must *classify* the information by deciding how items are related.

CRITICAL THINKING:
Classifying Ideas and Details

When you classify, you try to group similar details under a heading that explains what they have in common. Here is a classification of the writer's list of details for the subject "deer."

Types of deer in U.S.
  White-tailed deer of northeastern U.S.
  Key deer (Florida Keys)
  Black-tailed deer of the Pacific Coast
  Mule deer of the plains and western U.S.
Dangers to deer
  Natural dangers
    Lack of food (caused by flooding, winter)
    Animal predators
    Disease
  Dangers caused by people
    Hunters
    Cars

In the process of classifying, the writer has created more than one heading, so the relationship of the groupings has to be clarified. Two of the headings, "Natural dangers" and "Dangers caused by people," are actually subdivisions of a main heading, "Dangers to deer."

Classifying may also suggest missing details or reveal unnecessary ones. In this example, the writer has included in the outline several details that were not in the original list of brainstormed ideas—information such as other types of American deer. On the other hand, the writer chose to omit many details from the original list of brainstormed information because of the limited space of a short composition.

Techniques for Prewriting. Use the following questions to help you classify a list of ideas and details.

- Which items have something in common? What is it? (Use the common element to write a heading.)
- Are some items or groupings more important than others? If so, which ones?
- Which items are subdivisions (examples, parts, etc.) of the main ideas? (If you have not listed any subdivisions for your main ideas, return to the information-gathering techniques.)
- Do some items not fit within your groupings? (Discard these for the present paper; you may use them later to develop another limited topic.)

EXERCISE 17. Classifying Ideas and Information. Read the following list of ideas for a composition on cave-dwelling animals. Decide which ideas can be grouped together, and write a heading for each group. (Note: The headings are not in the list.) Then write the ideas under their proper headings. Put secondary headings under main headings if necessary. You may omit items that do not seem to fit.

a. cave-dwelling animals called *troglodytes:* salamanders, fish, insects, and crustaceans (shrimps, crabs, crayfish)
b. animals are blind—eyesight not useful in complete darkness
c. scarcity of food, must be brought in (by stream, bird droppings) from outside
d. animals have no pigment (all white)
e. no vegetation in caves; no light
f. weather not a threat—temperature fairly constant
g. environment usually small; fewer predators than at surface, less competition for food
h. high humidity, advantage for skin-breathing animals such as some salamanders
i. slower metabolism (rate of body functions) than surface animals; can exist on less food
j. troglodytes—fewer and larger eggs; newborns—better chance to survive
k. longer legs than surface relatives—can search for food more easily
l. *Ursus spelaeus*—extinct species of cave bear; fossils in caves

ARRANGING INFORMATION

23h. Arrange your ideas in order.

After classifying your ideas under main headings, you must consider the best order in which to present the information. With this sequence decided, you have an informal outline for your paper. Often your purpose suggests an order. Chronological order is appropriate, for example, when your topic is a step-by-step process, such as "preparing for a college-entrance examination." Arranging ideas in order of importance is more logical, however, if you are trying to persuade readers to visit residents of a nursing home.

In expository compositions background information is often necessary for the reader to understand what you have to say. Such background information, as well as technical terms that need to be defined for your audience, should be presented first. Then arrange your ideas in the order you think will be clearest and most interesting for your audience. (You will learn more about types of order in Chapter 24.)

REVIEW EXERCISE A. Following the Steps for Prewriting. Prepare to write a paragraph or short composition on a topic of your choice. Choose a subject, and limit it to a suitable topic. Decide on your purpose and audience, and consider your attitude and tone. Using at least one of the techniques for gathering information, list specific details to include. Classify the details under main headings, decide on an appropriate order, and write the order down as an informal outline for your writing.

WRITING THE FIRST DRAFT

All of the prewriting steps prepare you for the second stage of the writing process, the actual writing of a first draft.

WRITING THE FIRST DRAFT

23i. Write a first draft, keeping your audience and purpose in mind.

Your goal in writing a first draft is not perfection, but the clear expression of your ideas in complete sentences. With your notes and outline in front of you, recall your purpose and audience. Then write freely. You will take time later to evaluate, revise, and proofread.

CRITICAL THINKING: Synthesis

Synthesis is a creative process: the making of a new whole from smaller parts. All writing is therefore a synthesis: the combining of ideas and words into unique letters, essays, plays, or stories. Because writing is creative, the process itself often gives you new ideas. During a first draft you may rethink earlier decisions. You may alter your tone, delete a weak detail, arrange ideas more logically. Do not hesitate to use the discoveries that arise from synthesizing.

EXERCISE 18. Writing a First Draft. Using the prewriting notes you developed for Review Exercise A, write a first draft of your paragraph or composition.

EVALUATING

A draft, by definition, is not a finished piece of writing. All writers—professionals as well as students—must evaluate their first drafts to correct and improve them. To complete the writing process, you must be able to recognize the weaknesses, as well as the strengths, of your writing.

EVALUATING YOUR WRITING

23j. Evaluate your first draft.

Evaluating writing is the process of judging what works and what does not work. You are already evaluating when you make changes as you write a first draft. After you finish the draft, however, you must evaluate it as a whole, and this step requires distance: you examine the writing as if it were someone else's. You also judge the writing in its entirety: content, organization, and style. A thorough evaluation requires several rereadings of your first draft. By using different techniques, you can gain new insights from each review.

Techniques for Evaluating. To gain different perspectives on your draft, use the following techniques:

- Set your draft aside for awhile so that you are seeing it fresh.
- Read aloud, to "hear" what you have said. Listen for confusing statements, missing details, inappropriate language or tone.
- Have a classmate or someone else read your draft and comment on strengths and weaknesses. (Professional writers almost always have a friend or an editor who evaluates their writing.)

CRITICAL THINKING: Evaluating Content, Organization, and Style

When you *evaluate,* you judge your writing on the basis of *criteria,* or standards, that can be grouped under three headings:

Content	What have you said?
Organization	How have you arranged your ideas?
Style	How have you used words and sentences?

The following Guidelines for Evaluating apply to almost any form of writing. With this checklist, you can identify problems in your draft and mark them for later revision.

GUIDELINES FOR EVALUATING

Content

Purpose	1. Do the paper's ideas and details support the primary purpose: to explain, describe, persuade, or tell a story?
Audience	2. Will the intended audience find the paper interesting? Does the paper contain adequate background information and explanations of terms?
Topic Development	3. Is the information sufficiently detailed for the audience's understanding? Is any information unnecessary?

Organization

Order	4. Is similar information presented together, or must the reader jump back and forth among ideas? Does the order of the information make the main idea clear?
Transitions	5. Are sentences smoothly joined by connecting words? Does one idea lead clearly to another, or does information seem to be missing?

Style

Tone	6. Does the choice of words and details effectively communicate the writer's attitude toward the topic? Does the paper sound serious enough, or light enough, for its purpose?
Sentence Structure	7. Do the sentences vary in length and structure to avoid monotony?
Word Choice	8. Are words precise and specific rather than general and vague? Is meaning clear rather than fuzzy? Are descriptive words vivid?

EXERCISE 19. Evaluating a First Draft. Read the following draft, intended for an audience of high-school students, and evaluate it using the guidelines on page 369. Number your paper as the guidelines are numbered, 1–8, and write *yes* if the guideline is met and *no* if it is not. Give at least one specific example from the paper to support each "no" answer.

Caves are dark, damp hollow places within the earth. Sometimes they are hollowed-out places in hillsides. Because no light can reach the inside of a cave and light is necessary for photosynthesis to take place, no plants grow inside of caves, and it is plants that we associate as a source of food for animals. You would expect that caves should be empty of animal life, but that is not true. Thousands of animal species live full-time in caves. They have a special name: troglodytes, or "cave dwellers." Many other species of animals live part-time in caves (bears, bats, some tropical birds), but this paper is about full-time cave-dwelling animals.

A cave isn't the easiest place in which to live, as you can probably imagine. It is dark all the time—*pitch* dark—because no light from the sun can enter the cave except at the cave entrance. There is also very little food in a cave—no plant food, as we have mentioned already. What little food there is must be "imported" from the outside. Usually, it comes into the cave from a stream or, if bats live in the cave, from droppings.

So why would any animal want to live in such a hostile environment? They do. One of the advantages to living in a cave, if you are a troglodyte, is that the weather poses no threat. Usually the temperature inside of a cave remains pretty much the same, unlike the surface world with its extremes of heat, cold, and storms. Life in a cave may be more peaceful than life on the surface, because there are usually fewer predators and less competition for the existing food supply. Some animals that require high humidity to breathe through their skins, like the salamander, are delighted by the high humidity inside of a cave; they never would make it in the outside world.

Troglodytes look different because of the adaptations they have made to living in total darkness. For one thing, most are blind or have no eyes at all and have lost the power to see because it has been unused for generations. Also, troglodytes are white because they have no pigment. Apparently, pigmentation has the purpose of protecting creatures from the effects of the sun. These cave-dwelling creatures have adapted to their environment in other ways. They have longer legs than their relatives on the surface, apparently to enable them to search more easily for food on the craggy surface of the cave walls. Also, their meatabolism rate is slower; this slower rate enables the cave-dwellers to get by with less food. They have adapted to their environment in one more way, too, in the way in which they reproduce. Compared to their surface relatives, they lay fewer eggs and the eggs are bigger. This means that the newborn creatures are bigger and more likely to survive in the challenging environment of the cave.

EXERCISE 20. Evaluating a First Draft. Using the Guidelines for Evaluating, evaluate your first draft from Exercise 18 or any other piece of writing. To write your evaluation, number your paper 1–8 and indicate whether each guideline was met. Explain why any guideline was not met. You may exchange papers with another student to evaluate one another's draft.

REVISING

When you evaluate your paper, you locate problems in your writing. When you revise, you find a specific way to correct each weakness in your paper.

REVISING YOUR FIRST DRAFT

23k. Revise your first draft.

Four basic revision techniques can correct most problems in writing: adding, cutting, replacing, and reordering.

Techniques for Revising. To improve your evaluated draft, use the following techniques:

- *Add:* add new information (ideas or details), sentences, or words
- *Cut:* take out information, sentences, or words
- *Replace:* take out information, sentences, or words and substitute something more relevant or appropriate
- *Reorder:* move information, sentences, or words to another place in the paper

These four techniques can be used for problems in content (what you say about your topic), organization (how you arrange ideas about your topic), and style (how you use language to discuss your topic). Notice how one writer used these techniques to revise the following paragraphs. (See Revising and Proofreading Symbols on page 380.)

Topic: The value of S.A.T. preparation courses
Purpose: To inform
Audience: Classmates and teacher

Many high-school ~~students~~ enroll in S.A.T. prepara- replace
tion courses. ~~They hope to improve~~ their S.A.T. (Scho- replace/reorder
lastic Aptitude Test) scores ~~that most colleges require as~~ reorder/replace
~~part of an entrance application~~. Do these preparation cut
courses ~~have any effect in improving~~ test scores? ~~Course~~ replace
~~givers~~ say "yes"; the Educational Testing Service, which replace
administers ~~the~~ S.A.T.'s, says "not ~~really~~." ~~An~~ indepen- cut/replace
dent study ~~recently released~~ analyzed a large number of add/replace
individual studies. ~~The report~~ concluded that ~~"reason-~~ replace/cut
~~able gains could be made on S.A.T.'s through relatively~~ cut
~~small amounts of coaching."~~ The average improvement cut
after a coaching course is 15 points on the verbal section
and 20 points on the mathematics section. ~~The word~~ cut
~~*average* infers that~~ some students ~~may make~~ considerably replace
higher ~~scores~~; ~~some~~ less. One ~~student~~, Donna Sukenik of replace
Shaker Heights, Ohio, ~~complains~~ that ~~her verbal score~~ replace
~~actually was lower after a coaching course. "I think they~~ replace/cut
can be very helpful in math, where ~~you can refresh your~~ replace
~~memory about formulas and things like that," she said.~~ replace/cut
"But I needed help in verbal—and my verbal score went
down." According to ~~the~~ Educational Testing Service add/reorder/replace
study, ~~it would take~~ 40 hours of class time and ~~a lot of~~ cut/add/replace
~~extra~~ homework ~~to~~ answer two or three questions cor- replace/add
rectly in each section for an average gain of 13 points on add
verbal and 21 points on math. add

The following chart shows how the revision techniques (adding, cutting, replacing, and reordering) can be combined with the evaluation guidelines to solve writing problems. The other composition chapters contain charts that apply the four revision techniques to each specific form or type of writing.

REVISING A DRAFT

PROBLEM	TECHNIQUE	REVISION
Content		
The ideas and details do not help to explain, describe, persuade, or tell the story.	Add/Cut	Add explanations, supporting arguments, descriptive details, or narrative details. Cut information unrelated to the purpose of the composition.
The reader will not be interested.	Add/Replace	Add interesting examples, anecdotes, dialogue, or more narrative details. Replace details unrelated to the audience's interests or background.
Unfamiliar terms are not explained.	Add/Replace	Add a definition or explanation to the composition. Replace any unfamiliar terms with more familiar ones.
The information is insufficient for the audience to understand the topic.	Add	Add details, facts, examples, etc., to support the topic.
Some information does not support the topic and may confuse or distract the reader.	Cut	Cut the information (sentences or parts of sentences) that does not relate directly to the topic and purpose.

PROBLEM	TECHNIQUE	REVISION
Organization		
The reader cannot follow the ideas.	Reorder	Check the order set in the informal plan. Move the draft's ideas or details to clarify meaning.
Connections between ideas are not clear.	Add	Add transitional words to link sentences: *this, when, then, first, in addition, as a result,* etc. Add missing information.
Style		
The tone is unsuitable for audience and purpose.	Replace	Create a lighter tone by replacing formal words with less formal ones (slang, contractions, etc.). Create a more serious tone by replacing slang and contractions with standard vocabulary.
The tone does not convey the writer's intended attitude.	Add/Replace	Add words or details consistent with the attitude (angry, approving, comic, etc.), or replace inconsistent ones.
The sentences are monotonous.	Add/Replace/ Reorder	Combine sentences by joining them with *and, but, for,* or *or;* by making one subordinate to another; or by making one a modifying phrase. Change word order to begin sentences in different ways.
The words are dull or vague. Meaning is not clear.	Replace	Replace general terms with precise, exact words. Replace uninteresting descriptions with vivid, sensory details.

EXERCISE 21. Revising a First Draft. Using the evaluation you completed for Exercise 19, revise the excerpted paragraphs. For each problem that you found, identify a technique to correct it (add, cut, reorder, or replace). Then make the necessary improvements, referring to the preceding revision chart.

EXAMPLE

Evaluation Unnecessary information is included.
Technique Cut part of the sentence.
Revision One of the advantages to living in a cave, if you are a troglodyte, is that the weather poses no threat.

REVIEW EXERCISE B. Revising a First Draft. Using the evaluation from Exercise 20, revise your first draft.

PROOFREADING

When you have finished revising, you turn to the next stage in the writing process, proofreading: finding and correcting errors in grammar, usage, and mechanics.

PROOFREADING YOUR WRITING

23I. Proofread your revised version.

Proofreading your own writing requires particularly keen attention. Some techniques will help you focus on this task.

Techniques for Proofreading. To improve your accuracy in proofreading, use the following techniques:

- Put your paper aside for a while. You will see errors more quickly.
- Cover the lines below the one you are proofreading. You will not read ahead and pass over an error.
- Read the paper twice: once sentence-by-sentence and once letter-by-letter. You will catch errors in usage and grammar as well as in mechanics.

CRITICAL THINKING:
Applying the Standards of Written English

The purpose of proofreading is to apply the standards of written English to your writing. These standards, summarized in the Guidelines for Proofreading that follow, are the rules generally used in books, magazines, and newspapers. Writers follow these standards to prevent readers from being confused because of inaccurate writing or distracted by mistakes.

GUIDELINES FOR PROOFREADING

1. Is every sentence complete? (pages 277–80)
2. Does every sentence end with a punctuation mark? Are all punctuation marks correct? (pages 215–56)
3. Does every sentence begin with a capital letter? Are all proper nouns and appropriate proper adjectives capitalized? (pages 199–214)
4. Does every verb agree in number with its subject? (pages 79–93)
5. Are verb forms and tenses correct? (pages 118–28)
6. Are subject and object forms of personal pronouns correct? (pages 100–113)
7. Does every pronoun agree with its antecedent in number and in gender? Are pronoun references clear? (pages 294–99)
8. Are frequently confused words (such as lie and lay, fewer and less) used correctly? (pages 129–34, 167–91)
9. Are all words spelled correctly? (pages 257–74)
10. Is the paper neat and free from obvious crossed-out words and erasures? (pages 377–78)

EXERCISE 22. Applying the Standards of Written English. In each sentence, find and correct the error in grammar, usage, or mechanics. If you cannot correct an error, you may use other sections of this book for reference. Then make the correction.

1. One of the girls know the answer. (subject-verb agreement with indefinite pronouns)
2. Please give me the loaf of bread, that is on the bottom of the front row. (punctuating restrictive adjective clauses)
3. Between you and I, we've just run out of time. (using the objective case of pronouns for the object of a preposition)
4. Where did you put the tickets. (punctuating questions)

5. Whenever I don't get enough sleep or feel really tense and nervous. (sentence fragments)
6. I wish you wouldn't be so late, you know how I like to get to places on time. (run-ons)
7. The boat had sank to the bottom of the lake. (forming the past participles of irregular verbs)
8. She felt badly when she lost the tennis match. (using adjectives and adverbs correctly)
9. She had lain the box on the kitchen table, but it disappeared. (correct use of *lie* and *lay*)
10. Elaine goes to John F. Kennedy junior high school in North Miami Beach. (capitalizing names of specific buildings)

EXERCISE 23. Proofreading a Revised Draft. Proofread the draft you revised for Review Exercise B or another revised paper. Use the preceding Guidelines for Proofreading and the Revising and Proofreading Symbols (page 380).

WRITING THE FINAL VERSION

CORRECT MANUSCRIPT FORM

The last step in the writing process is to prepare a final, clean copy of your revised and proofread paper. Although there is no single correct way to prepare a manuscript, the Guidelines for Correct Manuscript Form that follow are widely accepted standards. Your final recopying of the paper is also the time to correct common errors in abbreviations, number usage, and word divisions.

23m. Write the final version in correct manuscript form.

GUIDELINES FOR CORRECT MANUSCRIPT FORM

1. Use lined composition paper or, if you type, $8\frac{1}{2}$ x 11-inch white paper.
2. Write on only one side of the paper.
3. Write in blue or black ink, or typewrite using double-spacing.
4. Leave margins of about one inch at the top, sides, and the bottom of a page.

The left-hand margin must be straight; the right-hand margin should be as straight as possible.
5. Indent the first line of each paragraph about one-half inch.
6. Follow your teacher's instructions for placing your name, the class, the date, and the title on the manuscript.
7. Number all pages. Place the number in the upper right-hand corner, about one-half inch from the top.
8. Write legibly and neatly. If you are typing, do not strike over letters or cross out words. If you must erase, do it neatly.
9. Before handing in your final version, proofread it carefully to make certain that your recopying has been accurate.

Abbreviations

(1) Use only customary, accepted abbreviations.

In most writing, you should spell out words rather than abbreviate them. Some abbreviations, however, are acceptable.

The abbreviations *Mr., Mrs., Ms., Dr., Jr., Sr., Rev.,* and *St.* are used with names. Spell them out in other uses. The college degrees, *B.S., Ph.D.,* etc., may be used with or without a name.

EXAMPLES I called **Dr.** Lee for the junior varsity player.
The pastor of **St.** John's Church is **Rev.** E. W. Miller, **Jr.,** who holds an **M.A.** in history as well as a **Ph.D.** in theology.

The abbreviations *A.D., B.C., A.M.,* and *P.M.* are acceptable when used with numbers (**30 B.C., A.D. 642, 1:30 P.M.**). Abbreviations for organizations are acceptable if they are generally known (**EPA, Y.W.C.A., UN**). Note that periods are usually omitted in abbreviations of governmental agencies.

Numbers

(2) Follow the rules for writing numbers.

The general rule for number usage is to spell out numbers that can be expressed in one or two words and to use numerals for others (**five million, $1.99, the forty-first yardline, 342, 1987**). Numbers in writing, however, do not easily conform to a single rule, and common usage requires several exceptions. A number beginning a sentence is spelled out. Days of the month and page numbers are written as numerals. A mixture of numbers—some one or two words, some longer—should all be written in the same way, either as words or as numerals. Statistical and technical writing generally expresses all measurements as numerals.

EXAMPLES **One hundred ninety** people died in the crash on **April 3** (either April 3 or the third of April, not April 3rd).

How could a team of **5** researchers discover what an association of **250** scientists could not?

In the experiment, **74 percent** of the subjects could not convert **3 liters** into a nonmetric measurement.

Hyphenation

(3) Divide words correctly at the ends of lines.

When you must divide a word at the end of a line, hyphenate it between syllables. Use the following general rules, but consult a dictionary if you are unsure of a word's syllables.

Do not divide a one-syllable word. Divide a word with double consonants between the consonants. Hyphenate words with prefixes and suffixes between the root and the prefix or suffix. In addition, avoid dividing words so that a single letter ends a line or only two letters begin a line. In these instances, a slightly uneven margin is preferable to an awkward hyphenation.

EXAMPLES laughed (not laugh-ed); com-mitment; trans-mission; fall-ing (not fal-ling; *ing* is a suffix); evac-uate (not e-vacuate); acces-sory (not accesso-ry)

EXERCISE 24. Writing the Final Version. Write the final version of the paper you proofread for Exercise 23. Follow the rules for correct manuscript form or your teacher's instructions. Be sure to proofread your recopying carefully.

CHAPTER 23 WRITING REVIEW

Applying the Writing Process. Write a paragraph or brief composition on a topic of your choice. Complete each step of the prewriting stage. Then write a first draft, evaluate it, and revise it. Finally, proofread your final revision and recopy the paper in correct manuscript form.

REVISING AND PROOFREADING SYMBOLS

Symbol	Example	Meaning of Symbol
≡	Maple High school	Capitalize a lowercase letter.
/	the First person	Lowercase a capital letter.
^	the first of May	Insert a missing word, letter, or punctuation mark.
^	separate	Change a letter.
	during after the dance	Replace a word.
	Tell me the the plan	Leave out a word, letter, or punctuation mark.
	an unussual idea	Leave out and close up.
	a water fall	Close up space.
	recieve	Change the order of the letters.
tr.	the last Saturday of September in the month	Transfer the circled words. (Write tr. in nearby margin.)
¶	¶"Help!" someone cried	Begin a new paragraph.
⊙	Please don't go	Add a period.
	Well what's new?	Add a comma.
#	birdcage	Add a space.
	the following ideas	Add a colon.
	Houston, Texas St. Louis, Missouri and Albany, New York	Add a semicolon.
=	two teenagers	Add a hyphen.
	Sallys new job	Add an apostrophe.
stet	An extremely urgent message	Keep the crossed-out material. (Write stet in nearby margin.)

CHAPTER 24

Writing Paragraphs

STRUCTURE, DEVELOPMENT, PURPOSES

As a unit of thought, a paragraph may be complete in itself or part of a longer piece of writing. In this chapter you will review the structure of the paragraph and learn to apply the stages of the writing process to the paragraph form. You will also learn methods of developing paragraphs for different purposes.

THE STRUCTURE OF A PARAGRAPH

THE MAIN IDEA

24a. A paragraph is a series of sentences that presents and develops one main idea about a topic.

An effective paragraph introduces one main idea and develops it clearly by presenting additional, more specific information. The ideas are arranged in a logical order and smoothly connected. In the following paragraph the writer, a native American, develops one main idea by giving specific examples.

> **The widespread use of cloth brought on many new variations to women's dresses.** One popular style used a cape, decorated with beadwork and shells, which could be worn over any plain calico dress. Some capes were actually the

decorated remnants of worn-out cloth dresses. Some cloth dresses were decorated with buckskin additions that were fringed. Some dresses were made of velvet, with decorations of ribbons and metal sequins. The most valuable dresses had their tops covered with elk teeth or cowrie shells.

BEVERLY HUNGRY WOLF

THE TOPIC SENTENCE

24b. The topic sentence states the one main idea of a paragraph.

In most paragraphs, like the one above by Beverly Hungry Wolf, the main idea is expressed in a single sentence. This *topic sentence* controls the content of the other sentences by focusing on one particular aspect of the topic.

Often, the topic sentence is the first sentence of the paragraph. Placing the topic sentence at the beginning helps readers by giving them a clear idea of what is going to be discussed in the paragraph. Stating the main idea at the beginning also helps writers keep clearly in mind the main idea they are going to develop.

The topic sentence may appear elsewhere in the paragraph. In the following paragraph, for example, the writer concludes with a topic sentence that summarizes the details presented.

Convinced that he had identified "the African," about whom his grandmother had spoken, [Alex] Haley searched through shipping records in London and Annapolis to trace Kunta Kinte's arrival in America in 1767 and his sale to the Waller family of Spotsylvania County, Virginia. After that line was established, his job was largely a matter of working through census records to trace the family's migrations from Virginia to North Carolina and, after emancipation, to Tennessee. ***Roots* is Haley's account of his family, from Africa to America, from freedom to slavery and on to freedom again.**

DAVID HERBERT DONALD

The Implied Main Idea

In your reading you will find that not every paragraph has a topic sentence. In some paragraphs, particularly narrative and descriptive ones, the main idea is implied, or suggested, rather than stated directly. The details themselves answer the question "What happened?" or create a main impression or mood.

The main idea of the following paragraph describing Sylvia Beach, who was a patron of many writers during the 1920s, is implied rather than stated directly. What is the paragraph's main idea?

> When I first saw her, in the early spring of 1932, her hair was still the color of roasted chestnut shells, her light golden brown eyes with greenish glints in them were marvelously benign, acutely attentive, and they sparkled upon one rather than beamed, as gentle eyes are supposed to do. She was not pretty, never had been, never had tried to be; she was attractive, a center of interest, a delightful presence not accountable to any of the familiar attributes of charm. Her power was in the unconscious, natural radiation of her intense energy and concentration upon those beings and arts she loved.
>
> KATHERINE ANNE PORTER

The implied main idea of this paragraph is that Sylvia Beach's attractiveness had more to do with her intelligence and personality than with her appearance.

For most of the paragraphs you will write in this chapter, you will be asked to state your main idea in a topic sentence. Learning to write effective topic sentences provides valuable practice in determining your main idea and expressing it clearly.

Topic and Restriction Sentences

Sometimes two sentences work together to express the main idea of a paragraph. The first sentence introduces a general idea; the second one restricts or limits that idea by focusing on one particular aspect of it. These two sentences are called *topic and restriction sentences.*

> [TOPIC] **Crisp is a splendid word, blessed with a great etymological pedigree that runs parallel to its onomatopoeia: the word's sound helps evoke its meaning.** [RESTRICTION] **Crispy is an itsypooism.** It's O.K. to say *crunchy,* because the imitative noun, *crunch,* needs a *y* to turn it into an adjective, but *crisp* is an adjective that later was used by English potato-chip makers as a noun. One of the senses of *crisp* is *short;* surely this adjective needs no lengthening. Stick with *crisp;* resist itsypooisms.
>
> WILLIAM SAFIRE

SUPPORTING SENTENCES

24c. Other sentences in the paragraph provide specific information that supports the main idea.

The other sentences in the paragraph must give enough details to make the main idea clear. In general, three or more details (facts, examples, reasons, etc.) are needed to develop a main idea adequately.

The supporting sentences should present additional, more specific information, not just repeat the main idea in different words. Compare the following two versions of a paragraph.

WEAK **Every student can benefit from engaging in some extracurricular activity.** A student needs experience in such activities. No student should leave school every day when the final bell rings, having no definite interest to follow in after-school hours. Everyone can benefit from extracurricular work. No one should think of school as solely a place to study.

IMPROVED **Every student can benefit from engaging in some extracurricular activity.** Through extracurricular activities you learn to work and play harmoniously, to give and take, to win and lose. When, as a member of a club, you are given a job to do, you learn to assume responsibility and to work unselfishly for the good of the group. In a radio or photography club, you can acquire practical skills that may prove useful in the long run. Similarly, if you work hard in dramatics or in musical organizations, you will develop talents that will be satisfying to you all your life. Finally, extracurricular activities can broaden your perspective by expanding your circle of friends.

EXERCISE 1. Revising Weak Paragraphs. Each of the following paragraphs is weak because it does not contain enough information to develop the main idea clearly and specifically. Revise each paragraph, adding more supporting information. (You may need to do some research to find the information.) You may also revise the topic sentence.

1. Learning to handle a checking account is one of the uncelebrated milestones on the way to becoming an adult. It is important to pay bills promptly. You need to be able to figure out how much money is in the checking account. Bouncing checks is not good.
(*Hint:* Tell why it is important to pay bills promptly and what the disadvantages are of bouncing a check. Give other reasons that explain why handling a checking account is a sign of maturity.)

2. Psychologists and interior decorators know that colors can influence people's moods. Yellow is supposed to stimulate mental activity. Blue is restful and relaxing.
(*Hint:* Tell about other colors, and give more information about each color's effects.)

3. If you could watch every single television show broadcast, you would probably find that TV programs can be categorized. There is the situation comedy. There are dramas. There are soap operas and news or educational programs.
(*Hint:* Vary the sentence structure, and give examples or more specific information about each type of program. Consider whether there are other categories of TV programs, and if there are, mention them also.)

THE CLINCHER SENTENCE

24d. A paragraph may end with a clincher sentence.

A **clincher,** or **concluding, sentence** may restate the paragraph's main idea. It may also summarize the paragraph's main points, reveal an insight the writer has gained, or suggest a course of action. In the following paragraph, the writer restates the main idea expressed in the topic and restriction sentences.

> **The interpretation of words is a never-ending task for any citizen in modern society. We now have, as the result of modern means of communication, hundreds of thousands of words flung at us daily.** We are constantly being talked at, by teachers, preachers, salesmen, public officials, and moving-picture sound tracks. The cries of the hawkers of soft drinks, soap chips, and laxatives pursue us into our very homes, thanks to the radio —and in some houses the radio is never turned off from morning to night. Daily the newsboy brings us, in large cities, from thirty to fifty enormous pages of print, and almost three times that amount on Sundays. The mailman brings magazines and direct-mail advertising. We go out and get more words at bookstores and libraries. Billboards confront us on the highways, and we even take portable radios with us to the seashore. **Words fill our lives.**
>
> S. I. HAYAKAWA

Not every paragraph needs a clincher sentence. Avoid weak concluding sentences such as "Now you know why baseball is my favorite sport," and do not simply tack a clincher sentence on to a paragraph that is effective without it.

EXERCISE 2. Writing Clincher Sentences. For each of the following paragraphs, try writing several different versions of a clincher sentence. Choose the version that you think is most effective.

1. If your vision needs correcting and you prefer not to wear eyeglasses, you can choose from at least four different types of contact lenses. Hard contacts, which are made of Plexiglas, are the oldest type and probably the least popular. The softer gas-permeable lenses allow oxygen to reach the eye, which makes them more comfortable to wear. Soft contact lenses are cellophane-thin, flexible, porous pieces of plastic. The latest development in contact lenses, extended-wear lenses, may be left in the eyes up to thirty days.

2. College students have many opportunities to participate in short-term overseas study programs. Organizations such as Experiment in International Living offer students a chance to attend seminars and travel around countries doing research and writing about their observations. Some organizations, such as the American-Scandinavian Foundation, sponsor overseas programs that enable students to work at a wide variety of jobs. Earthwatch, which sponsors museum work and anthropological research, matches interested students with research projects. Other overseas programs are sponsored by the Future Farmers of America, the President's International Youth Exchange Initiative, and the International Association for the Exchange of Students for Technical Experience.

THE DEVELOPMENT OF A PARAGRAPH

The writing process, with its many writing and thinking steps, can be used to develop a paragraph.

PREWRITING

CHOOSING AND LIMITING A SUBJECT

24e. Choose a subject and limit it to a topic that is suitable for a paragraph.

Although paragraphs vary in length, most are only about 150 to 200 words long. To find a topic that you can develop adequately in such a restricted space, you must limit a broad subject considerably. (See pages 355–57 for more on choosing and limiting subjects.)

EXERCISE 3. Choosing and Limiting a Subject. Choose one of the following subjects or another subject that interests you. Limit it to find at least three suitable topics for a paragraph, and choose one topic to write about.

1. Electronics
2. The American Revolution
3. Musical notation
4. The Super Bowl
5. Pollution

CONSIDERING PURPOSE, AUDIENCE, AND TONE

24f. Determine your purpose for writing, identify your audience, and consider your attitude toward your topic.

A paragraph may contain elements of more than one of the four basic types of writing (exposition, persuasion, narration, and description). Usually, however, a writer has one main purpose. An expository paragraph may include an incident, for example, but its primary purpose is to inform or to explain. Determining what your primary purpose is helps you gather appropriate details and select an effective pattern of organization.

Considering the needs and interests of your audience also helps you plan your paragraph. Although you cannot predict precisely how your readers will respond to your writing, you can adapt your writing to their reading and comprehension skills. For example, if you are aware of the specific backgrounds and interests of your audience, you are able to select language and examples or details that the audience will understand and appreciate. When you know your readers, you know what terms you should define, and you know what they will find offensive or pleasing.

Considering your attitude, or point of view, toward your topic is also important as you plan your paragraph. This attitude is expressed in the tone of your writing and is conveyed through the language and details you choose to write about your topic. The tone of a paragraph, as with other writing, can be serious or humorous, positive or negative, formal or informal.

(Review the information on pages 350–55 and 357–58 on how purpose, audience, and tone affect writing.)

Techniques for Prewriting. To consider how your purpose, your audience, and your attitude toward your topic will affect your writing, ask yourself:

- Is my primary purpose to explain or to inform, to persuade, to tell a story, or to describe?
- What topic will most interest my audience?
- What background information will they need to understand my ideas? What language will best convey my ideas to this audience?
- What is my attitude toward my topic, and how will I express this through the tone of my writing?

EXERCISE 4. Identifying Purpose, Audience, and Tone. Bring to class three paragraphs from newspapers or magazines. Be prepared to identify the primary purpose, the intended audience, and the tone of each paragraph.

GATHERING INFORMATION

24g. Gather information on your limited topic.

Use one or more of the information-gathering techniques (see pages 358–64) to collect details on your topic. Be sure to take detailed notes, and remember to keep your audience and purpose in mind.

EXERCISE 5. Gathering Information. Gather information on the topic you chose for Exercise 3 or on another suitably limited topic. Save your paper for later use.

DEVELOPING A PARAGRAPH PLAN

24h. Develop a paragraph plan: write a topic sentence; select supporting details and arrange them in a logical order.

Writing Effective Topic Sentences

An effective topic sentence meets the following three requirements:

(1) A topic sentence should be neither too limited nor too broad.

The main idea in a topic sentence must be one that can be developed by the other sentences in the paragraph. For this reason, a single fact is usually too limited to serve as a topic sentence. On the other hand, a statement that cannot be developed clearly and precisely in a single paragraph is too broad for a topic sentence.

TOO LIMITED Milk is a good source of Vitamin D.
TOO BROAD Vitamins are good for you.
SUITABLE Vitamin D, one of the vitamins essential for healthy bones, can be found in many foods.

(2) A topic sentence should state the paragraph's main idea precisely.

An effective topic sentence is neither vague nor wordy. Replace vague words with precise ones, and eliminate unnecessary phrases such as "This paragraph is about. . . ."

VAGUE There are some new devices to help deaf people.
WORDY A new device recently invented helps hearing-impaired people to "hear" when they are using the telephone because the telephone tones are changed from tones to print that they can read.
PRECISE A new device for hearing-impaired persons converts a telephone's touch tones into printed messages.

VAGUE Some people are really annoying.
WORDY I am going to talk about those annoying people who always like to give advice on what should have been done or what might have been done long *after* something has already happened.
PRECISE A "Monday-morning quarterback" is someone who criticizes others' decisions about past events.

(3) A topic sentence should arouse the reader's interest.

Try to catch the attention of the reader by including a vivid detail or by addressing the reader directly.

WEAK Money can be many things.
IMPROVED A remarkable variety of items other than bills and coins—from stones to dried fish—have served as money.

WEAK Everybody should know how to do the Heimlich maneuver.
IMPROVED If you have ever choked on a piece of food, you have some idea of how important the Heimlich maneuver can be.

Techniques for Prewriting. To evaluate your topic sentence, ask yourself:

- Is it neither too broad nor too limited?
- Does it express my main idea directly and precisely?
- Will it catch the interest of my audience?

EXERCISE 6. Revising Topic Sentences. Revise each of the following topic sentences, adding any information you need to make it more effective.

1. Some people work too hard.
2. I'd like to tell you something about what it was like, according to my grandmother, growing up in the days before television.
3. An hourglass measures time.
4. Most birds fly, but not the ostrich.
5. There are four basic blood types: A, B, AB, and O.
6. I'm going to tell you some interesting information about penguins.
7. The human ear is very complicated.
8. A great many people are extremely afraid of every snake that they ever see, but everyone should be made aware of the fact that most snakes are beneficial to people.
9. Have you ever tried to use a potter's wheel?
10. The sitar is a stringed instrument of India.

EXERCISE 7. Writing Topic Sentences. For each of the following lists of details, write an effective topic sentence. You will not necessarily use all of the details in a paragraph.

1. *Details:*
   a. Israeli scientists using inexpensive technique for measuring air pollution
   b. Using vegetable plants sensitive to different kinds of air pollution
   c. Alfalfa plants sensitive to sulfur dioxide
   d. Eggplant sensitive to ozone and nitrates
   e. Tomato, lettuce, and cucumber plants measuring amounts of nitrates in the air
   f. Research scientists at Technion Institute in Haifa and Hebrew University in Jerusalem
   g. Damage to plants grown at various distances from industrial sites reflects relative air quality

2. *Details:*
   a. Survey results: less leisure time for Americans in 1983 than in 1973
   b. Average leisure time per week 26.2 hours in 1973, 18.1 hours in 1983
   c. Average work week 47.3 hours in 1983, 40.6 hours in 1973
   d. Leisure time activities: watching TV, attending sports events, exercising, eating out, attending concerts and movies
   e. Women average 23 percent less leisure time per week than men: women 15.6 hours, men 20.3

3. *Details:*
   a. Vitamin D necessary for body to absorb calcium and to maintain strong, healthy bones
   b. Vitamin D in skin activated by exposure to sunlight; approximately 15 minutes in midsummer for young, light-skinned people; more time for elderly or dark-skinned people and for people using sunscreens
   c. Increased need for Vitamin D during winter, when sunlight weaker and less time spent outdoors
   d. Doctors suggest that people, especially elderly persons, get outside during winter for half-hour walk or "sunbath"
   e. Recent discovery that some types of depression triggered by lack of sunlight in winter

Selecting and Arranging Details

Analyze the information you have gathered, making sure that each detail is directly related to your main idea as you have stated it in your topic sentence. Remove any details that do not support your main idea, and arrange the remaining material in a logical order (see pages 394–400).

Techniques for Prewriting. To determine whether a detail is directly related to your main idea, ask yourself:

- Does the detail provide strong support for my main idea?
- Will it help my audience understand the main idea rather than confuse or distract them?
- How does the detail function within the paragraph—is it a fact? An example? A reason? A concrete or sensory detail?

REVIEW EXERCISE A. Developing a Paragraph Plan. Write a topic sentence for the limited topic on which you gathered information for Exercise 5. Then decide which details most effectively support your main idea, and arrange them in a logical order. Save your paper.

WRITING

UNITY

24i. Every sentence in a paragraph should be directly related to the main idea.

A *unified* paragraph is one in which all of the sentences are directly related to the main idea as it is stated in the topic sentence. Any sentences that do not help develop that idea should be removed. As you read the following paragraph, identify the two sentences that destroy its unity.

> Because in most cities and towns all the water we need gushes forth at the mere touch of a faucet and because water is cheap, we Americans use it lavishly. New York City alone consumes one and a half billion gallons a day. Every day each of us uses about eighty-three gallons: twenty-four for flushing; thirty-two for bathing, laundry, and dishwashing; twenty-five for other uses, such as swimming pools, watering lawns, etc.; and the mere two gallons we use for drinking and cooking. These figures are surprising enough, but they do not cover the much greater daily consumption of water in agriculture and industry. In 75 percent of the world, cities and towns lack any municipal supply of pure water. Citizens are forced to draw water from wells and streams, which are often contaminated. These facts about our consumption of water should make us wonder how long our supply will last if we continue to drain it so recklessly.

EXERCISE 8. Identifying Sentences That Destroy Unity. Identify the sentence(s) not directly related to the main idea in each of the following paragraphs. Copy them onto your paper, and be ready to explain how they destroy the paragraph's unity.

1. **A dishonest newspaper may warp the day's news either by hiding a story or by slanting headlines.** A paper with a strong political bias may hide a story favorable to the opposing party by placing it in an inconspicuous

position. On the other hand, it may give large headlines and a front-page position to news favorable to its own party. Newspapers may also change the total effect of a story by giving it a headline that is deliberately misleading or slanted. Headline writing is highly demanding work. Once considered the drudges of the newspaper office, headline writers have in recent years been accorded greater respect, as reflected in shorter hours and higher pay. MAYOR JONES CRACKS DOWN ON CRITICS, for example, gives quite a different impression from MAYOR JONES REPLIES TO CRITICS.

2. **The popularity of first names changes, with certain names in fashion for a generation or so.** For example, in 1928 the ten top names for girls were Mary, Marie, Anne, Margaret, Catherine, Gloria, Helen, Teresa, Jean, and Barbara. None of these names made the top-ten list for girls in 1983. That year the ten most popular girls' names were Jennifer, Jessica, Melissa, Nicole, Stephanie, Christina, Tiffany, Michelle, Elizabeth, and Lauren. Unusual-sounding names can cause problems for children. One California lawyer, for example, named his son Shelter because he wanted him to have a unique first name. The most popular boys' names have changed also. John, William, Joseph, James, Richard, Edward, Robert, Thomas, George, and Louis were the most popular boys' names in 1928. In 1983, however, the ten top boys' names were Michael, Christopher, Jason, David, Daniel, Anthony, Joseph, John, Robert, and Jonathan.

3. **Seminole Indians in Florida are pursuing a new venture to reduce the 47 percent unemployment rate on the Big Cypress reservation deep in the Everglades.** With the help of an electronics company, thirteen Seminoles are receiving training in electronics in preparation for the opening of Seminole Electronics, Inc., on the reservation, which is thirty to forty miles from the nearest town. Typical of the trainees is Josephine North, 31. North, until recently a part-time artist, will earn about $7.00 an hour as an employee of Seminole Electronics, Inc. The Seminoles are a 1,600-member tribe governed by a five-member tribal council. In the early eighteenth century, the Seminoles separated themselves (the name *Seminole* actually means "separatist") from the Creek Indians and later fled to Florida to escape capture by U.S. troops. The training program, funded by a government grant, is being supervised by Pocon, Inc., an electronics company in Pompano Beach.

COHERENCE

24j. The ideas in a paragraph should be arranged in a logical order and clearly connected.

A *coherent* paragraph is one in which the ideas flow smoothly from one sentence to the next, and the relationships between the ideas are clear. One way to achieve coherence is to arrange the ideas in a logical order. A second way is to provide clear transitions between the ideas.

Logical Order

Five ways to arrange the ideas in a paragraph are in chronological order, in spatial order, in order of importance, in an order that reveals comparison or contrast, and in an order that reveals an analogy.

Chronological Order

(1) Ideas may be arranged in chronological order.

Chronological order is used in narrative paragraphs to relate a series of events. In expository paragraphs it is used to explain the steps in a process. The following paragraph, for example, explains a simple process: an experiment to prove that sound waves travel through air. Each step in the experiment is described in the order in which it must be done.

> Light a candle. Put a tin can on its side with the open end of the can about two inches from the lighted candle. The flame should be near the center of the open end of the can. Hold the can firmly and tap it hard on the bottom. Notice what happens to the flame each time the bottom of the can is struck. The bottom of the can vibrates and sets the air in the can to vibrating. The vibrating air causes the flame to flicker or go out.
>
> ILLA PODENDORF

EXERCISE 9. Writing a Paragraph Using Chronological Order. Using the following information, write a paragraph in which the ideas are arranged in chronological order. You may combine or reword the sentences in any way you choose.

Topic sentence: The night of the Great Blackout turned out to be a lot of fun for our family.

a. We were all home by 7:00 P.M., when the power went off.
b. Dad had driven home from the plant by 6:00 P.M., and Mom had just come in from work when the lights went out.
c. We cooked hamburgers on a charcoal grill outdoors and made a big salad for dinner.

d. Since the telephones weren't working either, the house was quiet.
e. Jim found a transistor radio, and we listened to the news of the blackout.
f. People were trapped for hours in elevators and crowded subways; we were lucky to be home.
g. After dinner all five of us played a long game of *Scrabble*.
h. By 10:00 P.M. all of us were sitting around the fireplace telling funny stories about things we did when we were little.
i. The first thing we did was scramble to find candles and flashlights.
j. During the game, Dad and Jim got a fire going in the fireplace.

EXERCISE 10. Writing a Paragraph Explaining a Process. Write a paragraph telling how to do one of the following processes or a process of your own. Choose a process familiar to you, one which can be explained in a single paragraph. Give all the steps in the process in their correct order, and include any necessary equipment or supplies in your explanation. Define any terms unfamiliar to your audience.

1. How to study for a final exam
2. How to ask someone for a date
3. How to fly a kite (or a paper airplane)
4. How to hit a home run
5. How to see a movie

Spatial Order

(2) Ideas may be arranged in spatial order.

Descriptive writing usually uses *spatial order,* which shows where items are in relation to one another. The writer directs the reader's attention from one part of the scene to the next in an orderly, consistent way. In describing the Van Tassel farmhouse, for example, Washington Irving presents the house as a visitor would see it. Notice how the boldfaced transitional expressions clarify the positions of the objects.

> It was one of those spacious farmhouses with high-ridged but low-sloping roofs, built in the style handed down from the first Dutch settlers, the low projecting eaves forming a piazza **along the front** capable of being closed up in bad weather. **Under this** were hung flails, harness, various utensils of husbandry, and nets for fishing in the neighboring river. Benches were built **along the sides** for summer use, and a great spinningwheel **at one end** and a churn **at the other** showed the various uses to which this important porch

might be devoted. **From this piazza** the wondering Ichabod entered the hall, which formed the center of the mansion and the place of usual residence. **Here** rows of resplendent pewter, ranged **on a long dresser,** dazzled his eyes. **In one corner** stood a huge bag of wool ready to be spun; **in another** a quantity of linsey-woolsey just from the loom; ears of Indian corn and strings of dried apples and peaches hung in gay festoons **along the walls,** mingled with the gaud of red peppers; and a door left ajar gave him a peep **into the best parlor, where** the clawfooted chairs and dark mahogany tables shone like mirrors; andirons, with their accompanying shovel and tongs, glistened **from their covert of asparagus tops;** mock-oranges and conch-shells decorated the mantelpiece; strings of various colored birds' eggs were suspended **above it;** a great ostrich egg was hung **from the center of the room,** and a corner cupboard, knowingly left open, displayed immense treasures of old silver and well-mended china.

WASHINGTON IRVING

EXERCISE 11. Writing a Paragraph Using Spatial Order. Using the following information, write a paragraph in which the details are arranged in spatial order. You may add specific information (colors, types, etc.) and combine or reword sentences in any way you choose.

a. Small table beside the bed—clock radio, pile of magazines, box of tissues, red metal lamp
b. Bed against the wall—blue bedspread, newspaper and jacket on bed
c. Socks on floor; dirty laundry overflowing from wicker hamper
d. Three posters on the wall
e. Concert ticket stubs on dark cork bulletin board
f. Desk covered with books, papers, dirty clothes
g. Blue director's chair
h. Wooden dresser; trophies and books on shelves above dresser
i. Stereo and two speakers; record collection in orange-crate
j. Collection of caps and hats

Order of Importance

(3) Ideas may be arranged in order of importance.

Using order of importance in an expository or persuasive paragraph enables you to emphasize those reasons that provide stronger support for your main idea. Usually, the reasons are arranged with the most important one placed last, where it will linger in the reader's mind. When one reason is far more important than the others, however, the writer may begin with it. In the following paragraph, the actress Helen Hayes gives three reasons to explain why elderly people should write an autobiography. Identify the three reasons and the order in which she has arranged them.

> I also like to see older folks write an "autobiography." Writing is very therapeutic. In fact, experts say it promotes self esteem and personal integration. Personally, I think it also clears away the cobwebs and stimulates a fresh way of thinking and looking back at your life. Most important, perhaps, it leaves a private history of yourself and your family. Don't you wish your grandmother and her grandmother before her had done that?
>
> HELEN HAYES

EXERCISE 12. Writing a Paragraph Using Order of Importance. Choose one of the following topic sentences (*should* or *should not*). Then decide which of the reasons given support that topic sentence, list them in order from least important to most important, and write a paragraph. You may add information and combine or reword sentences in any way you choose.

Topic sentence: Employees (should, should not) be required to retire at seventy.

Reasons:

a. People who have been working all of their lives deserve to spend the last years of their lives relaxing.
b. Some people over seventy no longer have the necessary physical stamina.
c. People who work past seventy are taking jobs away from younger workers.
d. People over seventy have valuable experience unmatched by that of younger workers.
e. People who are willing and able to work past seventy should have the freedom to do so.
f. Many people over seventy need to earn money to survive.
g. People who derive their only satisfaction from their work feel unwanted when they retire.
h. Some people over seventy no longer have the necessary mental alertness.
i. People who develop outside interests earlier in life keep busy after they retire.

Comparison and Contrast

(4) Ideas may be arranged in an order that reveals comparison or contrast.

A *comparison* shows how two or more aspects of a topic are alike; a *contrast* shows how they are different. These patterns of organization may appear in any of the four types of writing. Facts, incidents, sensory or concrete details, and examples may be used to point out similarities or differences between two topics.

A paragraph of comparison or contrast may be arranged according to the *block method,* in which all of the ideas about one aspect of the topic are presented first, followed by all of the ideas about the next aspect of the topic. The following paragraph uses the block method.

If you travel over regions where the buildings were made in earlier times, you will notice great differences from North to South. In the North the roofs are steep to shed the snow, the windows small to keep out the cold, the building materials often easily worked soft woods provided by the abundant nearby forests. The ceilings are low to conserve heat, the chimneys numerous or large, the doors and windows arranged to baffle chilling drafts, and the hearth is the focus of the dwelling. As you move south, the roofs flatten, the windows grow larger, the ceilings rise, so that houses on the steamy James River, in Virginia, for example, have very high ceilings and also a through hall to permit easy cooling of the rooms. As you near the tropics, the woods become harder to work and more vulnerable to dampness and insects. The roofs may get still flatter unless the rainfall is torrential, in which case they steepen again as in Celebes. The patio usually replaces the hearth, and the walls of adobe or stone become thicker in order to preserve coolness; now the windows are small and deeply recessed to keep the hot sun from penetrating the interiors. All these practical arrangements were worked out empirically long ago.

topic sentence

buildings in the North

buildings farther south

buildings in the tropics

JOHN BURCHARD

The ideas in a paragraph of comparison or contrast may instead follow the *alternating,* or *point-by-point, method,* in which each feature of the topic is discussed one at a time, as in the following paragraph. The boldfaced transitional expressions signal the introduction of a new point.

In several respects, living in an apartment building is easier than living in a house. **For one thing,** there is no outside work to do in an apartment building. Apartment dwellers can forget those chores that keep homeowners busy, like mowing the lawn and repairing the porch. A **second advantage** to living in an apartment building is that the responsibility for maintenance falls on the building superintendent, not on the occupants. When a sink is stopped up or a short develops in an electrical circuit, homeowners must either solve the problem themselves or pay a plumber or an electrician. **Finally,** since an apartment is usually smaller and has fewer rooms, it is easier to clean than a house.

contrast 1

contrast 2

contrast 3

EXERCISE 13. Writing Paragraphs of Comparison or Contrast. Select two of the following numbered items or two other sets of topics. Write two paragraphs, one of comparison and the other of contrast. Use the block method for one paragraph and the point-by-point method for the other one.

1. A novel you have read and its movie or television version
2. Two types of cooking
3. Two heroes (or heroines) in a novel or movie
4. Going to the dentist and going to the doctor
5. Getting ready for a job interview and getting ready for a date

Analogy

(5) Ideas may be arranged in an order that reveals an analogy.

An *analogy* is an extended comparison, one that draws parallels between two basically dissimilar topics. It explores the nature of an unfamiliar topic by relating it to another, more familiar topic. In the following paragraph, for example, Eudora Welty discusses the points of correspondence between her fiction and the family trips of her childhood.

> I think now, in looking back on these summer trips—this one and a number later, made in the car and on the train—that another element in them must have been influencing my mind. The trips were wholes unto themselves. They were stories. Not only in form, but in their taking on direction, movement, development, change. They changed something in my life: each trip made its particular revelation, though I could not have found words for it. But with the passage of time, I could look back on them and see them bringing me news, discoveries, premonitions, promises—I still can; they still do. When I did begin to write, the short story was a shape that had already formed itself and stood waiting in the back of my mind. Nor is it surprising to me that when I made my first attempt at a novel, I entered its world—that of the mysterious Yazoo-Mississippi Delta—as a child riding there on a train: "From the warm windowsill the endless fields glowed like a hearth in firelight, and Laura, looking out, leaning on her elbows with her head between her hands, felt what an arriver in a land feels—that slow hard pounding in the breast."
>
> EUDORA WELTY

An effective analogy is neither self-evident nor strained. It is more effective to elaborate on only a few points of correspondence than to try to draw parallels where none exist.

EXERCISE 14. Writing a Paragraph of Analogy. Write a paragraph of analogy using one of the following subjects or one of your own.

1. Friends
2. Writing
3. Dreams
4. The future
5. Homes

REVIEW EXERCISE B. Choosing a Logical Order for Arranging Ideas. For each of the following topics, tell which kind of order you would use: chronological, spatial, order of importance, comparison and contrast, or analogy. (For some topics, more than one order is possible.) Be prepared to discuss your choices.

1. Why people should eat a balanced diet
2. An accident that you were involved in
3. A savings account and a checking account
4. Advertisements on television and advertisements in print media (newspapers and magazines)

5. The place where you would most like to live
6. Important safety tips for automobile drivers (or for pedestrians or for bicyclists)
7. Your earliest memory
8. Why people watch horror movies
9. A promise that was broken
10. Your room

Relationships Between Ideas

Direct references and transitional expressions clarify how ideas within and between sentences are related.

Direct References

(6) Connect ideas in a paragraph with pronouns, synonyms, or repeated words and phrases.

Direct references weave sentences together by reminding the reader of ideas mentioned earlier. These references may be pronouns, synonyms, or repeated words and phrases.

As you read the following paragraph, notice how the direct references (in boldfaced type) help the writer develop the main idea by *adding* specific information, not just repeating the same idea in different words.

> One final effect of radio and TV on the language must be noted. There is no doubt that **these great media of information** have cut down considerably the time that used to be devoted to reading, both of newspapers and of books. **This** means in turn that while **radio and TV** may enhance the **spoken language** (if indeed **they** do), **they** also tend to make of us a nation of functional illiterates, absorbing our **language** through the ear rather than the eye. Some may view **this** as a return to **language** in **its** original form and function; others may consider **it** a reversal, pure and simple, to the semi-**literate** Middle Ages.
>
> MARIO PEI

Transitional Expressions

(7) Keep the thought of a paragraph flowing smoothly from sentence to sentence by using transitional expressions.

Transitional expressions (sometimes called *linking expressions* or *connectives*) are words and phrases that indicate the relationships between ideas. Notice in the following paragraph how the boldfaced transitional expressions tie the ideas together and help make the writer's line of thought easy to follow.

> Much is said and written about the number of deer reputedly slaughtered by wolves. Very little is said about the actual numbers of wolves slaughtered by men. **In one case** a general falsehood is widely and officially disseminated; **in the other** the truth seems to be suppressed. **Yet** one trapper operating along the boundary between Manitoba and Keewatin, in the winter of the first year of my study, collected bounty on a hundred and eighteen wolves of which one hundred and seven were young ones born the previous spring. According to law he should have killed those wolves by trapping or shooting them. **In fact** he did what everyone else was doing —and still does in the Far North, with the covert permission of Governments: he spread strychnine so indiscriminately over an immense area that almost the entire population of foxes, wolverines, and many lesser flesh-eaters was wiped out. That did not matter **since** foxes fetched no price that year. Wolves were worth twenty dollars each for bounty.
>
> FARLEY MOWAT

Transitional expressions can be grouped according to the kind of relationship they indicate.

Transitional Expressions

To link similar ideas or add an idea

again	equally important	likewise
also	further	moreover
and	furthermore	similarly
another	in addition	then
besides	in the same way	too

To limit or contradict an idea

although	however	on the contrary
and yet	in spite of	on the other hand
but	instead	otherwise
conversely	nevertheless	still
even if	nor	yet

To indicate cause, purpose, or result

as	for	so
as a result	for this reason	then
because	hence	therefore
consequently	since	thus

To indicate time or position

above	beyond	nearby
across	eventually	next
afterward	finally	now
around	first (second, etc.)	opposite to
at once	here	thereafter
before	meanwhile	thereupon

To indicate an example, a summary, or a conclusion

as a result	in any event	in short
consequently	in brief	on the whole
for example	in conclusion	therefore
for instance	in fact	thus
in any case	in other words	to sum up

REVIEW EXERCISE C. Analyzing a Paragraph for Coherence. In the following paragraph, identify the direct references and transitional expressions that give the paragraph coherence. Be prepared to discuss your answers in class.

> A crow's morning greeting is something that has to be experienced to be believed. I don't know whether it corresponds to some timeless ritual of the species, but it was always the same, and it was so strikingly, so emphatically a demonstration of pleasure at seeing us, that today, still, decades later, I smile inwardly when I think of it. I see him again, standing on the windowsill, the blue-black of his feathers glistening in the soft morning light, beginning to bow. With slow dignity he lowered his head, and the bluish eyelids came down over his bright little eyes. At the same time he spread his wings out and down, fanlike, until the long feathers touched the windowsill. When he was fully into his *révérence,* he cooed in a gentle burble that was more like dove than crow. Two or three coos like this, raising and lowering the head with each one, and then it was time to get down to business again: inspection of the room, shoplifting, grabbing bits of food, disciplining us with a sharp blow of his beak if we got in his way.
>
> RUDOLPH CHELMINSKI

WRITING A FIRST DRAFT

24k. Write the first draft of your paragraph.

In shaping your ideas into your first draft, write freely, keeping in mind your purpose and audience. Remember that you will have time later to review and improve your writing.

Techniques for Writing. In drafting your paragraph,

- use your paragraph plan as a guide.
- keep your purpose and audience in mind.
- write freely, expressing your ideas as clearly as possible.
- add related details as you think of them.
- choose language that reflects the appropriate tone.

EXERCISE 15. Writing a First Draft. Using the paragraph plan you prepared for Review Exercise A (page 392), write the first draft of your paragraph.

EVALUATING

EVALUATING YOUR PARAGRAPH

24l. Evaluate the content, organization, and style of your draft.

As you evaluate your draft, use the following general guidelines. You will find guidelines for evaluating specific types of paragraphs in the section "Four Types of Paragraphs" on pages 410–30.

GUIDELINES FOR EVALUATING PARAGRAPHS

Main Idea	1. Is one main idea about a suitably limited topic either stated directly in a topic sentence or clearly implied?
Topic Development	2. Is enough specific information provided to develop the main idea clearly and precisely?
Unity	3. Is every sentence directly related to the main idea?
Concluding Sentence	4. Does the clincher sentence, if there is one, provide a strong conclusion for the paragraph?
Order of Ideas	5. Are the ideas arranged in a logical order that is appropriate for the purpose?
Relationships Between Ideas	6. Do the ideas flow smoothly from one sentence to the next? Are direct references and appropriate transitional expressions used to link the ideas?

Word Choice	7. Is the language specific and vivid? Is it appropriate for the audience? Are technical terms and difficult words defined or explained?
Sentence Variety	8. Are the sentences appropriately varied in structure and length?
Tone	9. Is the tone suitable for the purpose and the audience? Is it consistent?

EXERCISE 16. Evaluating a First Draft. Use the guidelines above to evaluate the following first draft. Answer each question from the guidelines, in writing, keying your answers to the numbers of the guidelines. Save your paper.

> Restaurant work, the kind of work teen-agers can get at a summer resort, has some good things going for it. It doesn't pay very much, though. If you work the evening shift, you can goof off all day. You can make lots of friends, in addition. And you get free food and a place to stay. Sharing a room is not my idea of fun, but my cousin Ramona met her future sister-in-law when she shared a room with her the summer they worked in the Poconos. In conclusion, it has certain advantages. And it gets you away from home.

EXERCISE 17. Evaluating Your Paragraph. Using the guidelines above, evaluate the draft you wrote for Exercise 15. You may also want to use the appropriate guidelines from the section "Four Types of Paragraphs" (pages 410–30). Save your paper for later use in this chapter.

REVISING

REVISING YOUR PARAGRAPH

24m. Revise your first draft.

Once you have identified which aspects of your paragraph need to be improved, you can use four basic techniques to revise your writing: *adding, cutting, reordering,* and *replacing*. The chart on the following page shows how these four revising techniques can be applied to the paragraph form.

REVISING PARAGRAPHS

PROBLEM	TECHNIQUE	REVISION
The main idea is not clear.	Add/Replace	Add a topic sentence. Add or replace details that imply the main idea.
The topic sentence is too broad.	Cut/Add	Remove words, phrases, or clauses that do not focus on one main idea. Add words, phrases, or clauses that qualify, and thus restrict, the topic sentence.
The topic sentence is too narrow.	Add	Add words, a phrase, or a clause that expands the scope of the main idea.
The topic sentence is dull.	Add/Replace	Add vivid details. Add an unusual comparison or a startling fact. Replace general words with specific ones. Address the audience directly.
One or more sentences do not directly relate to the main idea.	Cut	Remove the sentence(s).
The main idea is not developed.	Add/Replace	Add facts, statistics, examples, causes, effects, reasons, concrete or sensory details, or an incident. Replace vague statements with precise ones.
The paragraph trails off or ends abruptly.	Add	Add a clincher sentence: restate the main idea, summarize the information, emphasize an important point, or suggest a course of action.

PROBLEM	TECHNIQUE	REVISION
The ideas are not easy to follow.	Reorder	Rearrange the ideas in a logical order that the reader can follow easily.
The ideas do not flow smoothly.	Add/Replace	Add direct references and transitional expressions. Substitute more appropriate transitional expressions to connect ideas.
The language is dull.	Add/Replace	Add vivid nouns, verbs, adjectives, and adverbs. Replace general words with specific ones.
The language is too difficult.	Add/Replace	Add definitions and explanations. Substitute easier words and shorter, simpler sentences.
The sentences are monotonous.	Add/Replace	Combine sentences. Vary sentence beginnings. Vary sentence length.
The tone is inappropriate or inconsistent.	Replace	Substitute more formal/informal, humorous/serious, etc., terms.

The following example shows the changes one writer made in revising a first draft.

Educators
~~Many people concerned with education~~ are begin- replace
question
ning to ~~think about~~ whether ~~or not~~ computers are replace/cut
properly
being used ~~right~~ in the schools. In high schools, replace
computer literacy courses take up 64% of students'
of 1,082 schools made at Johns Hopkins University. Students
time according to a recent study ~~They~~ spend another add/replace

of their computer time *and about* *electronic*

18% in drill and practice. ~~Another~~ 6% in ~~recreational~~ add/replace

; word processing; and data retrieval.

games. Many teachers complain that drill and practice on add

high-school

the computer, for most students, is a waste of time. ~~The~~ reorder

software that uses the computer as *does*

computer ~~is nothing more than~~ a workbook page, ~~and it~~ cut/replace

not make good use of computers.

~~is cheaper and easier to use a workbook~~. One way in replace

which computers are being used well is in word process-

which teaches

ing, ~~teaching~~ students how to write and revise their replace

writing on the computer. And teachers of learning dis- cut

also praise the

abled and handicapped students ~~are crazy about the~~ replace

computer. But computer programs do not utilize the replace

simulation

computer's unique powers except rarely. In one ~~software~~ cut

program, students can dissect a frog and then put it back replace/add

together again. When the parts are put back in the right replace

reassembled

place, the frog jumps ~~up and~~ off the screen. Another replace/add/cut

to help high school

teacher uses a computer ~~hooked up to a piano to teach~~ replace

students sit at a

students to compose their own music. *keyboard, make up* cut

a musical phrase, program it into a computer, and

then improvise over it. The computer can even add

print out a student's original music in

musical notation.

EXERCISE 18. Revising a First Draft. Using your answers for Exercise 16, revise the first draft in that exercise. First, copy the paragraph as it is printed; then use the chart above to improve it by adding, cutting, reordering and replacing. Copy the revised paragraph on a separate sheet of paper.

REVIEW EXERCISE D. Revising Your Paragraph. Using your answers for Exercise 17 and the Revising Chart on pages 406–407, revise the draft of the paragraph you wrote for Exercise 15. Save your paper for later use.

PROOFREADING AND PREPARING A FINAL COPY

PROOFREADING YOUR PARAGRAPH AND PREPARING A FINAL COPY

24n. Proofread your paragraph, make a final copy, and proofread again.

Proofread your revised draft carefully, using the Guidelines for Proofreading on page 376. Then recopy the paragraph, following correct manuscript form or your teacher's instructions (see pages 377–79), and proofread it again.

EXERCISE 19. Proofreading Your Paragraph. Referring to the Guidelines for Proofreading on page 376, proofread and correct your paragraph. Remember to proofread your paragraph again after you make a final copy.

REVIEW EXERCISE E. Writing Paragraphs. Choose four topics from Review Exercise B (page 400) or four other topics. Write a paragraph on each topic, using a different order for each one: chronological order, spatial order, order of importance, analogy, and comparison or contrast.

PREWRITING First, make sure that the topic is limited enough for a paragraph; if not, limit it further. Next, determine your purpose, identify your audience, and consider your attitude toward the topic. Then gather information, select and arrange the details you plan to use, and write a topic sentence.

WRITING As you draft each paragraph, keep your purpose and audience in mind. Express your ideas clearly and make sure that the tone is appropriate and consistent.

EVALUATING, REVISING, AND PROOFREADING Use the Guidelines for Evaluating Paragraphs (pages 404–405) and the appropriate guidelines from page 369 to evaluate your writing. You may also ask a classmate to read and evaluate your paragraph. Then use the paragraph revision chart (pages 406–407) to revise it. Refer to the Guidelines for Proofreading (page 376) as you correct your revised draft and your recopied final version.

FOUR TYPES OF PARAGRAPHS

Most paragraphs can be classified into four types, depending on the writer's primary purpose:

1. An *expository paragraph* informs or explains.
2. A *persuasive paragraph* attempts to convince the reader to agree with an opinion and, sometimes, to perform a specific action.
3. A *descriptive paragraph* describes a person, place, or object.
4. A *narrative paragraph* relates a series of events.

Many paragraphs contain elements of more than one purpose. Description, for example, is often combined with narration. Usually, however, one purpose largely determines the content and the language.

THE EXPOSITORY PARAGRAPH

An expository paragraph may inform, explain, or define. It may be developed with facts and statistics, with examples, by means of cause and effect, by definition, or by a combination of these methods. It should be direct and unemotional in tone, avoiding vague words and emotional appeals, and it should be objective rather than subjective—the writer's personality should not intrude.

SUBJECTIVE When I lost my book bag full of schoolbooks and notes, I learned the hard way that people have got to have identification on their luggage, book bags, and other important stuff.

OBJECTIVE To ensure that luggage, book bags, and other valuables can be properly identified and returned if they are lost, tag all such valuables with your name, address, and telephone number.

Developing with Facts and Statistics

24o. Develop an expository paragraph with facts and statistics.

A *fact* is a statement that can be proved to be true; a *statistic* is a numerical fact that summarizes large quantities of data. The following paragraph, which gives information, uses facts to support the main idea.

Basic to all the Greek achievement was freedom. The Athenians were the only free people in the world. In the great empires of antiquity—Egypt, Babylon, Assyria, Persia—splendid though they were, with riches beyond reckoning and immense power, freedom was unknown. The idea of it never dawned in any of them. It was born in Greece, a poor little country, but with it able to remain unconquered no matter what manpower and what wealth were arrayed against her.

EDITH HAMILTON

The following paragraph uses facts to explain the formation of condensation trails.

Condensation trails, usually called contrails or vapor trails, are artificial clouds of water droplets or ice crystals that form in the wake of an airplane. They form because the water in the engines' exhaust condenses in the cold air. For a contrail to form, the air around the plane must be colder than −60° C. If the air is warmer, the warmth will prevent condensation of the moisture coming from the engines, and no contrail will form. Jets, which fly in the very cold upper layers of the atmosphere, are the planes most likely to produce contrails.

CRITICAL THINKING:
Distinguishing Between Facts and Opinions

To write effective expository and persuasive paragraphs, you must be able to distinguish between facts and opinions. A *fact* is information that can be proved to be true. It is a fact, for example, that the capital of Utah is Salt Lake City. An *opinion,* on the other hand, states a judgment or a belief; it can be explained, but cannot be proved. As a reader and a listener, you must be able to determine whether statements are accurate and verifiable or simply someone's opinion. Opinions often use words that indicate some kind of judgment, such as *most, should, should not, greatest, best.*

FACT Twenty-three students in this class have bought a particular brand of pocket calculator.
OPINION This is the best brand of pocket calculator.

FACT Public schools in this city close for two months during the summer.
OPINION Public schools should be open eleven months a year.

EXERCISE 20. Distinguishing Facts from Opinions. Some of the following statements are facts; some are opinions. Write *F* for each fact and *O* for each opinion. (Assume that statements that are written as facts are true.)

1. The number of corporate mergers has increased during the past fifteen years.

2. There should be more women executives in industry.
3. Local department stores reported record-setting sales in December of this year.
4. Men and women should wait until they are at least twenty-one years old to marry.
5. Cup for cup, tea contains less caffeine than coffee.
6. Anne McCaffrey is the best writer of fantasy.
7. For many years automobile companies in several nations have been researching the possible use of air bags as a safety device in automobiles.
8. A bibliography is an alphabetical list of the sources used for a research paper.
9. Every high-school student should be required to take two years of a foreign language.
10. Driver's licenses are renewable every four years; learner's permits must be renewed yearly.

EXERCISE 21. Writing Paragraphs Using Facts and Statistics. Write a paragraph based on the information given in each of the following numbered items. Refer to the material that follows Item 2 on page 413 as you plan, write, evaluate, and revise each paragraph.

1

Survey Question: Here is a list of things that people sometimes say are problems in professional sports. For each, tell me what kind of problem you think it is.

	BIG PROBLEM	SMALL PROBLEM	NO PROBLEM
Drug abuse	74%	24%	2%
High player salaries	55%	27%	18%
High ticket prices	54%	34%	12%
Alcohol abuse	52%	38%	10%
Unnecessary violence	41%	50%	9%
Team owners who meddle	34%	46%	20%
Too much TV pro sports	27%	25%	48%
Poor sportsmanship	24%	56%	20%
Fixed games	24%	35%	41%
Incompetent officials	23%	47%	30%
Too many pro teams	17%	27%	56%
Racial discrimination	11%	26%	63%

THE MIAMI HERALD

2

a. 1.8 million adults in United States enrolled in basic education courses
b. Federal government spending $75 million a year to support these programs; state and local governments spend about the same
c. Averages two dollars per year for each adult who is functionally illiterate (can't read or write)
d. Not enough space in programs for adults who want to learn basic reading and writing skills
e. More than 26 million Americans functionally illiterate—cannot read a notice, address an envelope, or write a check
f. Lisette Quinones, age 20, waiting for two years to begin a basic education course at LaGuardia Community College in New York
g. Critics: to eliminate long waiting periods, much more money needs to be spent for basic education courses for adults

PREWRITING Do not try to use all of the statistics or facts given in the numbered items; you do not want to overwhelm or confuse your audience. For each paragraph, decide first which four or five pieces of information will best suit the needs and interests of your audience. Arrange the material in an order that will be easy to follow, and write a topic sentence that expresses your main idea. Make sure that the information you have chosen effectively supports that idea.

WRITING Concentrate on expressing your ideas clearly in fairly formal language. Be sure to define or explain any terms your audience may find difficult or unfamiliar.

EVALUATING AND REVISING Ask yourself: Have I included neither too much information nor too little? Have I arranged the material in a logical order? You may also ask someone else to read your draft and tell you whether it is easy to understand. Then use the Guidelines for Evaluating Expository Paragraphs on page 418 to judge your writing, and refer to the paragraph revision chart on pages 406–407 as you improve it.

PROOFREADING AND MAKING A FINAL COPY Use the Guidelines for Proofreading on page 376 to proofread your paragraph. Remember to proofread again after you make your final copy.

Developing with Examples

24p. Develop an expository paragraph with examples.

An *example* is an item or instance that represents others of the same kind. Using examples helps you illustrate a general point concisely. In the following paragraph, the writer uses several examples to illustrate the point in the topic sentence.

> **Victoria was considerably more cultivated than some of her biographers allowed.** She spoke perfect German, excellent French, and adequate Italian; she was well-read in literature and history; she sketched charmingly, and she had a trained ear for music. Because as queen she was uncomfortable in the company of scientists of whose fields she was ignorant, it is sometimes assumed that she was less well-educated than she was. But few men of her era, let alone women, received any training at all in the sciences. Victoria was almost a bluestocking by modern standards.
>
> LOUIS AUCHINCLOSS

EXERCISE 22. Writing a Paragraph Using Examples. Write an expository paragraph developed with examples. You may use one of the following topics or one or your own.

1. American colonies founded on religious freedom
2. Popular musical groups whose fame results from a single recording
3. Gemstones associated with months of the year ("birthstones")
4. Outstanding dishes Italian cooking has contributed to the United States
5. Accomplishments of the U.S. space program

PREWRITING Begin by listing three or more examples and noting other details that will help you clarify the examples. (You may need to do some research.) Arrange the examples and supporting information in an easy-to-follow order, and write a topic sentence stating the main idea the examples illustrate. Then review your notes again, and remove any details that do not provide strong support for your main idea.

WRITING As you write your first draft, keep your purpose and audience in mind. Be sure to include enough supporting information to make each example clear.

EVALUATING AND REVISING Ask yourself: Have I included enough examples to make my main idea clear? Does each one truly illustrate my main idea? Then use the Guidelines for Evaluating Expository Paragraphs (page 418) and the paragraph revision chart (pages 406–407) to improve your paragraph.

PROOFREADING AND MAKING A FINAL COPY Proofread your paragraph carefully, using the guidelines on page 376. Then make a final copy and proofread it.

Developing by Means of Cause and Effect

24q. Develop an expository paragraph by analyzing cause and effect.

A *cause* is an event or situation that produces a result; an *effect* is anything brought about by a cause. Basically, there are two types of cause-effect paragraphs. In one type, you begin by stating an effect and then discuss the cause or causes. Such a paragraph answers the question "Why?" In the following paragraph, Barbara Tuchman explains why the combatants in World War I refused to accept U.S. President Woodrow Wilson's proposal to end the war without proclaiming either side the victor.

> Wilson's offer of December 1916 to bring together the belligerents for negotiation of a "peace without victory" was rejected by both sides. Neither was prepared to accept a settlement without some gain to justify its suffering and sacrifice in lives, and to pay for the war. Germany was not fighting for the status quo but for German hegemony of Europe and a greater empire overseas. She wanted not a mediated but a dictated peace and had no wish, as the Foreign Minister, Arthur Zimmermann, wrote to Bernstorff, "to risk being cheated of what we hope to gain from war" by a neutral mediator. Any settlement requiring renunciations and indemnities by Germany—the only settlement the Allies would accept—would mean the end of the Hohenzollerns and the governing class. They also had to make someone pay for the war or go bankrupt. A peace without victory would not only terminate dreams of mastery but require enormous taxes to pay for years of fighting that had grown profitless. It would mean revolution. To the throne, the military caste, the landowners, industrialists and barons of business, only a war of gain offered any hope of their survival in power.
>
> BARBARA TUCHMAN

The second type of cause-effect paragraph does not answer the question "Why?" Rather, it shows the effects, or results, of a cause. In the following paragraph, the writer discusses several different causes and their effects.

Strong gases and toxic fumes from such things as paint solvents and industrial chemicals may be absorbed in the soft-contact-lens plastic, causing eye irritation if the concentration is strong enough. Cosmetics, lotions, soaps and creams, hair sprays, or any aerosol discharges that come in contact with

cause 1
effect 1
cause 2

the lenses may also stick. Eye irritation may result, and the lenses may get coated to a point where they have to be replaced. Chemicals such as iron in ordinary tap water can also damage soft lenses. Hands should be washed and rinsed thoroughly, and dried on a lint-free towel, before soft lenses are handled.

effect 2

cause 3

effect 3

DR. JOHN A. DYER

EXERCISE 23. Writing a Cause-and-Effect Paragraph. Write an expository paragraph developed by means of cause and effect. You may use one of the following topics or one of your own.

1. Causes of shyness
2. Effects of a cold virus
3. Effects of high interest rates
4. Causes of the War of 1812
5. Effects of being left-handed in a "right-handed world"
6. Causes of low voter turnout in national elections

PREWRITING Begin listing at least three related causes or effects for the topic you have chosen. Review your list carefully to make sure that the items do not contradict one another, and, if necessary, gather additional information. Then arrange the material in order: You may find that presenting causes in order from most to least important is effective, while using the opposite order works well for effects. Finally, write a topic sentence that states your main idea clearly.

WRITING As you write, try to express your ideas as clearly as possible. Consider using transitional expressions such as *as a result, because, consequently,* and *since* to help your audience follow your line of thought.

EVALUATING AND REVISING Ask yourself: If my supporting sentences present causes, do they clearly explain why an effect came about? If they are effects, do they clearly show the consequences of a cause? Then use the Guidelines for Evaluating Expository Paragraphs (page 418) and the paragraph revision chart (pages 406–407) to evaluate and revise your paragraph.

PROOFREADING AND MAKING A FINAL COPY Refer to the guidelines on page 376 as you proofread your paragraph. Remember to proofread again after you make a final copy.

Developing by Definition

24r. Develop an expository paragraph by definition.

The definition of an object or idea first identifies, usually in the topic sentence, the general class to which the item belongs. The supporting sentences provide details that show how the item is different from all other members of that class. This two-stage method—general class and distinguishing characteristics—is also used to define abstract terms, such as *love, happiness,* or *success.* Since an abstract term does not have physical features, examples, incidents, and quotations from authorities are often used to clarify what the term means to the writer. In the following example the writers first define romantic fiction in a general way. Then they give many facts and examples to clarify the phrase "escape from reality."

> **Romantic fiction is primarily the kind which offers the reader an escape from reality.** It often deals with distant lands and times. The things that happen in it are more exciting or mysterious or adventurous or strange than the things that happen in real life. Often it deals with such things as tournaments and besieged castles and perilous journeys through hostile country. Sometimes its characters have long journeys to go alone through forests, . . . are besieged in lonely old houses, or are shut up on islands in the midst of faraway lakes, or lie in hushed hiding while a mortal foe treads close by. Sometimes there are pirates, hidden treasures, shipwrecks, thrilling flights from a close-pursuing enemy, last-minute rescues, ominous prophecies, missing heirs, disguised princes, intrigue, murder, breathless suspense. Again, romance is often pervaded by an atmosphere of strange things about to be revealed; often it deals with places and people now changed or forgotten or long since passed away. In short, romance shows life not just as it is, but as we like to imagine it to be.
>
> RALPH P. BOAS and EDWIN SMITH

EXERCISE 24. Writing an Extended Definition. Write an expository paragraph developed by definition. You may use one of the following terms or choose another term. Identify the general class to which the term belongs and include its distinguishing characteristics.

1. The Renaissance
2. Success
3. Bald eagle
4. Democracy
5. Lyric poetry

Techniques for Prewriting. As you prepare to write an expository paragraph,

- choose a method of development (or combination of methods): facts and statistics, examples, cause and effect, or definition.
- arrange the information you have gathered in a logical order that will be easy for your audience to follow.
- write a topic sentence that states your main idea clearly and directly.

Evaluating and Revising Expository Paragraphs

You can use the following guidelines for evaluating the expository paragraphs you write. Once you have determined which aspects of your paragraph need to be improved, refer to the paragraph revision chart on pages 406–407 for revision techniques.

GUIDELINES FOR EVALUATING EXPOSITORY PARAGRAPHS

Topic Sentence	1. Does the topic sentence identify a suitably limited topic and suggest that the purpose of the paragraph is to explain or inform?
Topic Development	2. Is the method of development (or combination of methods) appropriate for the main idea and for the audience? Are enough details given to make the main idea clear? Is the information clear, complete, and accurate?
Unity	3. Is each sentence directly related to the main idea as it is expressed in the topic sentence?
Conclusion	4. Does the clincher sentence, if there is one, provide a strong conclusion?
Order of Ideas	5. Are the ideas arranged in a logical, easy-to-follow order?
Relationships Between Ideas	6. Do the ideas flow smoothly from one sentence to the next? Are they linked with direct references and appropriate transitional expressions (*for example, because, etc.*)?
Word Choice	7. Is the language specific? Is it appropriate for the audience? Are technical terms and difficult words defined or explained?
Tone	8. Does the paragraph have an objective tone?

EXERCISE 25. Evaluating and Revising Expository Paragraphs. Using the guidelines on page 418, evaluate the following paragraphs. Then revise them on a separate sheet of paper, using the paragraph revision chart on pages 406–407.

1. One reason for the high dropout rate among high-school students in some schools is that students are tired of going to school. Another reason is that many students want or need to work, and some decide to work full time at part-time jobs they already have.

2. Americans move a lot. The average American moves ten times in his or her lifetime, and about 16 percent of the American population moves each year. This means that children change schools a lot. They have to keep making new friends. Adults find new jobs and are separated from their families sometimes.

REVIEW EXERCISE F. Writing an Expository Paragraph. Write an expository paragraph on one of the following topics or a topic of your own. Begin by planning your paragraph: Determine your specific purpose (to explain, to inform, or to define) and identify your audience; gather information; choose a method of development; arrange the information in a logical order; and write a topic sentence. Then write a first draft, and use the guidelines on page 418 to evaluate it and the paragraph revision chart on pages 406–407 to revise it. Proofread your revised draft, using the guidelines on page 376. Then make a final copy and proofread again.

1. The significance of *honor* in modern life
2. What a person's body language reveals
3. The benefits of having a part-time job
4. The effects of peer pressure on teen-agers
5. How to identify poison ivy or poison oak

THE PERSUASIVE PARAGRAPH

A persuasive paragraph attempts to convince the reader to agree with an opinion or to follow a course of action.

Developing with Reasons

24s. Develop a persuasive paragraph with reasons.

The topic of a persuasive paragraph should be a serious, debatable issue, one that has significance beyond that of a personal preference.

NOT APPROPRIATE Basketball is the best high-school sport.
NOT APPROPRIATE Rye bread is better than white bread.
APPROPRIATE One hour should be added to the school day.
APPROPRIATE Every high-school student should be required to take a one-year computer course.

The topic sentence, or *position statement,* should state the writer's opinion clearly and concisely. It should not be so brief that it is uninteresting, however.

The position statement should be supported by at least three *reasons*—statements that explain why the writer holds the opinion. Reasons are most convincing when they are supported by evidence in the form of facts, statistics, or examples. Together, the reasons and supporting evidence make up the writer's *argument.*

The United States' electoral college system is outmoded and ineffective, and it should be abolished; the President should be elected instead by direct popular vote. *(position statement)* Three times in United States history (1824, 1876, 1888) the loser in popular votes was actually sworn in as President. *(reason 1)* Under the present system, the candidate who takes a plurality of votes in a state takes all of the state's electoral college votes. *(reason 2)* Thus, millions of voters are in effect disenfranchised. Although 1.8 million Texans voted for Jimmy Carter in 1980, for example, Carter received none of Texas' electoral college votes. Currently, the weight of any person's vote depends on the population of the state in which the person resides. *(reason 3)* In Alaska, for example, 95,000 voters cast 3 electoral votes, while in Texas, a single electoral vote requires 372,000 voters. Write to your Congressional representative, urging him or her to work to replace the electoral college system with a system by which the President and Vice-President are elected by popular vote. *(call to action)*

One type of reason that you may use to support an opinion is a quotation by an *authority,* an expert in the field being discussed. In the following paragraph, a knowledgeable and experienced political science professor is cited (quoted) in support of the opinion that the electoral college should be abolished.

> Dr. Elizabeth McElderry, political science professor at State University, supports the movement for direct popular election of the President. "Why should the Presidency and Vice-Presidency be the only national offices that are not elected by direct popular vote? Surely each citizen of the United States should have an equal vote and a vote that, somehow, should be effective—not lost in the electoral college system."

If you were writing to support an opposing viewpoint—that the electoral college system should be retained—you could doubtless find an authority who agrees with you. That is what makes persuasive writing so challenging; you can create an argument in support of an opinion, and you can also create an equally effective argument in support of the opposite opinion.

Reasons in a persuasive paragraph are usually arranged in order of importance, with the most important reason last; this ends the paragraph forcefully. A paragraph that gives the most important reason first may also be effective. In either case, the reader should be able to distinguish important from less important reasons.

The clincher, or concluding, sentence in a persuasive paragraph may reemphasize the writer's opinion, summarize the argument, or specify a course of action. Such a sentence provides an effective ending by giving the paragraph a sense of completeness.

The tone of a persuasive paragraph should be serious and unemotional to convey that you have researched the issue thoroughly and that your argument is fair and reasonable. Avoid name-calling and using words with negative connotations. Be specific, accurate, clear, and forceful in presenting your ideas.

Techniques for Prewriting. In preparing to write a persuasive paragraph,

- evaluate your topic to make sure that it is a serious, debatable issue, not just a personal preference.
- express your opinion clearly and concisely in a position statement.
- gather at least three reasons that explain your opinion and evidence to support each reason.
- arrange the material in order of importance.

Evaluating and Revising Persuasive Paragraphs

You can use the following guidelines to evaluate the persuasive paragraphs you write. The paragraph revision chart on pages 406–407 will help you revise those aspects that need to be improved.

GUIDELINES FOR EVALUATING PERSUASIVE PARAGRAPHS

Topic Sentence	1. Does the position statement express an opinion on a serious, debatable issue? Is it clear, concise, and interesting?
Topic Development	2. Are at least three reasons given to explain the opinion? Is each reason supported by accurate evidence (facts, examples, quotations from authorities, etc.)?
Unity	3. Is each sentence directly related to the opinion in the position statement?
Conclusion	4. Does the clincher sentence, if there is one, provide a strong conclusion for the paragraph?
Order of Ideas	5. Are the reasons arranged in order of importance? Are the less important and more important reasons readily distinguished?
Relationships Between Ideas	6. Is the line of reasoning easy to follow? Are direct references and appropriate transitional expressions (*most important, finally,* etc.) used to link ideas?
Word Choice	7. Have name-calling and words with negative connotations been avoided?
Tone	8. Is the tone consistently serious and unemotional?

EXERCISE 26. Evaluating and Revising a Persuasive Paragraph. Using the guidelines above, evaluate the following paragraph. Then revise the paragraph, using the paragraph revision chart on pages 406–407. Write your revised version on a separate sheet of paper.

Just because they're still in high school, seniors shouldn't have to have a curfew. If you work, sometimes the only time you get to see your friends is late at night. And even if you don't work, the weekends are too short for all the things young people want to do before they graduate. For example, many students enjoy going to parties, shopping, and, my favorite pastime, playing in a band.

REVIEW EXERCISE G. Writing a Persuasive Paragraph. Write a persuasive paragraph supporting one of the following opinions or an opinion of your own.

1. Presidential elections should (should not) be held during a twenty-four-hour period so that the polls in all four time zones open and close at the same time.
2. Restaurants should (should not) be required to have non-smoking sections.
3. Students who are caught cheating on a final examination should (should not) automatically fail the course.
4. One member of the school board should (should not) be a high-school student.
5. High-school students should (should not) be required to pass a series of competency exams to graduate.

PREWRITING Once you have decided which position you will take, list all the reasons you can think of to support that position. Review your list, and select the three or four reasons your audience will find most convincing. Then gather evidence to support each reason, and arrange the material in order of importance. You may also reword the position statement to make it clearer or more interesting.

WRITING As you draft your paragraph, remember to avoid using words with negative connotations. If you decide to include a clincher sentence, decide what specific purpose you want it to perform—to reemphasize your opinion, to summarize your reasons, or to suggest a course of action.

EVALUATING AND REVISING Ask yourself: Is my argument logical and convincing? Have I established and maintained a serious, unemotional tone? You may also have someone else read your paragraph and comment on it. Then use the Guidelines for Evaluating Persuasive Paragraphs (page 422) and the paragraph revision chart (pages 406–407) to judge and revise your writing.

PROOFREADING AND MAKING A FINAL COPY Read your revised draft carefully, using the Guidelines for Proofreading (page 376). Remember to proofread again after you make a final copy.

THE DESCRIPTIVE PARAGRAPH

Descriptive writing creates images in the reader's mind by using language that appeals to the senses. Passages of description are usually woven into other writing. Most paragraph-length descriptions focus on one person, place, event, or object.

Developing with Concrete and Sensory Details

24t. Develop a descriptive paragraph with concrete and sensory details.

In the following paragraph, the writer describes part of a German city. Notice in this paragraph two important elements of description: (1) the use of many carefully selected concrete and sensory details and (2) the use of figurative language (in boldfaced type).

> Closer to the center of town a few dusty trees break the linear bleakness. Then on a boulevard, divided in the middle by a row of trees that meet overhead with trees on either curb to form two leafy tunnels, the traffic begins to swirl, dragging you mercilessly on, past a park into the unfinished glass and chrome and concrete world of the city. **Modest skyscrapers act as bookends** for lower structures, furniture showrooms and stores of electronic equipment. Vast windowless walls of concrete, some studded, some **quilted** for texture, loom over garages, amusement arcades, record shops, restaurants, and **potbellied trucks dribbling** their premixed concrete near the **hoardings** of a would-be skyscraper. At the end of a short street, drab with two-story buildings, rooming houses, and **dejected shops, squats** a miniature station, its newly painted **gingerbread eyebrows** giving it a **sullen expression. Half-defiant, half-apologetic,** a remnant of the past, it looks out on the wrong century.
>
> ANN CORNELISEN

The details in a descriptive paragraph may be given in either spatial or chronological order. Ann Cornelisen organizes her description spatially. In the following example, which combines narration with description, N. Scott Momaday uses chronological order; the details are given in the order in which the woman senses or imagines them.

> She went out into the soft yellow light that fell from the windows and that lay upon the ground and the pile of wood. She knelt down and picked up the cold, hard lengths of wood and laid them in the crook of her arm. They were sharp and seamed at the ends where the axe had shaped them like pencil points, and they smelled of resin. When again she stood, she inadvertently touched the handle of the axe; it was stiff and immovable in the block, and cold. She felt with the soles of her feet the chips of wood which lay all about on the ground, among the dark stones and weeds. The long black rim of the canyon wall lay sheer on the dark, silent sky. She stood, remembering the sacramental violence which had touched the wood. One of the low plateaus, now invisible above her, had been gutted

long ago by fire, and in the day she had seen how the black spines of the dead trees stood out. She imagined the fire which had run upon them, burning out their sweet amber gum. Then they were flayed by the fire and their deep fibrous flesh cracked open, and among the cracks the wood was burned into charcoal and ash, and in the sun each facet of the dead wood shone low like velvet and felt like velvet to the touch, and left the soft death of itself on the hands that touched it.

N. SCOTT MOMADAY

Often, as in these two models, the main idea of a descriptive paragraph—an impression or a mood—is implied rather than stated directly in a topic sentence. In the preceding paragraph, for example, the details and the writer's style create a silent, somber mood.

Techniques for Prewriting. As you prepare to write a descriptive paragraph,

- gather precise concrete and sensory details.
- select those details that will most effectively create a dominant mood or main impression, and arrange them in spatial or chronological order.
- decide whether you will state your main idea directly or imply it.

Evaluating and Revising Descriptive Paragraphs

You will find the following guidelines useful for evaluating the descriptive paragraphs you write. The paragraph revision chart on pages 406–407 will help you revise your writing.

GUIDELINES FOR EVALUATING DESCRIPTIVE PARAGRAPHS

Purpose	1. Does the paragraph focus on a single person, place, object, or event? Does it clearly state or imply a single main idea?
Topic Development	2. Are enough concrete and sensory details presented to enable the reader to visualize or otherwise mentally experience the topic?

Unity	3. Is every sentence directly related to the main idea?
Order of Ideas	4. Are the details arranged in spatial or chronological order?
Relationships Between Ideas	5. Do the ideas flow smoothly? Are direct references and appropriate transitional expressions (*over, past,* etc.) used to show where the details are in relation to one another?
Word Choice	6. Is the language specific rather than general? If figurative language is used, is it appropriate and effective?

EXERCISE 27. Evaluating and Revising a Descriptive Paragraph. Using the guidelines above, evaluate the following paragraph. Then revise the paragraph, using the paragraph revision chart on pages 406–407. Write your revised version on a separate sheet of paper.

The sunset was beautiful. The light seemed to change every moment. A lot of colors lit up the clouds, and the different colors changed. Finally, it was dark.

REVIEW EXERCISE H. Writing a Descriptive Paragraph. Write a paragraph describing one of the following topics or a topic of your own.

1. A football scrimmage
2. A stranger seen on a bus or a subway
3. The inside of a telephone booth
4. An alley
5. A garden

PREWRITING Begin by observing (or recalling) your topic. Take detailed notes on the sights, sounds, tastes, textures, and smells you experience (or remember). Then review your notes carefully, determine what mood or main impression you want to create, and decide whether you will state your main idea directly or imply it. Eliminate from your list any details that do not directly support that idea, and arrange the remaining details in an order that will help reinforce your main idea. If you plan to state your main idea directly, write a topic sentence.

WRITING Write your first draft freely, concentrating on using specific language. If other related details occur to you as you write, include them.

EVALUATING AND REVISING Ask yourself: Have I included enough concrete and sensory details? Do all of the details contribute to my main idea? You may also ask someone else to read and comment on your paragraph. Then use the Guidelines for Evaluating Descriptive Paragraphs (pages 425–26) and the paragraph revision chart on pages 406–407 to judge and revise your draft.

PROOFREADING AND MAKING A FINAL COPY Read your revised draft carefully, using the Guidelines for Proofreading (page 376). Proofread again after you make a final copy.

THE NARRATIVE PARAGRAPH

A narrative paragraph tells a story or relates a series of events. Most narrative paragraphs appear as parts of longer works, such as personal narratives, novels, or short stories. A one-paragraph narrative based on an experience that occurs within a short period of time may be complete in itself.

Developing with an Incident

24u. Develop a narrative paragraph with an incident or an anecdote.

In some narrative paragraphs, the topic sentence makes a point that is developed by the incident related.

> **Luck is sometimes the deciding factor in a game.** In the eighth inning of the deciding game of the World Series of 1924, the Giants were leading the Senators by the fairly comfortable margin of 3–1. A hard-hit ground ball struck a pebble and bounded over the head of third baseman Fred Lindstrom, and two runs came in, tying the game and sending the contest into extra innings. In the last of the twelfth, the Giant catcher, about to dash for a pop fly behind the plate, caught his foot in his mask and missed an easy out. The batter, given another chance, then doubled. The next man up hit another grounder toward third base. The ball again struck a pebble, soaring over the third baseman, and the Senators won the series.

Instead of a topic sentence that states the main idea directly, many narrative paragraphs have an introductory or concluding sentence that summarizes the action, tells how it came about, or comments on its significance.

Occasionally, narrative writing is combined with other kinds of writing. Narration and description are often combined, and sometimes an incident is used in an expository paragraph. In the following paragraph, which illustrates the combination of narration with description and exposition, the first two sentences summarize what the writer learned from the incident she relates.

> In my sensory education I include my physical awareness of the *word*. Of a certain word, that is; the connection it has with what it stands for. At around age six, perhaps, I was standing by myself in our front yard waiting for supper, just at that hour in a late summer day when the sun is already below the horizon and the risen full moon in the visible sky stops being chalky and begins to take on light. There comes the moment, and I saw it then, when the moon goes from flat to round. For the first time it met my eyes as a globe. The word *moon* came into my mouth as though fed to me out of a silver spoon. Held in my mouth, the moon became a word. It had the roundness of a Concord grape Grandpa took off his vine and gave me to suck out of its skin and swallow whole, in Ohio.
>
> EUDORA WELTY

Most narrative paragraphs are arranged in chronological order, which enables the reader to understand how one event leads to another. In longer narratives you may encounter *flashbacks,* sections that show what happened before the events of the main story. Such flashbacks are themselves generally organized chronologically too.

Techniques for Prewriting. In preparing to write a narrative paragraph,

- use the *5 W-How?* questions to gather details of the incident.
- arrange the ideas in chronological order.
- consider writing a topic sentence that makes a general point or an introductory or concluding sentence that summarizes the action, tells how it came about, or comments on its significance.

Evaluating and Revising Narrative Paragraphs

You will find the following guidelines useful for evaluating the narrative paragraphs you write. The paragraph revision chart on pages 406–407 will help you revise your writing.

GUIDELINES FOR EVALUATING NARRATIVE PARAGRAPHS

Purpose	1. Does a topic sentence make a general point, or does an introductory or concluding sentence summarize the action, tell how it came about, or comment on its significance?
Topic Development	2. Are enough details included so that the reader can understand what happened?
Unity	3. Have repetitive and unrelated details been left out?
Order of Ideas	4. Are the events arranged in the order in which they occurred?
Relationships Between Ideas	5. Do the ideas flow smoothly? Are direct references and appropriate transitional expressions (*later, before, in the meantime,* etc.) used to link ideas?
Word Choice	6. Are precise nouns, verbs, and modifiers used to help the reader picture the action? Is the language appropriate for the audience?

EXERCISE 28. Evaluating and Revising a Narrative Paragraph. Using the guidelines above, evaluate the following paragraph. Then use the paragraph revision chart on pages 406–407 to revise it, and write your revised version on a separate sheet of paper.

Some kinds of fun can be a lot of work. Last weekend my friends Al and Rosie invited me and Terry to go with them to a workshop on contra dancing, which is dancing in two lines with the partners lined up facing each other. I really thought I'd have a good time because I always enjoy watching dancing in old movies on TV. Unfortunately, the caller seemed to think that everyone in the group was already an expert. And most of the other people—including Terry, Al, and Rosie—caught on right away. But not me!

REVIEW EXERCISE I. Writing a Narrative Paragraph. Write a narrative paragraph using an incident to illustrate one of the following ideas or an idea of your own.

1. A simple misunderstanding can have long-lasting consequences.
2. A week without television can give you an extremely new perspective on life.
3. Setting a goal and working hard to achieve your goal is enormously satisfying.

4. Volunteers often receive more than they give.
5. What appears to be a bargain may turn out to be extremely costly.

PREWRITING Use the *5 W-How?* questions to make a list of details that the reader will need to know to understand the incident. Then arrange the actions of the incident in chronological order, and write an introductory or concluding sentence that makes a general statement which the incident illustrates. (If you are using one of the ideas suggested above, you may reword the sentence in any way you choose.)

WRITING With your notes in front of you, write your first draft freely, concentrating on trying to express your ideas clearly. Add related details as you think of them, but remember that your incident should keep to the point you are trying to make.

EVALUATING AND REVISING Ask yourself: Have I included enough details to make the incident clear and interesting? Have I left out unnecessary or repetitive details? Then use the Guidelines for Evaluating Narrative Paragraphs (page 429) and the paragraph revision chart (pages 406–407) to judge and improve your writing.

PROOFREADING AND MAKING A FINAL COPY Read your paragraph carefully, using the Guidelines for Proofreading on page 376. Proofread again after you make a final copy.

CHAPTER 24 WRITING REVIEW

Writing Paragraphs for Different Purposes. Write four paragraphs, one for each of the types of writing. You may use the same subject as a starting point for all four paragraphs, or you may use two or more different subjects. Remember to keep your audience and purpose in mind as you limit the subject for each paragraph. Gather information on your limited topic; arrange it in a logical order; and write a topic sentence that states your main idea. (For the descriptive and narrative paragraphs, you may instead imply your main idea.) Then write a first draft, and use the appropriate guidelines to evaluate your writing. Refer to the paragraph revision chart (pages 406–407) as you improve your paragraphs and to the Guidelines for Proofreading (page 376) as you correct them. Proofread again after you make your final copies.

CHAPTER 25

Writing a Research Paper

RESEARCH, WRITING, DOCUMENTATION

A research paper is an extended expository composition based on information gathered from a variety of sources to support the writer's ideas. In this chapter you will learn to use the writing process to prepare a research paper. You will also learn certain special procedures that apply primarily to papers based on research.

PREWRITING

SELECTING A SUBJECT

25a. Select a subject that interests you and that can be researched in the sources available to you.

In a way, the research paper requires you to become an authority on a subject. Thus, you should choose a subject that will hold your interest and that will lend itself to research in the available sources. For this reason, avoid subjects about which very little has been published, such as highly technical or recently developed subjects. No matter how interested you are in a subject, it will not be usable unless you have access to source material on it. Also, be certain that the subject you select can be presented objectively, or impartially. The purpose of a research paper is to explain or inform; you should therefore avoid controversial subjects that would be more appropriate for a persuasive paper.

Techniques for Prewriting. Consider the following suggestions to choose a subject for a research paper:

- To gather subject ideas, thumb through the subject cards in the library card catalog, skim articles in current magazines and newspapers, look at articles and pamphlets in the library's vertical file, or use techniques to search your own experiences (such as reviewing a writer's journal, brainstorming, or clustering).
- Avoid straight biography. If the subject is already famous, such a report would simply be a narrative, summarizing one or more biographies; if the subject is not well known, information would probably be difficult to locate.
- Check the library to be sure ample, up-to-date sources about the subject are available.

EXERCISE 1. Selecting a Subject. Using the preceding suggestions, list at least five subjects to research. Evaluate the suitability of the subjects and choose one to research. Save your work for later use.

GETTING AN OVERVIEW

25b. Do some preliminary reading to gain an overview, or general understanding, of your subject.

Begin your research by reading general articles in encyclopedias and scanning books to develop an overview, or broad understanding, of your subject. This overview will guide you as you limit the subject to a topic and determine the basic questions your research will answer. It will also be invaluable later as you begin to read and take notes. With a basic understanding of your subject, you will be more likely to use your time efficiently and less likely to take notes on unimportant or irrelevant information.

Techniques for Prewriting. To get an overview of your subject:

- Find two or more general articles about your subject in encyclopedias or specialized reference books (see pages 482–92). Note headings and subheadings in each article as possible ways to limit the subject. Then, begin a list of possible limited topics and basic questions about your subject.
- Look up your subject in the *Readers' Guide to Periodical Literature* (see pages 478–79) and read the titles of articles listed there.
- Using the subject cards in the card catalog, locate two or more books on your subject. Examine both the table of contents and major headings in the index and add to your list of possible topics and basic questions.
- Look for your subject in the library vertical file, skim available articles or pamphlets, and add any new ideas to your list of topics and questions.

EXERCISE 2. Getting an Overview. Use the preceding suggestions to get an overview of the subject you selected in Exercise 1. Save your notes for later use.

LIMITING YOUR SUBJECT

25c. Limit your subject to a topic that you can cover adequately within the assigned length of the paper.

If you try to write a research paper on a broad subject, you will either spend far too much time on the paper and exceed the assigned length or simply skim the surface of the subject. Taking the time to limit the scope of the subject now will save you time and energy later and result in a better paper. At the same time be careful not to develop a topic that is too limited; too little information might be available for you to meet the assignment's requirements.

Limiting a subject involves analyzing the subject to determine its logical divisions. (See pages 355–57.) For example, the writer of the sample paper on page 410 began with the general subject "parapsychology" and limited the subject as follows.

1. Parapsychology
2. Extrasensory perception (a specific branch of parapsychology)

3. Clairvoyance (a specific type of extrasensory perception)
4. Scientific studies of clairvoyance (a specific aspect of clairvoyance)

EXERCISE 3. Recognizing Suitable Topics. Indicate which of the following topics are suitable for research papers and which are too broad, too limited, or otherwise unsuitable (not expository). Then suggest how each unsuitable topic might be improved.

1. Why nuclear arms should be banned
2. Careers in the arts
3. The renovation of the Statue of Liberty
4. The contributions of Hispanics
5. The life of Sacajawea
6. The European Communities
7. Solar energy for industrial power
8. The Ferraro-Bush vice-presidential debate
9. Anthropomorphism in children's literature
10. Brain cell abnormalities in victims of Alzheimer's disease

EXERCISE 4. Limiting Your Subject. Analyze the subject you selected in Exercise 1 or another subject to develop at least five topics suitable for a research paper. Save your work.

CONSIDERING PURPOSE, AUDIENCE, AND TONE

25d. Evaluate your topic in terms of purpose, audience, and tone.

Before you begin your research, consider your limited topic in terms of the purpose, audience, and tone of a research paper.

CRITICAL THINKING: Evaluating Your Topic

Evaluating involves using criteria, or standards, to judge an idea or practice. The criteria for evaluating the topic of a research paper have long been established.

Begin by determining if your topic meets the expository purpose of a research paper: A topic such as "the special effects in the original *Star Wars* movie" might result in a good descriptive composition, but it is not appropriate for a research paper. Evaluate your topic to make sure that it will result in exposition. If not, limit your subject again to arrive at an expository topic.

Assume that the audience for your research paper is a general one: educated people of many different backgrounds who are interested in almost any topic that has some significance and that is developed with fresh and specific information. A general audience might be interested in reading a nontechnical explanation of the glacial formation of the Great Lakes. However, this topic would not be suitable for an audience of professional geographers, for it would offer them no new information. On the other hand, keep in mind that your audience is a general one and avoid highly technical topics appropriate for specialists.

The research paper requires a serious tone. Therefore, your topic should reflect a tone that is formal and impersonal. For example, the topic "my reactions to women's outlandish threads in the old days" is inappropriate; it uses the first-person pronoun *my*, and "outlandish" and "threads" are informal expressions. Recasting the topic as "women's fashions in the post-World War II era" instead conveys a serious attitude.

EXERCISE 5. Evaluating Topics. Indicate which of the following topics for research papers are appropriate in terms of purpose, audience, and tone. Then, rewrite those that are unsuitable.

1. Errors of calculation in Beethoven's symphonic orchestration
2. Hispanic voting patterns in the 1986 U.S. Senate elections
3. My super trip to a whale of a cave in Kentucky
4. Ethnic distribution of visitors to the 1984 New Orleans World Fair
5. Philosophical issues in the art of M. C. Escher

REVIEW EXERCISE A. Evaluating Your Topic. Evaluate the five topics you developed in Exercise 4 in terms of purpose, audience, and tone. Select one topic for your paper and, if necessary, revise it so that it is appropriate. (Your teacher may want to approve your topic before you begin your research.)

PREPARING A WORKING BIBLIOGRAPHY

25e. Prepare a working bibliography.

The first step in researching your topic is to compile a working bibliography of potential sources of information.

Research Aids

To find sources of information on your topic, you will use a number of the library research aids (card catalog, *Readers' Guide,* and reference works). These research aids are explained in Chapters 27 and 28. You might review those chapters before you continue your research to make sure that you are thoroughly familiar with the information in them. As you use the card catalog, in particular, do not confine your search to materials filed under your specific topic. If your topic is "clairvoyance," for example, you will probably find useful materials under more general headings, such as "Parapsychology" and "Extrasensory Perception." As you use library sources, note the titles listed at the end of general articles in encyclopedias and look for these sources. Then, when you find one source, check its bibliography to identify other possible sources. Also, always examine both the index and table of contents in a book to find out the extent of the information the source has about your topic.

Remember, however, that the library is not the sole source of information. Think creatively about what other possible sources may be. Bookstores carry many excellent books in paperback; government publications, personal interviews and correspondence can also be good sources. For a paper on your community's history, you might interview a local historian and examine records and documents at a local museum. If you plan to write for information, do so early enough to allow time for a response.

Scholarly journals can also be excellent sources. Like magazines, journals are published periodically (once a month, four times a year, etc.) However, unlike magazines, these journals are written for readers with specialized knowledge of a particular field. The *New England Journal of Medicine,* for example, publishes medical news for physicians and health professionals. These scholarly journals are not included in the *Readers' Guide,* but you can find articles by checking a specialized index for your area of interest. In large libraries, the reference librarians will be able to direct you to appropriate specialized indexes.

Evaluating Sources

Simply locating adequate sources will not insure that your research will result in an outstanding paper. Not all sources are equally valuable or reliable. Whenever you encounter a new source, take time to evaluate, or judge, its usefulness for your purposes.

Techniques for Prewriting. Ask the following questions to evaluate potential sources:

- Does the author appear to be an authority on the subject? Authors with several books and articles on a subject or those cited in other sources or bibliographies are usually reliable.
- Can the source be relied on for objective, impartial information? A book about a President's foreign policy written by a member of his staff may not be an objective source.
- For what audience was the work intended? Works written for younger readers often simplify topics or lack specific facts, while books for specialists may be too technical.
- How current is the information? A 1969 study of hazardous wastes is probably out-of-date and, therefore, unreliable. Even for topics about the past (post-Civil War reconstruction), recent articles may reveal previously undiscovered facts or new theories.
- Does an article appear in a scholarly journal, a special-interest magazine, or a general-interest magazine like those found on most newsstands? Does the periodical have a reputation for accurate, knowledgeable treatment of a topic?

EXERCISE 6. Evaluating Sources. Locate at least five potential sources of information about your topic. Evaluate each source by asking yourself the preceding questions. Replace any unreliable sources with more suitable ones.

Bibliography Cards

To compile your working bibliography, record each source on a separate card. Include *all* the information listed below; you will need it later, when you prepare your final bibliography. For books, you can obtain this information from the library catalog; for articles, from the *Readers' Guide.* For pamphlets and newspapers, you must check each source to find the necessary information.

BOOKS

1. Call number in upper right-hand corner of the card
2. Author's (or editor's) full name, last name first, for alphabetizing later (Indicate editor by placing *ed.* after the name.) If a book has two or more authors, only the name of the first author is written last name first; the names

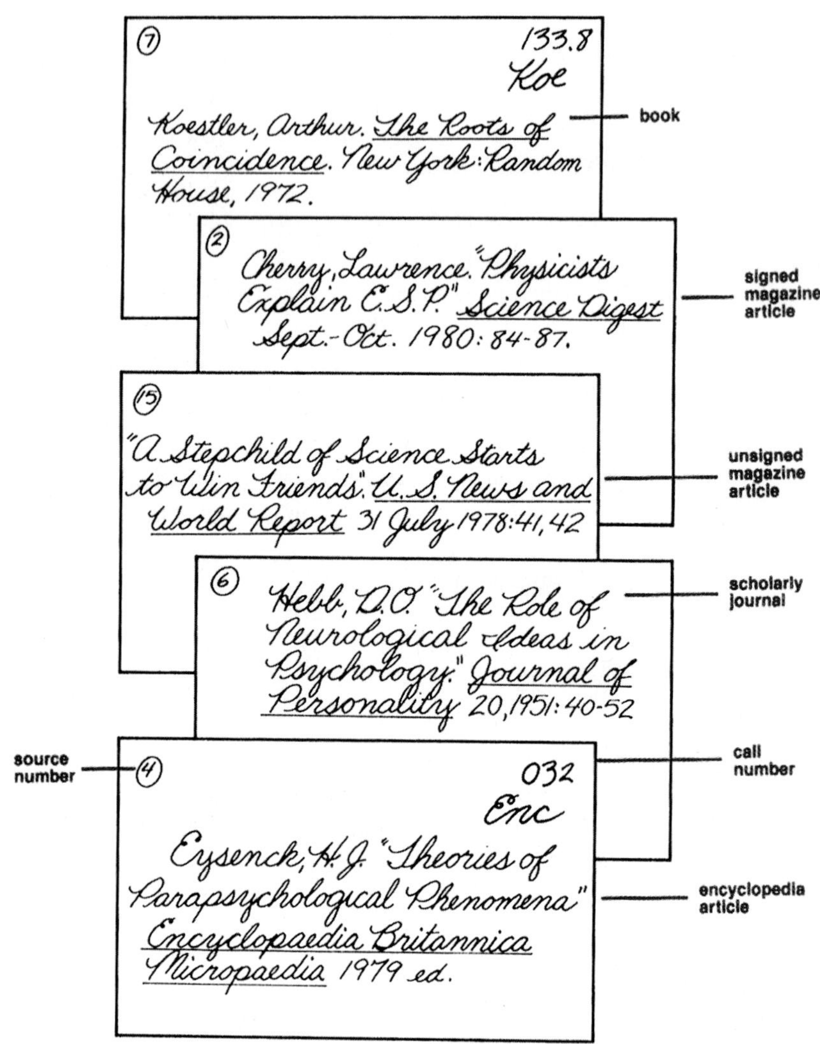

Cards in a Working Bibliography

of the others are written first name first. For three or more authors, write only the first author's name and add *et al.*, a Latin expression meaning *and others* (Rhine, J. B., et al.).

3. Title and subtitle, underlined (and editions, if second or later; and number of volumes, if more than one). Pamphlets only: series and number, if any
4. City of publication
5. Publisher's name (shortened, if clear)
6. Most recent copyright year (or date, for some pamphlets)

MAGAZINE, SCHOLARLY JOURNAL, NEWSPAPER, AND ENCYCLOPEDIA ARTICLES

1. Author's full name (unless article is unsigned)
2. Title of article, in quotation marks
3. Name of magazine, journal, newspaper, or encyclopedia, underlined
4. For popular press magazines: date and page numbers. For newspapers: date, edition, section, page numbers. For scholarly journals: volume, year of publication (in parentheses), page numbers. For encyclopedias arranged alphabetically: edition (if given) and year of publication.

For a book, the card catalog will list information needed for a working bibliography card, although it will not reveal much about the book's contents. To examine potentially useful books, go to the shelf in the library where sources are located according to call numbers. Nonfiction books are classified by subject, so by locating a source you will also find other books the library has on the subject on the neighboring shelves. A glance at the table of contents and the index in these books will tell you how useful each book might be. If the table of contents does not reveal information on your subject, look in the index to see whether the book includes information on your subject and, if so, how extensive the information is.

Assign each card in your working bibliography a number, and write it clearly in the upper left corner. Later you will use this number to identify the source on your note cards. Notice the arrangement and punctuation of the information on the previous sample cards.

EXERCISE 7. Preparing Bibliography Cards. Prepare bibliography cards for the items below. Add underlining and quotation marks where necessary.

1. A book entitled The Soul of a New Machine by Tracy Kidder, published in Boston in 1981 by Atlantic-Little.
2. An unsigned article entitled Personal Computers, published in the December 1983 issue of Consumer Reports on pages 73 through 88.

3. An article written by Michael Rogers, entitled Computer Culture Made Easy, published in the November 19, 1984, issue of Newsweek on page 102.
4. A book entitled Whole Earth Software Catalog, edited by Stewart Brand, published in New York in 1984 by Doubleday.
5. A book entitled Digital Deli, edited by Steve Ditlea, published in New York in 1984 by Workman.

EXERCISE 8. Preparing Your Working Bibliography. Prepare a working bibliography on your topic. (Your teacher may ask you to prepare a minimum number of bibliography cards.)

WRITING A PRELIMINARY THESIS STATEMENT

25f. State the preliminary thesis of your paper in one sentence.

To bring your topic into sharper focus before you research your potential sources, state the paper's thesis, or main idea, in one declarative sentence. This preliminary thesis statement further limits your topic and provides a guide for your research.

You may well revise this preliminary thesis several times as you continue your research and write and revise the paper. Expressing it as clearly as possible at this stage, however, will enable you to avoid gathering material that does not support your ideas. Be sure your thesis statement reflects an expository purpose and a serious tone.

The writer of the research paper on scientific studies of clairvoyance (pages 410–18) drew up the following *preliminary* thesis statement:

> According to the findings of some recent research, people with clairvoyance can "see" things without the use of the senses.

EXERCISE 9. Writing a Preliminary Thesis Statement. Keeping in mind the purpose, audience, and tone appropriate for a research paper, write a preliminary thesis statement for your paper.

PREPARING A PRELIMINARY OUTLINE

25g. Prepare a preliminary outline as a guide to your research.

Before you can take notes in an organized way, you must have some idea of the kinds of information you will be looking for. One way to do so is to formulate a series of *questions about the topic,* anticipating the questions your paper should answer. Your tentative answers to these questions can then become the headings and subheadings of a preliminary outline.

At this point, you do not need to concern yourself with matters of style or with the final organization of the headings. As you read and take notes, you may decide that some headings are irrelevant or are not covered well enough in the available resources. In addition, you will undoubtedly find other information to include. Like the preliminary thesis statement, the preliminary outline may be revised several times before you complete the paper.

Follow these suggestions in drawing up your preliminary outline:

1. Put the title of your paper at the top of a sheet of paper.
2. Below the title, write the word *Thesis* and your thesis statement.
3. Do not make the preliminary outline too detailed; you will add to it as you read and take notes.

The writer of the paper on scientific studies of clairvoyance formulated the following questions about the topic.

What is clairvoyance?
How do researchers conduct experiments on clairvoyance?
What kinds of experiments into clairvoyance have been conducted?
Do all scientists agree on the existence of clairvoyance?
What lies ahead for clairvoyance studies?

Using these questions, the student drew up the following preliminary outline. (You may want to compare this with the final outline on page 411.)

Title: Scientific Studies of Clairvoyance
Thesis: According to the findings of some recent research, people with clairvoyance can "see" things without the use of the senses.

1. Definition of clairvoyance
2. Scientific approach to clairvoyance
3. Experiments with clairvoyance
   —studies by J. B. Rhine
   —studies by Rhine's followers
4. Objections to experiments
5. Future of clairvoyance studies

EXERCISE 10. Preparing a Preliminary Outline. Develop questions about your topic and use them to draw up a preliminary outline.

GATHERING INFORMATION ON YOUR TOPIC

25h. Take notes on cards classified by the headings and subheadings on your preliminary outline.

Your working bibliography, preliminary thesis statement, and outline are a plan of action for your research. Always take notes *as you read;* your memory is not a reliable guide for detailed information and quotations. Without a complete, accurate record of your research, you will find it impossible to reconstruct information when you write the paper. With a package of 4 x 6-inch index cards, you are ready to read your sources. The note cards should be larger than working-bibliography cards for two reasons: First, the cards will accommodate longer notes; and second, you will be able to distinguish them from your smaller bibliography cards.

The following numbered items explain the entries on the sample card on page 393. Each explanation is numbered to correspond to the appropriate key number in the illustration. Be sure to use the same format on your note cards.

1. ***The "slug."*** In the upper left corner, write a point from your preliminary outline, called a "slug." Include only information related to that point on the note card. Some notes may not fall naturally under one of the headings or subheadings in your preliminary outline. If you find that your notes do not fit into your outline, revise the outline accordingly and enter the new slugs on cards. You also may delete points if you cannot find enough usable information on them. If you combine two headings, change your outline as well as the slugs on the appropriate cards. Be sure to put notes about different slugs on separate cards, even if the notes are from the same source.
2. ***The bibliographical reference.*** Enter the source number from your working bibliography in the upper right corner. This will save you from recopying the publication information onto the note cards. Several sources will often provide information on the same point; thus you will have several cards with the same slug, each representing a different source.
3. ***The note.*** To avoid taking unnecessary notes and to increase your overall understanding, start with a reliable, knowledgeable source that gives a detailed treatment of your topic. If other sources give the same information, you will not need to record it again. Then write most of your notes in your own words so that your research paper is not just a string of quotations. Also avoid a *derived* style, one that sounds like the

style of your sources rather than like your own style. Think carefully about the kind of note you want to take: *summarize* to record an author's main ideas; *paraphrase,* or restate in your own words, to record specific facts or details; *quote,* enclosing an author's exact words in quotation marks, to indicate when an author's language is as important as his or her ideas.

Whether you summarize, paraphrase, or quote, you must credit your sources. *Plagiarism*—the use of another person's words or ideas without acknowledging the source—is a serious, punishable offense, one you must always avoid.

When you take notes in your own words, save time by (1) using abbreviations for as many words as you can without affecting the clarity of your notes, (2) using symbols for short words (& for *and*), and (3) writing phrases rather than sentences. Always write legibly, and include all the information you will need to understand the note later.

4. ***The page reference.*** At the end of each note, write the page or pages on which you found the information. You may need to return to the specific page later to clarify a point, and you must include page numbers when you prepare citations for your paper. If information runs over from one page to the next, place a slash mark in the note to show where the page break occurs.

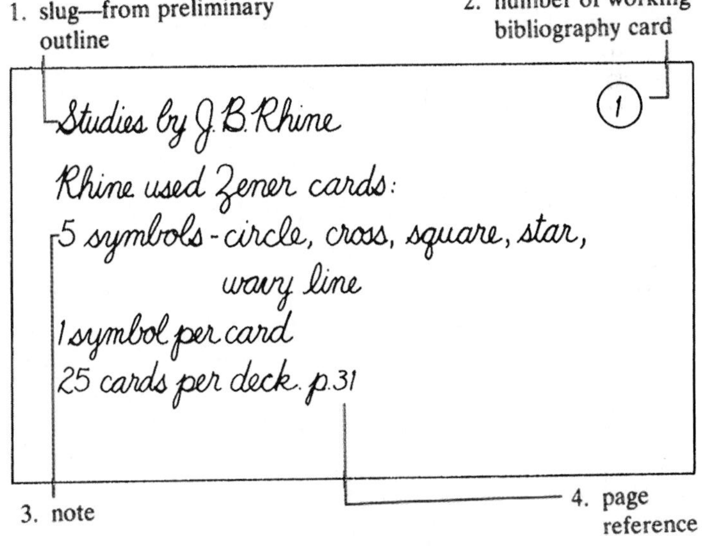

Sample Note Card

EXERCISE 11. Gathering Information on Your Topic. Read and take notes on your topic, following the preliminary outline you prepared in Exercise 10. Revise your preliminary outline as you find additional points to include or as you delete others.

CLASSIFYING AND ORGANIZING INFORMATION

25i. Classify and organize your notes, and prepare a revised outline.

Your preliminary outline was based only on a general understanding of your topic. Through research you probably have encountered new ideas and information. You may also have discovered that some points in your preliminary outline are not as significant as you originally thought. Now you should organize the notes you have gathered.

Taking time now to prepare a well-organized formal outline will give you a sound plan to follow as you write your first draft. Usually, the material for a research paper can be organized under six or fewer main headings. If you have more than six, review the organization of the material and the material itself to make sure that you have not included too much information or mistaken minor points for major ones. Also, your teacher may ask you to submit your revised outline with your completed research paper.

Techniques for Prewriting. To prepare a revised outline,

- Put all cards with the same slug (heading) in one group.
- Review each group of cards separately. Does each group adequately explain a point or should you gather additional information? Do any cards contain unrelated information? Does each group relate to your thesis, or should any be omitted?
- Compare each group of cards with the headings in your preliminary outline. What headings or subheadings should be added, omitted or revised?
- Think carefully about organization. Are headings and subheadings arranged in a clear and logical order? Is each subheading a logical division of that particular heading? Should you move any groups to another place in the outline? Should you rearrange the order of notes within a group?
- Prepare a formal outline, correctly using Roman numerals, capital letters, and Arabic numerals. (See page 461.)

REVIEW EXERCISE B. Preparing a Revised Outline. Classify and organize your note cards, revise your thesis statement if necessary, and prepare a revised outline. (Your teacher may want to check your note cards, thesis, and outline before you begin writing.)

WRITING

WRITING THE FIRST DRAFT

25j. Write the first draft from your revised outline.

With your revised outline, your notes, and your bibliography cards nearby, you are ready to write your first draft. Remember that the first draft is for your use only. You may start wherever you want; the important thing is to put your ideas in a form you can follow when you revise the paper. As you write, note two important mechanical considerations: to indicate you are omitting words from a direct quotation, use an ellipsis (. . .); to quote more than four lines (an extended quotation), set the quotation off from the text by indenting each line ten spaces.

CRITICAL THINKING: Synthesizing

The first draft of any composition is a synthesis, or putting together, of separate elements to form a new whole. Writing the first draft of a research paper is particularly complex because you must bring together information from many sources, digest it thoroughly, acknowledge your sources appropriately, and present your findings in a unified, coherent fashion.

As you write, keep in mind your purpose, audience, and tone. Use the information on your note cards to support your thesis clearly and effectively, and credit your sources for both ideas and quotations, using one of the methods explained below. Remember that ideas that become familiar to you during your research may not be as well known to your readers, who will be relying on transitions, definitions of technical terms, and logical sentence and paragraph structure to understand your paper.

Documentation

Three methods of documenting sources are used for research papers: parenthetical citations, footnotes, and endnotes. Your teacher may prefer that you use a particular method. No matter which method you use, remembering that your audience is a general one will help you decide which information to document, or credit.

Techniques for Writing. Use the following guidelines for documenting information from sources in your research paper.

- Always document the source of a direct quotation.
- Document the source of specific surveys, scientific experiments, public polls, and research studies.
- Document a new or unusual theory or opinion, or one held by a particular author, even if you present the author's ideas in your own words.
- Document rare, unusual, or questionable facts or statistics, especially if they appear in only one source. Usually it is not necessary to document facts or ideas that appear in several sources. Do not document facts widely available in reference books (Cleopatra was a queen of Egypt) or commonly accepted theories (comets are composed of frozen gases).
- Never assume too much knowledge on the part of your audience. If you do not know whether a particular fact is general or specialized knowledge, give its source.
- When possible, introduce source material with the name of the author or title of the work, so that source material will be clearly distinguished from your own ideas, and the paper will read more smoothly.

Footnotes

Footnotes are numbered notes which give information about a source: the author's name, the title, the publishing information, and a page reference. To indicate a footnote, write or type a number slightly above and to the right of the final punctuation mark at the end of a quotation or idea taken from a source. This number refers the reader to the footnote, which appears at the bottom of the page. You must plan each page so that there will be enough space at the bottom for the footnotes for that page. Number the footnotes consecutively, unless your teacher directs otherwise. Remember that you must document all quotations and all summarized or paraphrased information from your sources.

Use the following guidelines to prepare footnotes for your research paper. As you study the examples (taken from several research papers), notice the punctuation. Also note that months—except May, June, and July—are abbreviated, and that the first line of the footnote is indented.

1. The footnote for a book or pamphlet gives the name of the author (first name first); the title (underlined); the city of publication, the publisher, and the copyright date; and the page number(s).

EXAMPLES

[1]Doris Lessing, A Small Personal Voice: Essays, Reviews, Interviews (New York: Knopf, 1974) 47. [book by one author]

[2]Cleanth Brooks and Robert Penn Warren, Modern Rhetoric, 4th ed. (New York: Harcourt Brace Jovanovich, 1979) 179. [book by two authors]

2. The footnote for a magazine or newspaper article gives the author (unless the article is anonymous); the title (in quotation marks); the name of the publication (underlined); the volume number, if any (for scholarly journals only); the date; and the page number(s).

EXAMPLES

[3]Timothy Ferris, "Einstein's Wonderful Year," Science 84 Nov. 1984: 61–63. [article in a monthly popular press magazine]

[4]Carol Beckwith, "Niger's Wodaabe: 'People of the Taboo,'" National Geographic 164 (1983): 502. [article in a magazine that numbers its pages continuously throughout each volume year]

[5]"Navahos Upheld on Land Claims," New York Times, 30 June 1970, late ed.: A20. [unsigned newspaper article]

3. Different kinds of sources follow different footnote formats.

EXAMPLES

[1]Virginia Woolf, The Diary of Virginia Woolf, 5 vols. (New York: Harcourt Brace Jovanovich, 1979–84) 2: 115. [one volume in a multivolume work in which all have the same title]

[2]Robert Coles, Eskimos, Chicanos, Indians, vol. 4 of Children of Crisis (Boston: Atlantic-Little, 1978) 12. [one volume in multivolume work with different titles]

[3]Virgil, Aeneid, trans. Allen Mandelbaum (Berkeley: U of California P, 1971) 92. [translation; *U* stands for *University*, *P* for *Press*]

[4]Maxwell Perkins, "Thomas Wolfe," Thomas Wolfe: A Collection of Critical Essays, ed. Louis Rubin, Jr. (Englewood Cliffs: Prentice, 1973) 80. [one article in a collection of articles by different authors]

[5]Louis C. Faron, "American Indians," Encyclopedia Americana, 1984 ed. [signed article in an alphabetized encyclopedia]

[6]Florence Wright, personal interview, 4 May 1984. [interview]

[7]"Music in the Age of Shakespeare," PBS, WGBH, Boston, 17 Sept. 1980. [television program]

[8]MacWrite, computer software, Apple Computer, 1984.

[9]Frederic McDowell, "Recent British Fiction: Some Established Writers," Contemporary Literature 2 (Summer 1970): 108 qtd. in Paul Schlueter, The Novels of Doris Lessing (Carbondale: Southern Illinois U P, 1973) 75–76. [a quotation or an idea the author of a source has, in turn, taken from another author]

4. Once you have provided complete documentation for a source the first time you refer to it, you may use a shortened form for later references to the same source. The author's last name and the page number are usually sufficient.

EXAMPLES

[1]Doris Lessing, A Small Personal Voice: Essays, Reviews, Interviews (New York: Knopf, 1974) 47.

[2]Lessing 52.

5. If you use two or more sources by the same author, however, you must include a shortened form of the specific title each time you cite either source.

EXAMPLES

[4]Lessing, Voice 70

[5]Lessing, Stories 116.

6. If you mention the title of the specific work in your paper, you do not need to include the title in the footnote. Similarly, if you include the author's name in your paper, you may omit it from the footnote.

EXAMPLES

[8]Lessing, Voice 64. [neither name nor title mentioned in text]

[8]Lessing 64. [title mentioned in text]

[8]Voice 64. [name mentioned in text]

EXERCISE 12. Preparing Footnotes. Assign footnote numbers and write footnotes for the following five items, in the order given. Assume that neither the authors' names nor the titles are mentioned in the text. Add underlining and quotation marks where necessary.

Footnotes on page 1 of text:

a. An article entitled Psychic Research, by W. Stuckey, published in Science Digest volume 80, October 1976. Reference to page 32.
b. The same article as above, same page.
c. A book by C.E.M. Hansel entitled ESP and Parapsychology: A Critical Reexamination, published in Buffalo in 1980 by Prometheus Books. Reference to page 280.

Footnotes on page 2 of text:

d. An unsigned article in Discover volume 5, February 1984. Reference to page 8. Title of article: A PSI Gap.
e. An article entitled Clairvoyance, by Rex Stanford, in Psychic Exploration: A Challenge for Science, edited by John White and published in 1974 in New York by G. P. Putnam's Sons. Reference to pages 133–134.

Endnotes

Endnotes appear at the end of a research paper, rather than at the bottoms of the pages. They contain the same information as footnotes and follow the same format, but they are collected on a separate page headed "Notes," just before the bibliography. Endnotes should always be numbered consecutively within the manuscript.

Parenthetical Citations

Since 1984, the highly respected Modern Language Association (MLA) has recommended a simplified form of documenting sources. This form, called *parenthetical citation,* identifies sources in parentheses placed as close as possible to the borrowed words or ideas. Just enough information is given to refer the reader to the source in the bibliography. Usually, this information consists only of an author's last name and the page number or numbers from which the material is taken: (Smith 22). If the author's name is mentioned nearby in the text of the paper, even the name is not necessary: (22). When no author is given for a source in the bibliography—the entry is alphabetized by title—then a shortened form of the title and the page number or numbers are placed in parentheses: ("Navaho Claims" 84). If the title is mentioned nearby in the paper, then the title need not be used either: (84).

To use parenthetical citations to document sources for a research paper, follow these MLA guidelines:

1. In most instances you need only include in the parentheses the author's last name and the page number(s) from which the author's words or ideas have come. There is no punctuation between the author's name and the page number(s), only a space. Notice also that the words *page* or *pages* or their abbreviations do not appear in the citation. Place the citation as close as possible to the quotation or to the author's ideas. Usually, the parenthetical citation is placed at the end of a sentence before the final punctuation. If the material is quoted, close quotation marks, insert the parenthetical citation, and then place the closing punctuation mark.

EXAMPLES Clairvoyance, say scientists, is one of four categories of extrasensory perception: (1) telepathy—reading the thoughts of another, (2) precognition—sensing future events, (3) psychokinesis—affecting objects by thinking about them, and (4) clairvoyance—perceiving objects or events that are impossible to perceive by the normal senses (Cherry 84).

Remarks D. O. Hebb, professor of psychology at McGill University,"I do not accept ESP for a moment, because it does not make sense" (45).

The bibliography at the end of the sample research paper on pages 467–68 indicates that the information in the first example above was taken from page 84 of an article by Laurence Cherry titled "Physicists Explain ESP," appearing in the Sept./Oct. 1980 issue of *Science Digest.*

The second example above includes a direct quotation, so the citation appears after the closing quotation marks and before the final punctuation of the sentence. Only the page number from which the quote is taken appears in parentheses. The author's name is not necessary because it appears nearby in the paper.

2. If the bibliography lists two or more works by the same author, then use both the author's last name and a shortened form of the title in

the citation. In this case, a comma comes between the author's name and the title.

EXAMPLES (Stuart, The Thread 32)
(Stuart, The Land 134)

These references are to two novels by Jesse Stuart: The Thread That Runs So True, page 32, and The Land Beyond the River, page 134.

3. If your bibliography has two or more authors with the same last names, use both the first and last names.

EXAMPLES (John Smith 105)
(Mary Smith 134)

4. If the work has more than one author, you may use all the last names, separated by *and* and followed by the page number(s). You may also use only the last name of the first author, followed by *et al.* (and others) and the page number(s).

EXAMPLES (Johnson and Leiberman 53)
(Vasquez et al. 22)

The following examples show additional types of citations. Study also the citations that appear in the sample research paper on pages 460–68.

(Durant and Durant, Lessons 32) [two authors; more than one work by these authors in bibliography; the complete title is Lessons of History]

(J. B. Rhine et al., Extrasensory 108–110) [more than two authors; a work by another author with the same last name is included in the bibliography; the complete title is Extrasensory Perception]

(Woolf 2: 115–118) [the source is a multivolume work]

(McAllister) [the entire work, rather than a specific page, is cited]

(Bernstein 100; Strunk and White 81) [two sources are cited for the same information]

(qtd. in Bell 91) [original source not available; material quoted from an indirect source]

(2.1. 48–53) [quoted from Act 2, Scene 1, lines 48–53 of a play]

The Bibliography

Sometimes labeled "Works Cited," the bibliography provides the support for your research paper. It should include only those materials that you actually quote or paraphrase in the paper, not all of those you compiled for your working bibliography.

The following guidelines will help you arrange and style the bibliography entries.

1. Alphabetize the entries according to the last names of the authors (for an anonymous work, use the first important word in the title instead). Do not number the entries.
2. If you cite more than one work by the same author, do not repeat the author's name. Instead, alphabetize the works by title, and use three hyphens in place of the name for each work after the first one.
3. Indent all lines after the first line of an entry.
4. Place a period at the end of each entry.

The following examples are not in alphabetical order because most of them are drawn from different bibliographies. For a complete bibliography in alphabetical order, see page 468.

Lessing, Doris. A Small Personal Voice: Essays, Reviews, Interviews. New York: Knopf, 1974. [book with one author]

---. Stories. New York: Knopf, 1978. [book by the author of the previous entry]

Brooks, Cleanth, and Robert Penn Warren. Modern Rhetoric. 4th ed. New York: Harcourt Brace Jovanovich, 1979. [book with two authors; also the book's fourth edition]

Woolf, Virginia. The Diary of Virginia Woolf. 5 vols. New York: Harcourt Brace Jovanovich, 1978–84. Vol. 2. [one volume of a multivolume work used; reference to specific volume number appears in the text]

Coles, Robert. Eskimos, Chicanos, Indians. Vol. 4 of Children of Crisis. 5 vols. Boston: Atlantic-Little, 1978. [only one volume in multivolume work with different titles used]

Virgil. Aeneid. Trans. Allen Mandelbaum. Berkeley: U of California P, 1971. [translation; *U* stands for *University* and *P* for *Press*]

Perkins, Maxwell. "Thomas Wolfe." Thomas Wolfe: A Collection of Critical Essays. Ed. Louis Rubin, Jr. Englewood Cliffs: Prentice, 1973. 87–102. [one article in a collection of articles by different authors]

Ferris, Timothy. "Einstein's Wonderful Year." Science 84 Nov. 1984: 61–63. [article in a monthly popular press magazine]

Beckwith, Carol. "Niger's Wodaabe: 'People of the Taboo.'" National Geographic 164 (1983): 483–509. [article, continuous pagination magazine or scholarly journal]

"Navahos Upheld on Land Claims." New York Times 30 June 1970, late ed.: A20. [unsigned newspaper article]

Faron, Louis C. "American Indian." Encyclopedia Americana. 1984 ed. [signed encyclopedia article]

Wright, Florence. Personal interview. 4 May 1984. [interview]

"Music in the Age of Shakespeare." PBS. WGBH, Boston. 17 Sept. 1980. [television program]

EXERCISE 13. Preparing a Bibliography. Prepare bibliography entries for the following items. Add underlining and quotation marks where needed, and alphabetize the entries.

1. A magazine article by Charles Tart entitled Psychic Lessons in Human Behavior, volume 7, February 1978, page 51.
2. An unsigned magazine article entitled Science, the Media, and the Paranormal in Science News, volume 112, August 20, 1977, page 118.
3. A book entitled The ESP Experience: A Psychiatric Validation by Jan Ehrenwald, published by Basic Books, in New York, in 1978.
4. A book by Naomi Hintze and J. Gaither Pratt, entitled The Psychic Realm: What Can You Believe?, published by Harper & Row, in New York, in 1975.
5. A book of articles edited by Patrick Grim, entitled Philosophy of Science and the Occult, published by the State University of New York Press in Albany in 1982.

Charts, Diagrams, and Illustrations

Charts and diagrams may be included in your paper where they are of real value. For each one that is not your own, give the source from which you copied it. Never cut illustrations from library sources.

REVIEW EXERCISE C. Writing the First Draft. Write your first draft, incorporating your research findings and crediting your sources.

EVALUATING AND REVISING

EVALUATING YOUR RESEARCH PAPER

25k. Evaluate the content, organization, and style of your research paper.

Evaluation and revision are different, but closely related, activities. Evaluation involves careful examination of a piece of writing to determine where it succeeds and where it needs improvement. Revision involves making changes to eliminate weaknesses and to strengthen a piece of writing. It may be easier to combine evaluation and revision by examining and then improving one aspect of your research paper at a time.

Once you have prepared a rough draft of your paper, reread it critically, rethinking the scope of your ideas and looking for irrelevant material, unclear transitions, illogical arrangement of information, and unsupported assertions. Remember that your objective is to support your thesis, not simply to discuss or illustrate it.

CRITICAL THINKING:
Evaluating a Draft of a Research Paper

In order to evaluate a draft of a research paper, you need a set of criteria. The following Guidelines for Evaluating Research Papers provide standards against which you can judge your work. (You may also want to review the Techniques for Evaluating on page 368 and the Guidelines for Evaluating on page 369.) Ask yourself the questions in the guidelines each time you evaluate the paper. Evaluate your own paper as objectively as possible, since it will in turn be evaluated by your teacher with these or similar criteria.

GUIDELINES FOR EVALUATING RESEARCH PAPERS

Introduction	1. Does the introduction include a thesis statement that writer's attitude? Does the introduction catch the audience's attention?

Topic Development	2. Does each paragraph in the body develop one idea about the topic? Does each paragraph include specific details and examples from the writer's research?
	3. Is there enough information for readers to follow the line of reasoning? Is there any unrelated or irrelevant information? Are quotations and ideas from sources incorporated into the text to achieve the paper's purpose?
Conclusion	4. Does the end of the paper obviously conclude the presentation? Does it reinforce the thesis statement?
Coherence	5. Are ideas about the topic presented in a logical order, both in paragraphs and in sentences within each paragraph? Are there clear and logical transitions, or connections, between paragraphs and between major sections in the paper?
Emphasis	6. Is the emphasis on various ideas clear by means of the wording, placement, or amount of text devoted to them?
Word Choice	7. Is the language appropriate for a general audience? Are technical terms and unusual vocabulary defined or explained? Does the language reveal the serious tone appropriate for a research paper? Does the title clearly indicate the paper's topic?
Format	8. Are sources documented in the text, correctly using the MLA format (parenthetical notes) or some other acceptable format? Are short quotations incorporated into the text? Are longer quotations set off from the text? Are correct form and alphabetical order used in the bibliography?

EXERCISE 14. Evaluating Your First Draft. Evaluate the first draft of your research paper using the guidelines above and the Guidelines for Evaluating on page 369. Keep notes on your draft about items you need to improve. You may also want to exchange papers with a classmate to evaluate each other's papers.

REVISING YOUR FIRST DRAFT

25l. Revise your first draft to improve content, organization, and style.

After identifying parts of your paper that need to be improved, you are ready to make revisions, or changes, to strengthen your writing.

Revision involves analyzing, carefully breaking down and examining your writing to determine how to eliminate or correct weaknesses in it. To make changes, you should use the same basic techniques (adding, cutting, reordering, and replacing) you use to revise other forms of exposition. The particular technique you use will depend on the nature of the weakness you want to correct. Remember, as you make changes in the text of your paper, that you may also need to revise the outline, citations, and the bibliography. Use the revision chart on pages 373–74 to revise your research paper.

EXERCISE 15. Revising Your Research Paper. Revise your research paper, using the revising chart on pages 373–74. Be sure to check each revision against the chart. Your teacher may ask you to save your first draft to submit along with the revised paper.

PROOFREADING

PROOFREADING YOUR RESEARCH PAPER

25m. Proofread your research paper for grammar, usage, and mechanics.

When your research paper represents your best effort, proofread it carefully to check for and correct errors in grammar, usage, and mechanics. Remember that you want your audience to focus on the ideas and information in your paper, not on proofreading errors. (Review the Guidelines for Proofreading on page 376.)

EXERCISE 16. Proofreading Your Revised Draft. Proofread your paper carefully to correct the grammar, usage, and mechanics.

PREPARING A FINAL VERSION

PREPARING THE FINAL VERSION OF YOUR RESEARCH PAPER

25n. Prepare a final version of your research paper, following correct manuscript form.

Your final step is to prepare a clean copy of your revised and proofread draft. To make sure that you have copied correctly, proofread this version as well. Then assemble the parts of the paper, using the following MLA guidelines or your teacher's instructions.

1. Type or write your paper neatly and legibly on one side of acceptable paper.
2. Leave one-inch margins at the top, bottom, and sides of your page.
3. Double-space throughout, including title, quotations, and bibliography. (Long quotations are an exception; see note on page 246.)

You will also need to assemble the parts of the paper in the following order or the order your teacher requires:

1. *The cover.* Using staples, metal clasps, or other fasteners, bind your paper in a stiff cover. Give the title of the paper on the outside; make the cover simple but attractive.

2. *The title page.* Use a separate page as a title page. Place your name, information about your class (name and number of the course), and the date one inch from the top of the first page, even with the left margin. Double-space between these lines. The title is centered, with double-spacing between the information described above and the title. Do not put quotation marks around your title.

3. *The final outline.* Insert your revised outline directly after the title page. In this position, the outline serves as a kind of table of contents for your audience.

4. *The paper itself.* Begin the page numbering with the first page. Number consecutively all the pages of the paper, including the bibliography and those pages containing only charts or diagrams. Place page numbers in the upper right corner of each page, one-half inch below the top of the page and fairly close to the right margin. Use a number without the words *page, pages,* or their abbreviations. Write your title at the top of the first page, and quadruple-space between the title and the first line of your paper.

5. *The list of works cited.* Use as many pages as you need for the bibliography, allowing the same margins as those on the pages of the paper itself.

REVIEW EXERCISE D. Preparing the Final Version of Your Research Paper. Prepare the final version of your paper, and proofread it carefully. Then assemble the parts of your paper, following your teacher's directions.

CHAPTER 25 WRITING REVIEW 1

Writing a Research Paper Based on Personal Observation. Select a subject and analyze it to develop a topic that you can research in your own community through personal observation, such as site visits and interviews. Prepare a research paper based on your findings.

CHAPTER 25 WRITING REVIEW 2

Improving a Research Paper from Another Subject. Select a research paper you have written in one of your other content-area subjects. Evaluate this paper by applying the guidelines on page 369. Then revise the paper, using the chart on pages 373–74, and proofread it, referring to the guidelines on page 376. Be prepared to explain specific improvements you have made.

ABBREVIATIONS USED IN SOURCES

The following list explains a number of scholarly abbreviations you may encounter in your research. For the most part, you should avoid using these abbreviations in your own paper; exceptions are those shown in the examples in this chapter, such as *ed.* and *trans.*

c *or* © *copyright*; used before a date (©1965) to indicate when copyright was obtained. (The circled *c* is the international copyright symbol.)

c., ca. *about* (from the Latin *circa*, *circum*); used with dates—"c." or "ca. 1732" means "about 1732."

cf. *compare* (from the Latin *confer*); "cf. the Atlantic Treaty" means "compare with the Atlantic Treaty."

ed. *editor, edited, edition*

e.g. *for example* (from the Latin *exempli gratia*)

et al. *and others* (from the Latin *et alii*); also, *and elsewhere* (from the Latin *et alibi*)

f., ff. *following page, pages;* "p. 25f." means "page 25 and the following page"; "p. 25ff." means "page 25 and the following pages."

ibid. *in the same place* (from the Latin *ibidem*); no longer recommended by the MLA.

id. *the same* (from the Latin *idem*)

i.e. *that is* (from the Latin *id est*)

l., ll. *line; lines*
loc. cit. *in the place previously cited* (from the Latin *loco citato*)
ms., mss. *manuscript, manuscripts*
N.B. *note well* (from the Latin *nota bene*)
n.d. *no date*; publication date not given in book
op. cit. *in the work previously cited* (from the Latin *opere citato*); no longer recommended by the MLA.
p., pp. *page, pages*
q.v. *which see, whom see* (from the Latin *quod vide* or *quem vide*)
sic *thus* (from the Latin); used (in brackets) after an error in a passage, to make clear that the original was copied accurately
vide *see* (from the Latin)

Michael Davis

Psychology

April 8, 1990

CLAIRVOYANCE: INVESTIGATING A "SIXTH SENSE"

[The following sample pages are from a high-school student's research paper. Use them as a model in preparing your own paper.]

OUTLINE

Thesis: For many years, clairvoyance, the ability to "see" objects or events without the use of the senses, was not considered a suitable subject for scientific study; more recently, however, scientific studies have been conducted that attempt to prove the existence of this "sixth sense."

I. Definition of clairvoyance
  A. Comparison with other types of extrasensory perception
  B. Examples of clairvoyant ability
II. Scientific approach to clairvoyance
  A. Need for valid evidence
  B. Need for extensive evidence
III. Experiments with clairvoyance
  A. Studies by J. B. Rhine
    1. Method of card-guessing
    2. Interpretation of data
    3. Favorable results of studies
  B. Studies by Rhine's followers
    1. Use of separate rooms
    2. Use of categories for subjects
    3. Use of random-number generator
    4. Use of remote locations
    5. Use of hypnosis
IV. Objections to experiments
  A. Possibility of fraud
  B. Lower scores from tighter controls
  C. Variable results from repeated efforts
V. Future of clairvoyance studies

Clairvoyance: Investigating a "Sixth Sense"

One night a young woman was driving home with her husband. They came to a roadblock, where a police officer told them about an accident a half-mile ahead. After they had made a detour and had continued driving for a few minutes, the woman began to tremble and cry. She told her husband that her sister was lying dead on the road they had just left! Forty-five minutes after they had arrived home, the phone rang. The caller, a local doctor, told the woman that her sister was dead. She had been killed instantly in a car accident, the same accident the couple had heard of an hour before (Louisa E. Rhine, "Psychological Processes" 95–96).

Was this woman's experience simply a strange coincidence? Have you ever had a hunch or made a wild guess that proved correct? Such sudden insights, some scientists claim, may have been a form of extrasensory perception called clairvoyance. For many years, clairvoyance, the ability to "see" objects or events without the use of the senses, was not considered a suitable subject for scientific study; more recently, however, scientific studies have been conducted that attempt to prove the existence of this "sixth sense." [thesis]

Clairvoyance, say scientists, is one of four categories of extrasensory perception: (1) telepathy--reading the thoughts of another, (2) precognition--sensing future events, (3) psychokinesis--affecting objects by thinking about them, and (4) clairvoyance--perceiving objects or events that are impossible to perceive by the normal senses (Cherry 84). The category of clairvoyance includes such acts as guessing the unknown contents of a sealed envelope or describing the location of a lost child.

Was the woman's sudden knowledge about her sister's death an example of clairvoyance? Montague Ullman, a leading researcher of extrasensory perception, warns, "Scientifically, of course, such cases don't prove anything, because they can be called coincidence, unconscious self-deception, or deliberate hoaxes" (47). [direct quotation]

Ullman and other investigators insist that clairvoyance exists; yet in order to prove their claim, they recognize the need for reliable data. Accordingly, clairvoyance has been the focus of experiments based upon careful controls. Following the scientific method, scientists gather evidence from these experiments and use the evidence as the basis of proof.

During experiments, subjects may guess at hidden cards, locations, numbers, or a variety of other items. If enough of these guesses are correct, then scientists can be certain that more than mere luck is at work. However, as an added precaution against lucky guesses, scientists require extensive evidence, drawn from thousands of experiments. They may even repeat a particular experiment with one person hundreds of times before accepting its results.

This experimental research is relatively new. It began during the 1930's, when Dr. J. B. Rhine conducted experiments for all four categories of extrasensory perception (Bowles and Hynds 27). In his earliest attempts, he found clairvoyance the most suitable for research. He stated:

> Clairvoyance experiments are the easiest of all to conduct. . . . Not only is it easier to control against the more common experimental errors, but it is also easier to eliminate any alternative hypothesis that might be applied to the data (Rhine and Pratt 53). [extended quotation]

Enthusiastically, Dr. Rhine performed hundreds of experiments, testing the clairvoyant powers of ordinary people. His method was surprisingly simple; in fact, with patience and accurate record keeping, anyone can imitate it.

Rhine used a pack of cards called Zener cards, which contained five symbols: a star, a circle, a cross, a square, and a wavy line. One of these symbols was printed on each card. In the deck there were twenty-five cards, five of each symbol.

After shuffling the cards, the experimenter placed the deck on a table. Behind an opaque screen, which concealed the experimenter and the cards at all times, the subject either wrote down or called out in order the symbols in the deck (Bowles and Hynds 31). By pure chance, one would expect five correct guesses out of twenty-five in a single run-through of cards. Any scoring consistently higher than five correct guesses, Rhine concluded, was evidence of clairvoyance (Cohen 76).

[*The paper goes on to discuss Dr. Rhine's interpretation of his data, the favorable results of his studies, and the experiments of Dr. Rhine's followers. The following paragraphs make a transition from this section of the paper to the objections against clairvoyance experiments.*]

One recent development in clairvoyance research involves hypnosis. In tests, two groups of people perform Dr. Rhine's card-guessing experiment. One group is awake, while the other group is under hypnosis. The group under hypnosis has scored a significantly greater number of correct guesses than the other group. Although researchers find these results encouraging, they are performing further tests to measure the effect of hypnosis (Sargent).

As research into clairvoyance continues, however, opponents refuse to accept the findings. According to Bowles and Hynds, the unfavorable publicity the Rhines' work received may still be influencing the general public's attitudes toward psychical research (27). Critics cite three overwhelming problems in the studies: first, that researchers do not guard enough against fraud; second, that they get lower scores as they improve their testing methods; and third, that they cannot get the same results every time they repeat an experiment. **[transitional paragraph]**

[*The next section of the paper discusses each objection. The paper concludes as follows:*]

10

Defenders, meanwhile, claim that scientific standards, such as requiring similar results each time an experiment is repeated, need not apply to research into the human mind. Arthur Koestler writes, "[The standard of] repeatability [is] valid in the physical sciences, but less so in the frontiers of medicine and even less in those branches of psychology which involve unconscious processes . . ." (29).

Although Koestler and others claim that clairvoyance "is a hard reality" (23), many disagree, and the future of clairvoyance studies is uncertain. Philip H. Abelson, editor of the authoritative journal <u>Science</u>, sums up the controversy when he states that "these extraordinary claims require extraordinary evidence. Findings that question the basic laws of nature must be subjected to rigorous scientific scrutiny" ("A Stepchild of

Science" 42). Many, like Abelson, believe that statistical evidence charting an unknown power at work gives insufficient reason for abandoning assumptions about the way the mind works. Remarks D. O. Hebb, professor of psychology at McGill University, "I do not accept ESP for a moment, because it does not make sense" (45).

Skeptics like Abelson and Hebb may be unfairly dismissing the positive results of clairvoyance studies, which, compared with many other fields, are still very new. By demanding "extraordinary evidence" that extrasensory perception exists, they may be overlooking much of the evidence this paper has discussed.

On the other hand, scientists who claim that clairvoyance is a fact of life are exaggerating, for many questions remain. H. J. Eysenck, professor at the University of London, calmly states the crux of the issue:

> . . . very intriguing demonstrations have been given that suggest the existence of something outside the purview of physics and psychology, but no one has yet succeeded in bringing this something under adequate experimental control (1004).

Until scientists can present a reasonable explanation for clairvoyance, Eysenck contends, "it would be unwise to claim any more" (1004).

WORKS CITED

Bowles, Norma, and Fran Hynds. PsiSearch. New York: Harper, 1978.

Cherry, Laurence. "Physicists Explain ESP." Science Digest Sept./Oct. 1980: 84–87.

Cohen, Daniel. ESP: The Search Beyond the Senses. New York: Harcourt Brace Jovanovich, 1973.

Eysenck, H. J. "Theories of Parapsychological Phenonomena." Encyclopaedia Britannica: Macropaedia. 1979 ed.

Hansel, C. E. M. ESP: A Scientific Evaluation. New York: Scribner's, 1966.

Hebb, D. O. "The Role of Neurological Ideas in Psychology." Journal of Personality 20 (1951): 40–52.

Koestler, Arthur. The Roots of Coincidence. New York: Random House, 1972.

Palmer, John. "Progressive Skepticism: A Critical Approach to the Psi Controversy." Journal of Parapsychology 50 (1986): 29–42.

Puthoff, Harold E., and Russell Targ. "Remote Viewing: New Research Frontier." The Signet Handbook of Parapsychology. Ed. Martin Ebon. New York: New American Library, 1978. 78–90.

Rhine, J. B. The Reach of the Mind. New York: Smith, 1972.

Rhine, J. B., et al. Extrasensory Perception After Sixty Years: A Critical Appraisal of the Research in Extrasensory Perception. Boston: Humphries, 1966.

Rhine, J.B., and J. G. Pratt. Parapsychology: Frontier Science of the Mind. Springfield: Thomas, 1972.

Rhine, Louisa E. Hidden Channels of the Mind. New York: Sloane, 1961.

---. "Psychological Processes in ESP Experiences: Part 1, Waking Experiences." Journal of Parapsychology 26 (1962): 88–111.

Sargent, Carl L. "Hypnosis as a Psi-Conducive State." Journal of Parapsychology 42 (1978): 264–67.

"A Stepchild of Science Starts to Win Friends." U.S. News and World Report 31 July 1978: 41,42.

Taylor, John. Science and the Supernatural. New York: Dutton, 1980.

Ullman, Montague. "Can You Communicate with Others in Your Dreams?" The Psychic Scene. Ed. John White. New York: New American Library, 1974. 47–52.

RESOURCES FOR WRITING AND STUDYING

CHAPTER 26

The Library

ARRANGEMENT AND RESOURCES

Libraries, or media centers, as they are now frequently called, are sufficiently alike so that when you become familiar with one library, you can easily find your way in others. You should understand the following:

1. The arrangement of books in the library
2. The uses of the card catalog
3. The names and functions of the parts of a book
4. The use of the *Readers' Guide*
5. The use of the vertical file
6. The location of items in your library

If the library owns a book you cannot find, ask the librarian about it. It may be checked out, or it may be "on reserve" for various reasons. The librarian might place your name on a waiting list and notify you when it's available.

ARRANGEMENT OF BOOKS IN THE LIBRARY

26a. Learn the arrangement of books.

Fiction

By this time you know that books of fiction are usually arranged alphabetically by authors' last names. If your library contains numerous books by the same author, they are alphabetized by their titles, in that author's space.

Nonfiction: The Dewey Decimal System

All nonfiction books receive numbers in a classification system developed by the American librarian Melvil Dewey.[1] There are ten numerical subject classifications, with decimal points allowing an unlimited number of subdivisions. The value of this system is that all books on one subject are given the same number and are located together on the shelves. Dewey's broad classifications are shown below.

000–099	General Works (encyclopedias, periodicals, etc.)
100–199	Philosophy (includes psychology, conduct, etc.)
200–299	Religion (includes mythology)
300–399	Social Sciences (economics, government, law, etc.)
400–499	Language (dictionaries, grammars, etc.)
500–599	Science (mathematics, chemistry, physics, etc.)
600–699	Technology (agriculture, engineering, aviation, etc.)
700–799	The Arts and Recreation (sculpture, painting, music, photography, sports, etc.)
800–899	Literature (poetry, plays, orations, etc.)
900–909 930–999	History
910–919	Travel
920–929	Biography (arranged alphabetically by name of subject of biography)

Books having the same class number may be distinguished from one another by the author's name. For instance, all books on aviation are given the number 629.1. This number appears on the spine of the book.

[1] The Library of Congress system of cataloging, used in many public libraries but not commonly used in high-school libraries, classifies all books, both fiction and nonfiction. Each general subject category (Philosophy, Science, etc.) is assigned a code letter. In addition, whole categories are often subdivided by adding a second code letter to the first. Thus, the letter *P* (which designates Literature) may be followed by the letter *S* to specify American literature. Call numbers include the letter codes, followed by a series of numbers that identify specific books within a category. For example, the book *Responses: Prose Pieces 1953–1976*, by Richard Wilbur, an American author, has the Library of Congress call number PS 3545. A complete schedule of Library of Congress categories is usually available in any library using this system.

With the number appears the first letter of the author's name: if the author is Hood, the book's complete number is $\frac{629.1}{H}$. This number, including the first letter of the author's name, is known as the book's *call number*. To find the call number of a book, you look up the book in the card catalog.

LOCATING INFORMATION IN THE LIBRARY

The Card Catalog

Undoubtedly you have used the card catalog in your school or town library. You may not, however, know as much about it as you need to know in order to get the most help from it.

26b. Learn the uses of the card catalog.

In most libraries, the catalog cabinet holds at least three cards for each book in the library: at least one *author card*, the *title card*, and at least one *subject card*.

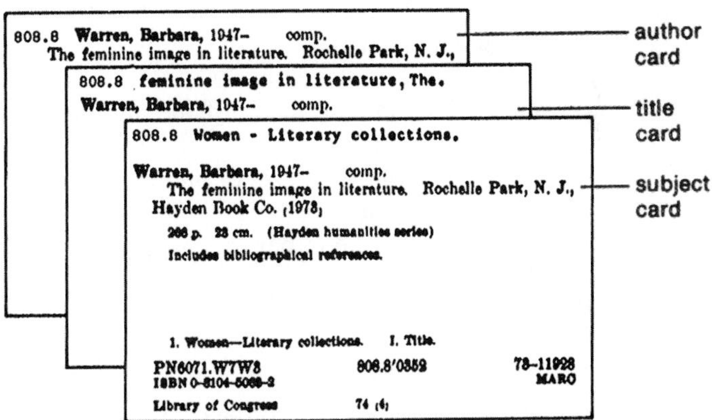

808.8 Warren, Barbara, 1947- comp.
The feminine image in literature. Rochelle Park, N. J.,
808.8 feminine image in literature, The.
Warren, Barbara, 1947- comp.
808.8 Women - Literary collections.
Warren, Barbara, 1947- comp.
The feminine image in literature. Rochelle Park, N. J.,
Hayden Book Co. ₍1973₎
1. Women—Literary collections. I. Title.
PN6071.W7W3
808.8'0352
author card
title card
subject card

The Author Card

The *author card* has the name of the author at the top. When there is joint authorship, there is a card for each author. Since the cards for all books by an author are placed together, you are able to find out what other books by the author the library owns. Cards for books *about* an author follow the cards for books *by* an author.

The Title Card

The quickest way to find a book in the catalog is to look it up under its title. Cards for books whose titles begin with *a, an,* or *the* are arranged alphabetically by the second word in the title.

The Subject Card

Subject cards are invaluable when you wish to find a number of books on a subject but do not know specific titles or authors. Under the subject heading "Political parties—United States," for instance, you will find a card for every book in the library on this subject. In fact, you may find a card for every book that contains as little as one article or chapter on United States political parties, so thoroughly is the cataloging done.

Information Given on a Catalog Card

A brief study of the sample catalog cards reproduced on page 473 will show you that a complete card gives a great deal of information. In addition to giving the title, author, and call number of a book, the card may give the following information:

1. *Facts about authorship:* full name of the author; names of joint authors and illustrators, if any.
2. *Facts about publication:* the place of publication; the name of the publisher; the date of publication.
3. *Facts about the book:* number of pages; whether the book contains illustrations, diagrams, etc.

"See" and "See Also" Cards

When you look for a certain subject, you may find a "see" card referring you to another heading. The "see" card tells you, in effect, "There is nothing here. You will find what you want under this other heading."

A second type of cross-reference card is the "see also" card, which refers you to another heading in the catalog where you may find additional titles on your subject.

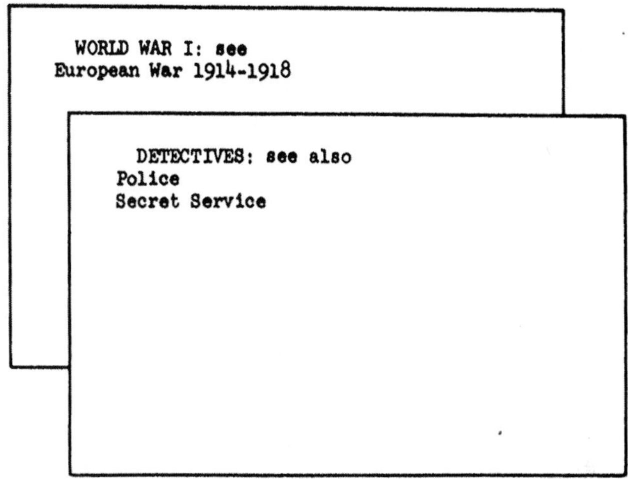
WORLD WAR I: see
European War 1914-1918

DETECTIVES: see also
Police
Secret Service

Sample Cross Reference Cards

EXERCISE 1. Using the Card Catalog. Using the card catalog in your library, write the title, author, and call number for the following books.

1. A history of American literature
2. A book about South America
3. A book by Edith Wharton
4. A book giving information about Edith Wharton
5. A book about space exploration

Using the card catalog, find answers to the following questions. Write the answers.

6. Does the library own any books by Willa Cather? If so, give the title and call number of one of them.
7. Give the title, author, publisher, and publication date of a book about George Washington Carver.
8. Does the library own the complete plays of Shakespeare in one volume? If so, give the exact title and the publisher of the book.
9. Give the title, author, and date of publication of a book of American poetry.
10. Does the library own a copy of Charlotte Brontë's *Jane Eyre*? If so, give the publisher.

The Parts of a Book

Once you have found the right book, you need to know the important parts of a book and the uses of each.

26c. Learn the names and functions of the parts of a book.

The Frontispiece

The frontispiece is a full-page illustration. If the book has a frontispiece, it faces the title page.

The Title Page

The first important page in a book, the title page gives the complete title, any subtitle, the name of the author or editor, the name of the publisher, and the place of publication.

The Copyright Page

The reverse side of the title page is the copyright page. Here you find the year in which the book was registered in the government copyright office in Washington. Before publishers release a new book, they send two copies to the United States Copyright Office. The office then issues a copyright, which gives to the copyright owner exclusive right to print the book or any part of it during the lifetime of the author and for a period of fifty years after the author's death. Sometimes publishers secure a copyright in their own name, sometimes in the name of the author.

Often you will find more than one date listed on the copyright page: "Copyright 1946, 1949, 1955." This means that the first edition of the book was copyrighted in 1946. In 1949 and 1955 new material was added and a new copyright secured to cover the new material. In books published since September 1957, the international copyright symbol is used: © 1980. The date of copyright is very important when you wish to know whether the material in a book is sufficiently up-to-date to be reliable.

Publishers sometimes indicate on this page which printing of the book this particular volume represents. Note the distinction between a new copyright date and a new printing date. The former tells when the book was last revised; the latter notes when it was merely reprinted.

The Preface, Foreword, Introduction

These terms are now used interchangeably to refer to remarks at the beginning of a book in which the author, editor, or publisher explains the purpose of the book, gives information that aids the reader in understanding the book, acknowledges credit and inspiration, etc.

The Table of Contents

The table of contents appears at the front of the book and consists of a list of the chapters and subdivisions with their page numbers. It provides a quick view of the content and organization of the entire book.

List of Illustrations (Maps, Diagrams, Charts, etc.)

Such a list cites illustrations with their page numbers and generally follows the Table of Contents. A very long list may appear at the end of a book.

The Appendix

The appendix contains additional information that the author did not include in the body of the book. It may include long quotations from other works on the subject, lists, diagrams and tables, etc.

The Glossary

A glossary is usually a list of definitions of technical or foreign language words used in the book. It is placed near the close of the book.

The Bibliography

The bibliography is a list of books consulted by the author in writing the book or recommended to the reader who wishes more information.

The Index

The index is an alphabetical list of topics treated in the book, given with page numbers. It is much more detailed than the table of contents. When you have found a book that seems likely to provide information on your topic, the index will tell you how much information there is and exactly where to find it.

The End Papers

The pages pasted inside the front and back covers of the book are the end papers. Sometimes they are used for a map or an illustration or to give a summary of the contents.

The *Readers' Guide*

A large part of the library reference work you will do in high school will deal with subjects of a contemporary rather than a historical nature. The best source of information, indeed very often the only source of information on truly current subjects, is a magazine. Without some sort of guide, you would have to spend hours hunting through magazines in search of articles on a subject. However, the *Readers' Guide to Periodical Literature* solves this problem for you.

26d. Learn how to use the *Readers' Guide to Periodical Literature.*

In the *Readers' Guide,* articles from some 170 magazines are indexed alphabetically by subjects and by authors. You may look up the subject in which you are interested and find the articles that have been written on it and the magazines in which they appeared.

Magazine stories are listed by title and by author; the complete entry is given with the author listing only. Poems and plays are listed by author.

Articles *about* moving pictures and plays are listed under the subject headings MOVING PICTURE PLAYS and DRAMAS, beneath the subheading **Criticisms, plots, etc.**

The *Readers' Guide* is published in paperbound pamphlets twice a month from September to June and monthly in July and August. Occasionally during the year a cumulative issue is published which includes the articles listed in preceding months as well as those for the current month. At the end of a year, a large volume is published containing all entries for the year, and every two years a volume covering a two-year period is published.

When you are taking down references from the *Readers' Guide,* you need to know what magazines your library has. You should know, too, whether the library has kept back issues of all these magazines or only of certain ones and for how many years back it has the magazines.

A sample excerpt from the *Readers' Guide* is reproduced on page 479. You can probably understand the many abbreviations used, but if you cannot, you will find them explained in the front of the *Readers' Guide* itself.

BALL, George Wildman
Options on Iran. por Newsweek 95:43 Ap 7 '80
Question of oil [interview by R. Christopher] por Macleans 93:50 Ja 7 '80
about
Mr. Ball's world. E. N. Luttwak. New Repub 182:12-14 Ap 5 '80 •
BALL, Leslie D. See Waldron, D. jt auth
BALLANTINE, H. Thomas, Jr
Role of government in health-care delivery in the 1980s [address, January 16, 1980] Vital Speeches 46:258-60 F 15 '80
BALLANTINE, Ian
Uses and abuses of enchantment. D. Weinberger. il Macleans 93:45-5 Ja 28 '80 •
BALLERINAS. See Dancers
BALLET
See also
Choreography
Cleveland Ballet Company
Dance Theatre of Harlem
Houston Ballet Company
Joffrey Ballet
Maryland Ballet
Merce Cunningham & Dance Company
Metropolitan Opera Ballet
Motion pictures—Dance films
New York City Ballet
Pittsburgh Ballet Theatre
Television broadcasting—Dance programs
Dance. J. Maskey. See issues of High fidelity and Musical America
Domestic reports: news and views from across the country. See issues of Dance magazine
Editor's log. W. Como. See issues of Dance magazine
Opera ballet:
Taming the two-headed monster. B. Laine. Dance Mag 54:51-3 F '80
Presstime news. See issues of Dance magazine
Reviews:
Ballet Metropolitan of Columbus. A. Barzel. Dance Mag 54:51-3 F '80
Dance Ring. A. Barzel. Dance Mag 54:44-6 F '80
Louisville Ballet. A. Barzel. Dance Mag 54: 50-1 F '80
Ohio Ballet. W. Salisbury. Dance Mag 54: 116+ F '80
Tulsa Ballet Theatre: old world style for a new frontier. J. Pikula. il pors Dance Mag 54:62-5 F '80

Bibliography

Dance books. il Dance Mag 54:106+ Ja; 121 F; 121 Mr '80

Directories

Dance directory. See issues of Dance magazine

International aspects

Foreign reports: news and views from around the world. See issues of Dance magazine

Study and teaching

Education briefs [ed by M. Pierpont] See issues of Dance magazine

Australia

Dance in Australia. A. Brissenden. il Dance Mag 54:12 F '80

Canada

See also
National Ballet of Canada

author entry
article by author
article about author
"see" cross reference to joint author
title of article
title and issue of magazine
subject entry
"see" cross reference
volume number
page reference
date of issue
illustration reference
secondary subject heading
"see also" cross reference

EXERCISE 2. Using the *Readers' Guide*. Write answers to the following questions.

1. Where are the bound magazines stored in your library?
2. What is the date of the latest *Readers' Guide* in your library? What period does it cover?
3. Select a prominent musician of today and look for an article about the person in the *Readers' Guide*. Give the complete listing.
4. Find and copy a "see" reference from the *Readers' Guide*.
5. Copy from the *Readers' Guide* the complete listing of a review of a motion picture.

Information Files

26e. Learn the nature and proper use of the vertical file.

Useful information on current topics is often found in pamphlets published by government agencies, industrial concerns, museums, colleges and universities, radio stations, welfare organizations, etc. Many libraries store such publications, as well as clippings and pictures from newspapers and magazines, in a special cabinet referred to as the vertical file. Consult the librarian to see if a file folder is available on the topic you are studying.

26f. Use microfilm and microfiche to find information.

Many libraries store some publications on microfilm or microfiche. *Microfilm* is a roll or reel of film; *microfiche* is a small sheet of film. Both types of film contain photographically reduced material which can be enlarged to readable size by special projectors. Consult your librarian for instructions.

26g. Use computers to find information.

Many media centers now store their lists of books and periodicals on computers. Instead of using the card catalog or the *Readers' Guide*, you type the information you need into a computer. You might have to read the list of available materials from the screen, or you might be able to get a printout. The librarian can provide information on the center's computer systems.

26h. Learn the location of resources in your library.

Your use of a library will be more efficient if you know the exact location of the principal items you may wish to use. If you will remember the information the following exercise calls for, you will save both the librarian and yourself a great deal of time.

EXERCISE 3. Locating Items in Your Library. Be prepared to state where each of the following items is located in your school or public library.

1. The card catalog
2. The *Readers' Guide*
3. The magazine rack and the newspaper rack
4. The pamphlet file
5. The fiction shelves
6. The encyclopedias
7. The biography shelves
8. The unabridged dictionaries
9. The computers
10. The microfilm and microfiche projectors

CHAPTER 27

Reference Books

SPECIAL SOURCES OF INFORMATION

Some media centers have bigger collections of reference books than others, but almost any media center will have most of the standard reference books described here. It may surprise you to find how quickly and easily you can locate needed facts, once you know that a reference book specifically made to supply them is in a nearby library. Familiarity with a library's reference books will increase your efficiency in looking up information.

ENCYCLOPEDIAS

27a. Get acquainted with encyclopedias: their plan, content, and indexes.

You have probably been using an encyclopedia in your schoolwork for some time. You know that it is a collection of articles in alphabetical order on nearly all fields of knowledge. Although written by experts with a high level of factual accuracy, the articles only give overall views, with details limited by space.

In any encyclopedia, the index or index-volume is important. If you looked in the *Encylopedia Americana* under the entry "Olympic Games," you would find an article several columns long. But in the index, you would find the volumes and page numbers of more than twenty other entries with information about the games. If you had not used the index, you would not have known about these other entries.

When using the *Encyclopaedia Britannica,* you should usually check the *Micropaedia* first. These first ten volumes contain shorter articles, with cross-referencing to the remaining nineteen volumes, called the *Macropaedia,* which have much longer treatments. Several encyclopedias publish yearbooks, which contain statistics, important events, and developments in every field pertaining to the year just preceding. Check these annuals if your topic involves a rapidly changing field.

Encyclopedias in Many Volumes

Collier's Encyclopedia
24 volumes
Bibliography and Index in Volume 24
Publishes *Collier's Yearbook*

Encyclopedia Americana
30 volumes
Index in Volume 30
Publishes the *Americana Annual*

Encyclopaedia Britannica
30 volumes
Cross-referencing throughout *Micropaedia*
Publishes the *Britannica Book of the Year*

World Book Encyclopedia
22 volumes
Research Guide and Index in Volume 22
Publishes an annual supplement

One- and Two-Volume Encyclopedias

Very often a brief, handy account of a subject is enough. For this purpose, a one- or two-volume "desk" encyclopedia is adequate. There are three well-known works of this kind. The *New Columbia Encyclopedia* and the *Random House Encyclopedia* are arranged alphabetically like dictionaries. The *Lincoln Library of Essential Information* has two volumes arranged in broad fields of knowledge with many subdivision articles and an index.

GENERAL REFERENCE BOOKS

Almanacs and Yearbooks

Although almanacs come out annually to cover a one-year period, many of their statistics include data for preceding years. Remember that an almanac tells about the year before its date: data for 1980 should be sought in the 1981 issue.

World Almanac and Book of Facts

Most popular of the handy annual reference books on the world today, the *World Almanac* gives facts and figures that are needed very often. Typical items are census tables, production quantities, export and import figures, election results, officeholders, sports records, Nobel and other prize-winners, and a summary of notable events. A full index is in the front.

Information Please Almanac

This almanac covers much of the same ground as the *World Almanac*, but in a different arrangement. Its full index is in the back. The *Information Please Almanac* covers fewer subjects, but its informal style is easy to follow and its articles are sometimes fuller.

The International Yearbook & Statesmen's Who's Who

The International Yearbook & Statesmen's Who's Who includes up-to-date information on international organizations and political, statistical, and directory information about each country of the world. A biographical section gives sketches of world leaders in government, religion, commerce, industry, and education.

Atlases

Don't think of an atlas as just a collection of maps. It contains information of many kinds: climate, rainfall, crops, topography, population, some history, etc.

Find out which atlases your library has and where they are kept. Because our day is marked by amazing numbers of new nations, an atlas even a few years old may be significantly inaccurate. To find out how up-to-date an atlas is, check its copyright date in the opening pages.

A few of the reliable atlases are listed here.

General Atlases

Hammond Contemporary World Atlas
National Geographic Atlas of the World
New York Times Atlas of the World

Historical atlases help us to visualize history by showing the world, or a region of it, as it was in one or more past periods.

Historical Atlases

The American Heritage Pictorial Atlas of United States History
Rand McNally Atlas of World History
Shepherd, William, *Historical Atlas*

BIOGRAPHICAL REFERENCE BOOKS

27b. Learn to use these handy biographical reference tools.

Many of the biographical reference works discussed here are likely to be on your library's shelves. Since their functions differ, be sure to find out what each can do for you.

General Biography

***Biography Index* (1946 to date)**

This work, as its name implies, is not a collection of biographies, but an index that tells you where to find material on the life of nearly anyone about whom a book or an article has been published. It indexes current biographical books and biographical material in periodicals, in much the same manner as the *Readers' Guide to Periodical Literature.* Like the *Readers' Guide*, the *Biography Index* is published regularly and in cumulative editions.

Dictionary of American Biography

This monumental work provides authoritative articles on notable Americans no longer living, from the earliest times virtually to the present. Individual articles are more detailed than those in any encyclopedia. The complete set of fifteen volumes includes a one-volume index, as well as updating supplements.

The New Century Cyclopedia of Names (3 volumes)

As the title may imply, this work deals with proper names of all sorts, including real, legendary, and mythological persons, places, and events, as well as literary works and characters and works of art—100,000 in all. Names hard to find elsewhere are often at hand in it, and historians commend its accuracy.

Webster's Biographical Dictionary

In this book, over 40,000 concise biographies appear in alphabetical order. Care has been taken to give the correct pronunciation of each name. Though the dictionary offers some details, it is not intended to provide the complete life of any person.

Who's Who, Who's Who in America, and *The International Who's Who*

These standard books, found in most libraries, give essential facts about notable *living* persons. Note that these are books of *facts;* they do not summarize the subject's life in any detail. Typical entries list parentage, place and date of birth, educational background, positions held, important achievements, writings and their dates, awards, religious and political affiliations, and present address.

Who's Who gives information about notable British persons and some famous persons in other countries. It comes out yearly.

Who's Who in America gives facts about notable Americans. It comes out every two years. Although persons listed in *Who's Who in America* are dropped after they die, entries for the most important persons thus dropped are preserved in a volume entitled *Who Was Who in America.*

The International Who's Who might prove useful to you in locating material on persons not listed in the above-mentioned sources. Well-known educators, artists, diplomats, etc., from various parts of the globe are included here.

Current Biography

Like the *Who's Who* books above, this monthly serial is concerned with *living* people. Each issue contains short, informal biographies of those currently prominent in the news. A picture of the person is often included. The scope is international.

Annually, articles in the twelve issues are put in alphabetical order in one bound volume. Currently, its cumulative index locates articles from 1971 on. A separate index covers those from 1940 through 1970. Biographies are also indexed by professions.

Books About Authors

Although the lives of authors are included in all biographical reference books and in the encyclopedias, the following books treat authors only. *The Writers Directory* briefly lists 18,000 of today's writers. It comes out every two years. Articles in the others are informal, longer, and include authors' pictures.

American Authors 1600–1900 by Kunitz and Haycraft
American Writers by Unger
British Authors Before 1800 by Kunitz and Haycraft
British Authors of the Nineteenth Century by Kunitz and Haycraft
Contemporary Authors: First Revision, Gale Research Company
Dictionary of Literary Biography, Gale Research Company
The Writers Directory, St. James Press, London/St. Martin's Press, N.Y.
Twentieth Century Authors by Kunitz and Haycraft
World Authors by Wakeman

Magill's *Cyclopedia of World Authors* is a popular reference that includes authors from all over the world. It gives biographical facts for each author and a critical sketch characterizing his or her works.

LITERATURE REFERENCE BOOKS

27c. Develop the habit of using reference books on literature.

You were just introduced to some standard reference books on authors. For information on literary works and their plots, characters, sources, quotations, etc., the following books are useful.

General

Benét's *The Reader's Encyclopedia*

This book describes itself aptly as "an encyclopedia of all the things you encounter in reading." It does have great variety: plots and characters, summaries of poems, allusions to myths and to the Bible, and descriptions of works of art, music, and so on. Though the Second Edition best meets today's interests, either is good.

Books of Quotations

At times you may want to find the source or exact wording of a quotation. Because books of quotations differ in arrangement, you need to learn how to find what you want in the one you are using.

Bartlett's *Familiar Quotations*

Bartlett's is probably the best known. It provides four kinds of information about quotations: (1) the author; (2) the source; (3) the exact wording; (4) famous lines by any author.

Stevenson's *Home Book of Quotations* and *Home Book of Proverbs, Maxims, and Familiar Phrases*

Using a different type of arrangement, these books group quotations according to subject matter, not by author. This plan is convenient when you want quotations on a particular subject—success, love, duty, etc.

H. L. Mencken's *New Dictionary of Quotations*

The choice of numerous quotations marked by epigrammatic wit or satire makes this collection unusual.

Magill's *Quotations in Context*

This book of quotations includes the contexts of the quotations.

Indexes and Collections of Poetry

Stevenson's *Home Book of Verse* and *Home Book of Modern Verse*

When you want to find a popular poem, it is a good idea to look for it first in these two big anthologies. The poems are arranged by subjects. Since the books are indexed in three ways—by author, by title, and by first line—you should have no trouble finding the poem you want if it is in either book.

Granger's Index to Poetry (sixth edition)

When you want to find a particular poem, *Granger's Index* can lead you quickly to a collection that includes it. It has three listings for each poem: by author, by title, and by first line. Whichever you use will give you the same information as the other two do.

Remember that the *Index* does not print any whole poems, but its listings are quick poem-locators for almost any poem you want to find.

Other Indexes

Other useful indexes include the following ones: *Short Story Index, Play Index*, and *Essay and General Literature Index.*

OTHER REFERENCE BOOKS

If you are researching a topic within one of these broad fields, check your library for the following reliable resources.

Literature

American Authors and Books by W. J. Burke and W. D. Howe, augmented and revised by Irving Weiss
Book Review Digest
Bulfinch's Mythology
Cambridge History of American Literature
Cambridge History of English Literature
Cyclopedia of Literary Characters
Contemporary Literary Criticism
Encyclopedia of World Literature in the Twentieth Century
Guide to Great Plays by J. T. Shipley
The New Century Classical Handbook
Nineteenth Century Literary Criticism
Oxford Companion to American Literature
Oxford Companion to English Literature
Oxford Companion to French Literature
Oxford Companion to Classical Literature
Oxford Companion to the Theatre
Thirteen Hundred Critical Evaluations of Selected Novels and Plays

Grammar and Usage

The Careful Writer: a Modern Guide to English Usage by Theodore M. Bernstein
A Dictionary of Contemporary American Usage by Bergen and Cornelia Evans

History and Social Studies

Cambridge Modern History
Dictionary of American History by J. T. Adams
The Dictionary of Dates by Helen R. Keller
Encyclopedia of American History by R. B. Morris
Encyclopedia of the Social Sciences
Encyclopedia of World History by W. L. Langer

Great Events from History
Statistical Abstract of the United States
Webster's New Geographical Dictionary

Science and Mathematics

Chambers Dictionary of Science and Technology
McGraw-Hill Encyclopedia of Science and Technology

Music and Art

Encyclopedia of World Art
Encyclopedia of the Arts, edited by Herbert Read
Grove's Dictionary of Music and Musicians
The Harvard Dictionary of Music, first edition, edited by Willi Apel. (The second edition contains additional and updated entries but abbreviates the first listings considerably. An abridged paperback edition is also available: *The Harvard Brief Dictionary of Music.*)
The International Cyclopedia of Music and Musicians
The McGraw-Hill Encyclopedia of World Art
The New College Encyclopedia of Music, edited by J. A. Westrup and F. L. Harrison (the handiest and best one-volume popular work)
Vasari's Lives of the Painters, Sculptors, and Architects, new edition in four paperback volumes

Colleges and Universities

American Universities and Colleges, American Council on Education
Barron's Profiles of American Colleges
Comparative Guide to American Colleges, edited by James Cass and Max Birnbaum
Lovejoy's College Guide

EXERCISE 1. Explaining the Uses of Specific Reference Books. Be able to explain the principal uses of each of the following resource books, its advantages and its limitations.

1. An encyclopedia

2. Yearbooks

   World Almanac and Book of Facts
   Information Please Almanac
   The International Yearbook & Statesmen's Who's Who
   Collier's Yearbook

3. An atlas

4. Biographical reference books

   Biography Index
   Webster's Biographical Dictionary
   Who's Who, Who's Who in America, Who Was Who in America, and *The International Who's Who*
   American Authors 1600 - 1900

5. Literature reference books

   Bartlett's *Familiar Quotations*
   Stevenson's *Home Book of Quotations*
   Stevenson's *Home Book of Verse* and *Home Book of Modern Verse*
   Granger's Index to Poetry

EXERCISE 2. Distinguishing Between Specific Reference Books. Answer in writing the following questions.

1. Distinguish between a world atlas and a historical atlas.
2. List three books that contain information about events of the past year.
3. Which literature reference book would you use to find the author of a poem whose title you know?
4. Arrange the following titles in order according to the frequency of their publication, listing the most frequently published first: *Who's Who in America, Who's Who, Current Biography.*
5. Contrast the arrangements of Bartlett's *Familiar Quotations* and Stevenson's *Home Book of Quotations.*

EXERCISE 3. Selecting Reference Books to Find Specific Information. Number your paper 1–10. From the books and reference works given in brackets, write the one you would use to get the specified information. Be prepared to explain your choices.

1. Names of the senators in Congress from your state. [encyclopedia, *Who's Who in America, World Almanac*]
2. Books in your library about reptiles. [*Readers' Guide,* card catalog, vertical file]
3. Life of the Secretary-General of the United Nations. [*Current Biography, Dictionary of American Biography, Webster's Biographical Dictionary*]

4. International records in track events. [*Information Please Almanac, Who's Who in America, Readers' Guide*]
5. The source of the common expression "All the world's a stage." [Stevenson's *Home Book of Verse, Webster's Dictionary of Synonyms,* Bartlett's *Familiar Quotations*]
6. Titles and authors of biographies of the President. [*Biography Index, Who's Who in America, Webster's Biographical Dictionary*]
7. A quotation about youth. [Bartlett's *Familiar Quotations, World Almanac*, Stevenson's *Home Book of Quotations*]
8. The body of water into which the Suwannee River flows. [*The International Yearbook & Statesmen's Who's Who, World Almanac,* atlas]
9. A picture of an author who came into prominence during the past six months. [encyclopedia, *Current Biography, Who's Who*]
10. Leaflets recently published by the National Safety Council. [card catalog, *Readers' Guide*, vertical file]

EXERCISE 4. Using Library Tools or Reference Books to Find Specific Information. Which library tool or reference book, including the encyclopedia, would you use to find the following items of information? Write your first choice. Be able to explain.

1. Titles of recent magazine articles on the latest fashions in dress
2. The special power that the mythological character Clotho had
3. The title of a book, owned by your library, on conservation
4. An account of the climate of Tahiti
5. The native state of the Vice-President of the United States
6. The ten most populous cities in the United States
7. An illustrated article on the Navajo Indians
8. Pamphlets published by the Foreign Policy Association
9. Any books the library may have on stamp collecting
10. Officials of the present government of Pakistan

CHAPTER 28

The Dictionary

CONTENT AND USES OF DICTIONARIES

Although dictionaries differ from one another in number of entries and method of presenting information, they all provide a report on the way language is used. Dictionary makers do not by themselves decide what words mean or how they should be pronounced and spelled. As a result of careful research, dictionary makers are able to record the way the majority of educated people use the language: the meanings such people apply to words and the ways they pronounce and spell words.

To people who want to make themselves understood and who wish to understand what they read, such a reliable report on language practice is of obvious value. No speaker of English knows all the words. Everyone needs help sometimes with the meaning, spelling, pronunciation, and use of a particular word.

KINDS OF DICTIONARIES

28a. Know the kinds of dictionaries.

Excluding the many special dictionaries—dictionaries of scientific terms, foreign-language dictionaries, etc.—there are two main kinds of dictionaries with which you should be familiar: the large *unabridged* dictionary, which you will probably use mainly in libraries; and the "college-size" dictionary, which you should have when you study.

College Dictionaries

The most practical dictionary for everyday use is the college dictionary, which usually has from about 100,000 to about 160,000 entries. Material in the front and the back often includes guides to punctuation, usage, and preparing research papers, and may contain other information useful to students. Because it is frequently revised, a college dictionary is likely to be more nearly up-to-date than an unabridged.

The four listed below are well known and reputable.

The American Heritage Dictionary of the English Language, Houghton Mifflin Co., Boston

The Random House College Dictionary, Random House, New York, N.Y.

Webster's New Collegiate Dictionary, G. & C. Merriam Co., Springfield, Mass.

Webster's New World Dictionary of the American Language, *Second College Edition,* William Collins Publishing Co., Cleveland, Ohio

Unabridged Dictionaries

The largest dictionaries—containing over 300,000 entries—are called *unabridged* dictionaries. *Unabridged* in this context means only "not cut down from a bigger one." Three (two American and one British) are listed below:

The Random House Dictionary of the English Language, Random House, New York, N.Y.

Webster's Third New International Dictionary, G. & C. Merriam Co., Springfield, Mass.

The Oxford English Dictionary, Oxford University Press, New York, N.Y.

An unabridged dictionary has two or three times the number of entries in a college dictionary. Many entries are likely to be more detailed and to give more facts. An unabridged dictionary is more likely to contain a rare or very old word, a dialect or regional word. *Webster's* and the *Oxford* use many actual quotations from named writers to show words in certain senses.

CONTENT AND ARRANGEMENT OF DICTIONARIES

28b. Familiarize yourself with the kinds of information in your dictionary and learn where and how each kind is given.

Although people most commonly use the dictionary to look up the spelling and meaning of words, to use it only for these purposes is to miss its many other kinds of information. The following study materials and exercises will help you discover the full resources of your dictionary and may lead you to refer to it more often and more efficiently.

Although all good dictionaries contain essentially the same facts, material may be arranged and handled quite differently. For example, some list items such as notable persons and places in the main alphabetical listing; others put them in separate sections. The location of abbreviations and foreign phrases may also differ.

EXERCISE 1. Understanding the Content and Arrangement of Your Dictionary. Using the dictionary with which you have been provided, write the answers to the following questions. Use the table of contents whenever it is helpful.

1. What is the full title of your dictionary?
2. Who is the publisher?
3. What is the latest copyright date? (Look on the back of the title page.)
4. Where does the complete key to pronunciation appear?
5. Is there a shorter key on each page? On every other page?
6. On what page do the explanatory notes on pronunciation begin?
7. On what page does the introductory article describing and explaining the dictionary begin?
8. What special articles are there on the history of the language, grammar, etc.?
9. On what page are abbreviations used in the dictionary listed?
10. Are the other abbreviations, such as A.D., C.O.D., and UNESCO, explained in the body of your dictionary or in a separate section at the back?
11. Are guides to spelling, punctuation, and capitalization given? If so, list the page on which each begins.
12. Is there a section giving the meaning of commonly used signs and symbols? If so, give the page it begins on.
13. Are the names of important people and places listed in the body of your dictionary or in a separate section?
14. Does your dictionary provide derivations of words? If so, do they appear near the beginning or at the end of an entry?

15. Are the names of literary, mythological, and Biblical characters listed in the body of your dictionary or in a special section? To find out, look up Hamlet, Poseidon, and Deborah.

EXERCISE 2. Using Your Dictionary to Find Specific Information. Look up in your dictionary the answers to the following questions and write the answers in a column on your paper. *After each answer write the page number on which you found it.* If any of the items are not in your dictionary, write the number of the question and leave a blank space.

1. What was the occupation of Maria Mitchell?
2. Give the meaning of the French phrase *comme il faut.*
3. Give the spelling rule for retaining the silent final *e* on a word when you add a suffix.
4. In what play is Iago the villain?
5. Where is Prince Edward Island?

A Dictionary's Information About a Word

Definitions

The main function of a dictionary is to give the meanings of words. Since a single word may have many meanings, an entry covering it must have a matching number of definitions. In some dictionaries, all definitions are simply numbered in sequence. In others, small subdivisions of meaning within a numbered definition are headed by letters in sequence.

Some dictionaries still put definitions in historical order, the earliest meaning first, the latest last. Others base order on frequency of use, the most common meaning first, the least common last. The first entry below shows historical order; the second, frequency of use.

mas·ter·piece \'mas-tər-ˌpēs\ *n* (1605) **1** : a piece of work presented to a medieval guild as evidence of qualification for the rank of master **2** : a work done with extraordinary skill; *esp* : a supreme intellectual or artistic achievement

mas·ter·piece (mas′tər pēs′, mä′stər-), *n.* **1.** a person's most excellent production, as in an art. **2.** any production of masterly skill. **3.** a piece made by a journeyman or other craftsman aspiring to the rank of master in a guild or other craft organization as a proof of his competence. [MASTER + PIECE, modeled on D *meesterstuk*, G *Meisterstück*]

A label usually shows the part of speech of the word being defined. For example, *n.* stands for noun, *v.* for verb, and so on. (Abbreviations used are explained in a dictionary's front matter.) In older dictionaries, a word used as more than one part of speech was given a new entry for each one. Now these once-separate entries are usually gathered into one main entry, with definitions still grouped and labeled by part of speech—noun definitions together, verb definitions together, etc. Definition numbers commonly start over for each new part of speech. College-size and bigger dictionaries cling to these practices.

When you look up a word's meaning, read all its definitions. Unless you do, you can't be sure that the meaning you select best fits the context in which the word is used.

Even though you have looked up the meaning, you should be wary of using a word you have encountered only once. A great many English words not only have more than one meaning, but they also have *implied* or *connotative* meanings, which are not given in a dictionary. Furthermore, there may be idiomatic uses of which a young student speaker or writer is not aware.

Spelling

The boldfaced word at the very beginning of a dictionary entry tells you the accepted spelling. When there are two or more acceptable spellings, the various spellings are given. Any spelling given has enough standing to justify use of it if you prefer it.

If grammatical change in the form of a word is likely to raise spelling problems, *inflectional* forms are given. (These are forms of a word resulting from its habitual usage, like the principal parts of verbs or the comparative and superlative forms of adjectives.) A dictionary is the best reference work to consult if you are uncertain about doubling a consonant, changing an *i* to a *y*, and so on.

Both the principal parts of irregular verbs you may have difficulty remembering and the spelling of frequently misspelled words can be found in any good dictionary. Think of the dictionary as the place to find the proper spelling (and forms) of:

a. the plural of a word, if the plural is formed irregularly
b. the feminine form of a foreign word: **alumnus; alumna,** fem.
c. the principal parts of an irregular verb
d. comparative and superlative forms of irregular adjectives and adverbs
e. case forms of pronouns: **who;** *possessive* **whose;** *objective* **whom**

Syllable Division

When a word must be divided at the end of a line, it should be divided between syllables. Syllable division is indicated in the boldfaced entry word and often in inflectional forms. The break is usually shown by a centered dot (**bas•ket**). In some dictionaries it is indicated by a space (**bas ket**). Look at the various sample entries throughout this chapter to see the different ways each dictionary shows syllable division.

Capitalization

Proper nouns and adjectives, commonly written with initial capital letters, are entered in most dictionaries with the usual capitals. *Webster's Third,* however, prints the entry word in small letters followed by a brief note such as: *usu cap* or *often cap,* short for *usually capitalized* or *often capitalized.*

Sometimes a word not capitalized in most of its meanings should be capitalized when used in one sense, or perhaps more than one. The abbreviation *cap.* following a definition number indicates that the word is capitalized when used in that sense.

EXAMPLE

cap·i·tol \ˈkap-ət-ᵊl, ˈkap-tᵊl\ *n* [L *Capitolium*, temple of Jupiter at Rome on the Capitoline hill] (1699) **1** **a** : a building in which a state legislative body meets **b** : a group of buildings in which the functions of state government are carried out **2** *cap* : the building in which the U.S. Congress meets at Washington

Pronunciation

Ordinary spelling cannot show the sounds of words precisely. Dictionary pronunciations respell each word, using one fixed symbol for each of the 42 or 43 common sounds of English. Most of the symbols look like ordinary letters of the alphabet, some with special marks added, but they work differently: each one stands exclusively and consistently for only one sound.

Each dictionary explains its symbols in a key, usually in the front of the book, and also prints a shortened key at the foot of each pair of facing pages. The key shows each symbol tied to its sound *as heard in one or two familiar words.*

In long words, one syllable, or sometimes more than one, may be spoken with more stress or force than the others. This stress is shown by accent marks: heaviest stress by a heavier mark, lighter stress by a lighter mark. The marks may be either slanted or straight, either above or within the line of type, and either before or after the syllable involved.

EXAMPLES **tax•i•cab:** tak' se kab′
'tak se kab
ták se kăb

When a word has more than one recognized pronunciation, all of the pronunciations are given. You will have to study your dictionary's way of giving pronunciations, since each of the most available dictionaries differs from the others in the system it uses.

Etymologies, or Word Histories

Most dictionaries show, by means of abbreviations and symbols, what language a word originally came from and what its original meaning was. They also explain the source of recently coined words, such as *quark.*

The abbreviations used to indicate the languages from which words derive are explained in the front of your dictionary. The following examples show how dictionaries vary in where they position an etymology within an entry. The symbol < means "from," like the abbreviation *fr.*

EXAMPLE

'**book** \'bůk\ *n* [ME, fr. OE *boc;* akin to OHG *buoh* book; perh. akin to OE *bōc* beech (prob. fr. the early Germanic practice of carving runic characters on beech wood tablets) — more at BEECH] (bef. 12c)

Restrictive Labels

Most of the words defined in a dictionary are part of the general vocabulary. Some, however, have to do with a special field or are used almost exclusively in a single region or are used at only one level of usage.

To indicate these words, dictionaries use restrictive labels—*subject labels* such as *Law, Med.* (medicine), *Chem.* (chemistry), etc.; *area labels* such as *southwest U.S.;* and *usage labels* such as *informal, slang,* or *dialect.*

Usage labels provide a good general guide to usage, but all writers must learn to make judgments about these matters on the basis of their own observations. Assigning a label such as *slang* or *informal* is necessarily a subjective judgment on the part of a definer, and not all dictionaries agree about labeling the same word. Your knowledge of the connotations of a word and the situation in which you want to use it should be your guide in choosing or rejecting a particular word or meaning.

Synonyms and Antonyms

Dictionaries often list other words of similar meaning (synonyms) and sometimes also words of opposite meaning (antonyms) at the end of an entry. At times they also append a slightly longer note comparing two or more words with similar meanings, showing fine shades of differences as well as similarities.

In the following example, synonyms (SYN) are discussed in detail, and antonyms (ANT) are also given.

EXAMPLE **brave** (brāv) ***adj.*** [Fr. < It. *bravo*, brave, bold, orig., wild, savage < L. *barbarus*, BARBAROUS] **1.** willing to face danger, pain, or trouble; not afraid; having courage **2.** showing to good effect; having a fine appearance **3.** fine, grand, or splendid [a *brave* new world] —***n.*** **1.** any brave man ☆**2.** [< 17th-c. NAmFr.] a North American Indian warrior **3.** [Archaic] a bully —***vt.*** **braved, brav'ing** **1.** to face with courage **2.** to defy; dare **3.** [Obs.] to make splendid, as in dress —***vi.*** [Obs.] to boast —**brave'ly** ***adv.*** —**brave'ness** ***n.***

SYN.—**brave** implies fearlessness in meeting danger or difficulty and has the broadest application of the words considered here; **courageous** suggests constant readiness to deal with things fearlessly by reason of a stout-hearted temperament or a resolute spirit; **bold** stresses a daring temperament, whether displayed courageously, presumptuously, or defiantly; **audacious** suggests an imprudent or reckless boldness; **valiant** emphasizes a heroic quality in the courage or fortitude shown; **intrepid** implies absolute fearlessness and esp. suggests dauntlessness in facing the new or unknown; **plucky** emphasizes gameness in fighting against something when one is at a decided disadvantage —***ANT.*** **craven, cowardly**

Encyclopedia Entries

Besides giving information about words, the college dictionaries listed in this chapter (but not some unabridged dictionaries) give facts about many people and places. These may appear as entries in the body of the dictionary or in special sections at the back.

Important Persons

A dictionary usually covers these items about a person:

1. *Name:* spelling, pronunciation, and given names
2. *Date of birth (and death if deceased)*

3. *Nationality (and country of birth if different)*
4. *Why famous*

Dictionary information about contemporaries soon goes out of date. It may be safer to refer to *Who's Who* or *Who's Who in America* for up-to-date facts.

Important Places

In treating a geographical entry, a dictionary usually gives the following information:

1. *Name:* spelling, pronunciation
2. *Indentification:* city, nation, lake, river, etc.
3. *Location*
4. *Size:* population, as of a city; area, as of a state, body of water, etc.; length, as of a river; height, as of a mountain
5. *Political importance:* If a city is capital of a state or nation, the fact will be noted, and the city may be named in the entry for the state or nation.
6. *Historical or other interest:* as Yorktown, site of surrender of the British
7. *Controlling country:* as in Guam, a United States possession

Be sure that a dictionary uses the latest census for its (undated) population figures before you trust them. Old data can be seriously misleading.

SPECIAL DICTIONARIES

28c. Learn the use of special dictionaries.

Along with general dictionaries, there are dictionaries of the special vocabularies of law, medicine, slang, and so on.

Books of synonyms are useful to people who do much writing. They help writers to vary their choice of words and to find the exact word needed.

Roget's Thesaurus of English Words and Phrases

This is the classic book of synonyms, over a century old. Originally, its words were grouped by classes and subclasses of meaning, with a huge index attached. Some recent editions retain this ingenious format. Others put the material in dictionary form—straight alphabetical order.

Funk and Wagnalls Standard Handbook of Synonyms, Antonyms, and Prepositions

This is also a standard book, listing in alphabetical order most of the words you might want to use and giving synonyms and antonyms for them.

Webster's Dictionary of Synonyms

This is valued especially for its able discussion of distinctions between words of similar meaning.

EXERCISE 3. Using Your Dictionary to Find Information About Words. This exercise is designed to test your knowledge of the information given about a word in the dictionary. With your dictionary before you, begin work at the teacher's signal. Look up the answers to the following questions. While your speed indicates to some degree your efficiency in using the dictionary, accuracy is the more important consideration.

1. Which is the more usual spelling: *judgment* or *judgement?*
2. In the first pronunciation for *research,* is the accent on the first or second syllable?
3. Copy the correct pronunciation of the word *comely,* using the respelling and symbols.
4. Copy the word *automatic,* dividing it correctly into syllables.
5. How many different meanings are given in your dictionary for the word *run* as an intransitive (*v.i.*) verb?
6. What restrictive label is given the word *shank* when used in the expression "the shank of the evening"?
7. Distinguish between the meaning of *councilor* and *counselor.*
8. What is the origin of the word *candidate?*
9. In what literary work does the character Mrs. Malaprop appear? For what was she noted?
10. Tell the story of Hero and Leander as given in your dictionary.

EXERCISE 4. Using Your Dictionary to Find Information About Words. Like the preceding exercise, this exercise will test your knowledge of the information given in a dictionary and your familiarity with the location of this information in the dictionary. At the teacher's signal look up the answers to the following questions. Accuracy is more important than speed, but speed is important.

1. Find two synonyms for the word *cowardly.*
2. Write the plural of *analysis.*
3. Write the comparative and superlative forms of *ill.*
4. What city is the capital of Burma?
5. What is the population of Dallas, Texas?
6. When did Queen Victoria reign?
7. What was George Eliot's real name?
8. What is the meaning of the symbol AA used by a doctor in writing a prescription?
9. Write two acceptable plurals of *octopus.*
10. What is the meaning of the Latin phrase *caveat emptor*?

CHAPTER 29

Vocabulary

MEANING THROUGH CONTEXT AND WORD ANALYSIS

Although it is likely that this may be your last year of systematic vocabulary study, the number of English words you know and are able to use will continue to be important throughout your life. Most immediately, you will see that a good vocabulary will help you to succeed in college or at a job. More important, however, your general knowledge or your knowledge of a specific field cannot be very deep or impressive unless you have a considerable stock of words at your command. The number of words you know is one indication of the pride you take in your mind. You owe it to yourself to have a vocabulary that fairly reflects your interests and abilities.

DIAGNOSTIC TEST

Selecting the Closest Meaning Number your paper 1–20. After the proper number, write the letter of the word or expression that comes closest to the meaning of the italicized word.

1. to *augment* the budget
   a) increase
   b) examine closely
   c) reduce
   d) disapprove of
2. to *ascertain* the facts
   a) cover up
   b) review
   c) find out
   d) testify to

3. a king known for his *avarice* — a) wisdom b) vanity c) deceitfulness d) greed
4. a *biennial* event — a) twice yearly b) every two weeks c) every two years d) twice daily
5. a *blithe* mood — a) bitter b) proud c) angry d) carefree
6. an offer to *capitulate* — a) confer b) mediate c) compromise d) surrender
7. a suspicion of *collusion* — a) robbery b) foolishness c) mistrustfulness d) agreement to deceive
8. to *conjecture* about the facts — a) talk b) lie c) guess d) conceal the truth
9. to *corroborate* testimony — a) testify about b) confirm c) deny d) question
10. to act under *duress* — a) compulsion b) misunderstanding c) difficulties d) bribery
11. an imposing *edifice* — a) natural wonder b) manner c) speech d) building
12. a leader's *foible* — a) weakness b) habit c) example d) follower
13. an *interminable* show — a) worthless b) endless c) tedious d) difficult to describe
14. to *nurture* a child — a) neglect b) give medicine to c) scold d) feed and bring up
15. a sign of *opulence* — a) poverty b) health c) wealth d) generosity
16. a *prosaic* sight — a) commonplace b) solemn c) stirring d) peaceful
17. a *prudent* action — a) unexpected b) ill-mannered c) sensible d) foolish
18. good-natured *raillery* — a) scuffling b) boisterousness c) competition d) banter
19. a well-deserved *reproof* — a) promotion b) reprimand c) apology d) recognition
20. a *volatile* temperament — a) changeable b) disagreeable c) sluggish d) easygoing

CONTEXT CLUES

29a. Find clues to meaning in context.

The words that surround a particular word in a sentence or paragraph are called the *verbal context* of that word. Consider this sentence, for example:

> Although she continued to predict victory, Captain Winters was really not *sanguine* about her team's prospects.

If you are not sure of the meaning of *sanguine*, the rest of this sentence provides some important clues. The first part suggests that there is something contradictory about the captain's predicting victory when she is not sanguine about her team's chances. From the whole sentence, you may reasonably conclude that *sanguine* must mean "hopeful" or "optimistic." Sometimes, of course, such reasoning will lead you into a wrong guess; but more often than not you will be right.

In addition to the other words, the situation itself often provides clues to the meaning of a word. In the example above, you would expect a captain to be concerned about her team's success. Thus, you would not suppose that *sanguine* meant "bored" or "disinterested." Clues provided by the situation being discussed often help in deciding between two very different meanings of the same word or of words that have the same spelling. For example, if you are reading about an argument, *retort* is likely to mean "a ready and effective reply." In a description of a scientific experiment, on the other hand, *retort* would probably mean "a vessel used in distilling."

EXERCISE 1. Using Context Clues to Determine Meanings of Words. Number your paper 1–10. After each number, write the italicized word in the sentence and write a short definition based on the clues you find in context. You may check your definitions with the dictionary later.

1. After listening to a good deal of coaxing, the mother finally *acceded* to her children's request.
2. After a *hectic* year in the city, George was glad enough to return to the peace and quiet of the country.
3. Although the risks were great, the dissatisfied officers met and formed a *cabal* against the commander-in-chief.

4. The last two lines of the poem are so *cryptic* that no two readers can agree about what they mean.
5. Any person who was not entirely *devoid* of honor would have been outraged at the suggestion.
6. The loud, *raucous* laughter of the troop irritated the lieutenant.
7. A large constrictor grabs its prey in its mouth and quickly coils itself around the victim to *immobilize* it. The harder the animal struggles, the tighter the snake constricts.
8. Eventually, the criminal *expiated* this murder and many other crimes on the gallows.
9. According to Bacon, scientists should learn about nature through *empirical* observations based on experiments and on careful study of the greatest possible amount of evidence.
10. Despite the awesome *fecundity* of certain species of fish, the balance of nature limits the population.

Common Clues to Meaning

Although a sentence may provide clues to the meaning of a word in a variety of ways, there are four kinds of context clues that are particularly helpful. Learning to recognize these four kinds of clues will help you determine the meanings of many of the unfamiliar words you encounter.

Synonym

Often writers use synonyms in sentences for variety. In such cases the meaning of one word is the clue to the meaning of the other word. In the following example, notice that the writer uses the word *avoid* as a synonym for *eschew* so that *eschew* does not have to be repeated in the sentence. (For a discussion of synonyms, see page 528.)

> A person on a reducing diet is expected to *eschew* greasy foods and, especially, to *avoid* sugar.

Example

Another technique that writers may employ to clarify meaning is including examples of an important word in a sentence. Expressions such as *for example, for instance, such as,* and *especially* will often indicate an example. In the following sentence, you can probably guess that the word *charlatan* means "a person who claims to have a skill which he doesn't really have" from the examples in the sentence.

> When hiring someone to do home repairs, be wary of charlatans such as carpenters or plumbers who do not have any references or tools.

Comparison or Contrast

The comparisons or contrasts used by writers often supply clues to meaning by pairing an unfamiliar word with a common word or phrase. Look for expressions such as *like, as, similar to,* or *in the same way* to precede comparisons. In the following sentence, the comparison of the word *buffoon* to the word *clowns* illustrates how comparison can be a good context clue.

> At parties William is a buffoon, just *like* all the other clowns in the class.

Contrasting meanings are often signaled by such words as *but, not, although, rather than,* and *however.* In the following example, notice that the word *dirge* is contrasted with *wedding march.*

> We were surprised at the bride's choice of music, for the processional sounded like a dirge *rather than* a wedding march.

Because it is contrasted to the wedding march, you can guess that a *dirge* is a music type that is not appropriate for a wedding. However, you might have to check your dictionary to discover that a *dirge* is specifically "a funeral hymn." Comparison or contrast clues will help you guess a word's meaning, but to be absolutely certain, look up the word in a dictionary.

Definition

When writers anticipate that their readers may not know the meaning of an important word, they often provide a definition. They may introduce the definition with an expression such as *in other words* or *that is*, or they may slip it in as an appositive without calling attention to it. The definitions or explanations in the following examples are italicized, and the words defined are in boldfaced type.

> The painting clearly shows the **aegis,** or *shield*, of Athena.
>
> A word is often defined by a **synonym**—that is, *a word of similar meaning.*
>
> His *observation* was *too obvious to mention*—a **truism**. [Notice that the explanation comes before the word defined in this example.]

People do not go to the trouble of explaining things unless they want to be understood. Be on the lookout for definitions of difficult words.

EXERCISE 2. Using Context Clues to Determine Meanings of Words. Number your paper 1–10 and after each number write the italicized word. Give a brief definition in your own words, based on the context.

1. Along with the discovery of the properties of poisons came the discovery of substances that had properties of combating the effects of poisons. These early *antidotes* were strange mixtures.
2. The border rebellion, *quiescent* during the winter months, broke out in renewed violence in the spring.
3. To the rest of us, the outlook just then seemed more ominous than *propitious*.
4. Most snakes are meat eaters, or *carnivores*.
5. The *salutary* effect of the new drug was shown by the rapid improvement in the patient's condition.
6. *Subterranean* temperatures are frequently higher than those above the surface of the earth.
7. Because the official could not attend the meeting herself, she had to send a *surrogate*, or deputy.
8. The method of reasoning from the particular to the general—the *inductive* method—has played an important role in science since the time of Francis Bacon.
9. If the leaders felt any *compunction* about planning and carrying out unprovoked attacks on neighboring countries, they showed no sign of it.
10. Formerly, a doctor who found a successful cure often regarded it as a trade secret and refused to *divulge* it to others.

EXERCISE 3. Using Context Clues to Determine Meanings of Words. Read the following passage and then write your own definitions for the italicized words. Consult your dictionary only after you have written your own definitions from context.

Most of the doctors who had treated cases of the peculiar disease were almost certain by then that the characteristic initial (1) *lesion* was the bite of some (2) *minute* creature, but they had little reason to suspect mites of being the guilty parties. At the time, it was generally believed that mites could transmit only two serious (3) *febrile* diseases—Japanese river fever and endemic typhus. Both of these are rarely found in the United States, and anyway both had been eliminated from consideration in this instance by laboratory tests. Moreover, the mouse, unlike the rat, had never been proved to be a reservoir for disease-bearing parasites. Mr. Pomerantz admits that hitting upon the mouse as the probable (4) *host* was largely intuitive. He is persuaded, however, that in singling out mites as the carriers—or (5) *vectors*, as such agents are known—of the disease he was guided entirely by (6) *deduction*.

Mites are insectlike organisms, closely related to ticks. Both are members of the Arachnida, a class that also includes spiders and scorpions. Compared to a tick, a mite is a minute animal. A mite, when fully (7) *engorged*, is about the size of a strawberry seed. In that state, it is approximately ten times its usual, or unfed, size. So far, science has classified at least thirty families of mites, most of which are vegetarian and indifferent to man and all other animals. The majority of the (8) *parasitic*, blood-sucking mites have to feed once in every four or five days in order to live. Most mites of this type attach themselves to a host only long enough to engorge, and drop off, (9) *replete*, after fifteen or twenty minutes. No one ever feels the bite of a mite—or of a tick, either, for that matter—until the animal has dropped off. Entomologists believe that both creatures, at the instant they bite, (10) *excrete* a fluid that anesthetizes a small surrounding area of the body of the host. Mites are only infrequently found in this country and until recently were practically unknown in New York City. Consequently, very few Americans, even physicians and exterminators, have ever seen a mite. Mr. Pomerantz is one of those who have. He came across some in line of duty on three occasions in 1945.

BERTON ROUECHÉ

29b. Look up unfamiliar words in your dictionary.

For those words that context does not make sufficiently clear, the dictionary will provide you with the help you need. But here, too, context is important. Most words have a number of different meanings. To find the one you want, you will need to keep in mind the context in which you originally encountered the word. Once you have found the meaning you want, read on through the whole definition. Most words have a range of different meanings; to know the word well, you should know more than one of its meanings. Moreover, learning the pronunciation, the derivation, and related forms of the word will help you to remember it. Once you take the trouble to go to the dictionary, you may as well get as much information as possible from it.

WORD ANALYSIS

29c. Use your knowledge of prefixes, suffixes, and roots.

In general, English words are of two kinds: those that can be analyzed into smaller parts (*unworkable, impolitely*) and those that cannot (*stone, money, winter*). The words of the first kind, those that can be divided, are made up of parts called prefixes, roots, and suffixes. Because these parts have broad, general meanings that remain essentially the same in different words, knowing something about word analysis can help you figure out the meaning of an unfamiliar word. However, there are some difficulties that make it unwise to depend entirely on word analysis for clues to meaning. It is not always easy to tell whether a particular group of letters is really the prefix or suffix it appears to be. The *-er* in *painter* is a suffix, but the *-er* in *winter* is not. To be certain, you have to know something about the origin of the word. Moreover, the original force of a combination of word parts may no longer have much to do with the modern meaning of a word. For these and other reasons, absolute dependence on word analysis would lead you to make as many bad guesses as good ones.

There are, however, some good reasons for having a general knowledge of the way English words are formed. Word analysis helps you to understand the peculiarities of English spelling and the connection between the related forms of a particular word. (Knowing about related forms often enables you to learn four or five new words as easily as one.) Also, word analysis gives you useful practice in taking a close look at words. In reading, you pass very quickly over words, hardly noticing more than their general shape. This is all very well for words you know well, but close examination is called for with unfamiliar ones. Most important of all, word analysis offers the key to the origin of English words. The fact that many different cultures have contributed to the vocabulary of English is one of its particular strengths. Educated people should know something about the history as well as the use of their words.

How Words Are Divided

Words that can be divided have two or more parts: a core called a *root* and one or more parts added to it. The parts that are added are called *affixes*—literally, "something fixed or attached to something else." An affix added before the root is called a *prefix;* one added after the root is called a *suffix.* A word may have one or more affixes of either kind, or several of both kinds. A root with no affixes at all is incapable of being divided. A word consisting of a root only is one like *stone* or *money*, to which word analysis does not apply.

The following table shows some typical combinations of affixes (prefixes and suffixes) and roots.

PREFIX[ES]	ROOT	SUFFIX[ES]	EXAMPLE
un-	work	-able	unworkable
post-	-pone		postpone
	friend	-ly	friendly
	fright	-en, -ing	frightening
il-	-leg-	-al	illegal
under	take	-er	undertaker
	truth	-ful	truthful
	child	like	childlike

Some of the affixes and roots in English are recognizable as complete words in themselves (*fright* in *frighten; child* and *like* in *childlike*). Most other affixes and roots were also once separate words, though the original words may no longer exist in our modern language. For example, *post* in *postpone* was a Latin word meaning *after*, and *pone* (*pono, ponere*) was the Latin word for *put*.

The Origins of English Words

In the lists that appear later in this chapter, prefixes and roots are grouped according to the language in which they originated: Old English, Latin (or Latin-French), and Greek.

Old English, or Anglo-Saxon, is the earliest recorded form of the English language. It was spoken from about A.D. 600 until about A.D. 1100, and most of its words had been part of a still earlier form of the language. Many of the common words of modern English, like *home, stone,* and *meat,* are native, or Old English, words. Most of the irregular verbs in English derive from Old English (*speak, swim, drive, ride, sing*), as do most of our shorter numerals (*two, three, six, ten*) and most of our pronouns (*I, you, we, who*). Many Old English words can be traced back to Indo-European, a prehistoric language that was the common ancestor of Greek and Latin as well. Others came into Old English as it was becoming a separate language.

As the speakers of Old English became acquainted with Latin, chiefly through contact with Christianity, they began to borrow Latin words for things for which no native word existed. Some common words borrowed at this time were *abbot, altar, candle, temple, fever,* and *lettuce.*

Many other Latin words came into English through French. In 1066, toward the end of the Old English period, the French under William the Conqueror invaded England and defeated the Anglo-Saxons under King Harold. For the next three hundred years, French was the language of the ruling classes in England. During this period, thousands of new words came into English, many of them words relating to upper-class pursuits: *baron, attorney, ermine, luxury.* English has continued to borrow words from French right down to the present, with the result that over a third of our modern English vocabulary derives from French.

Many words from Greek, the other major source of English words, came into English by way of French and Latin. Others were borrowed directly in the sixteenth century when interest in classical culture was at its height. Directly or indirectly, Greek contributed *athlete, acrobat, elastic, magic, rhythm,* and many others.

In the modern period, English has borrowed from every important language in the world. The etymologies in your dictionary trace the origins of words, often providing insights into their present meanings and into history as well.

EXERCISE 4. Finding the Etymologies of Words. Find out from your dictionary the origins of each of the following words. (For help in interpreting the etymology, see page 499 of this book.)

abscond	demon	quart
air	legal	tyrant
chase	loyal	votary

Prefixes

English borrowed not only independent words from Greek, Latin, and French, but also a number of word parts from these languages for use as affixes and roots. These sources are indicated in the following list of prefixes and in the list of roots on pages 520–23.

Prefixes have broad general meanings like *not, under,* and *against,* and a particular one of them may appear in hundreds of different words. In general, a knowledge of prefixes will help you to know when to double consonants in such words as *misspell* and *overrun*; when you are not sure, however, be sure to check a dictionary. Many prefixes have several different spellings in order to fit with various roots.

PREFIX	MEANING	EXAMPLES
Old English		
a-	in, on, of, up, to	afoot, awake
be-	around, about, away	beset, behead
for-	away, off, from	forsake, forget
mis-	badly, poorly, not	mismatch, misspell
over-	above, excessively	oversee, overdo
un-	not, reverse of	untrue, unfold
Latin and Latin-French		
ab-, a-, abs-	from, off, away	abduct, absent
ante-	before	antedate
bi-	two	bimonthly, bisect
circum-	around	circumnavigate
com-, co- col-, con-, cor-	with, together	compare, coexist, collide, convene, correspond
contra-	against	contradict
de-	away, from, off, down	defect, desert
dis-, dif-	away, off, opposing	dissent, differ
ex-, e-, ef-	away from, out	excise, efface
in-, im-	in, into, within	induct, impose
in-, im-, il-, ir-	not	incapable, impious, illegal, irregular
inter-	among, between	intercede, intersperse
intro-, intra-	inward, to the inside, within	introduce, intravenous, intramural
non-	not	nonentity, nonessential
post-	after, following	postpone, postscript
pre-	before	prevent, preclude
pro-	forward, in place of, favoring	produce, pronoun, pro-American
re-	back, backward, again	revoke, recede, recur
retro-	back, backward	retroactive, retrospect
semi-	half	semiannual, semicircular

PREFIX	MEANING	EXAMPLES
Latin and Latin-French (continued)		
sub-, suf-, sum-, sup-, sus-	under, beneath	subjugate, suffuse summon, suppose, suspect
super-	over, above, extra	supersede, supervise
trans-	across, beyond	transfuse, transport
ultra-	beyond, excessively	ultramodern, ultraviolet
Greek		
a-	lacking, without	amorphous, atheistic
anti-	against, opposing	antipathy, antithesis
apo-	from, away	apology, apocrypha
cata-	down, away, thoroughly	cataclysm, catastrophe
dia-	through, across, apart	diameter, diagnose
eu-	good, pleasant	eulogy, euphemism
hemi-	half	hemisphere, hemiplegic
hyper-	excessive, over	hypercritical, hypertension
hypo-	under, beneath	hypodermic, hypothesis
para-	beside, beyond	parallel, paradox
peri-	around	periscope, perimeter
pro-	before	prognosis, program
syn-, sym- syl-, sys-	together, with	synchronize, sympathy, syllable, system

EXERCISE 5. Understanding Prefixes in Words. Divide the following words into prefix and root, putting a slant line (/) at the point of division. Then give the meaning of the English word. Be ready to explain the connection between the meaning of the prefix and the present meaning of the word.

EXAMPLE 1. amnesia
1. *a/mnesia (loss of memory)*

1. absolve
2. amorphous
3. antipodes
4. biennial
5. circumspect
6. compunction
7. excise
8. hypodermic
9. impolite
10. subordinate

EXERCISE 6. Writing Words with Specific Prefixes. Find and write on your paper two words that contain each of the following prefixes: *de-*, *dia-*, *dis-*, *eu-*, *ir-*, *mis-*, *pro-*, *re-*, *syn-*, *ultra-*.

Suffixes

Suffixes, you will recall, are affixes added after the root, or at the end of a word. There are two main kinds of suffixes: those that provide a grammatical signal of some kind but do not greatly alter the basic meaning of the word and those that, by being added, create new words. The endings *-s, -ed,* and *-ing* are suffixes of the first kind; by adding them to *work (works, worked, working)* we indicate something about number and tense, but we do not change the essential meaning of the word. This kind of suffix is a *grammatical* suffix.

Grammatical suffixes are important in grammar, but in vocabulary we are more concerned with the second kind of suffixes—those that make new words. By adding *-ful* to *thank*, we get a different word: *thankful*. Adding *-hood* to *girl* gives us *girlhood*, again a different word. Suffixes that change meaning in this way are called *derivational* suffixes. Notice in the following examples that the addition of a derivational suffix often gives a new part of speech as well as a new meaning.

ROOT	DERIVATIONAL SUFFIX	RESULT
acid (n. or adj.)	-ity	acidity (n. only)
free (adj.)	-dom	freedom (n.)
accept (v.)	-ance	acceptance (n.)

Since derivational suffixes so often determine the part of speech of English words, we can conveniently classify them according to parts of speech. The meanings given for the suffixes are very broad. Often they have little connection with the meaning of the resulting word.

NOUN SUFFIXES	MEANING	EXAMPLES
Old English		
-dom	state, rank, condition	freedom, wisdom
-er	doer, maker	hunter, writer, thinker
-hood	state, condition	childhood, statehood
-ness	quality, state	softness, shortness
Foreign (Latin, French, Greek)		
-age	process, state, rank	passage, bondage
-ance, -ancy	act, condition, fact	acceptance, vigilance, hesitancy
-ard, -art	one that does (esp. excessively)	coward, laggard, braggart

NOUN SUFFIXES	MEANING	EXAMPLES
Foreign (Latin, French, Greek) (continued)		
-ate	rank, office	delegate, primate
-ation	action, state, result	occupation, starvation
-cy	state, condition	accuracy, captaincy
-ee	one receiving action	employee, refugee
-eer	doer, worker at	engineer, racketeer
-ence	act, condition, fact	evidence, patience
-er	doer, native of	baker, westerner
-ery	skill, action, collection	surgery, robbery, crockery
-ess	feminine	waitress, lioness
-et, -ette	little, feminine	islet, cigarette, majorette
-ion	action, result, state	union, fusion, dominion
-ism	act, manner, doctrine	baptism, barbarism, socialism
-ist	doer, believer	monopolist, socialist, capitalist
-ition	action, state, result	sedition, expedition
-ity	state, quality, condition	paucity, civility
-ment	means, result, action	refreshment, disappointment
-or	doer, office, action	elevator, juror, honor
-ry	condition, practice, collection	dentistry, jewelry
-tion	action, condition	creation, relation
-tude	quality, state, result	fortitude, multitude
-ty	quality, state	novelty, beauty
-ure	act, result, means	culture, signature
-y	result, action, quality	jealousy, inquiry

ADJECTIVE SUFFIXES	MEANING	EXAMPLES
Old English		
-en	made of, like	wooden, golden
-ful	full of, marked by	thankful, masterful
-ish	suggesting, like	childish, devilish
-less	lacking, without	helpless, hopeless
-like	like, similar	childlike, dreamlike
-ly	like, of the nature of	friendly, cowardly
-some	apt to, showing	tiresome, lonesome
-ward	in the direction of	backward, homeward
-y	showing, suggesting	hilly, sticky, wavy

ADJECTIVE SUFFIXES	MEANING	EXAMPLES
Foreign		
-able	able, likely	capable, affable, changeable
-ate	having, showing	animate, separate
-escent	becoming, growing	obsolescent, quiescent
-esque	in the style of, like	picturesque, statuesque
-fic	making, causing	terrific, soporific
-ible	able, likely, fit	edible, flexible, possible, divisible
-ose	marked by, given to	comatose, bellicose
-ous	marked by, given to	religious, furious

ADJECTIVE OR NOUN SUFFIXES	MEANING	EXAMPLES
-al	doer, pertaining to	rival, animal, autumnal
-an	one belonging to, pertaining to	human, European
-ant	actor, agent, showing	servant, observant, radiant
-ary	belonging to, one connected with	primary, adversary, auxiliary
-ent	doing, showing, actor	confident, adherent
-ese	of a place or style, style	Chinese, journalese
-ian	pertaining to, one belonging to	barbarian, reptilian
-ic	dealing with, caused by, person or thing, showing	classic, choleric
-ile	marked by, one marked by	juvenile, servile
-ine	marked by, dealing with, one marked by	marine, canine, divine
-ite	formed, showing, one marked by	favorite, composite
-ive	belonging or tending to, one belonging to	detective, native
-ory	doing, pertaining to, place or thing for	accessory, contributory

VERB SUFFIXES	MEANING	EXAMPLES
Old English		
-en	cause to be, become	deepen, darken

VERB SUFFIXES	MEANING	EXAMPLES
Foreign		
-ate	become, form, treat	populate, animate
-esce	become, grow, continue	convalesce, acquiesce
-fy	make, cause, cause to have	glorify, fortify
-ish	do, make, perform	punish, finish
-ize	make, cause to be	sterilize, motorize

Some of the words in the above lists make independent sense without the suffix (*employee, employ*). Others, however, do not (*delegate, deleg-*).

Because the English language has been exposed to so many different influences, the pattern of adding suffixes to form related words is often inconsistent. Things made of wood are *wooden*, but things made of stone are not *stonen*. We do have some regularities: verbs ending in *-ate* usually have a related noun ending *-ation (prostrate, prostration)*. We have such regular patterns as *differ, difference, differential, exist, existence, existential,* etc., but we have many other examples that are not so systematic. This irregularity is one reason why it is so important to learn related forms of the new words you add to your vocabulary. You cannot derive the noun form of *reject (rejection)* by knowing the noun form of *accept (acceptance)*. You have to learn it separately. In a sense, you do not really know a word until you know its important related forms.

EXERCISE 7. Writing Related Nouns of Specific Verbs. What nouns, if any, are companion forms of the following verbs? Write the noun after the proper number. Do not use gerunds.

EXAMPLES 1. convene 2. decode
1. *convention* 2. *decoder*

1. cavil
2. collate
3. demur
4. disburse
5. intercede
6. intervene
7. prescribe
8. proscribe
9. stultify
10. verify

EXERCISE 8. Writing Related Verbs for Specific Nouns. Number your paper 1–10. Give a related verb for each noun below if there is one. If there is no verb form, write 0 after the proper number.

1. asperity
2. austerity
3. complaisance
4. defection
5. notation
6. raillery
7. remission
8. remuneration
9. turpitude
10. verification

EXERCISE 9. Writing Related Adjectives for Specific Nouns and Verbs. Number your paper 1–10. Give a related adjective for each of the following nouns and verbs.

1. austerity
2. complaisance
3. deduce
4. increment
5. environment
6. essence
7. excess
8. prescience
9. prescribe
10. vituperate

Roots

A root is the core of a word—the part to which prefixes and suffixes are added. To find the root, you have only to remove any affix there may be. For example, removal of the affixes *a-* and *-ous* from *amorphous* leaves us with *-morph-*, a root meaning "form or shape." The root *-clysm*, meaning "falling," remains after we remove the prefix *cata-*, meaning "down," from *cataclysm*.

Roots have more specific and definite meanings than either prefixes or suffixes and appear in fewer different words. The following list contains some of the common foreign roots in English words.

ROOT	MEANING	EXAMPLES
Latin		
-ag-, -act-	do, drive, impel	agitate, transact
-agr-	field	agriculture, agrarian
-am-, -amic-	friend, love	amatory, amicable
-aqu-	water	aquatic, aqueduct, aquarium
-aud-, -audit-	hear	audible, auditorium
-ben-, -bene-	well, good	benefit, benediction
-brev-	short, brief	abbreviate, breviary
-cand-	white, glowing	candor, incandescent
-capit-	head	capital, decapitate
-cent-	hundred	century, centennial
-cid-, -cis-	kill, cut	suicide, regicide, incision

ROOT	MEANING	EXAMPLES
Latin (continued)		
-clin-	bend, lean	decline, inclination
-cogn-	know	recognize, cognizant
-cred-	belief, trust	incredible, credulity
-crypt-	hidden, secret	crypt, cryptic
-culp-	fault, blame	culpable, exculpate
-duc-, -duct-	lead	educate, conductor
-equ-	equal	equation, equanimity
-err-	wander, stray	erratic, aberration
-fac-, -fact-, -fect-, -fic-	do, make	facile, manufacture, defective, efficient
-fer-	bear, yield	transfer, fertile
-fid-	belief, faith	fidelity, perfidious
-fin-	end, limit	final, indefinite
-frag-, -fract-	break	fragment, fracture
-fus-	pour	transfuse, effusive
-gen-	birth, kind, origin	generate, generic
-jac-, -ject-	throw, hurl, cast	adjacent, eject
-jud-	judge	prejudice, adjudicate
-jug-	join, yoke	conjugal, conjugate
-junct-	join	junction, disjunctive
-jur-	swear, plead	adjure, perjury
-leg-, -lig-, -lect-	choose, read	eligible, legible, lectern
-loc-	place	locus, locale
-loqu-, -loc-	talk, speech	colloquial, locution
-magn-	large	magnitude, magnify
-mal-	bad	malady, malevolent
-man-, -manu-	hand	manicure, manual
-mit-, -miss-	send	remit, emissary
-mor-, -mort-	die, death	mortuary, immortal
-omni-	all	omnipotent, omniscient
-ped-	foot	pedal, quadruped
-pend-, -pens-	hang, weigh	appendix, suspense
-pon-, -pos-	place, put	postpone, interpose
-port-	carry, bear	transport, importation
-prim-	first, early	primitive, primordial
-punct-	point	punctuation, punctilious
-reg-, -rig-, -rect-	rule, straight, right	regent, incorrigible, rectangular
-rupt-	break	rupture, interrupt

ROOT	MEANING	EXAMPLES
Latin (continued)		
-sang-	blood	sanguine, consanguinity
-sci-	know, knowledge	omniscient, prescience
-scrib-, -script-	write	inscribe, proscribe, manuscript
-sent-, -sens-	feel	presentiment, sensitive
-sequ-, -secut-	follow	sequel, persecute, consecutive
-son-	sound	consonant, sonorous
-spir-	breath, breathe	expire, inspiration
-strict-, -string-	bind tight	constrict, stricture, stringent
-tract-	draw, pull	traction, extractor
-uni-	one	unity, universe
-ven-, -vent-	come	intervene, supervene
-verb-	word	verbal, verbiage
-vid-, -vis-	see	evident, television
-vit-	life	vitality, vitamin
Greek		
-anthrop-	man	anthropology, misanthropic
-arch-	ancient, chief	archaeology, monarch
-astr-, -aster-	star	astronomy, asterisk
-auto-	self	automatic, autonomy
-bibli-	book	bibliography, bibliophile
-bio-	life	biology, autobiography
-chrom-	color	chromatic, chromosome
-cosm-	world, order	cosmos, microcosm
-cycl-	wheel, circle	cyclone, bicycle
-dem-	people	democracy, epidemic
-gen-	kind, race	eugenics, genesis
-geo-	earth	geography, geology
-gram-	write, writing	grammar, epigram
-graph-	write, writing	orthography, geography
-hydr-	water	hydrogen, dehydrate
-log-	word, study	epilogue, theology, logic
-micr-	small	microbe, microscope
-mon-	one, single	monogamy, monologue
-morph-	form	amorphous, metamorphosis
-neo-	new	neologism, neolithic
-orth-	straight, correct	orthodox, orthography
-pan-	all, entire	panorama, pandemonium
-path-	feeling, suffering	apathy, pathology, sympathy

ROOT	MEANING	EXAMPLES
Greek (continued)		
-phil-	like, love	philanthropic, philosophy
-phon-	sound	phonology, euphony
-poly-	many	polygon, polygamy
-proto-	first	prototype
-psych-	mind	psychology, psychosomatic
-soph-	wise, wisdom	philosophy, sophomore
-tele-	far, distant	telegram, telepathy
-zo-	animal	zoology, protozoa

EXERCISE 10. Writing Words with Specific Roots. List two English words (other than those given as examples above) containing each of the following Latin roots.

EXAMPLES 1. -verb-
1. *adverb, verbose*

1. -aud- (hear)
2. -crypt- (hidden, secret)
3. -duc- (lead)
4. -fin- (end, limit)
5. -junct- (join)
6. -man-, -manu- (hand)
7. -mor-, -mort- (death)
8. -port- (carry)
9. -vid-, -vis- (see)
10. -vit- (life)

EXERCISE 11. Writing Words with Specific Roots. Follow the instructions for Exercise 10 for the following Greek roots.

1. -arch- (chief)
2. -auto- (self)
3. -bio- (life)
4. -chron- (time)
5. -cycl- (wheel, circle)
6. -dem-, -demo- (people)
7. -gram- (write, writing)
8. -hydr- (water)
9. -mega- (large)
10. -poly- (many)

Limitations of Word Analysis

Knowing something of the way in which prefixes, suffixes, and roots combine to form words provides insights into the history of our words and into their meanings. However, it would be misleading to suggest that the original meanings of the parts are always clearly reflected in a modern word.

It may happen that following the method of word division will lead you to a meaning that is so far from the modern one as to be of little help. For example, the words *admonition* and *monetary* have an element

(*-mon-*) in common. The first means "warning" and the second "pertaining to money." What is the connection? There is one, but it is remote: in ancient Roman times, money was coined in or near a temple of Juno, a goddess known as "the warner." This is interesting, but not much of a clue if you do not already know the meaning of both words. Word analysis can often help you to make a plausible guess at what a word may mean; it can rarely be absolutely depended upon.

Semantic Change

One obvious reason that word analysis does not always work as a way of finding meaning is that words change their meanings. This change in meaning—called *semantic change*—is extremely common.

There are several ways in which this change comes about. Sometimes a word that has had a general meaning comes to have a specific meaning. The word *starve* once meant "to die." It only later took on the special meaning of "to die from lack of food." In Old English, any crawling creature—including the dragon in *Beowulf*—could be called a *worm*. Now the word is used only to mean earthworms and the like.

Words also take on new meanings in the opposite way—from specific to general. Originally *barn* meant "a storage place for barley," and *lord* meant "loaf guard or bread keeper."

When a word acquires a new meaning, it may lose the old meaning, as *worm, starve,* and *lord* have. When this situation takes place, the word has become detached from the root meaning, although it retains the original root form. The *-jure* of *adjure* is related to *jury* and originally had to do with swearing in a legal sense. But usually the word now means "to entreat," and the meaning connection with the root has been lost.

Sometimes both old and new meanings are retained. Indeed, often it works out that a word will have six, eight, or ten meanings. Some of these meanings may be close to the original meanings of the word elements; some may vary from them considerably. The word *aegis* meant originally a shield or breastplate, especially one associated with the goddess Athena; then it also came to mean "protection" and "patronage, sponsorship." Depending on the context, it can mean any of these things in modern English. As a result, we may say that a lecture or exhibit is held under either the auspices—originally, bird watching—or the aegis—originally, shield—of a certain group. *Insular* means "pertaining to an island," but it has also come to mean "isolated, detached" and also "narrow, provincial." *Sanguine* may retain the root meaning and indicate "bloody," but it is more likely to mean "quite optimistic." Because there are so many situations involving semantic change, careful use of context clues or steady use of the dictionary is likely to give a more accurate sense of word meanings than word analysis alone.

EXERCISE 12. Writing the Original Meanings of Specific Words. List the following words and write after each its original meaning as given in the dictionary: *abeyance, challenge, derive, detriment, dirge, farce, lampoon, melancholy, monster, pedigree.*

USING EFFECTIVE DICTION

The word *diction* comes from the Latin *dicere,* meaning "to point out in words." Knowing that, you will not be surprised to learn that diction means two things—the words a speaker or writer selects and the specific ways in which the words are put to use. Diction may be either *formal* or *informal,* depending on its purpose.

If you are writing a report on the Civil War or on DNA, you will use formal diction. If you are writing a letter to a friend, you will use informal diction—probably with some informal expressions and slang, if slang is part of your personal "voice." If you write a profile of your neighborhood for a newspaper, you most likely will use formal diction, possibly with a few informal expressions but without slang. If you accept a young-adult magazine's invitation to write a book review of Isaac Asimov's *Foundation* series, you will choose diction that the young subscribers understand. Of course, if you write the same sort of review for an adult magazine, you will be free to use more complex words and discuss more complicated ideas.

Whatever the audience, your choice of words can make all the difference between a vigorous, clear writing style and a weak or ambiguous one. In each of the following pairs the first passage is vague and uninteresting; the second is detailed and vivid.

a. About half way between West Egg and New York the motor road goes alongside the railroad to avoid an ash dump.
b. About half way between West Egg and New York the motor road hastily joins the railroad and runs beside it for a quarter of a mile, so as to shrink away from a certain desolate area of land. This is a valley of ashes—a fantastic farm where ashes grow like wheat into ridges and hills and grotesque gardens. . . .

F. SCOTT FITZGERALD

a. The San Bernardino Valley is very different from the moist coast of California because it is subject to the hot winds from the Mojave Desert.
b. The San Bernardino Valley . . . is in certain ways an alien place; not the coastal California of the subtropical twilights and the soft westerlies off the Pacific but a harsher California, haunted by the Mojave just beyond the mountains, devastated by the hot dry Santa Ana wind that comes down through the passage at 100 miles an hour and whines through the eucalyptus windbreaks and works on the nerves.

JOAN DIDION

a. You don't know me unless you have read a book entitled *The Adventures of Tom Sawyer,* but that doesn't make any difference. That book was written by Mark Twain. He chiefly told the truth in that book, but I never knew anyone who told the truth all of the time.
b. You don't know about me without you have read a book by the name of *The Adventures of Tom Sawyer;* but that ain't no matter. That book was made by Mr. Mark Twain, and he told the truth, mainly. There was things which he stretched, but mainly he told the truth. That is nothing. I never seen anybody but lied one time or another, without it was Aunt Polly. . . .

MARK TWAIN

Notice that the professional writers are much more specific in their diction. Instead of vaguely relating that "the road goes alongside" the railroad, Fitzgerald tells us "it hastily joins" the railroad. Instead of writing that the road "avoids" the dump, he makes it "shrink away" from it.

Notice, too, that the professional writers often use figures of speech, comparing one thing to something else that seems quite different. Fitzgerald compares the valley of ashes to a farm that grows grotesque gardens—a figure of speech that ironically reminds us that ashes cannot grow anything.

The professionals also use sensory words to help us experience what they are describing. Didion tells us that the Santa Ana wind is "hot" and "dry" and that it "whines." The westerlies, on the other hand, are "soft." In addition to concrete words, Fitzgerald and Didion both draw on words with strong emotional effects: "desolate," "fantastic," "alien," "haunted," "devastated."

Mark Twain's diction would not be appropriate in a report to the chairman of the board in a corporation. However, the genius of his novel *Huckleberry Finn* is that Twain decided to use the conversational diction of his late-nineteenth-century hero, not the standard English of an impersonal narrator. Through this use of language, Twain makes his hero come alive.

Exact Meanings of Words

29d. Know the exact meanings of words.

Some fine distinctions among word meanings are interesting chiefly to purists. The following verse depends for its humor on the thin difference between the alligator and the crocodile:

THE PURIST

I give you now Professor Twist,
A conscientious scientist.
Trustees exclaimed, "He never bungles!"
And sent him off to distant jungles.
Camped on a tropic riverside,
One day he missed his loving bride.
She had, the guide informed him later,
Been eaten by an alligator.
Professor Twist could not but smile.
"You mean," he said, "a crocodile."

OGDEN NASH

We laugh at Professor Twist, who is more concerned with diction than with the fate of his wife. Despite Nash's mockery of the pedantic professor, however, we are obligated to be certain we are using the correct word in our speaking and writing.

Many words are spelled so much alike that they are easily confused —*dessert* and *desert*, for example. Other words have such subtle distinctions in meaning that a writer often carelessly chooses the wrong one—or really intends the sense of another, as in choosing *uninterested* when *disinterested* might be the proper choice.

EXERCISE 13. Choosing the Correct Words. Look up the words in parentheses below. Choose the word that best completes each sentence. Be prepared to give the meanings of the incorrect words.

1. Denise makes a big point of (flouting, flaunting) the rules.
2. "Scrambled" is a more (livid, vivid) verb than "went."
3. The old man looked at his first Christmas tree in (childish, childlike) wonder.
4. The spy received (oral, verbal) directions, rather than written ones.
5. Pulver (inferred, implied) that he would give up watching soap operas.
6. Cicero's name was on the (prescribed, proscribed) list, which meant he was a criminal who could be killed by anyone.

7. The Puritans believed that God was (immanent, imminent) in all of the natural world.
8. Ellsworth will (persecute, prosecute) his case against the fast-food chain.
9. Nora told yet another (anecdote, antidote) about her trip to Pikes Peak.
10. Which European leaders (capitalized, capitulated) to the Nazis?

Synonyms

29e. Recognize differences in meaning between synonyms.

Synonyms are words that have the same, or almost the same, meaning. We can say "a hard task" or "a difficult task," because *hard* and *difficult* are synonyms. We can say that New York is a large city or a metropolis, and *city* and *metropolis* are therefore synonyms.

It is often said that there are very few pairs of words in English that are entirely interchangeable, because there are usually slight but important differences between synonyms. Sometimes one synonym is noticeably more learned than another; *edifice* is more learned and pretentious than *building, domicile* more so than *home* or *residence. Daily* is the ordinary English word, *diurnal* and *quotidian* quite learned. Sometimes one of a pair of synonyms is noticeably informal; *smidge* or *smidgeon* is less formal than *particle.* Often learned words are rather specific in their suggestions; the sphere in which they can be used is narrow. Both *terrestrial* and *mundane* mean "pertaining to the world." But *terrestrial* is likely to suggest contrast between our world and other heavenly bodies, described by words like *lunar* and *solar;* and *mundane* carries with it suggestions of the practical, routine, everyday affairs of this world, as contrasted with more spiritual matters. Synonyms may differ, too, in expressing value judgments; to be *resolute* is a virtue; and to be *obstinate* is a fault.

The wealth of synonyms in English gives us a variety of ways of expressing ourselves, but challenges us to decide on the most appropriate of them.

EXERCISE 14. Understanding the Difference Between Pairs of Synonyms. Use each of the following words in a sentence which illustrates the specific meaning of each synonym.

1. donation, gift
2. venomous, toxic
3. vapid, inane
4. void, vacuum

5. reverent, pious
6. lean, gaunt
7. meditate, ruminate
8. gracious, cordial
9. congenital, hereditary
10. handle, manipulate

Mixed Idioms and Metaphors

29f. Avoid mixed idioms and metaphors.

An *idiom* is an expresson that is peculiar to a certian language and cannot be taken literally. We can say one thing when we mean another—for example, "lose your head"—and get away with it because everyone else knows the meaning we intend. We could not translate "make believe" and "fall for" literally and expect those idioms to make any sense. "Stephanie fell for Carl" does not mean that Carl was supposed to fall but Stephanie agreed to do it for him.

A *metaphor* is a comparison that shows a likeness between two otherwise dissimilar things. The "roof of the mouth," the "arm of the chair," the "foot of the table," the "nose of the plane" are all metaphors. William Shakespeare's "All the world's a stage," Psalm 23's "The Lord is my shepherd," and Emily Dickinson's "Hope is the thing with feathers" also are metaphors.

Sometimes people mix idioms or metaphors, often giving us absurd or humorous mental images as a result. For example, if you said that "The ship of state went into a tailspin," you'd be mixing two metaphors and calling up just such an image. A ship, of course, cannot go into a tailspin.

EXERCISE 15. Identifying Mixed Idioms or Metaphors. Tell what idioms or metaphors the writer is mixing in the following sentences. Then write a sentence explaining what each statement means.

1. In 1969 the moon became another place where "the hand of man had set foot."
2. A senator speaking about the American spirit: "It's vital to find out whether we will keep that spirit bright or let the light dim to keep the boat from rocking."
3. A memo from a corporate executive: "The President is sitting on a time bomb and he's running out of gas."
4. A legislator reports after a visit to constituents: "I've been keeping my ear to the grindstone."
5. An agency concerned with protecting the environment warns: "We're steamrolling our way down the drain."

Connotations and Loaded Words

29g. Learn to recognize connotations.

Semantics is the study of the meanings of words, changes in those meanings, and the *connotations* of words. When you are selecting the right words, you must be aware of their connotations. Connotations are the various emotions and associations that a word may suggest. A connotation is distinct from a word's *denotation,* which is the word's strict dictionary definition. Not all words have connotations. *Pen, paper, set, off,* and *listen,* as examples, suggest no particular emotions or associations. But such words as *skinny, slender, green, gray, intellectual,* and *egghead* do.

Connotations become attached to words through usage and common experience. The words *log cabin,* for example, refer literally to a dwelling made of logs. Suppose several people are looking at such a structure. One might think of it in terms of simplicity, strength, our pioneer past, and Abraham Lincoln. Another might describe it as a shack, associating it with poverty and unpleasantness. Yet another person might describe the dwelling as a "lodge," a word we associate with country retreats and hunting. Still another might see it as a "chalet," which suggests Switzerland and perhaps a ski resort.

Suppose you want to write about someone who is not working. You might refer to that person as "unemployed," "out of work," "at leisure," "at loose ends," or "between jobs." None of those terms have strongly negative connotations. If you described the person as a "freeloader" or a "moocher," however, your word choice would load your readers' feelings against the person.

The story is told that, during the Boer War, the Boers were described in the British press as "sneaking and skulking behind rocks and bushes." The British forces, when they finally learned from the Boers how to employ tactics suitable to veldt warfare, were described as "cleverly taking advantage of cover."

EXERCISE 16. Recognizing Connotations. The words in the following pairs have similar denotations, or dictionary definitions. Their connotations are different. Some differences in meaning are subtle; some are obvious. Which word in each pair has a positive connotation? Which suggests negative feelings? In a sentence, explain the distinctions between the words in the pair. In your sentence (or sentences), tell what emotions or associations are suggested by each word.

1. cautious / timorous
2. courageous / foolhardy
3. optimist / Pollyanna
4. hopeful / presumptive
5. lie / equivocate
6. concise / laconic
7. solemn / grim
8. guidance / manipulation
9. curious / nosy
10. freedom / license

EXERCISE 17. Defining Connotations. The names of animals often carry strong connotations, depending on characteristics we associate with them, whether or not those associations are based on scientific evidence. Tell whether each of the following names would have positive or negative connotations if applied to a person. What mannerisms or habits of each animal account for the name's emotional effect?

1. snake
2. owl
3. swine
4. lamb
5. worm
6. toad
7. bat
8. whale
9. skunk
10. cat

Loaded Words

29h. Learn to recognize loaded words.

Words or phrases that are heavily connotative are often referred to as *loaded* words. Because such words can be used to "slant" writing, they are often regarded with suspicion. Loaded words are often used in commercials and advertisements, where the intelligent consumer recognizes them as attempts to manipulate.

Connotation is an important element in our use of language, particularly when we want to express our own attitude toward a subject and possibly influence the attitude of our audience. Here, for example, are reports on a trial from two newspapers with different points of view about the defendant. Their biases are clearly shown in the way they "slant" their descriptions of testimony. The first newspaper's account:

> Deathly silence prevailed this morning in the courtroom when in a monotone Halevy described in detail what he saw. The jurors listened transfixed to Halevy's story and the feeling among observers was that this was David Halevy's day.

This is the other newspaper's description:

> The atmosphere in the court was one of exhaustion when *Time* correspondent Halevy continued giving evidence and described the period of heavy bombing of Beirut. Three of the ten members of the jury fell asleep and even the judge, Abraham Sofaer, yawned just before the noon break.

EXERCISE 18. Recognizing Loaded Words. The sentences in each of the following pairs have more or less the same denotative meaning yet suggest different feelings toward the subject. Which words load the sentences positively? Which words load the sentence negatively? Can you explain the emotions or associations attached to the "loaded" words in each sentence?

1. Lenahan dines every evening at 7.
2. Lenahan eats every night at 7.
3. The President has been obstinate as a negotiator.
4. The President has been firm as a negotiator.
5. Armand is fastidious about commas.
6. Armand is a nitpicker about commas.
7. The Nets squandered their ten-point lead.
8. The Nets lost their ten-point lead.
9. The subway was filled with the aroma of perfume.
10. The subway was filled with the stench of perfume.

EXERCISE 19. Using Connotative Meanings. Write two descriptions of a room, a meal, or a game. In one paragraph, use words that give your sentences positive emotional weight. In the other, use words that will give your readers negative feelings about the subject.

Colloquialisms

29i. Avoid colloquialisms in formal writing.

A colloquial writing style is the most informal style. It uses *colloquialisms*—words, idioms, and expressions that are characteristic of spoken English but not acceptable in formal written English. Dictionaries usually label colloquial usage (Colloq.). This label does not indicate that the usage is nonstandard or slang. Many colloquialisms have acquired enough permanence in the language to be accepted in informal writing. Writers of short stories, dramas, personal essays, plays, and even poems often use colloquialisms to create realistic dialogue and a convincing "voice." The following extracts use colloquialisms effectively.

> The most useful thing I could do before this meeting today is to keel over. On the other hand, artists are keeling over by the thousands every day and nobody seems to pay the least attention.
>
> KURT VONNEGUT

In the boondocks, we didn't wear shoes unless it was an absolute necessity.

GEORGE GRIZZARD

There were lots and lots of houses available. We heard this from a lady named Mrs. Black. . . . She took us to visit a house which would have been perfect for us and our books and our children, if there had been any plumbing.

SHIRLEY JACKSON

I used to get all revved up.

PHILIP BOOTH—THE NEW YORKER

These writers have deliberately used colloquial language to give their language a contemporary informal tone or add humor. But if you were writing a report for your history teacher, you would not say that "President Lincoln *keeled over* after John Wilkes Booth fired his shot." You would say he "collapsed" or "slumped over."

If you were writing a report for a corporation, you would not propose expanding its business "into the *boondocks.*" Notice in this case how imprecise the colloquialism is. This is a characteristic of colloquial language and is one of the reasons it is not acceptable in formal writing. In your corporate report, you would have to say exactly where you were proposing the expansion. By "boondocks," do you mean the suburbs, the small towns nearby, or the farming area?

If you were writing a report on *The Glass Menagerie,* you would not say that Laura has "*lots and lots* of insecurities." You would say she has "several insecurities," or "many," or "two main insecurities."

If you were writing a letter to a prospective employer, you would not say you were "*all revved up* about this *big deal* job." You would say you were "very excited about this important job."

In formal writing, then—in reports for school, in business letters, in office memos—you should avoid colloquial language. In your own informal writing, colloquialisms are acceptable as long as they express your meaning precisely.

EXERCISE 20. Replacing Colloquialisms with Formal Diction. Rewrite each of the following sentences, replacing each colloquial expression with precise formal diction. If you have any questions about which words or phrases are colloquial, check the dictionary.

1. Lillian has gobs of energy.
2. Ernesto says he has the stuff to be class president.
3. The *News* has pegged McNaughton as a man of action.

4. As an actress, Tina can deliver the goods.
5. Ellsworth fell for the guy's phony sales pitch.
6. The famous miser Silas Marner salted away his money for years.
7. The plan to make Madeline a beauty didn't pan out.
8. The salesman racked up a large bonus.
9. At 10:00 P.M. the boss called it a day.
10. Fred wore a stupid hat to the movie.

Slang

29j. Avoid slang in formal writing.

Slang consists of new words, or old words in new uses, that are vivid and colorful. High-school and college students enjoy adopting the latest slang. Most slang is short-lived. It enjoys a brief popularity and then is forgotten. For that reason, it is difficult to compile an illustrative list of slang terms that will be meaningful even a year later. The expressions in the following list were current a short while ago. How many of them do you recognize? Are any of them still in use?

SLANG

cool it	it's not my bag
groovy	heavy
uptight	nuts (crazy)
it's a drag	oddball
goof off	square
dig it	far out
cop out	bummer
off the wall	hang-up
bug off	weirdo
lousy	awesome

Occasionally a slang expression makes its way up the usage ladder and becomes acceptable even in formal writing, whereupon, of course, it is no longer slang. Slang should rarely be used in writing, and then only for a special purpose, as to reproduce dialogue. Although dictionaries label words *informal* or *slang,* you cannot rely on their arbitrarily drawn distinctions as a means of deciding whether a word is appropriate to your composition. A word that does not fit the general *tone* of your composition should not be used, regardless of its dictionary label.

The following sentences were taken from formal compositions. Note how inappropriate the italicized words are.

In any eighth-grade classroom where *kids* of the same chronological age are grouped together, we expect to find a physiological age range of six or seven years.

There is a grave danger that we may expose far too many students of only medium ability to the long course of professional study in our universities. The employment situation in some professional areas, we must admit, is *not so hot.*

Dickens' *bag* was to reveal the social evils of the day so that they could be destroyed one by one.

EXERCISE 21. Identifying Slang or Informal Language. Point out the words and expressions in the following passage that are slang or so informal as to be inappropriate to the general tone.

> While it is true that the students in the top ten percent of any grade are capable of doing good work in the grade above them, to undertake a general upward transfer of these students would produce more socially maladjusted kids than you could shake a stick at. Efforts to meet the problem by cutting out the arbitrary division of a school into grades have been successful in small schools, where the need to classify and control has not been great and where parents couldn't care less what grade their children are in. Today the schools that allow children to go at their own speed, with a child doing sixth-grade work in one subject and third- or fourth-grade work in another, are considered pretty far out. Eventually this method of school organization may become general practice.

Clichés

29k. Avoid clichés in formal writing.

A *cliché* is an expression so overused that it has become dull and nearly meaningless. The term comes from a French word for a plate used in printing. The same plate is used to make hundreds or thousands of impressions, all of them, of course, exactly alike. In the same sense, clichés are expressions used over and over again, lacking originality.

There are thousands of clichés in the English language. Many of them are figures of speech—metaphors, similes, or personifications. Many are hyperboles—exaggerations used for special effect. The expressions may have been considered original and forceful or amusing at one time, but overuse has dulled their effect. Here are three clichés based on figurative language:

cold as ice
fly off the handle
miss the boat

To say someone "flies off the handle" was once an original way of describing an erratic temper. The person with the temper might lose control and cause an uproar, just as an axe-head might cause a disturbance if it comes loose and flies off the handle when the tool is swung. To say someone "missed the boat" was once an original way of describing a person who missed out on a rewarding event or opportunity, just as a person who actually missed a boat would be deprived of a cruise.

Some clichés come to us so naturally that we use them without thinking. That is the point. They offer handy, ready-made comparisons and expressions. They help us avoid having to be original. In fact, clichés are so handy that it is often difficult to find fresh terms to replace them. We should try, nonetheless.

EXERCISE 22. Recognizing Clichés. The following interview with a cliché expert mocks our overuse of clichés. Read it and answer the questions that follow.

Q: You mean you get a handsome salary?

A: I prefer to call it a princely stipend. You know what kind of coin I'm paid in?

Q: No. What?

A: Coin of the realm. Not that I give a hoot for money. You know how I refer to money?

Q: As the root of all evil?

A: No, but you have a talking point there. I call it lucre—filthy lucre.

Q: On the whole, you seem to have a pretty good time, Mr. Arbuthnot.

A: Oh, I'm not complaining. I'm as snug as a bug in a rug. I'm clear as crystal—when I'm not dull as dishwater. I'm cool as a cucumber, quick as a flash, fresh as a daisy, pleased as Punch, good as my word, regular as clockwork, and I suppose at the end of my declining years, when I'm gathered to my ancestors, I'll be dead as a doornail.

Q: *Eh bien! C'est la vie!*

A: *Mais oui, mon vieux.* I manage, I'm the glass of fashion and the mold of form. I have a finger in every pie, all except this finger. I use it for pointing with scorn. When I go in for malice, it is always malice aforethought. My nods are significant. My offers are standing. I am at cross-purposes and in dire straits. My motives are ulterior, my circles are vicious, my retainers are faithful, and my hopefuls are young. My suspicions are sneaking, my glee is fiendish, my stories are likely. I am drunk.

Q: Drunk?
A: Yes, with power. . .

FRANK SULLIVAN

1. Identify at least five clichés in the interview that are based on figures of speech.
2. Rewrite a portion of the interview, replacing the clichés. Is it always clear what the cliché expert is saying?
3. Answer one of the interviewer's questions with a litany of clichés of your own.

EXERCISE 23. Replacing Clichés with Fresh Comparisons or Descriptions. Each of the following sentences contains a cliché based on a figure of speech. Eliminate the cliché and replace it with a fresh comparison or description of your own. (The directions in parentheses might help.)

1. Mildred is as straight as an arrow. (Describe Mildred's character without the cliché.)
2. The typist is as busy as a bee. (Describe the typist's movements without the cliché.)
3. Uncle Morty is as old as the hills. (Describe Uncle Morty so the reader gets a visual sense of his age without the cliché.)
4. The goalie is as tough as nails. (Describe the goalie's abilities and character, suggesting toughness, without the cliché.)
5. Uriah's hand feels as cold as ice. (Describe Uriah's handshake without the cliché.)

Jargon

29I. Avoid jargon in formal writing.

Jargon can have two meanings. First, it can refer to the specialized language of a particular group of people who do the same work or who have the same interests. Military personnel, computer users, editors, truck drivers, doctors, astronauts, and baseball players all have their own jargon. A waiter uses jargon when he calls into the kitchen, "Two eggs, wreck 'em!" An actress uses theater jargon when she says to a colleague going on stage, "Break a leg!" (In theater, this means "Good luck!") A sportswriter uses jargon in writing, "Carl Furillo popped out to shortstop."

In all these cases, jargon is perfectly acceptable. But jargon in a second sense is not acceptable in any kind of writing. That's when it consists of language that is incoherent and cumbersome, obscuring meaning rather than clarifying. This kind of jargon uses unnecessarily long and complicated words, often of Latin origin, as well as too many words to express a thought. Thus, this kind of jargon always delivers much less meaning than it seems to promise.

Here is a famous little proverb restated in jargon:

> A plethora of culinary specialists has a deleterious effect upon the quality of purees, consommés, and other soluble pabula.

In plain English this says:

> Too many cooks spoil the broth.

Can you translate the following jargon into the plain English of the original proverb?

> A mobile section of petrified matter agglomerates no bryophytes.

At times, a writer or speaker will use jargon deliberately to obscure an unpleasant meaning. He or she replaces a truth with a euphemism. Thus, people who steal computer programs are not called robbers or cheats but "pirates." Government bureaucrats refer to increased taxes as "revenue enhancement." A nuclear power plant official speaks of an "energetic disassembly" instead of an explosion, "rapid oxidation" instead of a fire, and of a "normal aberration" instead of a reactor accident. One state no longer has a Death Row; it has a "capital sentences unit." A large corporation recently circulated a memo that referred to "eliminating redundancies in the human resource area," instead of referring to layoffs or firing people.

Such pompous language is often called *gobbledygook,* a word coined by a United States Representative who had heard enough of such "official talk" in Congress. The origin of the word *jargon* also points to the emptiness of such use of language. The word is ultimately of "echoic" origin, meaning it reproduces a particular sound in nature. *Jargon* comes from a Middle French word meaning "a chattering of birds."

EXERCISE 24. Identifying Examples of Poor Diction. The following speech is a parody of the kind of speech a modern government official might write, if he or she were composing the Gettysburg Address today. That address, of course, is one of the greatest of all American speeches. It was delivered by President Abraham Lincoln at the dedication of the Soldiers' National Cemetery on November 19, 1863. The parodist's intent is not to mock the Gettysburg Address, but to contrast Lincoln's effective, eloquent diction with the kind of empty talk used by many politicians. Find the parody's examples of the misuses of diction that have been pointed out in this chapter—imprecise words, mixed idioms and metaphors, colloquialisms that are out of place in a formal speech, clichés, and jargon. Next to each example, write the simple, eloquent words used by Lincoln.

> I haven't checked these figures but 87 years ago, I think it was, a number of individuals organized a governmental set-up here in this country, I believe it covered certain Eastern areas, with this idea they were following up based on a sort of national independence arrangement and the program that every individual is just as good as every other individual. Well, now, of course, we are dealing with this big difference of opinion, civil disturbance you might say, although I don't like to appear to take sides or name any individuals, and the point is naturally to check up, by actual experience in the field, to see whether any governmental set-up with a basis like the one I was mentioning has any validity and find out whether that dedication by those early individuals will pay off in lasting values and things of that kind.
>
> Well, here we are, at the scene where one of these disturbances between different sides got going. We want to pay our tribute to those loved ones, those departed individuals who made the supreme sacrifice here on the basis of their opinions about how this thing ought to be handled. And I would say this. It is absolutely in order to do this.
>
> But if you look at the over-all picture of this, we can't pay any tribute—we can't sanctify this area, you might say—we can't hallow according to whatever individual creeds or faiths or sort of religious outlooks are involved like I said about this particular area. It was those individuals themselves, including the enlisted men, very brave individuals, who have given this religious character to the area. The way I see it, the rest of the world will not remember any statements issued here but it will never forget how these men put their shoulders to the wheel and carried this idea down the fairway.
>
> Now frankly, our job, the living individuals' job here, is to pick up the burden and sink the putt they made these big efforts here for. It is our job to get on with the assignment—and from these deceased fine individuals to take extra inspiration, you could call it, for the same theories about the set-up for which they made such a big contribution. We have to make up our minds right here and now, as I see it, that they didn't put out all that blood, perspiration and—well—that they didn't just make a dry run here, and that all of us here, under God, that is, the God of our choice, shall beef up this idea about freedom and liberty and those kind of arrangements, and that government of all individuals, by all individuals and for the individuals, shall not pass out of the world-picture.
>
> OLIVER JENSEN

REVIEW EXERCISE. Selecting the Definitions of Words. Number your paper 1–20. After the proper number, write the letter of the word or expression that comes closest to the meaning of the italicized word.

1. *amorphous* clouds — a) formless b) romantic c) jar-shaped d) commonplace
2. under the *auspices* of the state — a) protests b) sponsorship c) opposition d) observation
3. struggle for *autonomy* — a) fair treatment b) self-esteem c) survival d) self-rule
4. the last chance to *capitulate* — a) turn the tide b) surrender c) negotiate d) compromise
5. *circumspect* behavior — a) improper b) cautious c) surprising d) praiseworthy
6. to *collate* two documents — a) preserve b) seal up c) duplicate d) compare
7. feeling no *compunction* — a) satisfaction b) ambition c) remorse d) pride
8. to *conjecture* about a motive — a) guess b) mislead c) lie d) find out
9. the soldier's *defection* — a) weakness b) decoration c) desertion d) wound
10. not daring to *demur* — a) whisper b) appear c) object d) tell the truth
11. *devoid* of sympathy — a) full b) without a trace c) deserving d) undeserving
12. without *divulging* the answer — a) guessing b) revealing c) suspecting d) peeking at
13. to *expiate* a crime — a) profit from b) witness c) atone for d) facilitate
14. a *judicious* choice — a) illegal b) required by law c) wise d) laughable
15. a *minute* creature — a) short-lived b) quickly moving c) very small d) very young
16. *mundane* concerns — a) worldly b) tedious c) religious d) dishonest
17. *parasitic* followers — a) loyal b) living off others c) disloyal d) fanatical

18. a *propitious* start	a) proper b) false	c) sudden d) favorable
19. an unusual *pseudonym*	a) last name b) antonym	c) pen name d) honorary title
20. an act of *temerity*	a) cowardice b) rage	c) uncertainty d) foolish daring

Word List

Make it a habit to learn unfamiliar words from the following list regularly; ten each week is a practical number.

aberration
abeyance
abject
abnegation
abscond
absolve
abstruse
acrimonious
adjudge
adjure

admonish
adroit
affront
allay
amorphous
anarchy
antipathy
antipodes
apostasy
artifice

ascetic
ascribe
aspersion
assiduous
assimilate
atrophy
augury
auspices
austerity
avarice

aver
banal
bauble
bellicose
benevolence
biennial
blazon
bode
bravado
broach

buffoon
bullion
burnish
cadaverous
cajole
calumny
candor
capitulate
capricious
captivate

caricature
cessation
charlatan
chastise
chauvinism
chicanery
choleric
circumvent
civility
clandestine

coerce
cognizant
colloquy
commensurate
commiserate
commodious
conciliate
confer
configuration
connoisseur

consign
consternation
contingency
copious
corollary
corroborate
cosmopolitan
dearth
decorum
deduce

demagogue
denizen
deplore
desist
detriment
devoid
differentiate
dirge
discrepancy
discursive

disparity
dissent
distraught
diurnal
doggerel
dogma
duress
effusion
elegy
elicit

elocution
emaciate
emanate
empirical
engender
enigma
ennui
epitome
equanimity
equivocal

erudite
esoteric
espouse
ethereal
ethnology
eulogy
euphemism
euphony
evanescent
exhilaration

exhort
expatriate
expound
extant
extenuate
extol
extort
extraneous
extricate
facetious

facile
farcical
feign
festoon
fiasco
finesse
firmament
fissure
foible
foment

fortuitous
fresco
frugal
gambol
gauntlet
germane
glib
gratuitous
gregarious
guffaw

guile
hackneyed
harbinger
herculean
hiatus
homily
homogeneous
humdrum
hyperbole
idiosyncrasy

ignominy
illicit
immutable
impair
impassive
impeccable
incarcerate
incognito
inconsequential
incorrigible

indigent
indulgent
inexorable
infringe
ingenuous
iniquity
inordinate
inscrutable
intercede
introvert

inundate
inveigle
iridescent
irrevocable
lampoon
litigation
longevity
loquacious
ludicrous
lugubrious

magnanimous
maim
malign
malinger
maudlin
menial
mercurial
mesmerism
mete
misnomer

mollify
moot
mottled
mundane
munificent
nadir
nebulous
nefarious
nemesis
nettle

nondescript
nonentity
obese
obnoxious
obsequious
officious
omniscient
opulence
ostensible
pallor

proponent
propriety
prosaic
protégé
pseudonym
punctilious
purloin
quell
querulous
quiescent

scrupulous
scurrilous
sedentary
seraphic
solicitous
sonorous
specious
strident
subjugate
subversion

paragon
parsimonious
patrimony
pecuniary
perfidious
pervade
pestilence
phlegmatic
poignant
precocious

rampant
recant
refute
regimen
remonstrate
remuneration
renounce
repository
reprisal
residual

sumptuous
sundry
tacit
taciturn
temerity
tenable
tenuous
tenure
terra firma
testimonial

precursor
predispose
prerogative
prevaricate
primordial
proffer
progeny
prognosis
promontory
propitious

restitution
retaliate
retroactive
retrospect
revile
sagacity
salient
saline
sanguine
scathing

treatise
truism
usury
venal
venerate
vestige
vindicate
virulent
vociferous
voluminous

CHAPTER 30

Studying and Test Taking

WRITING TO LEARN AND TAKING TESTS

The writing requirements you face as a student might be even more complex than you have considered. They require a fairly wide range of skills.

Basically, you are called upon to summarize material, to take tests, and to write essays, either at home or during your exams. These activities require you to be good at comprehending what you read. You must have a good vocabulary and be a good speller, and you must know about such things as synonyms, antonyms, and verbal analogies. You must be able to recognize and correct errors, and you must be competent at revising sentences and organizing paragraphs.

WRITING THE PRÉCIS

A précis is a summary. It shortens some piece of writing—a passage, a chapter, an article, a report—to its bare essentials. In other words, the précis dispenses with all the examples, illustrations, quotations and other elements that fill out an author's basic points. It leaves only the central points themselves.

Précis-writing is an especially effective tool for sharpening your writing skills. It is also one of the best avenues to more attentive reading, since you must thoroughly understand material before you can summarize it.

In writing a précis, observe these rules:

1. *Be brief.* A précis is seldom more than a third as long as the material being summarized. It is often less than a third.

2. *Don't paraphase.* If you merely put each sentence of the original version in slightly different words, you will wind up with as much material as you had in the beginning.

3. *Stick to the central points of the material.* Avoid examples, illustrations, unnecessary adjectives, and repetitions.

4. *Use your own wording* instead of lifting phrases or sentences from the original.

5. *Be faithful to the author's points and views.* Don't insert your own ideas or comments, and don't use such expressions as "The author says" or "The paragraph means."

This is how to proceed with a précis:

1. Read carefully the material you are about to summarize. Keep reading it until you know precisely what it says. Look up any words or references you don't understand.

2. Write a brief sentence, in your own words, for each important point the author makes.

3. When you have gone all the way through the material, use your collection of sentences to write the rough draft of your précis.

4. Compare your rough draft with the original material, making sure you have accurately covered the important points.

5. Revise your draft until it is as concise and readable as you can make it.

Read the following paragraph two or three times. Then read the four précis of it given below. Each of them illustrates one major error in précis writing.

> The first thing that strikes the critical minority, as it looks at the whole cultural picture, is that ours is a nation of new-rich people, well washed, all dressed up, rather pathetically unsure just what it is washed and dressed up for; a nation convinced that a multitude of material goods, standardized, furiously and expensively advertised by appeals to greed and vanity, will in themselves make life worth the living. Because we are new-rich, we overvalue possessions. Almost any individual who makes a great deal of money very rapidly supposes that mere possession of wealth is evidence of worth. He also is apt to imagine that with his means he can buy happiness. These mistakes usually seem folly to the old-rich, to one who was born to property, whose father and mother were bred with it. Such a one knows that merely because he or his friends have it, it is no sign that they are worth it, but quite commonly the contrary. He has learned through experience that

money is not in itself very valuable stuff. Happiness, which is what all men desire, cannot be purchased; it is an illusive something not for sale. The old-rich know these things well enough, but the new-rich rarely discover them until they too have grown accustomed to possessions. So it seems to be with our society. We go in, almost without question and in all classes, for the sordid nonsense of supposing that externalities possessed ennoble the owners, that a full fist invariably indicates a fine spirit. [255 words]

Faulty Précis

1. Ours is a nation of new-rich people convinced that material goods will in themselves make life worth the living. Any individual who makes a great deal of money rapidly supposes that wealth is evidence of worth. He imagines that with his means he can buy happiness. These mistakes seem folly to one born to property. He knows that because he or his friends have it, it is no sign that they are worth it. Happiness, which all men desire, cannot be purchased. We go in for the nonsense that a full fist indicates a fine spirit. [96 words]

phrases and sentences merely copied from original

2. On the whole we are a nation of new-rich people who are well washed and well dressed, but we don't know what we're washed and dressed for. Our material goods are all standardized and expensively advertised. Advertisers appeal to our greed and vanity. We think these material goods are the means to wealth and happiness. The old-rich know that their friends aren't worth the money they have, but the new-rich don't know this until they have been rich for a while. [81 words]

précis misses point of original and emphasizes unimportant points

3. First, the critical minority says that we are a nation of new-rich people all dressed up with no place to go. We think the material goods advertised by appeals to our greed and vanity are what make life worth living. Anyone who makes a lot of

money thinks his money shows his worth and believes that it will make him happy. The old-rich, however, think that these ideas are foolish. Born into a rich family with property, these people know that money and property don't make them any better people. They know that the opposite is frequently true. They know that money in itself isn't worth much and that it won't buy happiness, which is the thing everyone wants. The new-rich, however, don't know these things until they have been rich long enough to find them out. Almost everyone, regardless of social class, believes that possessions make their owners better, and the more you have the more worthy you are. This is nonsense. [163 words]

précis too long—nearly two-thirds the length of original

4. The critical minority says we are a nation of new-rich people who are victims of newspaper, magazine, and television advertising which, by appealing to our greed and vanity, tries to convince us that all we need for happiness is a lot of possessions. We don't need most of the advertised stuff such as appliances, cars, and fur coats, but the rest of the world judges our worth by what we have. In many other countries, people don't have the material goods we have. We can't all be as lucky as the old-rich, who don't have to worry about money because they already have it. [104 words]

writer of précis injected own ideas

Acceptable Précis

Critics of American culture see us as a new-rich people who, because we are new-rich, think that material goods make life worth living. We think that money is an indication of worth and that wealth brings happiness. The old-rich know better.

ideas stated in précis writer's words

Born to property, they do not believe that just because they have it, they are worth it. They know that happiness cannot be bought. The new-rich, however, mistakenly believe that possessions indicate the worth of their owner. [78 words]

less than one-third the length of original

EXERCISE 1. Writing Précis. As your teacher directs, use the following passages for practice in précis writing.

1

Rapidity in reading has an obvious direct bearing on success in college work, because of the large amount of reading which must be covered in nearly all college courses. But it is probably also a direct measure of the special kind of aptitude which I am calling bookish, because rapidity of reading usually correlates with comprehension and retention. Generally speaking, the more rapidly a reader reads, the more effectively he grasps and retains. The median reading speed of college freshmen has been found to be around 250 words a minute on ordinary reading matter, and a student who reads more slowly than that will certainly have difficulty in completing his college tasks within reasonable study periods. To be a really good college risk under this criterion one should readily and habitually cover not fewer than 300 words a minute on ordinary reading matter. [143 words]

2

The major struggle between writer and subject is fought here, in the arena of reputation. A biographer may or may not choose to reveal the intimate, amorous details of a life, but he must, if he is good at what he does, probe beneath its public self. The doubts and vulnerabilities, the meannesses, ambitions, and private satisfactions that are hidden within a social personality yield him his greatest insights. Seeking to reveal what his subject filters out as unworthy or perhaps only as uninteresting, he becomes for him, we have seen, an adversary to be frustrated, coopted, or even outsmarted ("It will read charmingly in your biography," Jane Carlyle wrote bitingly of an insincere letter from her husband). A life taken only at its own crafted word is imperfectly and even unjustly rendered. Fine biography challenges the pose to find the personality. [145 words]

3

Ever since a group of men first developed a government, there have been opposing ideas of the relation between the state and its members. One view puts the state above the individual. The individual has no existence except as a member of the community, carrying out its will, living for its welfare, ready to die in its service. He is not supposed to separate his identity or his personal profit from that of the nation. The community has a right to interfere in his affairs; he has no private life in which it is bound not to interfere. The state is more than the sum of its members. Its continuance must be assured at whatever cost. The state is a *totality* in which they are completely submerged. This view of the state is held by all absolute rulers, including modern dictators. We usually speak of it as *totalitarianism* or *fascism*. It prevails over a large part of the world.

The other view puts the individual above the state. The state exists for the individual, not the individual for the state. The government has no other purpose than to serve the people; they may alter its form or, if need be, revolt against it, should it fail to carry out their wishes. Public and private life are quite distinct. The state may not interfere with the individual's private life so long as he does no injury to others. The individual has numerous rights which the state may not restrict except to protect the rights of other individuals. This view came to be widely held in England and northern Europe in the 1600's and 1700's; from there it spread to the New World. It took shape in the democratic form of government. [295 words]

4

What is strange about this new passivity, regarding both travel and broadcasting, is that not so long ago the reverse was considered normal; that is, flying was once a highly participatory activity—as was automobile driving, as was broadcasting. Thirty-five years ago, the driver of an ordinary car was intimately involved with the event of driving, by means of direct access to his steering wheel, brakes, transmission, and the outside environment. In the same period, a listener to Edward R. Murrow's broadcasts from London was directly involved with the event of broadcasting as well as the events of the Second World War that Murrow was describing. Since then, however, the automobile driver has given up his direct involvement in favor of power controls, automatic transmissions, and sealed-in passenger interiors, while the television audience has largely given up its involvement with drama and news in favor of undemanding, mechanical entertainment and uninvolving news. Nowadays, only aggressive people insist on direct, or participatory, driving, by means of sports cars; at least they are owned by people who are willing to appear aggressive. And only an aggressive minority, perhaps of a different, cultural, nature, appears to prefer participatory television, such as the music and serious drama programs that now and then are shown on public television. [215 words]

WRITING IN OTHER COURSES

30a. Use writing to explore concepts and topics in your science courses.

Writing about concepts and topics from a content-area subject, such as a science course, can enable you to understand the class better. Book reviews and journals are two forms of writing you can use to improve how you learn course content.

A book review examines and evaluates the contents of a book. You can write book reviews about fiction or nonfiction works that discuss scientific periods, discoveries, figures, or events. By doing so, you combine your scientific understanding and your judgment of how well a writer treats a particular concept.

Like other kinds of critical reviews, a book review in a science course should discuss the work's major points. It should also present your evaluation of the work's strengths and weaknesses, supported by specific details from the work itself and from reference works.

Begin your work on a review by doing a close reading of the book. As you read, take careful notes about important details and concepts in the book. Decide which major points you should discuss, and decide what your evaluation of the work is. Review your notes to locate specific details that support your views.

You should also consult reference works and other sources on the same subject to check the accuracy of the book you are reviewing. Then, write your book review. As you plan and write your review, keep the following questions in mind:

- *How does this book broaden your knowledge or your understanding of science?*
- *How does this work enable you to better grasp the content of your science course?*
- *Does the author present a biased, or slanted, view of the subject—and if so, how is this bias justified?*
- *In a fictional work, how probable and believable is the role of science and technology?*

After you write your review, evaluate, revise, and proofread it—just as you would with any other piece of writing.

If you want to write a book review about a fictional work, remember that science fiction is especially appropriate for a book review in a science course. For example, you might consider reviewing works by Isaac Asimov, Arthur C. Clarke, and Ursula K. LeGuin. If you choose to review a nonfiction work, you will find many possible choices, including works like Tracy Kidder's study of computers, *The Soul of a New Machine,* and Lewis Thomas's collection of essays, *The Lives of a Cell: Notes of a Biology Watcher.* Whether you review a fiction or a nonfiction work, try to select a book that has some relation to the content of your science course.

Another way to use writing in a science course is to keep a journal, just as you might keep a writer's notebook in an English class (see page 360). For example, as you conduct an experiment, you can record the specific procedures you follow, the results you observe, and your reactions to each phase of the experiment. You can also discuss why procedures succeeded or failed, and you can try to account for unexpected results. Journal entries like these can provide the information for a laboratory report about the experiment, using the format your science teacher provides. You can also use your journal to record field studies, demonstrations, and other class activities.

You can also use your journal to discuss the scientific concepts and topics you are studying. For example, you might write a journal entry about any of the following concepts:

- *Explain the differences between nuclear fission and nuclear fusion.*
- *Describe the process of mitosis.*
- *Discuss three practical applications of the laws of aerodynamics.*

By writing about scientific information you are studying, you can organize your thoughts and discover where your understanding needs to be improved. You can also practice applying your knowledge of expository writing to answering essay questions or to writing compositions in your science courses.

To improve your writing in all of your courses, always be sure to use what you have learned about the writing process in Chapter 23.

EXERCISE 2. Writing in Science. Following the steps in the writing process, complete one of the activities below.

1. Write a book review of a fiction or nonfiction work about a scientific concept, event, or figure. In your review, answer at least one of the questions on page 550.
2. For several days, keep a journal about the progress of an experiment, field study, or class demonstration. Write a brief essay that summarizes the procedures and results of the experiment and the specific ways that this activity added to your scientific knowledge.
3. Prepare a journal entry about any concept you are studying. Use one of the above three concepts or one your teacher suggests.

TAKING TESTS

No matter what your plans for the years following high school, you will most likely be asked to "take some tests." The most commonly administered tests include measures of verbal fluency, reading comprehension, and/or grammar and composition.

Among the tests of this type used for college entrance, the best known are probably the *Scholastic Aptitude Test—Verbal,* or SAT—V (including the *Test of Standard Written English*), and the *English Composition Test,* or "English Achievement" test. Both are administered by the College Entrance Examination Board. Another well-known test is the *American College Testing Program* (ACT) *Assessment Test.*

Some schools and colleges do *not* require tests for admission but do administer tests for placement in courses and for guidance purposes. The military and other employers may also administer tests of English language skills for certain jobs.

Tests with the word *aptitude* in their titles are used mainly to predict future success, whether in school or on the job. They do not, on the whole, measure what you have learned in particular courses. They measure the language skills which you have been developing all your life. *Achievement* tests, on the other hand, concentrate on specific skills and information which you have learned in academic courses.

Cramming is *not* an appropriate or helpful way to prepare for tests of this nature. There are, however, a number of good test-taking practices that will help you to do your best on any examination. These may be summarized as follows:

SUMMARY OF TEST-TAKING PRACTICES

1. Take a positive approach to the test.
   a. Try to do your best even though you may be nervous. Don't panic.
   b. Regard lapses of memory as normal. If you "block" on a certain question, go on and come back to it later if you can.
   c. Don't expect to answer every question correctly. Some of the tests are built so that the average student will answer only about half of the questions correctly.
2. Use your time wisely.
   a. Look over the test before you start to work. Get a feel for its length and difficulty.

b. Plan your time. If you have a time limit of 20 minutes for a 40-question test, check that you are on or beyond question 21 after 10 minutes. But avoid too much clock-watching; it uses up your time and heightens anxiety.
c. Work rapidly but carefully. Answer the easy questions first. If you don't know an answer right away, leave it and go on.
d. If you have time after finishing the test, try some of the questions you left out the first time. (On the ACT, you are not penalized for guessing.)

3. Avoid careless errors.
   a. Pay close attention to directions. Do the sample questions even though you're sure you understand the task.
   b. Read each question carefully. Be sure you know exactly what it is asking you to do.
   c. Look at all the choices before you answer. In many cases the correct answer is not *absolutely* correct; it is the *best* among the choices.
   d. Avoid careless mistakes in marking the answer sheet. Keep it lined up with the booklet if possible. The scoring machine can't tell when you were "off" by one question or one row.
   e. If you change an answer, be sure you erase the first answer thoroughly. If the machine "reads" both marks, it will count the question as unanswered.

One of the best ways to prepare for any test is to become familiar with the types of tasks you will be asked to perform. Many test questions will be familiar, while others may be new to you. The purpose of this chapter is to show you some of these question types.

TESTS OF WORD KNOWLEDGE OR VOCABULARY

Vocabulary tests measure your understanding of the meanings of words, either in isolation or in context. Often, the relationships among words—the way they are related in meaning—will be tested. Examples of three types of vocabulary questions follow.

Word Meanings

The simplest type of vocabulary question asks you the meaning of a word. Usually, the format is an incomplete statement to which you add one of several choices to complete the meaning. The following is a sample question of this type.

EXAMPLE **A** To whet one's appetite is to ——

a wean it
b salve it
c sharpen it
d appease it
e dampen it

Answer:[1]

A ⓐ ⓑ ● ⓓ ⓔ

Some questions of this type ask for a choice between *phrases* explaining the word's meaning or use; others offer *single words* and ask you to choose a synonym of the key word.

EXERCISE 3. Choosing the Correct Meaning. Read the beginning of each sentence below and the choices that follow it. Choose the answer which best completes the sentence.[2]

1 A person who is talkative is ——

a fervent
b reticent
c jocular
d loquacious

2 To be nimble is to be ——

a gracious
b agile
c numb
d earthy

3 Material you can see through is called ——

a opaque
b potential
c imaginary
d transparent

[1] Answer: ⓒ *sharpen it.* When you have marked your answer sheet for ⓒ, this is the way it will look. You will black in the circle containing the letter of the correct answer. Answers are shown this way for all sample test items throughout this chapter.

[2] Answers for this and all the following exercises will be found on pages 573–74.

4 Something that is powerful must be ——

- **a** lavish
- **b** lenient
- **c** potent
- **d** malicious

5 To condense something is to ——

- **a** abridge it
- **b** accelerate it
- **c** abolish it
- **d** acclaim it

Synonyms and Antonyms

In a test on synonyms or antonyms you are asked to select, from four or five choices, the word *most similar* in meaning (synonym) to the word given *or* the word *most nearly opposite* in meaning (antonym). *Pay attention!* These are sometimes mixed together. There are few true synonyms or antonyms in English; the "correct" answer, therefore, is the one most nearly the same or most nearly the opposite in meaning.

Following are two sample questions in which you are to find the word *most similar* in meaning (synonym) to the underlined word.

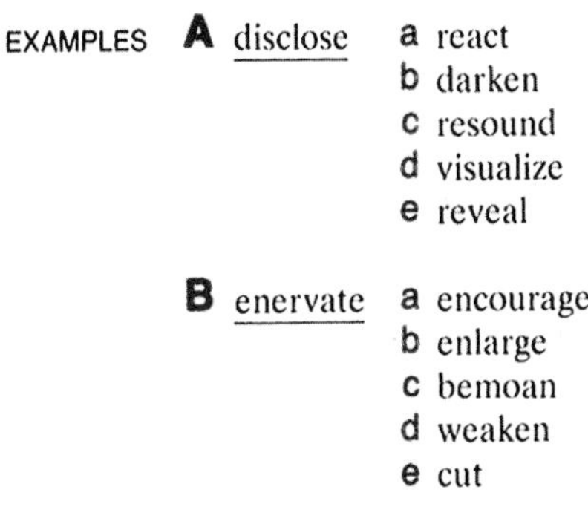

EXAMPLES **A** <u>disclose</u>

- **a** react
- **b** darken
- **c** resound
- **d** visualize
- **e** reveal

B <u>enervate</u>

- **a** encourage
- **b** enlarge
- **c** bemoan
- **d** weaken
- **e** cut

Answer:

A ⓐ ⓑ ⓒ ⓓ ●
B ⓐ ⓑ ⓒ ● ⓔ

The last question includes a common misconception of the word's meaning among the choices. Many people are confused as to whether *enervate* means to take "nerve" away or to give it; hence *encourage* is given as an incorrect choice.

EXERCISE 4. Choosing the Antonym. For each of the following questions, choose the word *most nearly opposite* in meaning (antonym) to the underlined word.

1 abstract
- a extract
- b general
- c concrete
- d ideal
- e difficult

2 chronic
- a occasional
- b habitual
- c public
- d unimportant
- e healthy

3 detriment
- a complement
- b loss
- c damage
- d attribute
- e benefit

4 abate
- a fall
- b shrink
- c subside
- d increase
- e release

5 transient
- a swift
- b permanent
- c polite
- d sure
- e passenger

Verbal Analogies

Analogies measure your understanding of relationships among words. Here is a sample set of directions and one question.

EXAMPLE In the items below, the first and second words are related in a certain way. The third word is related in the same way to one of the four words which follow it. You are to choose the word related to the third word in the same way that the second word is related to the first.

A *Inch* is to *foot* as *ounce* is to ——

a weight
b meter
c yard
d pound

Answer:

A ⓐ ⓑ ⓒ ●

In this sample question, the relationship tested is that of a unit of measurement to a larger unit in the same scale. An inch is a division of a foot. The correct answer is *pound,* since an ounce is a division of a pound.

Analogies may also be presented as shown in the following example:

EXAMPLE Below is a list of five pairs of related words. Choose the pair of words whose relationship is most like that of the first pair.

A INCH : FOOT ::

a quart : measure
b weight : peck
c ounce : pound
d mile : length
e meter : yard

Answer:

A ⓐ ⓑ ● ⓓ ⓔ

Again, *ounce* is related to *pound* as *inch* is related to *foot.* But here you are to find the whole pair. In the first example, the first part of the second pair was given to you. It may help to turn them into sentences such as the one in the first example.

Suppose the first pair of words were *glance* and *gaze.* Both name ways of looking at something. But a *glance* is a quick look, while *gaze* has the idea of a long or thoughtful look. Which of these pairs of words, then, has the most similar relationship?

EXAMPLE **A** GLANCE : GAZE ::

a blink : scowl
b glimpse : stare
c observe : note
d skim : peek
e peruse : study

Answer:

A ⓐ ● ⓒ ⓓ ⓔ

Option b presents the pair which completes the analogy, since *glimpse* also implies a quick once-over and *stare* gives the notion of a long and concentrated look. Another way to check your understanding of the analogy is to compare the first and third parts, and then check to see if the second and fourth parts have the same relationship. In the original example, this check would take the form: "*Inch* is to *ounce* as *foot* is to —— ?"

EXERCISE 5. Completing Analogies. In the items below, the first and second words are related in a certain way. The third word is related in the same way to one of the five words which follow. Choose the word related to the third word in the same way as the second word is related to the first.

1 *Clear* is to *cloudy* as *definite* is to ——

a sunny
b vague
c bright
d positive
e short

2 *Reckless* is to *cautious* as *rash* is to ——

a hasty
b impudent
c careless
d prudent
e smooth

3 *Gaggle* is to *goose* as *pride* is to ——

a lion
b vain
c king
d bear
e eagle

4 *Calm* is to *storm* as *quell* is to ——

a traffic
b crowd
c ink
d riot
e nerve

5 *Encourage* is to *scold* as *chide* is to ——

a punish
b praise
c query
d insult
e forbid

In the following items, choose the pair of words whose relationship is most similar to that of the first pair given.

6 LIMP : WALK ::

a snore : sleep
b walk : ride
c whistle : sing
d stutter : speak

7 QUARRY : STONE ::

a rock : mineral
b mine : ore
c soil : field
d oil : drill

8 SALVE : WOUND ::

a eraser : pencil
b drink : thirst
c save : money
d sword : scabbard

9 LAVISH : STINGY ::

a quick : average
b late : earlier
c bright : brightest
d profuse : grudging

10 RELEVANT : PERTINENT ::

a wasteful : efficient
b thoughtful : reasonable
c implicit : explicit
d quiet : slow

READING ACHIEVEMENT

Your grasp of the meaning of what you read is often measured in tests for school or vocational guidance. Reading abilities are usually measured in one of the two ways described below.

Sentence Completion

This question format could be called "fill in the blanks." Sentences are presented with one or two blanks, each indicating that a word has been left out. You are to choose the word which fits best in the sentence.

EXAMPLE **A** We laughed at the clown —— he performed funny tricks.

a but
b until
c because
d unless
e although

Answer:

The sentence clearly calls for a conjunction, but the only one that makes any sense is *because.* Questions like this look for your ability to recognize the logic and coherence of the sentence—one aspect of comprehension.

Reading Comprehension

Reading tests are not concerned with testing whether you understand, word by word, what you have read, but rather how well you can draw conclusions and make judgments about what you read. The questions about the passage you read should not require outside information, but should be based upon the information within the passage itself. Here is a sample passage followed by three questions.

EXAMPLE Two days after his sudden death on June 9, 1870, Charles Dickens was honored in a *New York Times* obituary covering more than five of the seven long columns on the front page. The length of this article accurately reflected Dickens' position among the American reading public of a century ago, when entire households waited anxiously from month to month to discover the fate of Little Nell, or Oliver Twist, or whichever Dickensian hero figured in the novel currently being serialized for United States audiences. In later years, the novelist's reputation diminished; critics dismissed him as a "popular" writer rather than a true craftsman. His remarkably vivid characterizations were considered caricatures, even though numerous outstanding writers such as Feodor Dostoevski, Joseph Conrad, and Henry James expressed their indebtedness to "the master." But during the 1940's, writers like Franz Kafka and Edmund Wilson brought readers to a fresh awareness of Dickens' unforgettable delineations of personalities whose very names—Scrooge, for instance—have assumed an independent meaning for people around the world. Readers today are also impressed by Dickens' vision, more than 100 years ago, of what the modern city was to become. For Dickens' London was a place of smoke and filth and a decaying social fabric, rather than the rich, bustling, upper-class London of virtually all his contemporaries.

A The main thrust of this article has to do with ——

a modern attitudes towards Dickens
b Dickens' descriptions of London
c changes in Dickens' literary reputation
d Dickens' treatment of fictional characters

B Dostoevski, Conrad, and James indicated that ——

a their writing was influenced by Dickens
b Dickens wrote for a lower-class public
c they had learned about London from Dickens
d Scrooge was a caricature

C Apparently other British authors of Dickens' day ——

a were upper-class Londoners
b ridiculed Dickens' London
c believed Dickens an expert on city life
d pictured London as an attractive place to live

Answer:
A ⓐ ⓑ ● ⓓ
B ● ⓑ ⓒ ⓓ
C ⓐ ⓑ ⓒ ●

These sample questions illustrate several types that may be asked. Question A, for example, asks for the main idea of the passage. Question B asks for a restatement of an idea clearly stated in the passage. And question C asks for an inference which the reader must draw from the passage. Other types of questions may ask for the meaning of a term or phrase as used in the passage, a recognition of the author's intent, or the identification of bias, exaggeration, or value judgments.

EXERCISE 6. Drawing Conclusions from Reading. After reading the following passage, answer the questions given at its conclusion.

The computerized age in which we live, while enabling us to land people on the moon and accomplish vast feats of arithmetical figuring in seconds, has raised many new problems. One of these, according to Dr. Lee McMahon, a psychologist at the Bell Telephone Laboratories, is the need for communication between computers and between humans and computers. In order to facilitate such communication, Dr. McMahon developed, in 1966, a new "language" designed to eliminate computer confusion about the relation of words in a sentence. The language is called FASE, for Fundamentally Analyzable Simplified English, and although at first it appears indistinguishable from ordinary English prose, it is actually quite different, for FASE reduces English to a strict form in which syntax is absolutely clear and free of ambiguity. The resulting grammatical structures can be broken down easily by a computer, while ordinary English cannot. For example, consider how a computer would interpret the phrase "time flies." The computer would have to decide whether this meant "time speeds by" or "clock the speed of certain insects," and such a choice, unaccompanied by human guidance, is beyond the capacity of even the most advanced computers. But a computer programmed to "read" FASE would have no trouble with the phrase, for FASE is based on a strictly maintained sequence of subject, verb, and object, with other parts of speech falling regularly into line. FASE lacks the beauty of English, then, and its spontaneity, but can be very useful in indexing scientific documents, which would be punched on cards and stored in a computer until needed. Locating a particular subject would be a comparatively simple matter for the computer, since there would be no ambiguity of meaning. "Time flies," for instance, would be "FASE-indexed" under time, rather than speed or insects.

1 FASE was developed by a ——

a psychologist
b computer programmer
c physician
d linguist

2 A FASE-programmed computer could correctly interpret the phrase "time flies" because ——

a the phrase is an idiom
b computers work so speedily
c the phrase contains a verb
d the subject comes before the verb

3 Sentences written in FASE are probably rather ——

a ambiguous
b idiomatic
c boring
d spontaneous

4 The writer implies that a computer's ability to make decisions is ——

a unlimited
b limited to choices about grammar
c nonexistent, even in sophisticated machines
d controlled by the use of FASE

5 In which of the following lines is a value judgment expressed?

a lines 24–25
b lines 27–28
c line 7
d line 16

STANDARD WRITTEN ENGLISH

The best way for someone to "test" your ability to write standard English is to have you write. This is not always practical, so multiple-choice tests have been developed to measure your knowledge of correct spelling and usage, your skill in organizing material, and your sensitivity to nuances of tone, style, and choice of words. The paragraphs which follow give examples of some of the more commonly used methods of testing skills in standard written English.

Spelling

Spelling may be tested in any number of ways. One of the most common formats consists of four words, one of which may be misspelled. You are to indicate the word spelled incorrectly or mark a choice indicating no errors. Another type of question involves the misuse of homonyms —words which sound alike but differ in spelling and meaning, such as *to, too*, and *two*. In this sort of test question, four phrases with different homonyms are usually given, and you are asked to choose the phrase in which a homonym is used correctly or incorrectly.

EXAMPLE **A** a *too* hot
b grizzly *bear*
c *peace* of pie
d rough *seas*

Answer:
A ⓐ ⓑ ● ⓓ

EXERCISE 7. Identifying Misspellings. For each of the following questions, choose the one word that is misspelled. If no word is misspelled, mark the answer N for no error.

1
a seize
b percieve
c righteous
d salutary
N

2
a ruse
b laughter
c explannatory
d traveler
N

3
a bumble *bee*
b *bowl* weevil
c string *bean*
d acting *troupe*
N

4
a bare *feet*
b boat's *sail*
c *bail* of hay
d filet of *sole*
N

5
a pint of *beer*
b carving *board*
c *right* to work
d wild *hoarse*
N

Error Recognition

Error recognition questions ask you to detect or correct errors in written passages. Some questions ask you only to indicate that an error is present; others ask you to specify the type of error it is. Here are samples of three types of questions.

EXAMPLES TYPE 1.

Mark the letter of the line containing an error in spelling, punctuation, capitalization, grammar, or usage. If there is no error, mark N for no error.

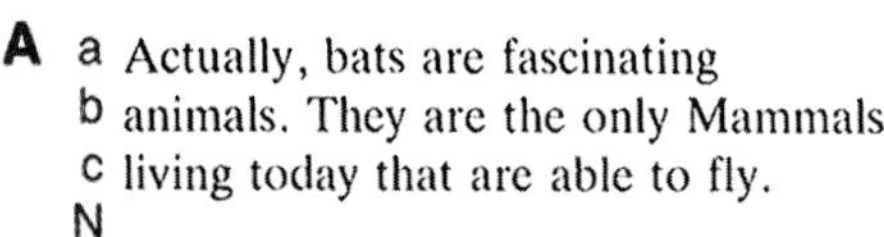

A
a Actually, bats are fascinating
b animals. They are the only Mammals
c living today that are able to fly.
N

Answer:

TYPE 2

Mark the letter of the underlined part that must be changed in order to make the sentence correct. (Be sure to note whether underlining includes the punctuation.) If there is no error, mark *e*.

B During <u>the colonel period,</u> (a) many colonies had <u>their own flags,</u> (b) the <u>earliest of which</u> (c) was based on <u>the British flag.</u> (d) <u>No error</u> (e)

Answer:

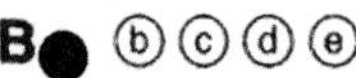

TYPE 3

Some of the sentences below contain errors; others are correct as they stand. For each sentence, mark your answer sheet:

a —if the sentence contains an incorrect choice of words (error in diction)
b —if the sentence is wordy (verbose or redundant)
c —if the sentence contains an overworked expression (cliché) or mixed metaphor
d —if the sentence contains an error in grammar or structure
e —if the sentence is correct as it stands

1 Each day it was a daily occurrence to see the mail truck arrive.

2 The mass of detail is not penitent to the question at hand.

3 The young man was fit as a fiddle as he started work.

Answer:

1 ⓐ ● ⓒ ⓓ ⓔ
2 ● ⓑ ⓒ ⓓ ⓔ
3 ⓐ ⓑ ● ⓓ ⓔ

EXERCISE 8. Identifying Errors in Written English. Following the appropriate set of directions, record your answers to each of the following questions.

TYPE I. Mark the letter of the line containing an error in spelling, punctuation, capitalization, grammar, or usage. If there is no error, mark N for no error.

1 a Russias woman astronaut may have been
b the first woman to explore outer space,
c but she wasn't the first woman explorer.
N

2 a As long ago as 1805, woman were helping
b men find their dangerous way across
c the uncharted Rocky Mountains.
N

3 a Sacajawea whose name means "Bird Woman," was
b only 13 when she was captured by a tribe of
c enemies.
N

4 a She was living with them in North Dakota
b when Lewis and Clark asked her help
c in accomplishing this difficult feat.
N

5 a Charbonneau, her French-Sioux husband,
b was hired in the autumn of 1804
c as a guide for the exposition.
N

TYPE II. Mark the letter of the underlined part that must be changed in order to make the sentence correct. (Be sure to note whether the underlining includes the punctuation.) If there is no error, mark *e*.

6 Sacajawea's (a) geographical knowledge and her usefulness as (b) a guide was limited (c) to her native region of western Montana. (d) No error (e)

7 Nevertheless, (a) she traveled all the way from Fort Mandan, N.D., (b) to the Pacific Ocean (c) and back again with the exploring (d) party. No error (e)

8 The first-hand reports (a) of the expedition by Lewis, Clark, (b) Gass, and others praised (c) her highly but, not her husband. (d) No error (e)

9 Shortly before the expedition left to find (a) its way (b) to the coast, a healthy son (c) was born to Sacajawea on February 11, 1805. (d) No error (e)

10 Her son, who (a) was given the name Jean-Baptiste Charbonneau made (b) the entire trip with (c) his mother and father. (d) No error (e)

TYPE III. Some of the sentences below contain errors; others are correct as they stand. For each sentence, mark your paper with one of the following letters as appropriate:

a—if the sentence contains an incorrect choice of words (choice in diction)
b—if the sentence is wordy (verbose or redundant)
c—if the sentence contains an overworked expression (cliché) or a mixed metaphor
d—if the sentence contains an error in grammar or structure
e—if the sentence is correct as it stands

11 Charbonneau was given five hundred dollars for his services as a guide, but Sacajawea received no pay.

12 It was generally agreed by the leaders of the project, Charbonneau mistreated his wife and was unworthy of his pay.

13 Their son returned back to St. Louis, Missouri, with William Clark, who brought him up and paid for his education.

14 After all was said and done, Sacajawea faded from view and, to make a long story short, it is not known what fate befell her in her later years.

15 Though it is a mistake to say that she guided the expedition, it is entirely possible that the roll played by Sacajawea made the difference between its success and its failure.

Error Correction

Error correction questions indicate the inappropriate part of the sentence and ask you to choose a suitable correction from the choices provided. Here are some samples.

EXAMPLE **A** Eating, drinking, and *to stay up* late at night were among her pleasures.

a correct as it stands
b she liked staying up
c staying up
d to remain up

B *On the snow-covered branch, two sparrows, they huddled close together.*

a correct as it stands
b On the snow-covered branch, two sparrows huddled close together.
c On the snow-covered branch, two sparrows, huddled close together.
d Closely, on the snow-covered branch, huddled the two sparrows together.

Answer:
A ⓐ ⓑ ● ⓓ
B ⓐ ● ⓒ ⓓ

Sentence Revision

This type of question requires you to mentally restate a *correct* sentence, using a given phrase. Using the phrase will require change in other parts of the sentence as well. Then you must choose, from among the choices given you, a word or phrase that will appear somewhere in the restated sentence. (It may not necessarily follow directly after the given revision.) Study the sample given below.

EXAMPLE **A** Sentence: When night came and the temperature fell, my father lit the fire in the bedroom.

Revision: Begin with "*Each night . . .*"

a that the temperature
b upon the temperature's
c because the temperature
d when the temperature

Answer:
A ⓐ ⓑ ⓒ ●

There will often be several ways in which the new sentence could be completed. If none of the choices given is in your revised sentence, think of another way to rephrase the sentence, and check the choices again. But be sure not to change the meaning of the original sentence when you revise it.

EXERCISE 9. Selecting the Best Revision. Following the appropriate directions, answer each of the following questions.

Error Correction. Choose the letter which indicates the best correction for the underlined part of each sentence. If the sentence is correct as it stands, mark *a*.

1 Traffic on the highway was blocked for an hour, this causing many drivers to have cold suppers.

a correct as it stands
b causing
c thus having necessitated
d which was responsible for

2 I haven't but a few more pages to write for this report.

a correct as it stands
b have scarcely
c haven't any except
d have only

3 Everyone due to the continued storm sat and sang around the fireplace.

a correct as it stands
b Sitting and singing around the fireplace were everyone, while the storm continued.
c The storm continued while everyone sits and sings around the fireplace.
d Everyone sat around the fireplace and sang while the storm continued.

4 Harry, although tired, worked late, typed long into the quiet summer evening.

a correct as it stands
b lengthily typing
c and he typed late too
d typing long

5 Suppose you tell us exactly where you hid and a thorough report of your precise reasons for doing it.

a correct as it stands
b and a report on why.
c and give us a report of your reasons.
d and precisely why you did it.

Sentence Revision. Mentally revise each of the following sentences according to the instructions given for each. Then choose the letter of the phrase most likely to occur in the sentence as revised.

6 Sentence: Leaning on the arm of her granddaughter, the old woman slowly entered the room.

Revision: Begin with: *The old woman leaned*

a so that she could
b for her entrance
c as she
d to slowly enter

7 Sentence: Aside from his dread of snakes, he was afraid of almost nothing.

Revision: Begin with: *He had a dread*

a but otherwise
b still
c outside of that fear
d and so

8 Sentence: What have we been doing all week but preparing for the holidays?

Revision: Change to a declarative sentence.

a had done
b anything all week more than
c nothing all week but
d does

9 Sentence: Bonnie told me she hadn't been there and didn't find out about what had happened until long after all of the excitement was over.

Revision: Change the indirect quote to a direct quote.

a told me, "I'd never been there and didn't find out
b told me, "I wouldn't have gone and
c told me, "I wasn't there. I didn't find out
d told me, "I won't go. I'm not going to find out

10 Sentence: She leapt to her feet and yelled, "I heard you say, 'What are they really worth?' "

Revision: Make the last direct quote an indirect quote.

a "I heard you say What are they really worth?"
b "I heard you ask what they're really worth."
c "I heard you ask What they're really worth."
d "I heard you say what they're really worth."

Organizing Paragraphs

Another writing skill often tested is organization. The most frequent exercise designed to measure organizational ability is the scrambled paragraph. This exercise takes a paragraph and presents the sentences in random order. Your job is to figure out the order that will make a well-knit paragraph.

Here is the way the directions are likely to go:

DIRECTIONS Each group of sentences in this section is a paragraph presented in scrambled order. Each sentence in the group has a place in the paragraph; no sentence is to be left out. You are to read each group of sentences and decide the best order in which to put the sentences so as to form a well-organized paragraph.

Before trying to answer the questions, jot down the correct order of the sentences in the margin of the test book. Then answer each of the questions by blackening the appropriate space on the answer sheet. Remember that you will receive credit only for answers marked on the answer sheet.

A sample paragraph follows:

EXAMPLE

P As you read, however, concentrate only on main ideas; don't try to remember everything.

Q If you develop an interest in what you read, you are more likely to remember the factual information in a passage.

R Finally, when you have completed the passage, pause to summarize the main ideas in your mind.

S You will have an even stronger motive for remembering those facts if you understand their importance to you.

1 Which sentence did you put first?

a sentence **P**
b sentence **Q**
c sentence **R**
d sentence **S**

2 Which sentence did you put after sentence **S**?

a sentence **P**
b sentence **Q**
c sentence **R**
d None of the above. Sentence **S** is last.

3 Which sentence did you put after sentence **Q**?

a sentence **P**
b sentence **R**
c sentence **S**
d None of the above. Sentence **Q** is last.

Answer:
1 ⓐ ● ⓒ ⓓ
2 ● ⓑ ⓒ ⓓ
3 ⓐ ⓑ ● ⓓ

Note the use of words such as *finally, however,* and *even stronger*. These words refer to previous statements. You may also find clues in sentences using pronouns or adjectives clearly referring to some noun in a previous sentence (*those* facts). Before you answer any of the questions, determine the correct order for all the sentences and write it down for your own reference. Most tests, however, will not ask you to give that order all at once. They will be designed so as to give you credit for each correct relationship you detect between the individual sentences.

EXERCISE 10. Organizing Paragraphs. Read the following sentences carefully and write down their correct order before answering the questions. Then choose your answer for each question that follows.

P Swim out and approach the victim from behind in order to avoid struggling.
Q Then go into the special procedure called a "carry," and swim back to shore with the victim.
R In order to save a drowning person, you must jump into the water, keeping your eye on the victim at all times.
S Bring the victim into a horizontal position by pulling back on the chin and resting the body on your hip, using your arms as a lever.
T Stick your elbow in the middle of the victim's back and cup the chin with your hand.

1 Which sentence did you put first?

a sentence **P**
b sentence **Q**
c sentence **R**
d sentence **S**
e sentence **T**

2 Which sentence did you put after sentence **P**?

- **a** sentence **Q**
- **b** sentence **R**
- **c** sentence **S**
- **d** sentence **T**
- **e** None of the above. Sentence **P** is last.

3 Which sentence did you put after sentence **Q**?

- **a** sentence **P**
- **b** sentence **R**
- **c** sentence **S**
- **d** sentence **T**
- **e** None of the above. Sentence **Q** is last.

4 Which sentence did you put after sentence **R**?

- **a** sentence **P**
- **b** sentence **Q**
- **c** sentence **S**
- **d** sentence **T**
- **e** None of the above. Sentence **R** is last.

5 Which sentence did you put after sentence **T**?

- **a** sentence **P**
- **b** sentence **Q**
- **c** sentence **R**
- **d** sentence **S**
- **e** None of the above. Sentence **T** is last.

Answers to Exercises

Ex. 3, p. 554	Ex. 4, p. 556	Ex. 5, p. 558	
1-d	1-c	1-b	6-d
2-b	2-a	2-d	7-b
3-d	3-e	3-a	8-b
4-c	4-d	4-d	9-d
5-a	5-b	5-b	10-b

Ex. 6, p. 561
1-a
2-d
3-c
4-c
5-a

Ex. 7, p. 563
1-b
2-c
3-b
4-c
5-d

Ex. 8, p. 565		
1-a	6-c	11-e
2-a	7-b	12-d
3-a	8-d	13-b
4-N	9-e	14-c
5-c	10-b	15-a

Ex. 9, p. 568	
1-b	6-c
2-d	7-a
3-d	8-c
4-d	9-c
5-d	10-b

Ex. 10, p. 572
1-c
2-d
3-e
4-a
5-d

ESSAY TESTS

Essay questions require that you organize and write down your understanding and analysis of a specified subject in a set time. Your answer is considered deficient if it is not organized according to the directions provided, not supported with sufficient detail, or is incomplete in the treatment of the subject matter.

Studying for Essay Tests

The best preparation for an essay test is to write out your own questions. In doing this, you must review the material and identify the most important points. Once you have written several questions, close the book and outline the answers. You will be testing your command of the material and exercising the skills you need in the actual test.

Scheduling Your Time

Always scan the complete test before you begin to work. Note the number and types of questions to be answered in the time allowed as well as the point value of each section. Then schedule your time accordingly. As a general rule, count on about two minutes of planning and one minute of revising for each five minutes of actual writing.

Analyzing the Question

Always read an essay question carefully and thoughtfully before you begin your answer. You usually have some choice about what to include;

however, teachers often specify the following ways in which you are to treat the material.

Identify Key Terms

Key terms indicate the organizational pattern you are expected to use. Answers that do not use the approach specified in the question may be evaluated as incorrect, even if the information given is correct. For example, if you have been asked to compare two characters in a short story, you must talk about two characters in terms of their similarities and differences. Your discussion of how one character was developed in the story might be accurate, but it would not show the comparison that was asked for.

The chart below gives the four main patterns of exposition and key terms associated with each.

PATTERN	KEY TERMS
1. Comparison and contrast	compare, contrast, show the differences, have in common, find likenesses, in what way are . . . similar/dissimilar
2. Cause and effect	analyze, explain, criticize, defend, show why, give factors that lead to, tell the effect of
3. Sequence or placement	list and discuss, trace, review, outline, give the steps, locate
4. Description	describe, identify, give examples of, write the characteristics of, define

Identify Specific Points to Be Included

Most essay questions require that you complete more than one task. Take time to note exactly what points you must include in your answer.

EXAMPLE In literature, as in life, there are many forms of heroism. One fictional character is a hero because of a single act of valor. Another is heroic because of living a life of quiet endurance. Sometimes the heroic act is one of physical strength and stamina. In other stories, the hero manifests moral courage. How do you define heroism? Choose two characters, each from a different short story read this semester. Evaluate each character in terms of the characteristics of heroism that you included in your definition of a hero. Show by contrast that one character is a hero and the other is not. Use specific details to support your evaluation.

In your answer you must write a definition of a hero which makes clear the characteristics that you consider essential to heroism. You must evaluate two short story characters (each from a different story) in terms of your definition. You must contrast the characters, explaining why one is a hero and the other is not. You must use specific details from each story to support your evaluation.

EXERCISE 11. Analyzing Essay Questions. Read through the following essay questions for a one-hour test on computer use. For each (a) tell how much time should be scheduled for the answer; (b) list the key term or terms and identify the pattern of organization called for; (c) identify the number and kinds of examples or support that must be included.

1. (15 points) Discuss the technical developments that resulted in powerful, small-sized computers.
2. (10 points) List three to five ways a computer might be used in a small business office.
3. (15 points) Show the advantages of word processing programs over traditional typewriters. Include at least three specific points in your comparison.
4. (30 points) Describe how either programmed learning or simulation games take advantage of the computer's capacities. Include three or more examples of specific programs.

Writing Essay Answers

Do not leave out any of the stages of the writing process.

1. Plan your answer by formulating a thesis statement and very briefly outlining your major points of support.

2. Write your answer in complete sentences. Judge from the amount of time available whether you should write a single paragraph or develop each of your main points in a paragraph of its own. Be sure to include specific examples or details to support your thesis.

3. Read through your answer to make sure you have covered all the points specified in the question. Proofread your paper carefully.

EXERCISE 12. Planning and Writing an Essay Answer. Following your teacher's directions, compose your own essay question on a topic you are studying in one of your classes. Assign it a point value in a test meant to take 40 minutes. Exchange questions with another student, or answer your own question.